"One of the very best books I have ever read of the life and times of a totally engaged and committed priest. The narrative of the author's life is written in a lucid and captivating style. One can hardly put the book down to find out the next adventure of this extraordinary man and his ministry. The book is filled with engrossing incidents in the priestly career of the Reverend Lester L. Westling, but its greatest value is in the counsel offered to clergy persons, young and old, and to the Church, as how best to fulfill the Gospel injunction 'to go forth and make disciples of all people.' An excellent book; an excellent read."

—THE REV. WILLIAM A. JOHNSON, PH.D., TEOL. DR.
Albert V. Danielsen Professor of Philosophy and Christian Thought, Brandeis University
Canon Theologian, Cathedral Church of Saint John the Divine, New York City

"Les Westling faithfully chronicles his life answering God's Call. Here is a life of service that led in new directions of ministry: as a civilian, in the military, and as a missionary. In Hanoi's prisons creative minds kept us alive through years of uncertainty and moments of terror, so I particularly appreciate the creative innovations Les consistently brought to ministry. Here is a great encouragement for pastors, chaplains, and lay persons alike as they are faced with unexplored, uncharted, and unexpected challenges in presenting the Good News of Jesus Christ to the world."

—DAVE CAREY
Captain, United States Navy (Ret.), Speaker, Consultant, Coach & Trainer
Author of *The Ways We Choose: Lessons for Life from a POW's Experience*

"As we rush down our road of life at traffic speed, Chaplain Westling challenges us to be aware of the merit of those around us and in ourselves. This book is the author's legacy to church and nation, inspiring us to seek and find the God-given gifts that propel us to perform acts of courage beyond our expectations. Not every soldier's valor is noticed; not everyone who struggles for a personal victory receives acclaim. The events recorded in this book demonstrate that all such efforts are true, and are rewarded with the true gold bestowed by our creator when we answer his unique call for each of us, and respond by following the Savior."

—ROBERT E. BUSH, C.M.H.
Past President, Congressional Medal of Honor Society
U.S. Navy Hospital Corpsmen, WW-II Veteran

"*All that Glitters* is a high adventure "page-turner" that chronicles Les Westling's fifty years of service as a minister, Navy chaplain, and missionary during the turbulent latter-half of the twentieth century. Written in bite-size chapters that keep you hungry for 'just one more,' it reveals a world of devotion, duty, and honor that is both inspiring and humbling. From migrant farm camps in California's San Joaquin Delta, to mining camps in the northern Philippines, to Marine combat camps in Viet Nam, it is a world where action speaks, and faith is proclaimed through works of love in real-life situations that are commonly dirty or difficult, and sometimes very dangerous.

In an era of growing confusion about the proper role of men in society and the church, *All that Glitters* presents a strikingly clear picture of true masculinity and its source and power in Jesus Christ. This is the story of a man's man, living for the glory of God and the good of all peoples, and it is a vitally important story for the world to hear."

—RIC ERGENBRIGHT

Author, *The Art of God*, ECPA Gold Medallion Winner 2002 Best Gift Book

All that Glitters...

Memoirs of a Minister

The Reverend Lester Leon Westling, Jr., M.A., D.Min., LMFT
Captain, Chaplain Corps, U. S. Navy (Retired)

THIS BOOK IS DEDICATED AS A MEMORIAL

to

The Reverend Joseph Henry Thomas, D.D.,
sometime Rector of Saint Clement's Parish of
Berkeley, California,
who showed me as a youth what a Priest should be;

to

Lester Leon and June Holmes Westling,
my parents,
who showed me how to live as a Christian;

and to

The Reverend John Booth and Rebecca Miller Clark,
whose lives inspired me to share a missionary life
with their daughter.

Contents

Preface and Introduction

The memoirs of this minister are those of a priest of the Episcopal Church. Rather than writing an autobiography, I have composed this book as a collection of memorable events in my life or which I have observed, presented as vignettes. Each of these was selected because I believe it bears some measure of teaching for both clergy and laity. I composed this volume as an extension of pastoral ministry beyond retirement, and I pray that it will be found helpful for generations to come.

The title of this book is an abbreviation of a well-known proverb, so written as to allow the reader's recollection of it to complete its sentence. My purpose in doing this is to stimulate the imagination so as to encompass a double meaning. The rewards that have come to me in this life of service have been twofold. The joys have far exceeded the gold that any mine could produce, the experiences of love and glory no earthly fortune could provide. But some of the glitter that covers the image of the ministerial life in the popular view is a disguise that masks the agony that is often the cost of love that demands integrity and courage. All that glitters is not gold.

I was to learn in the course of a life of service that courage is not just to be found on battlefields. The word "courage" finds its derivation from the Latin *cor* meaning "heart." Courage often is the result of the birth pains of love. Courage is fear that not only has faith, but heart as well. I learned courage from the valor demonstrated by scores of brave people—my parents, my wife, my sister, my parishioners, many prophetic clergy, as well as my comrades in arms. I have tried to introduce the reader to as many as I could in this volume. This book is a tribute to many souls, both living and dead—some mentioned by name, many more not—whom God sent into my life to make this ministry possible.

I believe the greater pain for Jesus was not the physical torture on the Cross but the spiritual conflict in the Garden of Gethsemane. There, it was

His duty to divine the Will of His heavenly Father. His friends could go no farther than the garden gate. No other could bear for Him the heavy weight of decisive prayer. His loneliness and bloody-sweat bore witness to the earnestness of His search. There are times in ministry when our only consolation can be found in Gethsemane with Him, times when no other mortals can share the secrets of our hearts.

We who are called to follow the Master will not be perfect as He, but our commission takes us on a perpetual search—with His Risen companionship—both to our Mounts of Transfiguration as well as to His Garden and to His Cross. The Savior has granted us in His Service minute glimpses of the cost of His Easter victory. In this great Hallelujah Chorus we call "Ministry," it is the constant challenge of those who would be the stewards of the mysteries of Christ to be sure that our words match His music.

I have been truly blessed by God with a life partner who has been infinitely patient with my preoccupations throughout the last 44 years. Among these endeavors during the last decade has been the writing of this book. Marjorie and my daughter, Karla Westling Bakke, independently read the entire manuscript as meticulous proofreaders, spending hours ferreting out pesky typographical errors, word duplications, and misspellings which had successfully eluded the reviews of the author. Karla has shared editing responsibilities with me, and her proficiency in Asian languages and research on my behalf at the National Archives, were great assets to this volume. It will be my pleasure to introduce the reader more fully to the members of my family in chapters that follow.

I wish to express my sincere gratitude to my sister, Harriet Westling Shank of Seattle, Washington. Harriet has been my reader, candid critic, and companion, in the building of the manuscript. She is a Harvard/Radcliffe-educated French and Latin scholar, and she has continuously struggled with my composition to keep it pure and more readable. Harriet is legally blind, but has used a closed-circuit television device to magnify my manuscript pages in the arduous pursuit of the task of reviewing my work. As a 'cellist, retired after years with the Seattle Symphony, she pursues her music by memorizing great portions of scores to provide accompanied solo performances. Her courage has been an inspiration to me, and her proficient feedback has been a significant factor in the completion of this book.

It was Captain Ronald H. Botts, USN (Retired), who introduced me to Jason Milliken of Global Publishing Services and Katherine Lloyd, Project Manager of this book. This insured that the messages that were bursting within me to share eventually made it into print. I knew Ron when I was a missionary in the Philippines, and he was a Lieutenant Commander pilot stationed with Fleet Air Wing Two at USNAS Sangley Point. He loved the Lord and flew a Navy Santa Claus with me into the mountain barrios of Luzon.

The crew of Crown Camera in Redding, California, have labored long and hard to revive images from 8mm film and old photographs in order to illustrate historical events described in the text. I am grateful to them as well.

Now I need to shift to some more mundane matters of ecclesiastical and literary terminology to ease the task of my readers.

The Church through which God Called me to discipleship and to ministry is endowed with the Sacred Ministry in three Holy Orders: Bishops, Priests, and Deacons. Ordination into each of these Orders is held to be as eternal as one's Baptism. However, ministers in each Order are assigned to various jobs or positions in the Church. These positions bear titles which identify the minister's temporary responsibilities, such as Rector (of a self-supporting parish) or Vicar (of a Mission congregation which has as its Rector either the Bishop of the diocese or the Rector of a neighboring parish, whichever provides its financial supplement). Other examples of such positions referred to herein are: Curate (an assistant with the "cure of souls" or pastoral care duties), and Chaplain to an agency or institution and its personnel. (I have capitalized these titles here for emphasis.) It may appear that bishops are mentioned an inordinate number of times in the stories, but this is a book about a priest. As with other clergy in this Church, my bishop is my pastor. In the same way that a lay person looks to the parish pastor for guidance, healing compassion and encouragement, my bishops have had a prominent role as the primary source of succor in my life through seminary and since ordination. My bishops have shaped my development, or, at rare times, have limited my effectiveness, in ministry. Where in the text the words "Call" and "Vocation" begin with capital letters, the bidding and guidance of the Lord is implied.

I have ended sections of this writing with a verse or two of Scripture. When a reference is followed by "f," in accordance with documentation procedures, the following verse is included. If the verse should be followed by "ff," the verse noted and two following apply. The note "a" following a number indicates the first portion of a verse only, whereas "b" would indicate the latter part of a verse. Each vignette in the book has been inspired by the Scripture that is noted at its conclusion. When a verse refers to an event in the life of Our Blessed Lord, I ask that the reader understand that the author has experienced the companionship and compassion of Jesus in the material recorded. Nothing more is presumed; nothing less is to be construed. These references bear witness to the fact that the Christian life and the Christian ministry receive their vitality and maintain their direction when they are anchored in the Word.

I write this in the autumn of my life. Even though I move about with more aches than I did five decades ago (after five fairly recent surgeries), I am vigorously blessed with renewed good health. I offer these reflections as an act of thanksgiving for this life and for the wonderful lady who has shared all of the joys and the dangers of most of it with me, and who has given us three grown children of whom we are justifiably proud. But in the season between the summer and winter of our lives we watch as the leaves begin to fall. Most of my seminary colleagues have now retired, and some of my lifelong friends have "fallen asleep." On the other hand, spring comes to mind as many children I ministered to have grown to maturity, some of them sharing with us through photographs and visits their own growing offspring. Many now join with our own precious adult children as they look to Marjorie and me as loving parents-in-the-Lord. It serves as a reminder that being called "Father" is an earned title, and it gives me happiness to hear Marjorie sometimes called "Mother" by them as well. Where we may have earned such notability, we shall enjoy being known that way in spite of Reformation-bred controversies to the contrary. And when I address pastoral bishops who have cared for me as "Reverend Father-in-God," I mean it, even though the 1979 revision of the *Book of Common Prayer* has expunged those words.

It is my fond hope that the stories which follow will convey a valid view from within the pulpit and from behind the Altar, as I have gazed for fifty years from those stations into the eyes of many beholders. Please remember, however, that this is just *my* view, which I believe to be true and for which I take responsibility. Clergy receive comments both critical and complimentary, but rarely does the minister feel completely free to answer with candor in return. I have taken this opportunity to "talk back." It is my earnest hope that the honesty of this response will be found both useful and godly. If so, an additional reward of appreciation will be added to the many that have so lavishly enriched my life in the Christian ministry and as a priest of the Episcopal Church throughout the past half century.

Lester L. Westling, Jr.
Redding, California
Epiphany, 2003

The Author at age 14 - an ROTC Cadet at Harvard School. (Page 20)

CHAPTER ONE

The Burning Bush

***M**y* life experiences have convinced me that with God there are no blind streets. I know that He has guided me, and I believe He guides us all in ways that accumulate both tools and memories by which our future contributions to His Kingdom can be built. In this journey I am among the most fortunate.

I was born in 1930, the second child of a family that was in the midst of surviving the Great Depression. This imprinted my generation with distinctive precautionary mindsets that were learned from observing our elders even when we were much too young to understand their incentives. My father was a creative marine design engineer and inventor who never forgave himself for leaving the University of Nebraska less than a year short of completing his engineering degree. My mother was a piano teacher whose two-year degree at Drake provided the necessary credentials at that time in history to teach music. With my mother doubling as the family business manager, frugality preserved our home and future. Both parents were perfectionists in their fields and in their lives, and they both labored at their professions as long as health permitted.

My father created and restored ships from 1916 until his retirement in 1958. He converted his beloved Matson "white ships" from luxury liners into troop transports for World War II, then pioneered bulk sugar cargo handling and shipping—thus saving the Hawaiian sugar trade when it was deprived of Ceylon's hemp transport sacks during World War II. He became an international authority in intermodal refrigerated cargo transport as a final thrust in his career—always innovative—creative "before his time."

Although older than the nation's average youth that were called to arms, my parents were the best of "The Greatest Generation" described by Tom Brokaw in his recent book (New York: Random House, 1998).

When my mother once was asked: "Do you teach piano?" I heard her reply, "I teach children." She continued to teach throughout her final seven-year bout with cancer, and to my knowledge taught her last keyboard pupil some eighteen hours before she died in great pain in Peralta Hospital. My father was known as "Wes" to every steamship company executive and every stevedore Walking Boss on the San Francisco waterfront in its most active years. The ladies who worked in the Matson laundry that he designed and had built in San Francisco to service the company's liners and Honolulu hotels sought his counsel as they would a pastor's. My mother was a virtual family counselor to her pupils and their families.

Both my parents were employed: Father full-time on the piers across the bay from our Oakland home; Mother both parenting and teaching in the home (pioneering as a working woman in pre-World War II days, when wives commonly limited their expectations to tasks of house and children). Dad sang baritone in the Oakland Orpheus Club. When Oakland's first radio station began to broadcast, Mother accompanied him as they provided some of the first programs on KLX.

As a child, I remember our house filled with a background of pupils' endless scales and repetitious melodies punctuated by occasional false starts. Mother finally gave up on my music lessons, first on the piano, then, after a brief trial, on the violin. She declared that if the instrument had a crank and a gearbox, I might have enjoyed more of a success with music. My father taught me to sing and use breath control, which was his expertise. This provided me status in a musical family and a place in our occasional musical family evenings. The training he gave me has proven to be a significant contribution to my liturgical ministry in a chanting Church.

My Great Aunt Minnie was the hunchback widow of a Spanish-American War veteran. When Jake died of a post-war illness in the Ozarks, she, alone except for their dog, dug his grave, sang a few hymns, and buried her husband. She joined our family before I was born. Aunt Minnie assisted my mother in the juggling act of running the house, raising two children, and cooking meals, while Mother kept her full schedule in the living room that doubled as the piano studio. It was Aunt Minnie who coddled my eggs and gave me my morning dose of cod liver oil. When "the bums," victims of the Great Depression, came knocking on the back door asking for a handout, Aunt Minnie would cook up a complete hot meal for them as long as they would eat it on the back porch so as not to invade the household. As she performed routine tasks around our home, she sang such hymns as "He walks in the Garden with me" and "Jesus loves me, this I know" (with an occasional "Little Brown Jug"). She would play these tunes on the harmonica and listen to sermons on the radio when she was resting. I think everybody should have a Great Aunt Minnie!

Both parents were obsessed with providing their offspring with educations which would prepare them for honorable and productive futures. The upshot of all this is that my parents were furiously ambitious for my sister and for me, and when I started working as a dishwasher at eleven years of age for twenty-five cents an hour, we all understood without question that it was so that I could go to college.

One of the jobs I held during high school days was that of a file clerk and occasional trucker's helper with a confection, tobacco, and liquor distributor in Oakland's Chinatown. This was during the mid-1940s, when China's sufferings were prominent in the minds of most American West Coast dwellers. Chinese children attended late afternoon sessions at "China School" after public school had dismissed for the day, and several would pass by the warehouse loading dock on their way home. It was from such a student that I purchased my first Chinese dictionary (which I still have), and with whom I struggled to write my first Chinese characters (which I have kept as well).

My father had patented a chainlink ladder for engine room escapes when American shipping was a principal target of enemies in both oceans. This not only saved lives, but it produced an income which provided me my eighth grade year at Harvard Military School which had just moved from Los Angeles to North Hollywood. This Episcopal Church school was historically a preparatory school for Harvard University, hence its distinguished name. It was here that my young life received a direction which would ultimately integrate all others into a common and predominate purpose to which all other experiences seemed to contribute.

The academic year was 1943–44. R.O.T.C. and the military regimen and uniform gave my life structure and a dignity that compensated for my somewhat average academic performance. As a boarder, I grew accustomed to rising with the others in "Cottage C" once a week at 4:30 A.M. to scrub and wax dormitory floors for inspections, and I learned how to carry a trombone (if not to play it well) in the front rank of Harvard's marching band as we participated in war bond rally parades in the Los Angeles area.

One morning while crossing busy two-lane Coldwater Canyon Boulevard (which separated my dormitory-cottage from the main campus) I carried the usual armload of books. A car stopped in the far lane and motioned me to cross. When I reached the center-line, I felt a sudden pressure on my shoulder pushing me forward, and in response and without thinking I suddenly ran the rest of the way past the front of the stopped vehicle. Down, down the inclined path on the campus side of the road I ran. As I did so, a sudden crash thrust the car that had stopped for me forward as the gravel truck behind it, having lost its brakes, landed down the path just behind me with such an impact that the front wheels broke from their axles. Instinctively I headed for the chapel instead of the classroom. To a twelve-year-old, this was unnerving. I could still feel the push that I had felt thrust upon my shoulder and that had literally propelled me beyond the jaws of certain death under twisted steel. I did not know what that meant, but I was just beginning to come to terms with the conviction that I was preserved for a purpose.

One of the teachers was ordained Deacon in the chapel, and I was pleased to be chosen to serve the Altar for the bishop at this service. Because this diocesan school had as its President the episcopal visitor, Suffragan Bishop Robert Gooden, our chapel was a "chapel of ease" of the cathedral. When we joined other acolyte guilds at festivals at Saint Paul's Cathedral in downtown Los Angeles, we wore *purple* cassocks. We were a pretty proud bunch! The soon-to-be-Deacon was very popular with the cadets. His room on campus had its door always open. After dinner he hosted informal gatherings where stories and jokes were exchanged, and where plans were formulated for annual summer educational jaunts to England, which he conducted. Sometimes I stood at the door and listened, but I never felt comfortable entering and joining the banter. This was partly because I was just an underclassman, and partly because I heard talk elsewhere of how there was a rising anticipation of the time when he would replace "the old priest whose sermons were so boring." This gossip became increasingly offensive to me even as a youth, because our chaplain, Father Fredrick M. Crane, had become very important to me. I loved his gentle kindness. I thought to myself in these very words: "When I get to be his age, I want to look like he does." He did not have to preach. He just smiled, and to me his face was the face of Jesus. It was his smile that led me to Baptism and to the Christian Life. And as I reflected on it in later years, it was his smile and his example that nurtured in me God's Call to the Priesthood.

I asked Florence Hamilton, a lifelong friend of my parents, a widow in frail health, to be my Godmother. I knew she was a very devout Episcopalian, but as a lad of thirteen I had no idea what an effort would be required of her to attend the service. Coming by a succession of trolley and interurban trains from the far reaches of southwest Los Angeles to the San Fernando Valley, then walking blocks up hill to the school meant a trip starting hours before dawn in order to be with me on that precious moment of new birth. Over a decade later, in January 1956, by then in her 90s, she would kneel at the Altar Rail of the Chapel at Saint Peter's Church in Redwood City to kiss the hands that would bestow on her my very first Priestly Blessing. On the following day she would be there to receive Holy Communion at my First Mass.

My senior high school was completed in the rarified atmosphere of a small preparatory school in Berkeley. My physical education consisted of throwing horseshoes at a stake, while my courses consisted of content aimed at collegiate requirements. My track was essentially scientific. I graduated, with my eleven classmates, in three years, after taking entrance examinations for M.I.T., Rensselaer Polytech, Cal Tech, and Stanford.

But there was another side to the education I received during this period. I found a home at Saint Clement's Parish Church under the shadow of Berkeley's Claremont Hotel, and in the big heart of its Boer War veteran rector, Father J. Henry Thomas. My father would drive me to the church in Berkeley from our Oakland hills home in time for the early services. Father Thomas was a perpetual optimist who could see sunshine beyond any storm. Gathered around him I met seminarians of mature years, most of whom were studying on the G.I. Bill after discharge from World War II military service. Father Thomas left his mark on all of us because he was the epitome of what a priest should be. He was the tonic I needed during accelerated high school years. When I discovered that he had no Acolytes and that I was needed, I found a precious continuity with what I had loved most about Harvard School. However, when this kindly priest observed how I served with the rigid precision I had been taught, he was quick to urge me to relax and to worship through my serving. He cautioned with perception: "Lester, when you are here for the right reasons, you never need fear making a mistake."

One day Father Thomas would present me to Bishop Walters as a Postulant for Holy Orders, because the San Joaquin Valley at the time was a missionary district and needed clergy. I can recall his telling me about the priestly life by saying: "Son, there are them that builds it and them that oils what others built. You must decide which you will be." And his favorite tutorial was: "A doorbell punching parson makes a growing parish."

Those seminarians that gathered around Saint Clement's, all of whom became prominent bishops, archdeacons and rectors in their ministerial lives, rather adopted me, and I became a frequent visitor at the Church Divinity School when its student body was only thirteen. The tug-of-war between their plans for my future and those of my parents was a loving source of tension in my life, from which I would have to escape to begin my own self-discovery.

A day following high school graduation I signed on a Standard Oil tanker as an engine room wiper. I found at sea such an exciting release from being tied to the future that I began to believe that, between the opposing poles that had demands upon me, I would find neutrality in a life in the Merchant

Marine. I remember vividly my first encounter with a member of the crew—most of whom were several decades older than I was. "Slim," a tall wiper of about 35, directed me to look at my hands before I began my work shining handrails and cleaning oil out of the bilges beneath the engine and boiler rooms. They were the soft clean hands of a school kid. "Look at your hands!" Slim said. "They will never look the same again." And so they would not, for I was about to learn the dignity of hard work and the discipline of surviving extreme heat while violently discharging the contents of my digestive system due to severe motion sickness. But in the midst of it all, I had found a home that would fashion my values as life unfolded in realms yet unimagined. Not only my hands, but my life would never look the same again.

My father, who had left me at the dock with tears of pride in his eyes as I went aboard a Standard Oil tanker at age 16 for my first departure, was there at the end of summer with determination in his eyes to wrench me from my new-found haven to get me to Stanford in time to matriculate. As I look back on it, I am very grateful he did this, because I know he was playing his part in the drama of my life, of which God was the playwright. I thank God that my parents were ambitious for their children. My older sister was to be a teacher or a musician, while I was to be either a physician or an engineer. Private high school curricula were chosen and financed at the cost of great sacrifices by them. My sister was masterfully placed in the picture frame God had evidently designed for her. She graduated from Radcliffe College of Harvard University, achieved a Master's Degree in Performance at the University of Texas, taught 'cello and piano to students of all ages, was on a college faculty, and spent most of her career as 'cellist in prestigious symphony orchestras. It is obvious to me that she found her Vocation fulfilled in her music, which radiates her love for life and for the Lord.

When I found myself a freshman in physics and engineering at Stanford at the age of 16, my only escapes from pressures I did not understand at the time were two. I carried the trombone in the Stanford Marching Band at football games and rallies (playing with music I laboriously translated into slide-position numbers). And I surreptitiously purchased and, although not enrolled in his class, studied Shau Wing Chan's course books in Elementary Chinese.

Although this contributed naught to my sagging grade point average, I was invited to return to Stanford as a Sophomore.

I escaped my academic dilemma by a return to the sea. This time I was able to gain a position in the engine room on an army transport out of Fort Mason. We took the U.S. Army First Cavalry to Inchon, Korea via Guam and Yokohama. After this three-month voyage I chose to spend my second college year in the Merchant Marine Academy's first year Cadet School—then on the Gulf Coast. There I found success too easily achieved, and returned to a straight mechanical engineering major at Tulane University with both parental encouragement and sponsorship. I made it as far as my senior year as an honor student, but that was as far as I could go in a scenario I knew would not be right for me.

I left the university, served summers at sea in engine rooms of tankers and transports; alternately spent tumultuous school years employed at various company-owned Standard Stations (in days when service stations did more than just dispense gasoline). Now I was "on my own," yet unable to afford my hopes of returning to Stanford to pursue a classical or humanities major. I gratefully accepted a half-tuition scholarship as a pre-enrolled (Episcopal) theological seminary student at the Methodist affiliated College of the Pacific in Stockton. There I literally devoured, like a starving man eating a steak, every course I could compress into the academic year and two summers required of me, with transferred credits, to earn a Bachelor of Arts Degree in Pre-theology. I wanted this to prepare me to enter the Episcopal Church Divinity School of the Pacific in Berkeley. C.O.P. (now the University of the Pacific) benefited me greatly, and the staff were very gracious and encouraging to me. Dr. Colliver taught me Scriptures that I had longed to know, and I got as much of the behavioral sciences and literature as I could. I also gained a zeal from "old Methodism" for a ministry of community outreach and social service that the Episcopalians who surrounded me in later ministerial years confessed some difficulty in understanding.

When I first arrived in Stockton, a college housing officer introduced me to Edna Livoni, the widow of a Methodist Minister. Her house near the campus had been renovated into four small apartments. For only ninety-nine dollars a month and the ability to withstand the intense heat of the valley, I had very good quarters in the attic. Part of the deal, however, was that in response for her interest in my ambitions I promised to graduate in the cap, gown and hood of her late husband. Following C.O.P. summer semester and my first academic year in seminary, I returned to the campus to do so, and she proudly attended the ceremony. When Dean Betts put the Bachelor's Hood over my head (in a procession of hundreds of other graduates) he whispered discretely in my ear, "Les, you finally took it away from us, didn't you!" Yes! I was going to be a priest, one day. I knew with great sureness why I was pushed out of the way of that crash on Coldwater Canyon Boulevard in 1943; I knew full well Whose Hand it was that did it. On the day of my college graduation I saw in my mind's eye, smiling approvingly from Paradise, the face of Harvard School's Father Crane.

My years in the seminary provided academic growth that resulted from a struggle to survive. No day goes by that I do not make use of something I learned there. It would be beyond present limitations to describe courses and professors whose strivings molded me into an Episcopal clergyman. I am so very grateful to them. It was stimulating, but it was never fun. Enjoyment for me has always been when I could be creative. Growing in preparation for my Vocation was hard work, yet this was what made seminary exciting for me.

In my life I had never had time to play. As a child of the Great Depression, I never learned how to play or to enjoy it. It is my greatest regret that I did not know how to teach my children to play (although they learned without me), and to this day that is an art I seem not to have acquired. Lessons of honest labor would have to serve as part of my education. I could only hope that this would be an asset to future ministry and a substitute for all my deficiencies as recreation leader and sportsman. In retrospect, I can see how God made use of these experiences so I could touch the lives of many in subtle ways of understanding. Although I believe I was born to be a priest, I know better than to define myself by what I do or by what I have accomplished. I know who I am. I am a Child of God.

I joined the Coast Guard Reserve and drilled weekly with them to contribute to the Korean War effort, even though I was exempt from the draft as a seminarian. Many of my good friends were on the front, and I felt obligated to help in some fashion. I would go overseas one day, but only after I had my Vocation to equip me. I worked during two seminary summers as a petroleum quality control analyst in the Martinez Shell Oil Refinery, and before my Senior Year I returned to the engine and boiler rooms of a military transport. It was a personal challenge to return "to the fo'c's'le" of the Merchant Marine and its ports of call, not only for wages, but also as a Christian sailor—before donning the collar of the Christian Ministry and having the "protection" of the expectations that it provides. I did not reveal to crew members that I was preparing for the ministry.

I found a kindred spirit in the older fireman who shared boiler room watches with me in the transport USAT *Simon B. Buckner.* He played the bass drum for the Harbor Light Salvation Army Citadel in San Francisco when we were in home port, as an act of gratitude for his sobriety. During the academic years in seminary, weekends were devoted to internships in parishes which paid well, and I was able to stay awake in Greek and sleep through Hebrew. Two generous Knights' Templar Scholarships encouraged me and helped a great deal. Fortunately all grades then were "Pass-Fail" and I had the credits to graduate with my class in 1955. This was another academic miracle of God!

Mother and Dad attended my graduation with pride, as they acknow-ledged my struggles and achievement. They were unable to travel to Bakersfield for my Ordination as Deacon, but my "Priesting" was gloriously shared with them. My father commented (with all of the candor of his waterfront career): "All right, Son. You got this far. Now preach to beat hell."

When I was a youth, I told my mother that I wanted to be a priest. Her instantaneous reply was: "You cannot be. You are not good enough." Don't condemn her when you read this. She was right! Her background shaped this conviction. She was raised in a devout Puritan Christian family. Her father was a Minister who died at the age of 42 while active as a pastor. He was a saint. I have read some of his work. Mother was right. I was not good enough. So God let me pursue other goals just long enough for me to obtain the training He wanted me to have for the unique life I was to live. Then, when it was God's good time, my pastor Father Thomas put his big arm around me and said:

"Of course you are not good enough. None of us can be. Only Jesus was good enough. But He loves you. If He has Called you, that is all you need to know."

My father was the Episcopalian. An annual ritual we shared was to meet in San Francisco on Good Friday and take the cable car from the waterfront up California Street to the end of the line, then walk to old Trinity Church to participate in the noon-day meditations. As we would walk up the hill beyond Van Ness Avenue he would tell me how much the Church had meant to him as he grew up. He would reminisce about his youth in Fairbury, Nebraska where he stoked the church furnace, shovelled winter snow, taught Sunday School, led Morning Prayer, and where he would serve as Acolyte when a priest or the bishop could come monthly for Communion. He told me how my mother's father pastored the Christian Church there and headed the local Temperance Union while a few blocks away his father would brew beer in his basement. He would rehearse the *Prayer of Humble Access* from memory as we climbed the hill, and I think of him each time I offer it now.

We never talked religion in our home because of this myth that my parents' beliefs were so very different. I found my way to various Protestant Sunday Schools on my own as a child, walking miles on Sunday mornings, and I learned the heart of religion from Aunt Minnie. As a boy I never thought to question the way we lived. I never really examined it until it was time for my mother to die. I was a Navy Chaplain at the time, getting ready to leave for the Submarine Squadron and the Tender USS *Proteus* on Guam. My mother asked me to tell her what it would be like for her when she was "called Home." I wanted to respond to this sincere invitation, yet simultaneously I wanted to be sensitive to her needs. I knew my own faith believed that the Bible taught of an Intermediate State called Paradise in which we will grow to be prepared for the Return of Christ in Glory—while many Protestants reject this concept by teaching we will go to heaven or hell at death. Not wanting to take advantage of her fragile situation to convince her of anything that might be contrary to her father's teachings, I called the Minister of the Fruitvale Christian Church to consult with her. He spent time with her, and together they planned her Memorial Service.

I came home on emergency leave some months later in time to have a final two days with Mother along with my father and sister, and then to attend Mother's funeral. In his eulogy, the Minister used an excerpt from the very eulogy given for her father's burial, in accordance with their plan. The Scripture text was I Thessalonians 4:13-18, and his message was exactly what I, as an Episcopalian and as a priest, would have explained to her. I was caught up in the tragic waste of years during which we could have shared so many vital things. I was sad as I contemplated the "unhappy divisions" that had kept us unnecessarily spiritually apart as a Christian family over years we could never reclaim.

—◦⁄◦◦⁄◦—

I rejoice that I have been given this time after five decades of very active ministry to write and to understand things that were happening when I was too busy living them. What I have just described are some of the burning coals that welded together my Vocation as a minister in the crucible of the life I have been given. It is essential for each of us to understand our Vocation in life, and even in retrospect to understand it from the very beginning. I believe that God has a wonderful destiny for each of us, but the discovery of it is best done when we can see the pattern and trace it back to the sparks that ignited our consciousness of it. For some, the fire burns slowly, evenly; for some there is an explosion at the start or at the moment of recognition. For some the fire burns with great brilliance—but for some it burns too bright and burns out too soon. However, what truly validates one's Calling is whether the fire lasts. But surely there is and has been for each of us, just as there was for Moses, a bush that burns to light the way before us.

Of the traditional burial sentence, "We commit his body to the ground, earth to earth, ashes to ashes, dust to dust," Jack London wrote this obscure commentary on his inevitable demise: "I would rather be ashes than dust." I strongly agree, and to this I would add: "...because dust has always been dormant, but ashes come from a fire that once was blazing and which could have provided light, warmth and power for those who would make good use of it."

—EXODUS 3:2–4; ISAIAH 64:8

Crossing the International Date Line in the crew of the U.S. Army Transport *General Simon B. Buckner* en route to Inchon, Korea (Page 24)

Almost 35 years later, the Author crossed the Equator for the first time, enduring the appropriate rituals. It was at Latitude and Longitude 00 - 00, just off the Ivory Coast, granting him and his shipmates the title "Royal Diamond Shellback". At the time he was Chaplain of USS *Carl Vinson* (CVN-70) and Battle Group "C". (Page 322)

The Author as seminarian (standing at far right), serving the Rector at the Altar of St. Peter's Parish Church, Redwood City, California - 1953. (Page 42)

Photo by Darrell W. Meacham, San Carlos, CA

Congratulating the newly ordained Priest, Suffragan Bishop of California, Henry Shires; California Diocesan Bishop Karl Morgan Block, and the Bishop of San Joaquin Sumner Frank Dudley Walters - January 7, 1956. (Page 43)

CHAPTER TWO

Early Ministries

One World's End
Was the Beginning of Another

*T*he Right Reverend Sumner Francis Dudley Walters, the Episcopal Bishop of San Joaquin, introduced me to the Emmanuel Mission, a red chapel that stood in the field laborers' camp at Terminous. He explained that Helen Wagstaff (whose stature inspired many of the clergy secretly to call her "Flag Staff"), Diocesan Director of Christian Education, would be my advisor, and that he would provide me with a small stipend and mileage allowance for my travel and some books. I was to be his "lay vicar" in the fields while studying at the College of the Pacific.

Terminous, California is not the end of the world, but when I ministered in Terminous I thought we could see it from there. Actually, this place was the location of the Atkins-Kroll packing shed, one of those so-called factories in the fields, on the peat islands of the San Joaquin Delta.

In those days this was the terminous of a railroad line where the harvested and processed asparagus and celery were loaded onto box cars to be freighted to market. There were other box cars there—in the mud and off their trucks. They were the homes of field workers who performed stoop labor in the rain and under the scorching valley sun. They were the homes of the families of those who made the harvests possible. Some were migrants, and others lived there the year around in the shadow of the levee that protected them from the waters of the junction of the Mokelumne River and Potato Slough.

Emmanuel Mission was my first experience of leading worship, providing a "sermon," and teaching in the Church. I think this was also part of the good bishop's intrigue to teach me to modify my "high church" background to more nearly conform to his own, and I soon learned the necessity of tailoring the degree of formality to the environment.

For most of those who attended on Sunday mornings, a very simplistic worship experience was most appropriate, to say the least. I can still hear Mrs. Fisher's voice like fingernails scratching across a blackboard. In the second line of *What a Friend We Have in Jesus*, the tune goes up and then goes down again at the singing of the words: "What a privilege to carry...." Dear Mrs. Fisher, in great voice, but oblivious to melody, would just keep ascending against the descending tide of the other voices. She was the wife of a packing shed foreman and provider of stability for the mission, so I learned to practice elementary parish diplomacy by avoiding that hymn unless she might request it.

The closet-sacristy of the chapel still contained a shelf of Bibles and copies of the *Book of Common Prayer* in Japanese, unused since that population was evacuated from the fields and confined to internment camps never to return to Terminous. The migrant camp was mostly composed of Latinos and White laborers whose living conditions and sanitation were barely on a survival level, and whose lives seemed devoid of any hope of change. In order to do home visiting in the winter mud among the immobilized box car dwellings, I mounted the directional mud tires backwards on the rear wheels of my little 60-horsepower Ford, with the theory that "I could always get out of what I got into." Occasionally I held parties for the children on Saturday nights at the chapel in order to provide a diversion from the bar on the levee, and I had occasion to be of assistance to the principal of the small Terminous School by encouraging parents to send their children to classes before the county truant officer might come after them with the force of the law.

Bishop Walters was a true evangelical Christian leader, and when he commissioned me to serve Emmanuel Mission, he explained that on the monthly reports I was to "count every breathing body" that attended every service and every event. He took great pride in the progress of the mission and read these reports with great interest. I rang the donated locomotive bell in the small steeple prior to services, and I left the doors open when the building was occupied to demonstrate a welcome to those who might join us.

At the conclusion of a 1950 fall catechism class, the bishop came and conducted Holy Confirmation for the few candidates. In celebration of this achievement in the life of the mission, while observing with annoyance the many flies that distracted the worship during his visitation, and, as a Christmas present to the congregation, he provided for the installation of a pair of screen doors for the entrance.

The report for the month of January showed a marked decrease in the attendance figures. I was called to the bishop's office in his Stockton residence to explain. Standing tall before his desk, like a sailor "before the Mast," I had to explain that in obedience to our original agreement I had counted every living creature that entered the worship services and gatherings at Emmanuel Mission, and following the installation of the screen doors the dogs, cats, and chickens that routinely came to church were unable to gain unaided entry. I was dismissed without comment, but I am sure the bishop enjoyed the humor of it once I was out of his sight and hearing.

The offerings at the services were mostly "in kind." That is, the basket that was passed on Sunday mornings regularly came to the Altar filled with celery or asparagus "seconds" discarded from the packing shed, together with some coins and currency. A little aged Mexican lady lived across the canal and was physically unable to walk well, much less navigate the narrow highway bridge (which has long since been replaced) to attend services. She requested and received regular pastoral visits from me at her little cottage where we had prayers and chatted. Her weekly offering was one egg from her chickens behind the house. I had permission to keep the edible portion of these offerings as a means of maintaining myself.

It would be mid-afternoon before I returned to Stockton following my sabbath activities. On my way home I would stop by the beautiful Morris Chapel at the college for a brief moment of prayerful thanksgiving. I soon observed that the bowl of the baptismal font in the baptistry alcove of the narthex was frequently used as a wishing well by Saturday afternoon or Sunday morning visitors who lacked any understanding of the purpose of that piece of ecclesiastical furniture. "Feeling my oats" as a *proper* Episcopalian, and assuaging my conscience with the thought "it would be going to a worthy cause," I would take advantage of the vacant chapel (devoid of witnesses) to empty the coins that "desecrated" the holy font. I would then proceed to a restaurant on the avenue to enjoy a hearty and balanced Sunday meal.

Terminous looks different these days. I understand that some years after I left Terminous, a delegation of "do-gooders" from Lodi came out there to survey the deplorable living conditions in the camp, and were able to get the old box cars that offended them demolished—leaving families in the camp to live in tents in the same mud where they had always lived and where their children had played before.

When I recently motored down State Route 12, I drove over new bridges across canals I remembered and through the vast islands of fertile fields framed by levees. The roadway is still two-lane, but it is somewhat improved. The rail line that gave Terminous its name was gone. The packing shed, the workers, and their camp behind that shed had all vanished, as had the little red chapel with the short steeple and the bell. In place of it all, I saw mature shade trees that sheltered the mobile homes in a park by the levee, and, on the water side of the settlement, there is a marina of sport boats and a yacht.

I can no longer remember the names of many of the people of the mission in the era when I was the Lay Vicar of Terminous, but in my mind there are vivid pictures of many faces. I wonder if Mrs. Fisher now sings off-key in Paradise, and if the Sunday School children I entertained on Saturday nights stayed out of the bar. I wonder where those who used to work those fields live today, or if they have all been replaced by machines. I wonder if the descendents of the residents of the Terminous I knew remain trapped in that depressive cycle of working for little and spending more than their incomes. Such a cycle kept them stooping in the sun and rain, and obliged their children, who migrated with them for the harvests, to avoid school and to belong nowhere. I wonder if the crusaders from good homes who came to change Terminous ever returned to see the results of their crusade.

But I shall always be grateful for this beginning to my life in church leadership which immersed me in fellowship with brothers and sisters who struggled to survive and to know God under the burning sun. After this experience, I could never allow church life, where I could guide or influence it, to be a meaningless charade. I thank God for the good bishop who pointed me in the direction of a Terminous where I would be stamped with its indelible beginning for a life in the service of Jesus. I continue to pray that the presence of that little red chapel in the field inspired those who came to it, and those who may only have seen it there, to look above the demanding and necessary tasks required for their survival to see God's vision for them and to know His love. I hope that the little mission taught many that "Emmanuel" really means "God (is) with us" and that with Him each of us has infinite value.

—St. Luke 12:32,37

Location, Location, Location

*T*he church is on the corner of Emerson and Wall Streets. "Where?" came the response; "What is it near?". . . I responded, "Here, I'll draw you a map."

You see, Tracy was only a town of 10,000 in 1954, and finding things was not all that difficult then, even where the most direct route was impeded by stop signs every few blocks and the intersecting streets did not connect through to easily identified boulevards. The only big industry in the area then, other than the surrounding ranches, was the Heinz catsup plant. The west branch of the Lathrop Army Distribution Center was nearby. Deuel Vocational Institute, then a maximum security prison under the California Youth Authority, was just moving from former military quarters in Lancaster,

California, to just south of the city in a newly constructed compound of concrete, watch towers, and razor-wire topped double fences. On "the campus" were residences for some of the relocated prison staff. This brought some interesting professionals into the congregation, and I made some visits to that facility as it became established in its new home.

The Reverend Morgan Sheldon, pioneering Vicar of Tracy's Saint Mark's Mission, married Margaret a year prior to his moving to Boise to be Canon of the Cathedral there, and he was followed in the interim by supply part-time clergy. My Rector in Berkeley had referred me to the Missionary District of San Joaquin for my training and apprenticeship because of the needs there. This is why I had served Emmanuel Mission, Terminous during college days in 1950 and 1951.

—◦◦◦◦—

At the beginning of my senior year in the seminary, in the fall of 1954, Bishop Sumner F. D. Walters of San Joaquin appointed me Lay Vicar for Saint Mark's, possibly grooming me for the permanent position there upon graduation and ordination. I commuted from Berkeley to Tracy for weekend Saturday home visits, youth activities, and Sunday and Holy Day services. Parishioners invited me for overnight hospitality, and I slept on one of the church pews on rare occasions. Father James Trotter came one Sunday a month from Saint Francis, Turlock, for Holy Eucharist and Baptisms, when I would exchange with him for Morning Prayer and Sermon, not uncommon for the main Sunday worship in those days in the liturgical history of the Episcopal Church.

The Tracy congregation was close-knit, a loving group of perhaps 50 Communicant Members. With considerable determination, they had purchased a quarter-block parcel of land and had constructed on one-third of the area a rectangular church building of basalt blocks, partitioning a quarter of its interior for sacristy, heating and air-conditioning machinery and office space. There was no problem finding volunteers for teaching Sunday School and for

Altar Guild services. I enjoyed my pastoral and preaching ministry there, and I became indoctrinated early in my ministerial life to "parish politics" and to how they intensify in small churches. I could see clearly the great potential for the growth of this congregation. Because of its geographic location, the city of Tracy *had to grow astronomically.*

However, before my year there had come to an end, I found myself asking far-sighted questions which, in unwelcome ways, would challenge an "old guard" who had sacrificially devoted their resources to a building which I feared would hold them back. I believed it was plain to anticipate the future that loomed on the horizon. As I grow older I am increasingly sympathetic to how change threatens those who have become secure in the *status quo.* Although then young, I do believe I was sufficiently pastorally astute to assess the sensitivities of devoted lay contributors who had accomplished so much from the beginning days of house church meetings. I exercised caution in explaining my recommendations for the future of the mission. But my choice upon graduation would have to be determined by where I would have the freedom to see the results of my efforts flourish in a predictable future.

As a young churchman in the Diocese of California, I had both observed and heard from Bishop Karl Block himself how, with great foresight, he had planted new churches in his diocese. Bishop Block gathered around himself an informal group of advisors composed of executives and program planners from the various utilities, real estate firms, and from local governmental entities. He would meet with them, and, with their aid, project where future populations would locate. He loved real estate, and he was unafraid to take risks for the Church. For example, he bought a corn field in what was then the rural outskirts of Concord. It now lies on the border between downtown and the residential area of that enlarged city. This property now adjoins the city park and is occupied by Saint Michael and All Angels' Parish Church and Preschool. I accompanied him when he bought a plot and nearby house in remote Carmel Valley before it became one of the most prominent (and impossibly expensive) settlements in the country. This would be my model for church planting in the future.

At the time I served Tracy, Tracy Boulevard was the western boundary of the city. A tract of about eight or ten blocks of new homes had "dared" to establish itself across that boulevard, a virtual invasion into the planted fields. But the advisors I sought out told me the city was about to explode in the direction of the Altamont Pass. It was then beyond any popular imagination that those farmlands to the west of the city would in a few years be in absolute demand by residential builders. Who would have thought in 1954, that before the turn of the century, workers would be commuting daily by car, bus, and train from as far away as Stockton, Manteca and Modesto—through Tracy—to their workplaces in Oakland, San Francisco, even San José?

Indeed, family homes in Tracy quickly became a premium among other valley commuter options! Toward the end of my year of ministry in Tracy, bulldozers were already at work clearing ground for the construction of McKinley Elementary School, with Monte Vista Middle School and a city park with a public swimming pool soon to follow. McKinley School was initially planned to be inset a block or so west of Tracy Boulevard. Adjacent to the street "apron" approach to the school, an open field composed of some acres fronted on the boulevard. Possibly for an offer, this could have been purchased with consideration for a possible swap for the then-coveted residential quarter block (awkwardly zoned for a church) at Emerson and Wall Streets. But the very thought of selling the church and plot, probed quietly with members of the governing "Bishop's Committee," was ruled out as an "anathema" with no room for discussion. (The property that I wanted for Saint Mark's is now divided between a Masonic Lodge and another church and its school.)

Today, a little over four and a half decades later, Tracy's population exceeds 54,000★—a growth of more than 540 percent! This growth has more than tripled the land-use of Tracy, and the new growth is essentially west of Tracy Boulevard and south along it—which includes modern infrastructures and schools. Tracy Boulevard bisects older well-established residences (that was all of Tracy when I served there) and the huge new additional developments to the west and south. This places churches and businesses along that thoroughfare in the enviable position of being very visible in their appeal to serve populations residing in both old and new Tracy.

The number of organized religious congregations★ has only doubled: from 21 in 1954 to 42 in 2000, yet individual growth figures for all of these groups are not available to report. The Church of Saint Mark added a "parish hall" wing across the back of the remaining lot and paved the remainder of it for limited parking. The Year 2000 edition of the Episcopal Church Annual reported no identifiable increase since 1955 in the Communicant Membership of Saint Mark's, Tracy, but since then the world had moved on!

There is a happy and exciting ending—no, a new beginning—to this story. Saint Mark's Mission, now called Saint Mark the Evangelist Episcopal Church, reluctantly sold their property in old Tracy forty-four years after I had recommended they do so. After holding services in a local high school for a year, the church was able to relocate on a 5-acre plot on Tracy Boulevard on the southern outskirts of the expanding city, surrounded by new upper-middle class family residences.

At the rear of the property, a former residence is being reconstructed as the transitional (Bishop) Schofield House Chapel. A projected quadrangle complex, pictured on a signboard, has been designed to occupy the field facing the boulevard. With the years, a more central location was sacrificed, but with an energetic outreach ministry the congregation could overcome the limitations of being located somewhat remotely and amid a select socioeconomic population. After decades of treading water, confined to the small enclosure of a virtually hidden property, dramatic growth in member-ship and service to the community is certainly predictable!

Did I do the right thing in not settling there and fighting for change? Of course this decision was not based on the single issue of where the buildings of the congregation would be located, but this issue was symbolic of determining factors both for those good folks and for me. I recognized that I was too young and too junior to act as a change-agent with this congregation. My experiences at Tracy brought me greater maturity, and with that maturity came the conviction that as a newly-ordained minister I would better serve the Church as an apprentice to a seasoned rector in an established parish for a start. I would then have models for future ministry—models either to copy or to avoid. Thus, I was convinced that it was neither the time, nor was Saint Mark's, Tracy, the place, for my next task upon seminary graduation. I accepted the Call of Saint Peter's Parish in Redwood City in the Diocese of California (the diocese where I had been raised) to be their curate—assistant to the rector—with the responsibility for the "cure of souls."

—PROVERBS 29:18a, ST. MATTHEW 5:14ff

★ Census estimates and numbers for congregations were provided by the Tracy Chamber of Commerce and the Tracy City Library on October 5, 2000.

The Laying on of Hands

*C*hurches that preserve the three-fold ministry of Deacons,★ Priests, and Bishops who are in direct succession from the twelve Apostles, do so with the Biblical injunction of the Laying on of Apostolic Hands with public prayer. It is commonplace in this tradition for the bishops (as the sole ordaining ministers) to gather their Candidates for the diaconate for ordination at the Diocesan Cathedral. Deacons who are to be advanced to the priesthood (after the canonical period of testing) are usually ordained by their bishop to that Order individually in their first parish or mission. This way they can be surrounded by their new congregation.

John Keester and I had been classmates for three years at the Church Divinity School of the Pacific, the Episcopal Church seminary in Berkeley. His parents and home parish were in Bakersfield, California. As we had been Postulants of the Diocese (then known as the Missionary District) of San

Joaquin, we would be ordained as deacons together by Bishop Sumner Walters. To accommodate John and his family, we approached the bishop with the request that the service be held in Saint Paul's Parish Church in Bakersfield instead of in the Cathedral in Fresno. Here John could be in the midst of family, friends and well-wishers who had known him for a lifetime, and I would await such an experience for my "priesting." Our request was approved.

Thus, on Saturday, June 13, 1955, John and I became deacons in the Anglican Communion of Christendom. The only person I really knew at the service, other than John, was the bishop. I did not even know the priest who formally presented me for ordination. The Reverend John Keester went on to Arvin and the oil fields south of Bakersfield to organize a congregation there. (Those were the days when rural missions were more commonly subsidized in order to have their own full- or part-time clergy.) I came alone and left alone, but I rejoiced that I had made my part of the day a gift to my seminarian-brother (now my brother deacon). I was thrilled to have at last entered Holy Orders by the Laying on of the Bishop's Apostolic Hands. My first and only prior experience like this was when I received the Sacrament of Holy Confirmation exactly ten years before.

Did I feel any different after the service? I guess I was too much in shock for it to register immediately. However, I remember how it all caught up with me when I made a brief rest stop on the way back to Berkeley. I bent over a drinking fountain for some water, and automatically brought my right forearm to my chest to restrain a necktie from getting wet. Guess what?—No tie!—Just a round collar that would identify me with my role as Christ's minister for the rest of my life. Father Thomas had taught me that wearing "the uniform" would make me available, and if I felt it inappropriate to wear the clerical collar somewhere, I probably should not be there! Now as I write, my memory humorously leaps eleven years forward in time to the Navy Chaplain School in Newport, Rhode Island. In the early morning, my Roman Catholic dormitory neighbor and I desperately struggled together before a mirror to recall the four-in-hand art of the cravat before our first inspection in the uniform of new Navy Chaplains.

I had been the Seminarian Assistant at Saint Peter's Church in Redwood City, California during my Middler academic year 1953-54. I spent every Saturday, Sunday and holiday there, supervising Christian Education with the assistance of the long-time Sunday School Secretary Edna Walker, leading the rapidly growing Acolyte Guild, organizing junior high and senior high youth groups, making home visits, assisting at Sunday worship and occasionally providing a homily.

During that time, I designed partitions at one side of the former church building so that Paul Jones, a retired builder, could fabricate three-sided cubicles for Sunday School classes along one wall of the large space that served as a parish hall. One incident that I shall never forget occurred while making my rounds of the children's Sunday classes in those cubicles (while the High Mass was being celebrated in the church). A small boy left his drawing at his table to approach me. I was wearing my black cassock in the course of my duties. Ever so gently he hugged my legs, looked up into my eyes with great innocence and love, then asked: "Are you God?" This shook me to my very being. Once I recovered, I sat down on the floor with him in that old auditorium and gently set the both of us straight. This was indeed a most humbling experience, an appropriate lesson for one preparing for a lifetime in the ordained ministry.

As I relate events that happened to me at Saint Peter's as a seminarian, I admit having some difficulty distinguishing some from other events that occurred after I returned to the parish a year later on August 1, 1955 as a deacon and then as priest. However, the greatest height of my life in the Sacred Priesthood came at its very beginning. It was planned with the ingenious imagination of the Rector of Saint Peter's, Father Charles Peter Boes. Like so much of what he did at the parish, it was executed in magnificent style. This was my service of Ordination to the Priesthood on January 7, 1956. He wanted this service to incorporate the greatest possible number of my family and clergy-friends, as well as the entire community. It was his recommendation that, although I was eligible sooner, I wait until the close of Christmastide and the beginning of the Epiphany. This season symbolizes not only the coming of the Wise Men to view the Christ Child and present their gifts, but also their mission to return to their distant lands to make Christ known to their people. Further, this would come at a time when the heavy seasonal obligations of the clergy would have abated and they would be free to participate. And so it was.

Bishop Block of California was the ordaining bishop and "President" at the Pontifical Eucharist. His Suffragan, Bishop Henry H. Shires, read the Litany for Ordinations. The Bishop of San Joaquin, who had followed me in my return to college and then through the seminary, the Right Reverend Sumner F. D. Walters, preached on the text Saint Matthew 9:36: "He had compassion for them because (they were) like sheep without a shepherd." The three "Sacred Ministers" assisting were my rector, Father Boes; my beloved seminary Professor of Church History, the Reverend Doctor Samuel Garrett, and Father James Trotter, Rector of the Parish of Saint Francis of Assisi, Turlock. He had been my hero since my Sunday School days at Saint Clement's, Berkeley, when we traced his work as a Missionary at Saint Francis of Assisi Mission, Upi, Cotabato, Mindanao in the Philippines.

Now the great day had arrived! 700 were assembled in the pews, while in the courtyard and down the sidewalk the procession of 200 awaited the cue to enter. Then the clarion call came from inside the church, loud enough to be heard by all. It was provided by the Sequoia High School trumpeteers in the choir loft. At this signal the procession crossed the threshold and narthex, and started down the center aisle of the nave. The brass sounded the introductory notes to the Entrance Hymn:★★

"Sol... So.So.So. Sol... Sol... Sol... Sol...!" Instantly 900 voices boldly entoned:

> *God of our fathers, whose almighty hand*
> *Leads forth in beauty all the starry band*
> *Of shining worlds in splendor through the skies,*
> *Our grateful songs before thy throne arise.*

I will not write out the entire hymn here. But I add the third stanza because it proved to be more prophetic than we could have anticipated on that exciting, warm, and peaceful morning.

From war's alarms, from deadly pestilence,
Be thy strong arm our ever sure defence;
Thy true religion in our hearts increase,
Thy bounteous goodness nourish us in peace.

So in they came. Led by the Master of Ceremonies and the Thurifer, three dozen vested Acolytes carrying processional crosses, torches, *Book of the Holy Gospels*, and everything liturgically acceptable. There were Lay Readers, Members of the Vestry, civic and local government leaders, a few local ministers, then 40 priests (all close friends), the Sisters of Saint Savior, Sisters of the Community of the Transfiguration, and the two surviving Sisters of Saint Anne (all Episcopal Church monastic Orders), seminarians, and of course the three bishops and their crozier-bearing chaplains appointed for the service.

The great service of Ordination and Holy Communion was immediately followed by the new priest granting his First Blessings in the adjoining chapel. 400 lined up for this, and I am choked with emotion as I recall it. The first to kneel at the altar rail was my Godmother, Florence Hamilton. In spite of frail health, she had travelled the long distance from her home in Fort Bragg, California. Accompanied by her son and his family, she was there to see for herself that her many prayers for me over the years had been fulfilled. Next to her were my dear parents. Others followed to hear the words of Blessing, to receive the Sign of the Cross, and to grasp and kiss my right and left hand that would the very next day Elevate the Sacred Host and Fracture Him at my first Mass.

At the luncheon that followed, Bishop Walters told jokes that many of us had heard him tell at previous gatherings, and, as a display of courtesy, the other bishops laughed heartily. Anne de Stephano, the Altar Guild Directress, gave me a green set of Eucharistic Vestments which she made. There were gifts of a new Pyx to carry the Sacrament to shut-ins (and later, on the battlefields of Viet Nam), a "Stock" or container for cotton wads impregnated with the Holy Oils of Unction and Baptism, and a portable Communion Set. I still use all these articles in the exercise of priestly ministry. As I do so, I recall these wonderful Christians and the memorable events that fulfilled my past dreams while setting me on an irreversible course for the future.

The next morning, two brothers in Christ, Bill Russell and Bert Romo, who had been devoted as laymen to a ministry which we had shared for the two years I had served the parish, flanked me on their knees to serve as Acolytes at my first Holy Communion celebration in the Chapel where I had given my first Priestly Blessings. In spite of my advance practicing, I did lose my place in the Missal Book during the *Prayer of Consecration*. I recovered and continued after a few awkward moments, during which loyal laymen supporters Bill and Bert thought that perhaps I was having a "Martin Luther" theophany (such as he had experienced at his first Mass). However, I was able to reassure them that although I was a bit anxious to find my place, no such ethereal crisis or "out of the body" experience had taken place. It was just that their friend had been through a few highly emotional and very tiring—yet wonderfully unforgettable—days.

—PSALM 110:4; ST. LUKE 10:1–11

---

*Capital initial letters of the three Holy Orders used here for emphasis.
** From *The Hymnal 1940*, No. 143, Copyright by Church Pension Fund. New York: The Church Hymnal Corporation. Words by Daniel Crane Roberts, music by George William Warren. Used by permission of Church Publishing Incorporated.

Seek and Ye Shall Find

My dear Godmother, Florence Hamilton, told me at the Ordination Luncheon about her participation at the Parish of Saint Michael and All Angels in the Northern California coastal city of Fort Bragg. She had moved there as a widow, to live on the property owned by her son. She confessed that, although she attended worship each Sunday, there were times when she was unable to receive Communion. "Why?" I asked. "Well," she replied, "about the time I am able to get out of the pew to walk forward, it is all over." "Do you make this known to the Priest?" I asked. "Well, I guess not. I am not proud of being so slow, embarrassed perhaps."

This was neither the time nor the place for me to lecture this dear soul who had come far to present me as a youth for Holy Baptism in North Hollywood, and had come again, now in advanced age, from Fort Bragg to the Bay Area for my Ordination. But I did advise her to report the matter to her Rector, and added that she should, in fact, be proud that she had made every effort to attend; that it would be easy to "fix" the matter. Either the Minister would be pleased to wait for her if she wanted to walk forward, or the Celebrant could bring the Sacrament to the pew for her and for others who might request this. Further, I went on to make her this promise. At every Mass from the very beginning of my priestly ministry, after most of the congregation had come to the Altar Rail and received Communion, I would turn to the people remaining in the pews holding out the Chalice and Paten (the cup of consecrated wine and plate holding the blessed bread) in a gesture of invitation. In this manner, I would look each time for those who might need to receive Communion at their pew or who might be hesitant to come forward because of physical infirmity. I have kept this pledge with great loyalty ever since. Even though my Godmother Florence entered God's Paradise some years ago, I call doing this brief act of searching: "Looking for Mrs. Hamilton."

My two years at Saint Peter's Parish consisted of my Middler Year as a Seminarian, then, following a year of absence, a return as Curate. Both periods were before the time when that parish had spawned Christ Church, Portola Valley to the west and Trinity Parish, Menlo Park had developed the satellite congregation of Saint Bede's to the south. Thus, the Redwood City parish boundaries included, in addition to modest homes within its city limits, forested estates in Woodside and beyond, and palatial homes in Atherton to the south. The congregation was vibrant with life, happy in spirit. In the words of a parishioner: "We just seem to understand each other and our common needs." The membership included a balance of "us common folk" and celebrities: tradespersons, professionals, and corporate executives; owners of small shops and owners of diamond mines and steamship lines. All seemed to pray together and work together remarkably well. In spite of the wide socio-economic range within the congregation, no one seemed too proud to enjoy such menial tasks as tending the church gardens, working in the kitchen or polishing the Altar brass. Funding never seemed to limit our program, but the clergy and staff had to be on our toes to keep up with the pace of this active membership. Indeed, this was an inspiring place to begin my ordained ministry. This community gave me an unforgettable model to seek to replicate through the years ahead!

The "Men's Club" met from time to time and held an annual barbecue—for purposes of *fun*-raising and *fund*-raising. This was just one of the many self-sustaining parish activities for all ages and genders. I single it out to identify it as the initial locus of a spontaneous gathering among its number of a smaller group who were seeking an even closer identification with the mission of the Church. About a half-dozen men ranging in age from 25 to

45 evolved into what became a Parish Chapter of the Brotherhood of Saint Andrew. We met weekly to fulfill the three-fold rule of that national men's organization: prayer, sacred studies, and service. Just as Saint Andrew had been compelled to find his brother Peter for the Lord, so this group of "brothers," armed with growing knowledge of the Scripture and the Church, devoted themselves to a relentless search of the parish for opportunities to help people and programs. In the "cure of souls" they shared this ministry with me, and became "the reaction force" for the parish as a whole.

Bill Russell (former WWII bombardier/navigator, bread truck driver by choice), Bert Romo (bank teller), Harry Walrath (Boy Scout Executive who later became a Priest), Gordon Robinson (buyer for a major grocery chain), and Warren Lutz (I cannot recall his occupation) composed our Chapter. Our number was later augmented by Juan Cuneo (classical violinist) and by a Mr. Salter who was somewhat older than the rest of us. These men scattered their talents throughout the parish where a need was identified. They trained and served as Acolytes, taught Sunday School, sang in the choir, assisted shut-ins and the elderly, were leaders in the annual Every Member Canvass and in the Capital Funds Drive, read Scripture and served as Lay Readers in parish worship, and gave rides to church for those in need of such assistance. They had been known to drive a flatbed semi-truck for the youth group's Christmas carolling hay ride, and they performed other tasks too numerous to list. Our Brotherhood was dedicated to a relentless search for a closer personal relationship with Christ, and through which to make Him known to others. It was this Parish Chapter of the Brotherhood of Saint Andrew and other chapters like it in the diocese that I knew I could count on when I needed help to revive the Good Shepherd Mission in West Berkeley. In my next assigned position they came joyfully when summoned to conduct a door-to-door invitational survey.

It was neither unusual nor surprising for adventures at Saint Peter's to have a humorous component. Such things kept us pursuing our mission without taking ourselves too seriously. A Capital Funds Drive was initiated under the guidance of a professional fund-raiser, in order to complete the conversion of the former church building into a modern parish hall and to make other improvements in the property. The Wells Organization had gathered members of the parish in the banquet facility at Ricky's Town House in Palo Alto. The event was to motivate the drive and to organize the canvassers into teams. The previously designated team captains were expected to explain procedures and recruit volunteers for their individual groups for the drive. Military terms were given to various aspects of the campaign, and this would be reflected in the speech of B.S.A. member and former Air Force Officer, Bill Russell. Bill took the matter seriously, and rehearsed in his mind how he would address the large gathering as he made his appeal. He introduced himself as a team leader, then appealed for people to join the teams. His talk reached a crescendo with the statement: "If I am to be one of the generals in this campaign, remember that the generals can do nothing without their privates." At this point, and to Bill's complete surprise, the gathering exploded in laughter. The banquet went on to be not only a success, but a rollicking good time.

—◦◦◦—

Our two-week summer Vacation Bible School required plenty of advance planning and staff recruitment to accommodate the huge number of pre-registered pupils plus expected late registrants. The sessions occupied mornings, and 50-minute periods were scheduled so that each class could move through the chapel service or other activities outside "their room" at pre-arranged times and in rotation—"just like the big kids do in high school!" Classes by age group were assigned to various teachers and rooms. There was a "recess" space where refreshments were served, or from which a nature walk illustrating the day's lesson could be initiated. The Chapel was designated for an informal worship service with an interactive talk on the day's Scripture selection adjusted for the age group attending. I designed the curriculum so that each day was progressively devoted to an event in the life and ministry of Jesus. Everything, from the crafts, Bible readings, exercises, and decorations, focused on the lesson for the day.

The above is background for the following incident. Two sisters were enrolled during the summer in question. The younger girl had been the victim of a most unfortunate automobile-versus-pedestrian accident in which her legs had suffered major injuries. Her life was spared, but this could have been fatal. Both girls came to Vacation Bible School. The younger sister, wearing steel braces, came in a wheelchair. She was attending a class in a room next to the Chapel, while the older sister was, at the time, in the Chapel session. Bernice Russell was playing the reed organ, and I was leading the prayers and giving the talk. The theme for the day happened to be one of the healing miracles of Jesus.

When it came time for a discussion to plumb the depth of the pupils' understanding, the older sister raised her hand with movement signifying that she had something of great urgency to share. "Yes?" I called upon her. "Jesus healed my sister!" she proclaimed with great gusto. "And I want to find her and show you." She rushed out the Chapel door, ran to the next room, and without any explanation rolled her sister out of her class, bringing her to us and her classmates before the Chapel Altar. "Here she is," she proclaimed proudly! "See, Jesus healed my sister!"

—◦◦◦—

The local Board of Education was searching for a solution to a certain problem. Their deliberations culminated in the very difficult decision that the Superintendent of Education was to fire the Principal of Sequoia High School. The Saturday edition of the local newspaper reported the matter with banner headlines, and the issues were hung out like unwashed laundry on a clothesline for all to view. People on both sides of the matter were undoubtedly grievously hurt, and the pupils would be upset and possibly divided as well. The matter was on most citizens' minds. That was Saturday.

I think I was the only one that noticed it. As I was administering the Blessed Sacrament at Holy Communion on Sunday, they were side by side at the Altar Rail, lifting their hands simultaneously to receive the Lord: the

Superintendent and the newly dismissed Principal. It was all in quiet reverence that they did so. No press. No other words than "the Body of Christ" and the Blessing before they went their separate ways. These men had privately found something that surpassed the objectives of any Board or that the harsh realities of public life could overwhelm. "The peace of God passes all understanding."

⟳

A crowd of children had searched the grass and shrubs in the small park two blocks west of the church for about 45 minutes. What they found were ovals of colored construction paper which could be redeemed in the parish hall after the Easter Eve service. As the "hunt" ended, the Easter Procession formed up on the street, headed up by a motorcycle policeman who blocked traffic as the procession advanced. The Thurifer blessing the city with incense, and vested Acolytes bearing the Processional Cross and Torches, also led the way for the children. Brothers of Saint Andrew, vested in cassocks and cottas, served as marshals for the event, and the cope-adorned priests brought up the rear. On our way, we sang Easter hymns *a capella* and with great exuberance. The assemblage reached the side door of the church at about 4:00 p.m..

Thereafter followed the Great Vigil of Easter: igniting the New Fire of Easter, the Lighting and Blessing of the Paschal Candle, and the reading of a selection of three of the nine appointed Bible lessons (called "The Prophecies"). The Easter Baptisms concluded with a brief explanation of what Easter eggs have to do with Easter. (As the chick breaks through the eggshell, so Christ burst the tomb on Easter morn.) The Mass of the Resurrection would await the dawn, and once again at mid-morning on Easter Day. At the conclusion of the service it was time for the youngsters to trade paper eggs for the chocolate ones that would reward their patience.

⟳

The common theme running through each of these recollections of events at Saint Peter's Parish in Redwood City is "The Search." It is the search for Jesus Christ, Who is to be found by a lovely lady reaching for the Blessed Sacrament; among a small group of Christian men seeking to serve "the least of these, their sisters and brothers" (St. Matthew 25:35–40). It is the search for Jesus Christ, Who was found by a little girl who claimed the healing of Jesus where most adults could only seek in sorrow; Who was found by two civic leaders divided by "the world," yet together in their Savior. Children searching for Easter treasures on the park green could discover the glorious Risen Jesus present in the celebration of His Resurrection and in the Sacrament of His New Life in the waters of Baptism. The Easter Christ is always at hand, and He always will be! The local Church fulfills its mission when it reveals the Savior and brings His Peace and Joy to a searching world.

—ST. MATTHEW 7:7–11; ST. LUKE 15:3–9; ST. JOHN 1:40f, 45

Inasmuch

I had my first introduction to prison ministry through a close association with Father Tod Ewald and his beloved wife Mary. After his seminary graduation and ordination they went directly to Holy Innocents' Parish in Corte Madera, California. Together they revived a pastoral ministry there and stayed to serve for well over three decades. This Marin County suburb was just over a small hill from San Quentin Prison. In addition to his parish ministry, Father Ewald went to the prison chapel every Saturday to hear Confessions and to celebrate the Holy Eucharist. He would take laymen from his parish with him, and during seminary days I was occasionally included to serve as Acolyte. The indoctrination such visitors received upon entering the facility included the following warning: "There will be no such thing as a hostage at San Quentin, and we do not want dead visitors!" In other words, do not get too close to anyone. However, in complete contrast to this, a meal at the Ewald's rectory was often shared with parolees who had been part of the "congregation within the walls." This was decades before the *Kairos* program was organized to bring lay-conducted ecumenical retreats into prisons. *Kairos* is based on *Cursillo* ("little course" in the Christian Faith), and this has claimed numerous life changes.

My association with Father Tod and Mary Ewald prepared me in good yet realistic ways for the time when I had opportunity as a Seminarian to make visitations in the new maximum security youth prison, Deuel Vocational Institution, that had just moved to Tracy. I was not naive about the fragile task of ministering to the incarcerated. I listened to many incredible stories, and was introduced to the concept of "hooks and crooks," by which some inmates attempt to snare inappropriate advocacy from well-intentioned outsiders. But I was determined never to rule out genuine needs, and this practice would serve me well later as both parish pastor and as a military chaplain. At Deuel Vocational Institution, I eagerly learned from such professionals as the Warden, Louis Nelson. A Lutheran, he and his family worshipped at Saint Mark's Episcopal Church, where I befriended them. He became an important mentor for me in this type of ministry, before he was later promoted to the position of Warden at San Quentin Prison. Although he was a compassionate man, he maintained a large collection of confiscated handmade lethal weapons that had been crafted by inmates from such items as combs, kitchenware, furniture parts, and broken masonry. These articles served to remind his staff what they might suddenly encounter.

After I was ordained a priest, Father Ewald invited me to "supply" for him at times when he was away. A member of his parish Brotherhood of Saint Andrew chapter accompanied me, and one of the inmates, a 23-year-old three time offender, served as Acolyte. The prison Main Chapel spaces were already prepared for the Protestant and Roman Catholic services on Sundays for the

General Population. So, as usual, Episcopal services were held on Saturday afternoons in a large hall adjacent to the Chapel. They were well attended. On a particular Saturday when I was the celebrant, I had casually selected at random hymns which I thought might be familiar and might have at least a remote connection to the homily I would offer. Surprisingly, one of the hymns spoke to me in a powerful way that day, and the experience returns to my mind each time it is sung by other congregations, even in years hence. It goes like this:

There's a wideness in God's mercy like the wideness of the sea;
 There's a kindness in His justice, which is more than liberty.
There is welcome for the sinner, and more graces for the good;
 There is mercy with the Savior; there is healing in His Blood.

There is no place where earth's sorrows are more felt than up in heaven;
 There is no place where earth's failings have such kindly judgment given.
There is plentiful redemption in the Blood that has been shed;
 There is joy for all the members in the sorrows of the Head.

For the love of God is broader than the measure of man's mind;
 And the heart of the Eternal is most wonderfully kind.
If our love were but more simple, we should take Him at His word;
 And our lives would be all sunshine in the sweetness of the Lord. ★

Each time I hear these words said or sung I am compelled to offer prayers of intercession for all who are incarcerated, especially those known to me. The words of this hymn I selected that day also remind me of my young days as a Merchant Seaman, when I first experienced the wideness and the miracles of the sea. It also may be a reflection of a quotation of Ben Jonson, the early 17th century playwright and poet, who is reputed to have said: "The only difference between a ship and a prison is that on a ship one has the additional hazard of drowning." Indeed, there, but for the grace of God, go any of us—including me.

When I became Vicar of the Church of the Good Shepherd in West Berkeley, I received my first request for ministry to a parishioner who had been sentenced to State Prison. Once a quarter, I travelled south to the California Men's Colony in San Luis Obispo, then housed in old military barracks and Quonset huts. This alerted me to the importance of such visitations as part of any parish ministry. I found this to be an often hidden need in every congregation I served—both civilian and military, regardless of socioeconomic status. I have spent hours in most of the California Department of Corrections prison visitors' rooms, and even longer waiting in lines in visitor processing areas. (I know what the interiors of Navy and Marine Corps brigs look like, as well.) On one occasion when a prison chaplain ignored my expressions of urgency, I went to the Board of Prisons in Sacramento to advocate for the transfer to a prison psychiatric treatment facility of an inmate whom I knew to be in crisis. Had my appeal been honored in time, a very serious suicide attempt would have been avoided, prior to his move to Atascadero State (Prison) Hospital.

In current times, modern translations of the Bible are commonly used as alternatives to the King James Version. Therefore, the seven letters that were squeezed into my California personalized automobile license plate, INASMCH, have been less recognized in recent years, because that one word has been dropped from newer translations. But my motto comes from Our Lord's teaching recorded in the Gospel according to Saint Matthew 25:35–40:

> *"...I was ahungered, and ye gave me meat: I was thirsty and ye gave me drink; I was a stranger and ye took me in; I was naked and ye clothed me; I was sick and ye visited me; I was in prison and ye came unto me.*
>
> *"Then the righteous answer Him, saying, 'When saw we Thee ahungered and fed Thee? or thirsty, and gave Thee drink? When saw we Thee a stranger, and took Thee in? or naked, and clothed Thee? Or when saw we Thee sick, or in prison, and came unto Thee?'*

"And the King shall answer and say unto them, 'Verily I
say unto you, INASMUCH as ye have done it unto one of the
least of these my brethren, ye have done it unto Me.'"

During my years as a Navy Chaplain when I was the Circuit Rider for
a squadron of ships out of Mare Island, California, a sailor off one of the
Ammunition Ships I served was arrested in Concord, California, accused of
rape. I visited him a number of times in the Contra Costa County Jail in
Martinez. I had no intelligence about the veracity of the claim against him,
but his incarceration was not solving the problem, because, if convicted, his
jail time would also count against him with the Navy as "Unauthorized
Absence"(UA). On the telephone, I brokered an arrangement with his
grandmother to pay his bail so that he could be returned to Naval Authority.
When I drove to the jail entrance to receive him, he came to my car in a
paper jump suit. All his clothing had been retained as evidence in the case.
He was barefoot, and the only thing of value that he had was the plastic
zipper on what he was wearing to keep him decent. I drove him to our
home in Concord where my wife rummaged through my son's closet to find
something for him to wear, including a pair of my shoes.

Meanwhile young Lester cooked up some hamburgers and prepared a
salad and a soda for him to eat. When he was ready, we went to my automobile
to transport him to be received at Naval Station Treasure Island. As he walked
around the front of the car in the afternoon sun, he paused and then broke
down in tears. I got out to see what was the matter. He explained that he had
read my license plate. He said: "I used to be a Christian, and I understand what
you have done for me." I replied, "We care about you, and so does the Lord.
Now put your shoulders back, tell the truth—whatever it may be—and care
about yourself so that the Lord will have less to worry about!"

Searches of every person entering and leaving prison or jail facilities are
absolutely necessary for everyone's safety and protection, and in civilian
confinement facilities the prohibition from wearing clothing the color of
prison garb is also a most reasonable requirement. But beyond that, visitors to

prison inmates, with notable exceptions, are often treated with decorum appropriate to the offenders themselves, subjected to a duplication of red tape, an attitude of suspicion, and inappropriate hours of delay. A clerical collar brings no expectations of privilege. California Correctional Officers are aware that among the inmates in San Quentin there is (or has been) a "Ministerial Association"—a group of convicted clergy. Usually I would be the only person in a given civilian parish and community who knew where the person I would visit for long stretches had gone and why. I found that loved ones who remain loyal and continue contact over long separations are rare, that divorces are common, and that friends forget. Most often my journeys were secret ones, "under the stole" in ecclesiastical jargon, and usually I have been the inmate's only visitor through years, even decades, of incarceration.

Throughout my life as a minister—both as a civilian pastor and as a Navy Chaplain—I have made my long-distance rounds (even after I have moved to other posts), keeping confidential track of prisoners. Hopefully, this loyalty as God's representative has encouraged recovery and restored self-respect. Indeed, I have observed sincere spiritual renewal demonstrated in the lives of many. One inmate I visited regularly said to me: "I had to go to prison in order to find freedom." Every one of us, man or woman, youth or senior, needs hope to live, and Christ is the ultimate source of hope and redemption.

I know that many re-offend after their release. This is known by the term "recidivism." According to social scientists, there are various reasons for this. I have observed parolees who have found themselves strangers in the world that has changed radically in the years they were apart from it, sometimes overwhelmed by even routine responsibilities that confront them "on the outside." Whether or not the motivation is a conscious one, a longing for what became a familiar home over years inside confinement can provoke behaviors that return one to prison. This can involve additional victims, and continue to waste the life of offenders, as well.

Parole Agents and Probation Officers have heavy case loads, and they need help to keep their contacts personal and positive. This is where an established and trusted pastoral relationship can be proactive in the avoidance of trouble.

Father Ewald taught me to give an alarm clock to each inmate upon his or her release, as a symbol of the fact that they must return to being their own timekeeper after months and years of being told every hour of each day where to go and what to do. I have learned to listen to parolees rejoice in seeing grass and trees, hearing birds' songs and voices of playing children. But it takes more than that to keep one's promises, no matter how sincere. The road back to crime or drugs, old associates or former violations, can be overwhelmingly tempting. A pastor's love can motivate careful listening, candid monitoring, and referral to other professionals, if needed. Parole is the time to redirect the person into his/her new environment and into a social climate which will be supportive of new intentions. A different and unfamiliar geographic location may be required for that to happen, but contacting another pastor in that new place in order to continue a pastoral relationship must be accomplished by the parolee him/herself to avoid any breach of confidentiality.

The creation of halfway houses for parolees is currently a rapidly developing industry. Indeed there is a need for mentoring personal adjustments upon release. But if the emphasis on the parolee's needs becomes lost in the providers' profit motive (as it may have become in many youth resettlement group homes), and where such projects become massive and are run by untrained or unlicensed supervisors, such developments become impersonal and suspect.

The Dominical Command quoted above (Saint Matthew 25:35–40) is an injunction of Jesus that directs His Disciples, certainly including His ordained Ministers, to visit the incarcerated, encouraging them not to lose sight of the fact that they were made in God's Image and that they are still His sons and daughters! Each mortal has the responsibility to face the consequences of his/her behavior. We are to bless the sinner, not the sin. It is the function of the justice system to exercise its best human judgment, hopefully, with Divine Guidance. It is not our function as ministers to pronounce that judgment. Perhaps justice has been misguided, perhaps not. Ultimately, that is between each person and God Himself "from Whom no secrets are hid." But I am convinced that no one can live without hope and without the knowledge that he or she is loved by the Savior.

Ministry to the incarcerated or to parolee/probationers should not necessarily be considered a "specialized" Prison Ministry reserved only for designated chaplains. It is a necessary part of parish pastoral care as well. Isolation and inactivity are the greatest of punishments, and in prison one who is conscientiously seeking to correct oneself can be very "lonely in a crowd." The pastor's visits and correspondence can break through the isolation, be positive incentives to anticipate, and these can be a major element in converting the punitive into self-motivated rehabilitation.

The criminal justice system is an unfortunate necessity in our civilization. "Original sin" is basic to human problems. The Creator has given us the freedom to make choices, so that when we chose to love and obey Him, it is spontaneously sincere—not a robotic response to a divine demand. People are people, wherever they may be. Actions have their consequences. God rarely sends His Angels to do for His Children what they can do for themselves. Yet, God's love prevails. A challenge universal for every ministry is most evident in dealing with this population, that is: "Tell the truth in ways it can be heard and accepted." A minister who does not care, does not count. May we be dispensers of His hope, stewards of His wisdom and mediators of His grace.

—ST. MATTHEW 10:16; ST. LUKE 15:20; ACTS 12:7f

* From *The Hymnal 1940,* No. 304, Copyright by Church Pension Fund. New York: the Church Hymnal Corporation. Words by Frederick William Faber, 1862. Used by permission of Church Publishing Incorporated. Faber's words in the third stanza of the hymn were altered when published in *The Hymnal 1982.* (In the opinion of this writer, the result is a significant change from the originally intended meaning.)

The Church of the Good Shepherd

A MISSION OF THE EPISCOPAL DIOCESE OF CALIFORNIA

Good Shepherd Mission Altar, West Berkeley, California - 1956. (Page 84)

CHAPTER 3

Good Shepherd

My First Solo

I enjoyed a rare bond with the Right Reverend Karl Morgan Block, the late Bishop of California. It was as though I were a son to him. After the loss of his dear wife Nancy, he would attack his work with such energy that he would become forgetful of himself. When he seemed near exhaustion, I would offer to drive him to his cottage in Carmel. We would pause on our way to buy produce at the stands beside Highway 101 south of San José, then a two-lane thoroughfare. On arrival at the Carmel house, he would go immediately to the kitchen, still in bowler and overcoat, to begin preserving and canning fruit—an activity reminiscent of his married years.

I was the Curate in one of his wealthiest parishes and a priest he had ordained not too many months prior to this visit to Grace Cathedral. He admitted me to his busy office and into his busy life when I might be in San Francisco. "What can I do for you today, my little rabbit?" he inquired as he looked up from the haystack of papers that covered his huge desk. This time he got an immediate response. "I want to become Vicar of Good Shepherd in West Berkeley," I responded. "What?" he exclaimed with such shock that his pince nez spectacles fell onto his lap, and I thought his great frame would fall over backwards, swivel chair and all. Knowing his penchant for real estate acquisition for the diocese, I added quickly: "And there is a house next to the church for sale. If we bought it, Good Shepherd would have a quarter of the block!"

"Well, don't just sit there, son. Get the realtor on the telephone, and let's see what they want for it." *Yes!* I thought. He was hooked. "Does anyone live down there?" the bishop asked. "Yes, bishop. Lots of people live there. They are not all the same color, but they work hard and I know they need Jesus."

Soon thereafter, I moved my belongings into the little cottage on Ninth Street. When it cleared escrow, the old house around the corner on Hearst Street was bought and became our Sunday School. I called this worshipping community "the remnant that remained" (a term popular with the Old Testament Prophets). They were composed of twelve elderly White and decidedly Anglican ladies, survivors of the old neighborhood, and three devout Black adult parishioners. The latter were dear "Mother" W. H. Carrington, whose parents wanted a boy, so, out of loyalty she kept the name William Henry; Mr. Hiram Jacobs, a recent widower; and the lone Crucifer, tall and jovial Austin Nottage, native of the West Indies. A multi-racial plethora of children composed a ready-made Sunday School.

This group represented those who had kept the church going for the 43 years that had transpired since Father William Higgs had been Vicar. He served simultaneously as an instructor at the Training School for Deaconesses in Berkeley, and was fondly remembered as "the one that walked with a limp." He had ministered at the Church of the Good Shepherd as their last resident priest prior to my arrival. Indeed, most of the "remnant ladies" still remembered worshipping with his leadership. In those days, this had been the prestigious area of town. People came to church in those days in the fancy flivvers of yesteryear. The one-ton bell in the steeple tower had been given by the San Francisco Fire Department as the first fire alarm for Berkeley.

In more recent times Good Shepherd had become both toy and training tool of the seminary on the hill, the Church Divinity School of the Pacific, from which I had graduated just fifteen months before. The congregation had gratefully accepted their role, "rolling with the tide" as succeeding groups of theological students came and went. There were seminarians who wore Geneva gowns, carried big Bibles, and participated in street preaching on the avenue. This group might be followed by another who would fill the little church with the sweet smoke of incense, as birettas crowned the heads of chanting worship leaders. Where else could this happen in Christendom but in the Episcopal Church in the mid-twentieth century?

The vision God gave me for Good Shepherd was twofold. The first goal was to open wide the doors of this portal to heaven and let the neighborhood enjoy the fact that God loved them. The second objective was long-range in scope. As a native of the East Bay, I could still drive by church buildings in the "flatlands" from West Oakland to Point Richmond—buildings that were once proud Episcopal churches: buildings that had become rescued by other faith communities or that had been secularized as eating establishments or antique shops. All of them now have been demolished, replaced in the name of "progress." But at the time, those which still stood served to be reminders that the Episcopal Church had "headed for the hills," once the carriage trade had bequeathed the land nearer the bay primarily to factories, warehouse industries, and to their laborers as residents. Old Victorian homes that once had demonstrated affluence became standing evidence of need.

This was an enormous field, ripe for the harvest by the Church. The name of Saint John's Parish moved from West Oakland to Montclair, leaving behind its historic structure sold to a sequence of Black churches, finally to be reduced to kindling for the construction of the Cypress Freeway. Old Saint Matthew's in South Berkeley was filled with a rejoicing Pentecostal congregation, then demolished and replaced by a library building. The Point Richmond congregation had scattered long ago, and its structure was occupied by secular enterprises. I felt a great burden of sadness that my Church had abandoned the inner city and the people who lived there, and I was convinced that it was time for action.

Before us was an opportunity to reclaim our rightful mission in the changing East Bay—a church of gracious invitation for all. Energetic parish calling began the awakening process in South and West Berkeley, and, in time, an embryonic "house church" began meeting in the Tillman home on Seventh Street near Cypress in West Oakland. Sunday carpools from there bolstered attendance at Good Shepherd and represented bold beginnings to larger dreams yet unfulfilled.

Good Shepherd's divine services continued with a few visitors, as the fall turned into the winter of 1956–57. Irma Vroman, one of the "survivors" who remembered Fr. Higgs, knew the ways of Altar Guilds better than I, and, together with Dorothy Bigge and Mother "Bill" Carrington, taught others to keep things beautiful and ironed altar linens correctly with military precision. Mrs. Bigge, an English widow of a World War I veteran, had served on the Altar Guild of Canterbury Cathedral. In a moment of indiscretion she revealed to me that her duties there included the dusting of Saint Augustine's Chair, "and once when nobody was looking ...I actually sat in it!"

Dorothy Foster, a Licensed Vocational Nurse on the closed psychiatric ward of Herrick Hospital, had for years served as Church Organist and organized an annual social event called "Choir Capers." When a graduate student at the Pacific School of Religion circulated a questionnaire to the prestigious churches of the Bay Area, Good Shepherd happened to receive one. Among its many inquiries, it asked: "What degrees are held by your choirmaster/organists?" I replied: "L.V.N." "Describe the machinery that powers your organ." I responded: "Our reed organ receives its air from an Electrolux vacuum hidden under the floor boards which is fixed to blow instead of suck." And to the question: "What is your endowment for church music?" I answered truthfully, "Our only endowment here is the Holy Spirit!" As you might imagine, I never heard from that researcher again.

Because the little cottage on the Ninth Street side of the church had only a small floor heater in its central hall, I contracted pneumonia as the cold weather set in. Father Albert Olson, the rector of neighboring All Souls' Parish, came to my rescue to hold my weekday Mass, and he provided for one Sunday as well. This, and the help of Irma Vroman's chicken soup, got me back in the pulpit once again.

The Episcopal Church has a men's organization called the Brotherhood of Saint Andrew. I had established a chapter at Saint Peter's Church in Redwood City. Again I gathered our growing number of men under the leadership of Hiram Jacobs, and we started a fledgling chapter at Good Shepherd as well. Because one of the stated missions of this fraternity is evangelism, I sent out an invitation to all of the chapters in the diocese to join us in West Berkeley on a Saturday during the 1957 Epiphany Season for a day for the exercise of this vow. Eighty-five men gathered from many parishes, first at the Altar for a corporate Communion, followed by a country breakfast served in the old parish hall by the indomitable ladies of Good Shepherd. After this I gave them instructions for the execution of "Operation Good Shepherd." Armed with "primitive punch cards" with coded numbers around their edges and a set of carefully worded and non-intrusive questions, they were dispersed by prearranged plan to canvass an appointed share of one hundred square blocks of residences that surrounded the church. About 2,500 cards were returned by 3 P.M. that afternoon. After the men left, our crew processed the information recorded on these cards, leaving it up to me in the weeks ahead to follow up where appropriate. However, the next day the Sunday attendance at the 11 A.M. service already swelled from the usual dozen to eighty-five.

After a 37-year absence, on Saturday, January 25, 1997, I was invited by the incumbent vicar to return to the Altar of the Church of the Good Shepherd to hold the Requiem for 94-year-old "Mother" Carrington. Her stepson, Walter, had come for the service from his post as American Ambassador to Nigeria. Oakland Mayor Elihu Harris paid tribute to the deceased and to Good Shepherd, and to what they had both meant to him as a child, and to the community where he had grown up. Lamitsoi Williamson, devoted church member, had arranged it all, and the event served as a reunion of the living and the dead in the Communion of Saints. At the reception following the service, a young-appearing lady, who happily identified herself as a grandmother, reminded me of an event in the summer of 1957. As a small girl, she and other children were playing in the nearby park on Eighth Street. A man in a black shirt and a white collar came into the playground and asked her and the others what they were doing that summer. She remembered answering: "Nuthin' much." They responded to the invitation to come to the church and attend a Vacation Bible School. "It was fun," she attested, "and I have belonged ever since." This greeting was for me one of the most significant events of the day of the Requiem.

Good Shepherd was the traditional recipient of the Thanksgiving food baskets that were donated by the parishes "further up on the hills." Just before Thanksgiving week of 1958, there had been a warning promulgated that the cranberry crops that year had been treated with an insecticide that was declared suspect. The U.S.D.A. had given permission for the cranberries to be marketed, but with the understanding that in uncertain cases there was the risk of illness or worse to the consumer. When the Thanksgiving food offerings were delivered to my vicarage, (you guessed it!) they were composed of no less than eighty percent canned cranberries! Unwilling to distribute the cranberries in question, as well as lacking much else to fill the boxes, I called for help. With a carload of confidants and with the permission of a generous nearby food market manager with whom we shared our secret, we spent the day scrambling through his warehouse, boxing every dented or excess (but declared safe) can of food that we could find.

It had been my privilege when living on the San Francisco peninsula to become an Associate Priest to the Episcopal nuns of the Community of the Transfiguration. I visited their Branch House in San Mateo, and would spend an occasional day there in retreat or relaxation, say Mass and hear Confessions. I continued this practice after I moved to Berkeley, although less often.

One day I sat talking with one of the older Sisters in their common room. She could tell by the twinkle in my eye that I was enjoying my first "solo" cure. "You're having a good time at Good Shepherd, aren't you?" she inquired rhetorically. "Yes Sister, I love it," I replied. "Well, I do not want to dampen your spirits in any way, but I would offer you this for consideration. Until you have the Devil scared, your work has not begun. When he starts fighting back, take heart. You are becoming effective." Her advice has proven to be among the greatest assets for ministry that I have ever received. Sisters wish to remain anonymous, but I shall never forget her or those words of hers that have proven to be a comfort to me through the years.

Miss Anna Head, once a loving benefactor of the children of declining West Berkeley and founder of the private girls' school that bears her name, gave the stained glass Good Shepherd window that dominates the church building with beauty and love. I often stood in an attitude of prayer before the Altar, which, like most others before the Liturgical Movement, was located against the so-called "East Wall" of the Sanctuary. Standing there, I would look above the dossal curtain to the feet of the Good Shepherd towering above me in that great window. I felt driven to meditate at the feet of the Master who had led His disciples over the hills of Galilee, and whose guidance had brought me to this place to serve. This church had narrowly escaped the wrecker's ball, surviving to welcome into the embrace of the Good Shepherd so many who, like us all, need God's love. Many who felt unwelcome elsewhere in the 1950s because they lacked a "Sunday wardrobe," or because their spouse was in prison or of another race, or because their secret partner was of the same gender, fell into the arms of the Good Shepherd here. The little century-old "plains Gothic" church was destined to provide Christian roots for one boy Acolyte who would become bodyguard to Huey Newton during his trip to China, and for his teammate who became a State Assemblyman and later the mayor of Oakland. The Mission was a trailblazer for the Church!

This was before the days of "church causes"—before media floodlights searched for remarkable stories to illuminate, thus motivating people to seek the limelight. What we did so naturally and with such quiet love at Good Shepherd had not yet become a popular "cause célèbre" for the Church. We were just a family which, devoid of self-consciousness, was providing its own unheralded witness to the neighborhood and to the world beyond as to "how to hold hands." The Mission became home for many who needed a home. As I beheld the feet of Christ standing in the window above the Altar, I gave thanks that He had brought me to His Home where *I* needed to be as well.

—PSALM 84:3f

Onward, Christian Soldiers

*B*ishop Block had pledged his support for the rebuilding of the Mission of the Good Shepherd, but in doing so he had let the small cadre of patient saints know: "this is your day in the sun."

This implied that it was "now or never." However, the parishioners were quite eager to share the vision, and when I suggested objectives to be pursued, intelligent discussion might follow, but all were eager to cooperate without exhaustive explanations or any delaying tactics. We would either grow or die, and we needed to integrate racially to reflect the population within the parish boundaries. At the time, the small adult congregation was predominately elderly and White; the Sunday School children were predominately Black. It was the fashion in the West to frown on the South for their protection of the American version of apartheid. However, in California, churches commonly were segregated on a voluntary basis—including local Episcopal parishes. I soon discovered a hidden reality. In order to have mixed races at dinner committee meetings or social gatherings in Berkeley in the late 1950s, it was necessary to call a restaurant ahead to be sure we could be served together.

I did not want to lose the support of the seminarians. Over the years, they had kept the doors of Good Shepherd open. But I needed to redirect their efforts, so as to mobilize the congregation and to bond my leadership with the people. Early in the sequence of things I accepted as interns one or two students from the Church Divinity School of the Pacific. I made it known that Sunday Evensong would belong to the seminarians, and a rotation of volunteer preachers and worship leaders for the evening service was established. This preserved the traditional contribution the Mission had made to the development of future clergy, as well as providing for the continuation of the recognized contribution seminarians had made to the Mission. They were indeed considered to be part of the church family. During my four years at Good Shepherd we enjoyed this mutually beneficial relationship with both faculty and students "on the hill." Generations of clergy remember with gratitude the love they received and the experiences they had as participants at Good Shepherd, West Berkeley.

Each of our members of the Mission accepted the fact that they were missionaries. Obviously they were not like the type of folk who might make a splash in the media; not the attorneys, surgeons, "top guns" or police who are features of television dramas. But they were heroes and heroines in their own right. I was a young priest; our core group were "senior citizens" who were much older and physically less able than I. We had great social inertias to overcome to make changes in mores with which our culture had too often grown satisfied. Although this was before the days of massive protests in Berkeley, we were determined to do what we believed to be right without demanding social change beyond our jurisdiction. I thought at the time that the kind of publicity that Bishop James A. Pike would later wish to focus on Good Shepherd would only convert a spontaneous effort to change ourselves into a conversion compelled by public opinion.

As the Vicar of Good Shepherd, it was my intention to follow the pattern for social change I perceived in Saint Paul's ministry. Paul had converted runaway slave Onesimus to Christ, then sent him back to his owner Philemon. In the Epistle to Philemon from his final imprisonment in Rome, Paul appealed for Philemon to accept Onesimus with equality as his Christian brother, not with severe punishment or death. This Onesimus was undoubtedly the one later mentioned in early Church records as Bishop of Ephesus. Righteous social changes that defy conquest by forcible means cannot resist the power of Christian love!

Gradually the little church filled to capacity with worshippers. People of the various races represented in the population of West Berkeley came to look us over. Then others came from other neighborhoods; then from other cities. Most loved what we were doing, wanted to become a part of it, and did so. If the Lord sent them, the Good Shepherd gathered them. We just set our own example. Others saw and chose to follow. At the time, what we were doing was different, but we did not appeal for external allies.

Initially, various artificial strategies were devised and utilized to help people feel welcome without making it too obvious. We mixed old timers with newcomers, simultaneously guiding people of various races to associate with each other in ways that, for some, were previously unfamiliar. For example, at parish dinners each table had an appointed host who would invite others according to a preplanned seating arrangement, and place cards reinforced the verbal introductions of the host. It was not with the intent of making us race tolerant (a phrase I despise), but to help us become friends. Diversity would enrich us. Our social experimentation of "priming the pump" was sufficiently diplomatic that it was never resented, and it was generally successful. Even now, as I write about our church members, I am not comfortable in having to report the race of each without special reason for doing so. For the most part I will leave that to the reader's imagination. By the grace of God we became a "salt and pepper" congregation with some cinnamon mixed in as well—friends of God and friends of one another.

Those who made history at this Mission Church were the lay people: the flock of the Good Shepherd. The story of the Mission cannot be told without paying tribute to Her people, how they demonstrated great courage in their daily lives, and how they contributed to the ministry in West Berkeley and in the Church beyond.

—◦◦◦—

I arrived at Good Shepherd in time to preside at the burial of Clarence Joseph Vroman, age 76, on August 5, 1956. His widow, Irma, had been Directress of the Altar Guild for many years, was knowledgeable and devoted to the task, and loved indoctrinating others into the mysteries of the sacristy and the Sanctuary. To fill the emptiness after loss of her husband, Irma volunteered to be my housekeeper during my bachelor days in the vicarage. She lived in a third floor walk-up attic apartment in one of Berkeley's older buildings that had been subdivided into multiple residences. Being short of stature and somewhat rotund, she experienced difficulty getting up and down three flights of stairs. However, second only to her loving loyalty, Irma's most lavish gift was her jolly sense of joy. After climbing those stairs to her apartment door and knocking three times (in the Name of the Father, and of the Son, and of the Holy Spirit), one could hear her laughter from within—even if she were two rooms away. Irma, known as "Tootsie" to her adult children and closest friends, made herself totally available to support the ministry of the Church.

Irma welcomed my request that she accompany me on visitations where having a witness would be an advantage. As trust grew in our "developing" neighborhood, telephone requests for consolation would come in to the vicarage both night and day. Most callers were invited to come to the office at a mutually convenient time. But there were tragedies, and such things as follow-ups to visits by police in incidents of domestic violence, rape or someone claiming to be in severe depression. These circumstances seemed to justify more immediate pastoral attention. On the other hand, intoxication and prostitution were not strangers in West Berkeley at the time. At any hour, a telephone call to Tootsie requesting a ride-along would be answered with a giggle and a response that she would meet me inside the front door of her apartment house as soon as I could drive there to fetch her. Her presence not only helped me build trust in the neighborhood, but she knew she was there to protect my personal image as well as that of the Church.

I believe Hiram Jacobs, a tall handsome gentleman from Panama, and his wife, were in their mid-thirties when she was taken suddenly ill. He rushed her to an emergency room, but she died on a gurney as he held her hand in a hospital hallway awaiting treatment. Hiram, a civilian employee at the Naval Aircraft Rework Facility at the Naval Air Station, Alameda, was left with their son Michael, who was about 5 years old at the time. This all occurred just before I arrived in Berkeley.

Hiram's brother, Father Solomon Jacobs, a parish priest serving then in the Diocese of Nebraska, came to his brother's side at the time of this loss. But Hiram was a man of courage, and he saw to it that Michael was dressed well, did good in school, and continued the violin lessons that his wife had wanted for him. Hiram served for extended periods on the Bishop's Committee and as Mission Treasurer. Many evenings were devoted to meetings as we got the church organized and brought it to financial stability. Hiram never revealed that his son Michael spent many of those evenings asleep in his car at the curb. When I finally learned this, I had regrets, but it was too late to make changes.

Little Michael, however, had involuntarily, in his own way, made his contribution to the development of the Mission in West Berkeley.

―⸱∿∿⸱―

Sophie Marshall, one of our delightful "seniors," had made her living as a milliner. She made ladies' hats for a major department store in San Francisco, and continued in retirement to work out of her solo apartment in West Berkeley. Sophie delighted in her craft, even as the need for it in our culture was dissolving. Rheumatoid arthritis was gnarling her hands and conquering her dexterity, and she could walk only with the aid of the steel braces that were strapped to both her legs. Still, Sophie kept her Altar Guild schedule, crossing four-lane traffic-laden San Pablo Avenue at her corner and walking four more blocks to the sacristy, where she would iron the linens and meticulously set up the Altar. We could only guess the amount of pain she endured constantly, because Sophie never complained. Good Shepherd was her family, and serving evidently gave meaning to her life.

―⸱∿∿⸱―

"With a name like O'Connor, are you Irish, Johnny?" When he would hear this commonly asked question: "Are you Irish, Johnny?" it would be met with a moment of silence in which his face would turn scarlet and the steam of emotions would rise almost to a bursting point. Then with hand on one hip and stump on the other, his reply would come: "No, by the Grrrace of Godt!" Johnny's brogue was indeed Scottish, and the strong determination in any task he put his mind to was a reflection of the kind of character that had developed in his ancestral highlands.

John, a Roman Catholic monk in former days, left the monastery for secular work in the Bay Area in which he had lost his right hand and forearm below the elbow in a plastics press. He gave up strong drink, resided with his sister Nell, and learned to live again. How does one tie shoes, paint houses, and drive and repair automobiles with one hand? Johnny demonstrated these tasks on a routine basis. Johnny found a home and family among us at Good Shepherd, and he loved the Episcopal Church (if it was "fittingly fancy"). During the rebuilding of our parish hall and the replacement of the foundations under the century-old church building, Johnny would be there pushing wheelbarrows loaded with dirt or cement, left hand on one handle and with the right handle in the inside crook of his other elbow. While I was in Connecticut for the "Outgoing Missionary Conference" in July of 1959, Johnny hung lily-of-the-valley wallpaper in a room in the vicarage that my wife Marjorie was preparing as a surprise for my return for a nursery for the baby we were expecting. Johnny had a clever name that had a Scottish twist to it for almost everything, and he kept everyone within hearing range constantly laughing.

—ɷɷɷ—

Ray Edwards was an engineer for the Naval Shipyard at Mare Island. To avoid breaking trust with him, I can only write that domestic life for him and for his small son was, in my opinion, a prolonged nightmare. Ray was a stalwart member of the Good Shepherd Chapter of the Brotherhood of Saint Andrew, served as Head Usher and was a dependable advisor to me as a friend and Bishop's Committee Member when I was vicar. Some years later, after Ray had retired and while I was serving as Chaplain to a squadron of Navy ammunition ships home ported at Mare Island, Ray called from his home in East Oakland and invited me to lunch with him at a restaurant in Vallejo. This was a reunion that I anticipated with gladness, but as we ate and looked out over the harbor, Ray's news was not good. I was the first person other than his physician to know that Ray was dying rapidly of cancer. We prayed together over a table of empty dishes. A few months later, when I was at sea, my beloved brother in Christ was gone, leaving his wonderful space in this world empty as well.

—ɷɷɷ—

I first met Esther Lee Brown while visiting door-to-door in the neighborhood. Esther was a single mother, raising her son Rodney from birth to maturity with every bit of energy she could muster. Esther suffered from a progressive neurological disease that did eventually confine her to a wheelchair. But even after that, Esther was a regular at church and at every social function the Church would hold, always dressed appropriately for the occasion. She would volunteer for any task she could handle, always filled with laughter. Esther had an extended family in the area, and before long she had them involved at Good Shepherd. With scholarship aid, Rodney attended a college preparatory high school on the East Coast as a boarder. Esther quickly became one of the Good Shepherd pioneers who shared our vision.

———*♫♫♫*———

Chief Petty Officer, U.S. Naval Reserve (Retired), Austin Nottage was the Master of Ceremonies of the Church of the Good Shepherd. He loved to carry the Processional Cross or serve as the Bishop's Chaplain during his visitations. Austin had come from the Caribbean originally, worked on the track crew, and later as a Porter for the Southern Pacific Railroad. When serving in the Navy as a lad, Austin learned to write his name for the first time, and then he learned to read. Mr. Nottage, as he was always known, carried himself with the great dignity that was becoming a Crucifer and Master of Ceremonies, and he never failed in his generosity, dress and demeanor. Austin Nottage was a proud gentleman of the Church and proud of his position at the head of the procession.

———*♫♫♫*———

Madge McKinnie was a strong minded Anglo-Catholic Episcopalian. Her English background included an inheritance of authoritative liturgical expertise, which was offered lovingly (but not always gently) in such a manner as to keep her priest from offending the Lord God. But this attitude kept dear Madge going, and it kept some of the rest of us in line as well.

Madge was approaching retirement from the Helen Keller Institute at the California State School for the Deaf, which then was in Berkeley. Madge would take me into the school to introduce me to the triple-handicapped, and to introduce these children to the Church as well. She taught me how to place one of their small hands on my face so that fingers touched my lips and my throat at the same time, enabling them to pick up the movement of my mouth together with the vibrations of my larynx, thus to "hear" what I was saying. She introduced them to me by having them feel the clerical collar around my neck. Madge knew and cared for those children in a way that could only be described as a loving miracle. By her very presence at Good Shepherd the teaching of the Faith was inevitable, because she lived and breathed Church.

Of course she was especially wonderful as teacher of our Mission's children. Madge was exceedingly generous to the Church, and did numerous benevolent deeds for people behind the scenes, always avoiding recognition. Without teaching after retirement, however, Madge's strength seemed to fail her. Sometime after I went overseas, she left for British Columbia to be near a daughter, where she spent her final days.

—*ᵥᵥᵥ*—

Eleanor Bliss and Lamitsoi and Bill Williamson, strong pioneers of the original group, still live in the East Bay Area, cherish precious memories, and share them with their grown children who were once a part of the Good Shepherd's flock as well. Lilian Vezey, who had a large role in the reconstruction of the buildings, died peacefully on November 9, 2002, three weeks and three days short of her 99th birthday. She was very active at the retirement facility in Oakland where I visited her. Dr. Bill Bouwsma, U.C. Professor of History, once so present with his family at the Mission, has retired. Sam White, sometime Chef at Spenger's Fish Grotto near the Mission, and his wife June, seem to have disappeared from the neighborhood without a trace. Elva Reynolds, who kept the "Women's Auxiliary" together through thick and thin, may have vacated her Ninth Street home as well.

"Mike" McHone, our first Bishop's Warden, died while I was in Asia. Mother "Bill" Carrington could no longer muster the energy to sing in the choir (and to kick off her red shoes when the sermon lasted beyond her expectations of propriety). She died after seven years of confinement to bed, with nursing care in her home. Clergy from the Good Shepherd consistently brought her the Blessed Sacrament, including during her final hours among us. Dorothy Foster, our beloved organist, was ministered to by retired Fr. William Fay of All Souls' Parish and his wife Marjorie during her final eight years in a crowded five-bed room in a local convalescent hospital. Austin Nottage died all but abandoned in the Livermore Veterans Administration custodial care facility. I replaced the jacket which had been taken off him while he slept. Mary Lawson, whose attentive sons were Acolytes as boys, died a few days short of 90 on April 26, 2001.

Most of the "elders" of our original "core group" have slipped away to be with the Master as well. After I returned to the United States and the West Coast, I was able to visit all of the now-deceased members I have mentioned except Sophie Marshall and Mike McHone. Undoubtedly there are others I have failed to mention (and perhaps to remember appropriately), who were beyond my ability to find and to see once again.

———

In the forty months I served the Mission of the Good Shepherd, 110 Baptisms were administered and recorded: 110 Souls brought to Christ! Many of the then-younger, early converts seem to have joined the transient tides so typical of Californians, and have moved on. We can only pray that what they learned of Christ at Good Shepherd has accompanied them. Other folk have come to take their place on the old pews and kneelers they left behind.

Good Shepherd survived my departure for the missionary ministry in the Philippines, then as a Chaplain on the battlefields of Viet Nam. The Mission survived the reign of the "hippies" that apparently overwhelmed those in charge for a period in the 1960s, who evidently encouraged the sale of the vicarage and abused the interiors of some of the other reconstructed church properties. Still, the Mission has survived to carry on a vital ministry in West Berkeley, and to house such activities so essential to the community as Head Start and Alcoholics Anonymous—adjuncts to Her Ministry of worship and pastoral care.

We of the racial majority can empathize to a certain extent, but we can never fully know what it is like to be a minority in this nation which makes hollow promises of equality, even seeks to legislate them. This was more beyond our understanding in the middle of the last century. This comment is added to pay tribute not only to majority adults who opened their hearts and invitation to those unlike themselves, but especially to those who accepted that invitation to join this congregation. The burning depth of personal affront to the unfairness that so many live with on a daily basis was beginning to erupt in the process of national integration that was not destined to be peaceful across our land.

Good Shepherd became a family because those involved mustered such a degree of spiritual strength that latent resistance to change among the majority and a potential for rage among the minorities were gracefully sublimated for the greater good. No such resources were required of persons who lived in a place and time still content to ignore the need to integrate the races, and those who were satisfied with (even voluntarily) segregated churches. But these sacrificed the powerful results of alliances that respected differences while being eager to learn from and be enriched by them.

The vision that we shared and saw develop during the last half of the decade of the 1950s in West Berkeley brought us together in an everlasting way. We prayed together, planned together, worked together and played together. That vision extends beyond the horizon of this age, and it has had a lasting effect on the lives of those who participated in its evolution. I miss these courageous saints more than words or tears can express. But *we shall meet again!* And *the* Good Shepherd will be there with us then too, just as He so gently and lovingly gathered us together once before in His Holy Flock on the eastern shore of San Francisco Bay.

—*Apocrypha* Ecclesiasticus 44:1f, 9–14;
St. John 10:14–18; Philemon; I John 3:1–3

Angels of Whom We are Unaware

ugh came to the Vicarage of the Good Shepherd Mission looking for help. This century-old church with its tall spire was visible from the Santa Fe tracks a few blocks to the east and the Southern Pacific mainline by the Bay nine blocks to the west, so appeals such as this one by transients were routine.

Hugh was a tall man whose weather-beaten frame betrayed him as one who had known hard times. As we talked, I learned that Hugh had been working in the car barns of the transit system, sweeping the trolley cars at the completion of their runs. But the trolleys had been towed off to the Emeryville Yards, where they had been rolled over on their sides and burned. The buses that replaced them were serviced elsewhere, and, eighteen months short of retirement, Hugh had been turned out without any identifiable livelihood. But Hugh wanted to work.

I was immediately interested in this rusty-haired, unkempt, social orphan, because he was looking for employment to give his life meaning, and, unlike most who came to my door in the middle of the week, he was not seeking a handout. My thought was to employ him to do some maintenance, cleaning, or gardening at the church. However, I soon learned that only the latter option was within the limits of his capabilities, and even that soon proved to be marginal. But he was indeed a Child of God, and as a young priest I was eager to exercise my role as quarterback on God's West Berkeley team.

In order to verify Hugh's story, I went to make a call on him at his stated place of residence. My trail led to lower Broadway in old Oakland, then through an obscure door between a dusty pawn shop and an unhealthy looking tattoo parlor next to a bar. I climbed a very long staircase, and proceeded down the long dark hall of the upper story of this fire-trap tenement with many numbered doors on either side. Just as I thought I had reached a dead end, the hallway twisted so as to connect with another narrow passage dimly lit by an occasional bare lightbulb hanging from the ceiling. This corridor took me into the upper story of an adjoining structure. No fire escapes were visible anywhere from inside this confining loft-dungeon. Finally I found Hugh's dingy room, evidently—by the ambient odor—not far from the door of the common toilet. Hugh's eyes sparkled when I announced to him: "Mister, you're hired." For a very miserly amount, Good Shepherd Mission had acquired a gardener.

It became evident to leading members of the congregation long before it came to my attention that Hugh had a brown thumb rather than a green one. The old roses in the garden that had survived generations of neglect began to display their displeasure with my choice of their caregiver. The shrubs and the grass also browned to display visible complaint, and the ladies of the parish expressed their dissatisfactions vocally, and with much less restraint. What was I to do with this Child of God?

Hugh's gratitude for his new sense of belonging also motivated him to undertake the long (and expensive for him) bus ride from West Oakland to West Berkeley on Sunday mornings to attend worship. Entering the church noticeably late, his boots would pound down the aisle to the front pew. There he would take up residence directly beneath the pulpit. (I must interject that one must come early to an Episcopal Church in order to get one of the back seats.) Yet Hugh liked to sit where he would see and hear. Once settled, he would open his brown bag and start eating its contents, pop the top on a Coke, and then cock his ear to listen intently to the sermon as he munched and swallowed. To complete my description of his appearance, I am forced to add that Hugh drooled from the partially paralyzed right side of his lower lip.

After a few weeks of patient endurance, I was met with the predictable delegation protesting my pastoral acumen and on the verge of insulting my spiritual and familial heritage. "Hugh has to go!" they demanded. Dear Madge, a devout supporter of the enriched liturgics which I espoused, was the leader of the protesting pack. I defended the very mission of the Christian Church which I believed justified his retention. What followed was a period of somewhat uncomfortable détente between pastor and people, with little change in the behavior of our new parishioner and gardener.

We suffered through Lent and Holy Week with liturgical penitence, but little redemption on either side of the standoff. Hugh, unaware of the firestorm that surrounded him, remained in his garden on weekdays and in his front pew on Sundays. Then came Easter morning of 1959. The sermon came right from the lectionary's appointed Gospel lesson, and, without any intrigue on my part, the Holy Spirit made full use of my humble pulpit offering.

The story told of how the grieving Mary at the entrance to the Tomb heard kind words from one she supposed to have been the gardener, but when she responded she found to her amazement that it was indeed the Risen Christ. The homily expanded the topic with a lesson on how Jesus comes among us in unexpected ways and through unexpected agents.

A repentant Madge came to me after that service with tears flowing. "Has Hugh been baptized?" she asked. I said that I doubted that he was, but I would ask him. "If not," she pleaded, "I would like to present him and be his Godmother." The Risen Jesus had indeed worked yet another miracle. That Easter Day the congregation adopted Hugh, not only as a Child of God but as their Christian Brother.

On the Sunday after the Ascension, after some brief instructions, Hugh Greer Hamilton appeared in church in a nice brown suit and tie (undoubtedly given him by an "anonymous donor"). He was surrounded by the very delegation that had strongly opposed his presence before the "Easter wonder." And Madge, dear Madge, took his arm proudly and marched him to the baptismal font. The congregation crowded around as I asked: "Name this Child." Madge led the people of the Church of the Good Shepherd as all exclaimed: "Hugh Greer!" And as I poured the water, my soul sang as I said boldly: "Hugh Greer, I baptize thee in the Name of the Father, and of the Son, and of the Holy Ghost. Amen."

I do not know where Hugh Greer Hamilton is today—yet I am sure he is in the Arms of Jesus. However, the additional miracle that I am able to report more than four decades later is that the ancient rose bushes in the gardens of the Good Shepherd Church in West Berkeley still bloom, and the grass beside the church is still green—in spite of my years there as Vicar, and in spite of our gardener with a brown thumb.

—ST. JOHN 20:14ff, 18

Restoring the Glory

*A*nna Titmus was a rather large woman. A widow living alone, a retired school teacher for whom the Church was family, Mrs. Titmus felt it was her duty to sit in the front pew each Sunday and to lead the congregation in their responses. Her classroom voice was always one word ahead of those who obediently followed her in unison, as she put us through the paces of the Apostles' Creed, the Venite, and the General Thanksgiving. In a congregation like Good Shepherd, Mrs. Titmus (never just "Anna") was understood and adored by all.

Several weeks into Advent 1956, preparations for Christmas began in earnest. A growing number of husbands came out of hiding to repair, varnish, and clean the Church. The wooden pews were removed during the first days of one week for the floorboards to be revarnished in time to dry by the following Sunday. It was a major project, initiated to prepare for the celebration of the Birth of the Savior and the Mission's first midnight Mass in decades.

In the process of replacing the pews, their order became inadvertently reversed. The one usually at the very rear of the nave, so placed because of the crack that ran the length of plank that made up the bottom of the seat, got placed up front. And, you guessed it, this was the very one that was occupied by our beloved, portly cheerleader the following Sunday.

Now the homiletical objectives of Advent include not only that of reminding worshippers and the world beyond their circle that the birthday of the Savior is approaching, but also to remind all that He will return, thus to herald the apocalypse. When our dear Mrs. Titmus first stood that Third Sunday in Advent to lead the congregation in their liturgical duties, the longitudinal crack in the plank that had temporarily spread in the support of her posterior simultaneously closed upon her as she arose. There is no doubt in my mind that the shriek she involuntarily gave, with all the volume her girth could muster, adequately alarmed all within several blocks of the old church that the end of the age was imminently expected.

What was to follow less than a fortnight later was to be my first Christmas Midnight Mass with my own congregation. The thrill of anticipation, coupled with a case of nerves, accelerated as Advent approached its final days. The ladies of the Altar Guild bustled about, beautifying the Sanctuary. I practiced with all the lay participants to ensure that the first of such services that had graced that congregation, long without a priest, would go off without a flaw.

It was 11:30 P.M., the announced time to begin, yet the choir was still vesting. When any scheduled event for which I am responsible starts late, I am uneasy throughout the event that follows. This was no exception. The processional party finally intoned "O come all ye faithful," and when we arrived at our places in the Chancel, I faced the Altar with my back to the congregation (as we did in those days) and solemnly began the prayers of preparation and chanted the Collect of Christmas. Then with my back still properly to the people, I awaited the Senior Warden, our beloved toothless plumber, to approach the lectern and announce the Epistle lesson, as he was accustomed to do on any given Sunday morning. We waited, and we waited, but no lector's voice broke the awkward silence. It seems that Mike had enjoyed a bit of Christmas cheer before the service began, with the result that he had lost his place in the order of things. After this significant pause, I, in my agitation, whirled around within the Altar Rail and, with book in hand, began to announce the Epistle. As I did so I found myself in a vocal duet with our tardy lector who, by then, with the assistance of family members, had recovered his equilibrium. I withdrew so that he could continue without my assistance. I swallowed deeply to contain my embarrassment.

On cue, two beautiful young Black Acolytes flanked me with lighted torch candles, and another held the *Book of the Gospels* before me. As they led me to the center of the Chancel steps for the chanting of the Holy Gospel, I recall that in contrast to the comfort their precision gave me, I still thought to myself almost audibly: *What on earth can go wrong next?* At the very instant we reached our station, midway between the lectern and the pulpit, ready for the Christmas Gospel to begin, sparks flashed and danced along the trail of ancient wires that electrified former gas lamps that illuminated the entire interior of the Nave. The next moment, we were bathed in darkness. I had the answer to my question.

The eyes of the Acolytes sparkled with delight as I sang the Gospel while the candles they held performed the function for which they were originally intended in the liturgy. At my direction, after the Gospel and the Creed, the boys stood tirelessly below the pulpit and raised their torches so I could see to deliver my well-prepared sermon. Our candlelit service was more inspiring than had we planned it that way. The first verses of the carols were familiar to all and were sung without the aid of lighting or reed organ. Also with the help of our torch bearers, no one fell on the chancel steps coming up to receive Holy Communion. That service ended with a blessing received—in more ways than one.

George Pascoe had retired from the Berkeley Unified School District as a maintenance man and custodian. Then in his mid-seventies, he undertook the bracing of the church bell tower with shoring timbers. The great bell had been stilled for years. This was in obedience to a legendary understanding of local law that the only bells allowed to be rung in the city were those on state property, namely those of the campanile of the University of California. I was warned not to risk arrest by breaking the silence of the sabbath. Long before civil disobedience would become a norm for Berkeley, I was persuaded that the risk would be worth taking. Incidentally, now church bells peal freely throughout Berkeley to announce the Lord's Day. Good Shepherd led the way! But another risk was involved. When the ringing of the heavy bell rocked the steeple, those assembled for worship were pelted with tiny particles of plaster, and the wooden building creaked and groaned like a sailing vessel in a storm. George Pascoe rigged ladders, blocks and tackle, and put an end to our fears of collapse. Later he scaled the steeple itself to repair loose shingles and to regild its cross.

The above examples were just a few of many vivid reminders that confronted us with this century-old steeple-crowned structure, the dilapidated parish hall, and the vicarage cottage that stood long neglected on the corner of Ninth and Hearst Streets. It took nearly four years to restore the buildings to a safe and respectable condition. The old single car garage fell over with a strong push, the rose gardens were refurbished, the lawns mowed, and new white paint lavishly covered the peeling surplus Navy gray—at least to heights where our ladders could reach. But the old church had to be jacked up and the crumbling foundation and footings had to be strengthened or replaced with new concrete. I devised a plan by which the aged cottage-vicarage could be joined to the old parish hall to form a central entry and a pass through kitchen. The cottage could then be used for classrooms and an office for the church. The old kitchen that reeked of leaking gas and which had provided a home for a family of rats, would be demolished from the far end of the hall where it had been added as a lean-to. The old hall needed to have its shingled sides stuccoed and broken windows replaced with steel framed ones that would open and close. Crash bar exit doors would be added for safety and to comply with current building codes. The house acquired by the diocese around the corner could then become a proper vicarage. The plan was a good one. The only thing lacking was a miracle to provide for it.

About this time there appeared an angel in the form of the son-in-law of two of the long-time members. Harry Attfield and his wife Thirza Mary Ellen Williams Attfield, immigrants from England years before, brought their love of the Church of England with them. They were a West Berkeley pioneer family. William Vezey, their son-in-law, had his own construction company. He and the Attfield's daughter, his wife Lilian, first offered to re-plaster the interior of the church and to wire and install new and adequate lighting fixtures. The result was beautiful, and it brought a new dimension of safety to the congregation as well!

The two banks of choir pews faced each other across the Chancel in traditional collegiate style. The Chancel floor between them was raised about seven inches to the same level as the choir pews. This change gave a more spacious appearance to the Chancel. The Good Shepherd window and the Scripture texts in calligraphy on either side of the window resembled a triptych of three arches above the Altar. The indented structural arch that framed all three was plastered in a slightly darker shade of tan, which brought unity and centrality to the worship center of the church.

The difference was awesome, and completely beyond our capabilities and our dreams.

Bill Vezey's next year's project was to paint properly the exterior of the historic structure, all labor and material being provided without cost by the Vezeys. Two decades later, the Church of the Good Shepherd was declared a California State Historical Monument.

It was safe to say that Bill Vezey and his wife Lilian were enjoying seeing the results of their creative gifts. What they had contributed was even more lovely than they could have imagined, and they were making history.

At a conference with Bill and his builders, I revealed my hopes for the parish hall and the cottage, and I asked what our congregation could do about it. Upon closer inspection, the contractor's crew quickly discovered areas of the hall floor that were sinking. The dangerous nature of the lean-to kitchen at the rear was blatantly obvious. We discussed the need for replacement of the antique pot-bellied stove, which was eventually sold for a very good price as a genuine antique. That stove had been the only source of heat for the entire cavernous interior of the hall. Vezey's men suggested the installation of a force-draft central furnace for the consolidated structure, once the old vicarage and the parish hall were joined with the kitchen and entry hall between them. We carefully sorted out what the people of the church would be able to do and estimated the funds that we needed to raise. We needed to provide for the use of some heavy equipment. We composed a two-year plan. I made it clear that I did not intend taking advantage of the generosity of the Vezeys, but we needed professional guidance and oversight. Likewise, the growing congregation needed to help themselves reach for these goals, so that any still needed philanthropic efforts would not overwhelm or cripple our Christian stewardship by making us too dependent, now that we had a good start.

I was an active member of the West Berkeley Lions Club, a service organization composed mainly of the industrialists whose factories and warehouses were located in this area adjacent to the bay shore. Our efforts on behalf of the community were known and respected. At a luncheon meeting of the club at Spenger's Fish Grotto, I gave a presentation that was overheard by a cheering section of the kitchen staff including parishioner, Chef Sam White. I suggested that if our parish hall could provide West Berkeley with a youth center and a place for such activities as "Head Start" and Alcoholics Anonymous, their industries might suffer less from intrusive vandalism and burglaries, and many Berkeley people would be helped.

I asked for "imaginative donations in kind" to help us with the construction. The equipment rental manager offered us the free use of compressors and jackhammers, the lumberyard gave us a discount, and, among other such offers, the Berkeley Pump Company provided the use of their printing and publicity department for two successive Saturdays.

During those two days, their professionals, together with our volunteers, designed and printed an illustrated appeal brochure with a return "business reply" envelope to be enclosed with each. Our church members set about mailing them to every business and potential donor we could envisage. It was obvious that we had struck a sympathetic nerve. Ten thousand dollars came pouring into our mail slot, quite a large response in those days. Our congregation was composed of people who knew the meaning of hard work. Many were artisans and laborers. Even handicapped persons demanded tasks they could accomplish. People of both genders mobilized around the vision, and reconstruction of the facilities was underway.

"Play Days" were organized by our loyal one-armed adult Acolyte, Johnny O'Conner (who would do anything as long as you did not call him Irish). "Bring your toys," he would announce in Church. "Your shovels, wheelbarrows, hammers, and brushes." Johnny called the ladies of the congregation "The Sisters of the Loose Habits," and he "summoned them" to "feed the lot of 'em," to paint and chip, and to help in a myriad of ways. Marjorie and I tarpapered and sealed the roof of the cottage in a single operation that lasted through the day and by floodlight until 4 A.M. the next morning. Bill Vezey and his builders watched over us and contributed what we were not able to do.

As our rebuilding and beautification continued, the neighborhood became gradually transfigured as well. The other churches for a mile around began to paint up and fix up. The old Victorian houses sprouted painted fences and colorful flower gardens. Cars on wide Ninth Street began to drive slower, and fewer dogs seemed to roam at night. A new self-esteem seemed to be radiating throughout West Berkeley. From the beginning to a point where we could see that the major goals of the dream for reconstruction had been accomplished required thirty months of hard labor. But the church was filled, the Sunday School flourished, and the church achieved self-support almost casually. Indeed, my years in West Berkeley were nothing short of an extended and developing revelation of the Lord for me, as I believe it was for all whose lives were in any way touched by this fellowship.

Those who gravitated to Good Shepherd were professors, garbage collectors, widows, mechanics, nurses, bankers, teachers, and accountants. We were invalids and robust laborers, children, adults, and the aged. We were people of every size, shape, and race. We shared joys and tragedies, sickness and health, convictions and redemptions, life and death. We prayed together, worked together, sang together, cried together. Many came among us, gained confidence by God's love that we shared, then moved up the social scale, up the economic ladder, and farther up into the hills. A third of the parish left us that way each year, and we rejoiced for them. But, in order to grow, we had to do much better than just replace "our losses" each year. We were happy to be "a pumping station for the Lord." We were grateful that each of us knew we were growing personally and together at the feet of the Good Shepherd, whose image over our Altar showed Him gathering His lambs unto Himself.

—I KINGS 8:26–30; PSALM 127:1

In Love and Peace Together

The congregation heard in the announcements that the Senior Warden would have some special news to share with the congregation at Coffee Hour. The Crucifer lifted the Cross and the

Choir followed down the aisle. As the Celebrant, I came behind with hymnal in hand, while all sang with gusto the recessional hymn based upon the 23rd Psalm. When we got to the third verse, I burst into laughter that could not be contained. These were the words that were the source of my amusement:

"Perverse and foolish oft I strayed
But yet in love he sought me,
And on his shoulder gently laid,
*And home rejoicing brought me."**

Our secret would soon be revealed. And it was a secret, closely guarded by me and by Marjorie, because we needed to discern our own destinies free from the designs of a well-meaning, yet somewhat patronizing, constituency. For this reason, we met and dated out of Berkeley for the eight months we felt were required for us to become friends, and, as it developed, to contemplate marriage.

Marjorie, then happily employed in a Berkeley bank, had moved with her twin sister and a girlfriend into an apartment a few blocks from Good Shepherd. They had been worshipping uptown at Saint Mark's Church. In order to find out if they would be the only White people who attended the Episcopal Church in their new neighborhood—not wanting to be exceptions—they decided to attend once to see. That first Sunday they came to the Church of the Good Shepherd, they found us to be a "salt and pepper" congregation where they felt quite welcome. They also found that the young priest was instantly solicitous of newcomers in general, but of these newcomers in particular. An invitation for lunch at a restaurant near the bank where Marjorie was employed soon followed. This meeting would be the last for quite some time to occur so blatantly close to home. Before the Coffee Hour announcement of my betrothal had been completed and the name of my intended had been uttered, some members of the congregation rushed toward another person that some of the ladies had "thoughtfully" planned for me to pursue. When the Church Warden had completed his reading of the contents of the sealed envelope revealing Marjorie's name, one dear lady seated at a card table that held her refreshments thrust her forehead onto it so forcefully in disbelief that the table shook and the coffee splattered.

Marjorie Clark and I spent the next six months in preparation for joining our lives. The house on Hearst Street was remodeled and furnished as a proper vicarage, even though the other cottage had not yet been incorporated into the parish hall construction. Both of us brought to completion all of our individual obligations, and we received the bishop's permission and pre-marriage counseling in anticipation of the appointed day.

All Saints was the name of Marjorie's Episcopal high school in Sioux Falls, South Dakota, and All Saints was the name of the seminary chapel at the Church Divinity School. Therefore, our nuptials would be solemnized on All Saints' Day (November 1st). Marjorie's dad, Father John B. Clark, Chaplain at Bishop Hare School on the Rosebud Reservation, would journey to Berkeley to marry us. Our beloved Bishop Karl Morgan Block, died shortly before our wedding. The Right Reverend James Albert Pike graciously consented to celebrate the Nuptial Mass at our service, deferring to the bride's father to consecrate our union.

Bishop Pike honored me with his confidence in many ways, and even though I shall always be grateful for that kindness, I knew from the start that I would not be able to follow him with complete sincerity. His mercurial leadership and insistence on micro-management frightened me. Further, I was wise enough to recognize that after the relationship I had enjoyed with Bishop Block, for whom I was grieving, not even the Holy Spirit would have satisfied me as his replacement.

Bishop Pike advised me that when a priest marries in a parish, or when major construction has been accomplished, "it is time to leave." He reminded me that as my time at the West Berkeley Mission approached four years, both had occurred. Knowing my strengths in evangelism strategy and my passion for reclaiming inner cities for the Church, he offered me a new position supervising the five old parishes "south of Market Street" in San Francisco. This exciting prospect was hard for a young priest to decline, but I heard myself reply that I had always wanted to be a missionary in Asia, and while I had youth, health, and a willing spouse, this was probably the time for me to answer that Call.

We were conscious that we were older than many who marry, and that we wanted children while the "biological clock" was still running in our favor. Karla Nancy was born that August. She was named for Bishop Karl Morgan Block and his late wife Nancy.

Our departure for the Philippines as missionaries was delayed until our infant was five months of age, old enough to receive the necessary battery of inoculations required of even so young an "Appointed Missionary" of the Episcopal Church. In the meantime, we packed and sold or gave away our belongings, including our station wagon.

While still Vicar of Good Shepherd, I participated in a very helpful Outgoing Missionaries' Conference at Seabury House in Connecticut. I was also able to attend, under the sponsorship of the Episcopal Church, an intensive summer course at Stanford in Chinese language. This course fulfilled a long-standing ambition of mine.

We left our beloved Good Shepherd on January 5, 1960 for Baguio City in the mountains of Luzon in the Philippine Islands, into the great unknown and a new chapter of life and ministry for the three of us. Our departure from this loving flock and church family was a tearful one. My parents drove us away from the newly painted and wallpapered vicarage beside the church on Hearst Street to the San Francisco International Airport. I can still hear the parting farewell comment uttered by our mission gardener and newly baptized Christian, Hugh Hamilton: "Why can't you just stay home and mind your own business?"

—PROVERBS 31:10, 25f

---

* From *The Hymnal 1940,* No. 345, (Second Tune) Copyright by Church Pension Fund. New York: the Church Hymnal Corporation. Words by Henry Williams Baker, 1868, based on Psalm 23. Used by permission of Church Publishing Incorporated

CHAPTER 4

Philippine Missionary Adventures Begin

Orientation to Our Next Destination

*L*ate 19th century history reveals that most non-Roman Churches confronted the enormous task of fulfilling "the Great Commission" in Asia by agreeing on comity arrangements designed to avoid a duplication of evangelistic endeavors. This explains the lasting territorial influence of certain denominations that have become identified with indigenous churches in various areas of that part of the world. For example, the Presbyterians dedicated missionaries to Korea, Christian and Missionary Alliance evangelized Indo-China, and portions of other countries were similarly agreed upon. This geographic apportionment of a century ago also can be observed in the theological and liturgical customs in the various districts (dioceses), individual parishes, and the leaders of the current consolidation of non-Roman Christian churches in the People's Republic of China.

Observing that comity, responsibility for missionary outreach in the Philippines was originally accepted by the American Episcopal Church for four distinct populations: British, European and American expatriates and embassy personnel, mostly in Manila; the Chinese in Manila; Igorot Tribes in northern Luzon, and the Morros in Zamboanga. The latter two populations had been abandoned by early Roman Catholic missionaries as being too difficult to convert.

Igorots are the aboriginal peoples of the Cordilleras Mountains. "Aboriginal" carries with it inappropriate derogatory implications of "primitive." However, a better definition is "earliest known, primary, or first inhabitants." Their history is not unlike that of the Celts, the aboriginals who seceded the lowlands of "England" to the invading Angles and Saxons, retreating to the highlands of what we know as Wales, Scotland, and Northumbria. There they made their stand and defended their independence and ethnicity. Igorots are proud that, although their ancestors surrendered the "Lowlands" to those who came to the islands later, they took to the rugged mountains and retained their integrity.

Life in the Cordilleras is harder, the weather colder, and the terrain more demanding. These are the folks whose ancestors created rice terraces on the mountainsides in pre-Christian times, which are now numbered among the wonders of the world. Through generations of acclimation to their rugged habitat, the Igorot people are genetically distinguished by their short but solid physique, hearty determination, and an independent way of life. In Bishop Brent's years of leadership, the Anglican Mission found a welcome with the Igorots, where the Roman Mission with its Spanish colonial mind-set had failed in its thrust. (The approach of the Roman Church evidently succeeded elsewhere in the Philippines).

From our first day in the Mountain Province onward, Marjorie and I recognized that we would be learning as well as teaching among a strong, proud, and admirable people, who had grown to love and worship Christ through a deep devotion to Anglo-Catholic faith and worship. We would always feel valued and loved by them. This was an awesome beginning to our overseas mission ministry, and it would leave upon us an unforgettable mark, for which we are lastingly grateful.

—ST. MATTHEW 28:18ff

Marjorie Felt Right at Home

We circled the airstrip surrounded by green fields lush with banana trees and tiger grass. We finally landed quietly next to a Quonset hut that was, at the time, the Manila International Airport. The flight from Honolulu had taken 23.5 hours, with fueling stops at Midway and Guam where we were not allowed to leave our seats. In January 1960, there were no airfields west of Hawaii that could accommodate jet airliners. Baby Karla, five-and-a-half-months of age, travelled in a small crib fastened to the bulkhead in front of our seats. As we circled Guam on our westward flight, we photographed her with the island jungle to be seen through the aircraft's porthole over her shoulder. That picture also showed outside the window the port side propellers and a beach far below—near which she would one day live. How could we ever know what might lie ahead for us?

Upon arrival, we were invited to stay briefly in the home of the Rt. Rev. and Mrs. Lyman C. Ogilby on the big church compound in Quezon City, the capital suburb of Manila. Our first night's sleep in the Bishop's Residence was brought to an abrupt and very early morning end with the crowing of roosters that neighbored at the adjoining Saint Andrew's Theological Seminary.

Soon Reinaldo, Bishop Ogilby's driver, would be whisking us in the diocesan van northward on Luzon's two-lane National Highway. He expertly avoided multiple potholes, horse-drawn two-wheeled *karetelas* (provincial "pickup trucks"), *kalesas* ("taxis"), and an occasional carabao (water buffalo) on the road.

The Kennon Road took us from the beaches of the China Sea to an elevation of over 4,500 feet in slightly more than a dozen hazardous zigzag miles, crossing river gorges far below on unsupported single-lane Bailey Bridges. We finally arrived at Baguio (meaning "storm" in local dialect), at the time a Chartered City of less than 30,000, nestled in pine forests. It serves as the southern entrance to the Mountain Province and the "summer capital" of the Philippine government. The Baguio Hotel was there, as was Camp John Hay, the American armed forces' R&R Center and golf course. This is the cool-weather location of residences of colonial expatriates. Many of these homes have passed to wealthy Filipinos and officials.

Baguio City is surrounded by gold and copper mines that had tunneled underground from the walls of great canyons carved by nature out of the Cordilleras Mountains. This is the territory where the Japanese troops fought the tough Filipino Scouts a decade and a half before we arrived. Prior to our departure from California, local newspapers reported—in small articles on back pages—the massacre of Christian missionaries at the remote northeastern base of this range.

We were greeted as celebrities on our arrival at Baguio City's Easter School. Mr. Esteban Bañga-an, Headmaster, and Mr. Eusebio Boteñgan, his assistant, welcomed us and baby Karla with open arms, and helped us unload at the former residence of Suffragan Bishop Wilner on the hillside just above the school. My position would be to serve with indigenous catechists and clergy on the staff of the missionary Priest-in-Charge, to provide Sacramental services and pastoral care as a circuit rider for thirty-five preaching "out-stations" of the Epiphany Mission headquartered at the church in La Trinidad (Provincial Capital adjacent to Baguio). In addition, I was to act as Director for two large elementary schools: Easter School in Baguio, and Saint Elizabeth's School, Acupan, at the head of the canyon where Benguet Consolidated Mines had their principal gold mining tunnel entrance and offices.

We were informed that the following Saturday we would be entertained by Easter School students and faculty, and by Baguio's Resurrection Parish children and adults, with a great circle and demonstrations of the Courting and War Dances of the Igorot Tribes.

In addition to the Benguet people native to this subprovince, many of those living in Baguio City at the time were representatives of tribes further north in the mountains. Many from these more remote tribes migrated to the Benguet area around Baguio City for purposes of employment. Gold and other precious ore mines in the surrounding canyons and the chromite mines south along the China Sea coastal mountains in Zambales Province provided Igorots four pesos a day (then equivalent to one U.S. dollar) pay for a miner once he was at his post far below the earth's surface. "Portal-to-portal pay" was an unheard of concept in that place and time.

———∞———

My latest visit to the Philippines was in 1985, and at that time I observed significant changes in infrastructures everywhere. The Manila International Airport is now a huge concrete structure that had survived a major fire several years before my visit. The National Highway no longer had men in tiger grass rain ponchos, standing by each major pothole during storms ready to shovel gravel back into "their hole" after each truck passed. The portion I traversed had become a four-lane divided freeway. The Bailey Bridges along the Kennon Road had been replaced with concrete two-lane spans. Easter School had expanded to include a high school department, and, more recently, has added a junior college as well. The Easter School Weaving Room and shop that Marjorie had managed were still in operation. All this made me feel that Marjorie, Karla, and I had been a part of the history of both the Church and the Nation. However, the squatter shacks and the open sewers (*esteros*) still occupied major portions of Manila. Some things on the planet are slow to change.

———∞———

I divert the reader's attention at this point to explain Marjorie's background and to tell about her family. My reason for this is that I wish to underscore my conviction that with God there are no blind streets! He guides our life experiences in ways that prepare us for our future journeys, and He does His Work with certainty.

Marjorie spent her formative teenage years in Mobridge, South Dakota. Her priest father, the Reverend John Booth Clark, was Superintending Presbyter of the clergy and catechist team on the Standing Rock Reservation. He was also Rector of Saint James' Parish in town (a church then considered to be in the "White Field" in the ministry of the diocese).

Marjorie was familiar with her father's pastoral duties of providing Divine Services in many places, making pastoral visitation rounds, and meeting with the Brotherhood of Saint Andrew on the Reservation. Her grandfather, the Reverend Aaron Baker Clark, had homesteaded in the Dakota Territory as an Episcopal priest when the Dakota Nation was yet on the warpath. Two of his sons, John and David, were educated at Trinity College, Hartford, and at Berkeley Divinity School when it was yet in Middletown, Connecticut.

Family rumor has it that the family patriarch, who was both priest and Master Builder, sent his sons, after their graduations, to his original hometown of Schuylerville in upstate New York, where they were to become journey-man carpenters before ordination. Upon their return to the Dakotas, the three of them not only would lead worship on the Reservations, but also would handcraft many of those "prairie Gothic" chapels that still make their witness on Indian lands. They were knowledgeable in the Dakota language, and able to preach and translate prayers and hymns in it accurately. Marjorie had a splendid model of a missionary wife in her own mother, Rebecca Miller Clark, who came to the Rosebud Reservation originally as a missionary teacher.

As we found ourselves in Baguio surrounded by Igorot Christians, I remembered one hot summer when Marjorie had taken me to South Dakota to attend the annual Church Convocation on a Reservation. She brought me there to meet her father during his active days in that ministry, and to observe the "tipis" brought from the other Reservations for this gathering. In my vivid recollection, I could smell the open cooking fires, so similar to the prevailing scent of the charcoal fires that identify every Igorot mountain barrio. The central point of the annual Convocation on the Reservation was a temporary flat-roofed "cathedral" erected of tree boughs and branches, having the capacity to seat several hundred.

In the distant past, on the approximate dates of this Christian Convocation, the ancestors of those gathered had created such a shelter for the performance of the Sun Dance rituals. Now, the current yearly gathering culminates in the Christian Eucharist commemorating the redeeming Sacrifice of Christ.

On another occasion, Marjorie had taken me to the Rosebud Reservation to visit the graves of seven of her forebear family members, including her parents. There is buried between her mother and father, an Indian lady. Her father gave his own grave to a Native American who needed it. I thought this to be appropriately symbolic for this couple who had dedicated their lives to the Sioux. With the death of the Reverend John B. Clark, one hundred years of "Clark Ministry" in the "Indian Field" of the Diocese of South Dakota and a generation of Marjorie's family's ministry among the Navajo came to an unheralded conclusion. I was the sixth male in Marjorie's extended family to be ordained to the priesthood and to make a commitment to the missionary ministry. When Marjorie, baby Karla, and I became Appointed Missionaries of the Episcopal Church, that family commitment was extended into its second century.

—◦◦◦—

Marjorie's vocation was undoubtedly shaped by a legacy of loving service. Her Calling has not been to seek ordination, but rather to be the spouse of a priest, and this priest has every reason to be thankful for this. Truly, as one reads the accounts in this writing, behind every event and between every line, the companionship, advice and support of this loyal and patient life partner must be found as evidence that without a Divine Calling, her long journey beside me would never have been possible. I believe being a pastor's wife requires a very special person with a very special and unique Divine Calling.

The Mountain Province of Luzon was an unknown, even frightening prospect for us prior to our arrival. But once we were surrounded by those so eager to welcome us, Marjorie was very much at home and again in love with a very strong and proud people. Throughout her years on the plains of South Dakota, God was preparing her for our life in the Philippines.

During our years in the Philippines, at least six adolescent Igorots shared our home and our table—three or four at a time—under Marjorie's guidance. They were indeed members of our family, and they will be introduced by name in the next vignette. These relationships proved to be mutually beneficial, as, to the best of our knowledge, all of them became fine adults with productive lives, families, and careers.

Also, as a loving yet careful homemaker, Marjorie's attentive culinary guidance brought the three of us—herself, young Karla, and me—back to the United States without intestinal parasites, after six-and-a-half years in the Philippine Provinces and in the Tondo District of Manila. (People who migrate to other lands do so without generations of immunities inherited by those of native birth and ancestry, and are therefore vulnerable to many diseases that their host people are not.)

Marjorie's church experiences in South Dakota could be more accurately described as "low church" in regard to liturgy and vestments, quite different from the colorful rituals and understandings of the Episcopal Church in the Philippines. However, the essentials of ministry were exactly the same. Marjorie felt very much at home with the Igorot families, their children, their congregations, and their needs.

—RUTH 1:16f; PROVERBS 18:22; ST. LUKE 1:38a, 46–50

Saint Trichinosis and Other Chapels

*J*ust as I elevated the Host (the Celebrant's large communion wafer) at the Prayer of Consecration accompanied by the ringing of the Sanctus Bell, I heard another sound from outside the hilltop shed we used as a chapel. It was the death-squeal of a large pig prior to its impalement for roasting on a bamboo pole. Shortly after the Blessing and dismissal, as I doffed my chasuble, one of my smiling flock presented me with edible delicacies: the victim animal's steaming liver and "lechon" (crispy chunks of surface meat with skin and some hair) on a banana leaf. The "Happy Happy" banquet was offered in my honor, to celebrate my arrival and first Mass at Antamok Tram, one of the many "preaching stations" I would be serving as a missionary member on the Outstation Circuit.

Recognizing that foreigners require boiled water for drinking, I was given a San Miguel Beer instead—boiling hot in the tropical sun. There was also a bottle of water prepared especially for me. It had been brought to a boil over the charcoal and wood fire that had "cooked" our feast, and it had in the fluid several tiny insects that had expired in the process. This lavish event was no mere coffee hour following the service. It represented great sacrifice by these mine employees and their families. Would I eat and drink with the congregation gathered in a circle to welcome me? Of course I would. Did I survive? Obviously!

Antamok Tram is atop a ridge between two steep canyons in which lie the entrances and support buildings of two gold mines once reputed to have been the world's third-largest gold producers. Today, with the decline in the price of precious metals, these once productive crevasses south of Baguio are silent except for families of miners who have gone alone to seek employment elsewhere. But in the days I served there, these were places of great activity.

Antamok Mine is to the east of the ridge where we were gathered on the day in question; Balatoc Mine in the canyon to the west. Each of these mines had large congregations to serve as well. Antamok Tram was on the height where pulleys supported cables that extended to the canyons below to either side. The huge uncut logs that were suspended from these cables were transferred from the forests to the mine portals. These timbers were used to brace the underground mine tunnels.

In the canyons below on either side of "Tram," many large multistoried "bunkhouses" provided crowded homes for miners and their families. The steep mountainsides that walled the canyons were dotted with shacks clinging precariously to the cliffs. These thatched huts and their banana trees and piggeries were the dwellings of those too independent to find comfort in the crowded quarters provided by the mine. Men folk had come from tribal areas further north in the mountains to pry high grade ores from subterranean veins and pry what wages they could from the European and American mine owners.

All this was in an accommodation to a money-economy that had rudely plucked them out of the Stone Age into the age of machines and communications. Manila was jammed with squatters who came continuously in incredible numbers from the provinces to settle in untaxable squalid shacks serviced by open sewers. They came in search of pesos unnecessary in the barter economies from which they came. A common phrase among missionaries who built schools in the provinces was: "If we do not prepare them to come out of the mountains and the provinces, then they will come out unprepared." As in so many "civilizations" of the world, a population tide in the Philippines flowing from the rural to the urban seems irreversible.

The hospitality and love Marjorie and I encountered in the Mountain Province of Luzon was incredible. Here among the Igorot people, we inherited a friendship that had developed with American missionaries decades before us. After the evangelism of this area had been abandoned by European Roman Catholics (who encountered the dwellers there as ferocious head-hunters), it was resumed by Episcopal missionaries who were able to win their hearts and souls while respecting their independence.

With head-axe and spear, past generations of Igorots guarded their freedom. Our Saint Mark's Church at the foot of the Kennon Road is in a barrio called *Saitan,* which means "sharpening stone." In earlier times, if one climbed into these mountains, the intruder had best first sharpen his "bollo" (machete) for self-defense. All this speaks of a period just a few generations prior to our ministry here in 1960. However, the bond with Americans forged by the Episcopal Church became even stronger during World War II, when American missionaries hid from Japanese soldiers with the tribes, supported them as they could, printed promissory dollars for exchange to be redeemed upon hoped-for victory, and in some cases stood before enemy firing squads on their behalf.

Easter School, the Weaving Room and its store, are located on the north side of Baguio's Guisad valley. We lived on the hill just above the school in a majestic three-story wooden structure, the former residence of the late Suffragan Bishop. This house had been used as headquarters for the detachment of the Japanese Army, and behind our house there were caves and tunnels the Japanese soldiers dug to be used as bomb shelters.

Baguio had been bombed and strafed by Japanese aircraft on December 8, 1941. Being west of the International Date Line, this attack occurred simultaneously with the attack on Pearl Harbor.

Father Charles Matlock and his wife, veteran missionaries, lived next door to the Filipino Rector and the Parish Church of the Resurrection, about five blocks from Easter School. Their mission house had served as the Treasury for the Japanese Forces. The Matlock's lawn was often perforated by trenches clandestinely dug by locals still pursuing gold that reportedly had been buried there by retreating officers. Bad memories of "Japanese Time" were vivid in the minds of adults, and rehearsed for the benefit of those too young to know or remember.

For example, when Filipinos were required by the invaders to shout out: *"Banzai"* (loosely translated: "Long Live" the Emperor!), they commonly shouted *"Bankai"* ("corpse" in dialect, with the undetected meaning of "Death" to the enemy). These mountain people resisted a national enemy, but at the same time they were defending their ancient right to independence.

Gavino Dao-añg, an adult Catechist with thirteen children, lived with his family not far from us in a small house on the hill overlooking Easter School. Gavino had served as a translator for the U.S. Army personnel who supported the Philippine Scouts during the war, and he was knowledgeable in the several dialects used throughout the circuit of mission outstations in the Benguet Subprovince (southwest part of the Mountain Province) and in Pañgasinan and Zambales Provinces in the lowlands.

In all these areas, Igorot families settled away from their home tribal areas and barrios where there were gold, copper or chromite mines to employ them. It was always startling to see men in G-strings working star-drills and other Industrial Age machinery.

It was a great privilege to spend days riding the Dañg-wa Tranco truck-bus beside Gavino, often sharing homily presentations in advance for him to translate for me at our next stop. As we journeyed and slept in mine camps and barrios, Gavino showed me streams and small waterfalls where we could bathe. Gavino collected my old *Reader's Digest* magazines, using them to perfect his reading of English as we rode for hours from one outstation to another. After my departure from the Philippines, Gavino Dao-añg graduated from Baguio Colleges, completed the course at Saint Andrew's Theological Seminary, and, when last I heard, he was the resident Vicar at Saint Mark's Church, Saitan, Pañgasinan.

—⚬⚬⚬—

During 1960, I had responsibilities as Director of Easter School and for services in its Saint Nicholas' Chapel in Baguio. I also had similar responsibilities for the large Saint Elizabeth School perched in a "pocket" at the head of the Balatoc Mine canyon at Acupan, where I went early Thursday mornings. But the real administration of the schools was done by Principal Esteban Bañga-an at Easter School and by Principal Josefa Suyayan at Saint Elizabeth's School.

I made reports to the Bishop, served as Chaplain, and maintained a political representation for the Mission with the governmental education authorities. Primarily I spent most of the time commuting on day trips or travelling for days at a time from our home in Baguio to the "Epiphany Mission Outstations" with Gavino. I loved being a circuit rider, not realizing what great preparation this would be for my future ministries in Viet Nam. We held services in chapels, bamboo and grass homes, in open fields, and in one case, in a shed occasionally used to store manure for fertilizer.

In the lowlands at the base of the Cordilleras Mountains where we went, houses commonly were elevated on poles so that the animals (carabao, pigs, chickens) could find shelter from the blazing heat and from monsoon rains. Roofs were thatched, and the floors of these houses were fashioned of strips of bamboo perhaps an inch wide with equally wide gaps between them for air circulation from beneath.

At Labayug, Pañgasinan, a twenty-minute *jeepney* ride through the jungle eastward from the National Highway and the bus route, I said Mass in such a house with Gavino as my translator. The usual ambient temperature was 120 degrees, the humidity was high, and what little wind that we had for cooling came through the floor after passing over the animals. Both here and in the manure shed mentioned above I learned to value the liturgical use of incense. "Reformation Asthma" (my name for resistance to the use of incense in many of our stateside congregations—without medical justification) was something unheard of in the Philippine Episcopal Church.

In the mountain barrios, Gavino Dao-añg ushered me into the circle of "Old Men" gathered to pass a rancid jelly glass of *Ta-poey* (rice wine) in a sort of communion of friendship in which it was expected that all would partake. He introduced me to many of the *pagano* customs, explaining in vivid terms what it was like to live compelled by constant fear, and how injurious pagan life was for his people prior to Christian conversion.

Gavino and I rescued from pagan sacrifices to medical care, little Albin at Antamok Mine and Juanita at Antamok Trail (whose story is told elsewhere). Marjorie and I watched Albin play baseball once again, after being restored from severe malnutrition by a physician's intervention. However, both children eventually succumbed as the result of the influence of witch doctors, demonstrating physical reasons supporting spiritual ones for the urgency of our labors.

Worship in the Mountain Province was colorful and joyous. At the schools and in most of the congregations, the *Missa de Angelis* was commonly sung *a capella* by parishioners who had never seen or heard a piano or an organ. The *Merbeck* setting was reserved for Advent, Lent, and other ferial or somber occasions. Good Friday street processions behind Cross and Choir were common. Maundy Thursday all night Vigil was kept with entire congregations commonly present.

During these Vigils, the Biblical Passion of Christ was continuously sung in local dialect, not ceasing until the coming of the dawn and the Mass of the Pre-Sanctified, when the one remaining Host—consecrated Altar Bread—was consumed by the Celebrant. This symbolized the morning Death of Christ on the Cross. Several generations of missionaries had sacrificed much to bring to these people in their native barrios a beautiful and dramatic expression of the Christian Faith which, through the folks who were now our hosts, ministered to us as well in unforgettable ways.

The exciting ways they worship married easily with the cultural heritage of the Igorot people. Once one has heard their "gongzas" (gongs) and witnessed the circular formations of their dances, the sounds and sights can never be forgotten. Think how they must make their indelible mark on those who have grown from childhood with these rhythms!

The most spectacular of the dances is the Bontoc War Dance. It recalls not-too-remote a time when the head-axe, the spear and shield were more than decorations—rather, genuine implements of combat. The shield carried by the leader is constructed of a balsa-type wood, so designed as to attract a spear thrust by an opposing warrior, causing it to stick fast in the shield—thus disarming the opponent. Upon hearing the haunting harmonious and rapid entonement of the dancers' gongs, one wants to arise and fight for the tribe!

Another dance is the Courting Dance, in which the lady to be courted dances in the middle of the circle with a kerchief to be surrendered to the accepted suitor. The G-strings and stiff woven bachelor caps (that double for a pocket) were originally worn by the men, but only occasionally were seen outside mines or demonstration tribal dances. The "tapis" skirt with woven tie belt is made on small looms harnessed between the weaver and a tree or post, woven in three narrow sections, then sewed together. Like the men's G-string loin cloths, they bear the distinctive colors that identify one's tribe. For example, Bontoc has red with a black longitudinal strip in the design, and Western Bontoc is similar in color but has a white and blue strip instead of the black at the center. The Benguet skirt and jacket top are quite uniquely constructed in a tighter weave of blue and gray.

I add all this because these folk are creative and artistic, and their conversion from primitive animism demands a demonstrative and musical expression of Christian worship, rich in symbolism, in order for it to become understood and assimilated into their culture.

Bailey Bridges were constructed by the U.S. Army Engineers, intended perhaps for a single crossing of invasion vehicles 15 years before our arrival. They were used for major highways during our years in the Philippines and for a decade thereafter, until they were replaced by wider (and safer) concrete and steel structures. (Pages 93 & 116)

An Igorot Dance presented by the Vestry and Churchwomen of Saint. Elizabeth's Mission congregation, Acupan, Benguet, Mountain Province. (Pages 104 & 119)

Saint Andrew's Church as completed at Kapangan, with the steeple Cross as the lightning rod that protected the surrounding valley. (Pages 109 & 110)

Looking up Balatoc Canyon from the gold mine at Saint Elizabeth's School perched on the side of a canyon supported on stilts on the riverside. Acupan, Mountain Province, Philippines. (Page 117)

Some of the students at Saint Elizabeth's School, Acupan, Benguet, Mountain Province. (Page 119)

Church and school bells in the Mountain Province are fabricated from the nose cones of "abandoned" dud 500-pound bombs. The powder was undoubtedly used by fishermen. (Page 118)

Cyril, Alfredo, Brigit, Margaret, Purissa, and Virginia came at various times to live with us. Brigit, Margaret, and Virginia moved with us to Manila when we were sent there by the Bishop. Some came as teenagers from the barrio, some from Saint Mary's Orphanage when they had outgrown its resources. They came to us as "domestic help" for a stipend, but unlike in the homes of other foreigners in their land (and to the consternation of some of the other missionaries!), they truly became members of our family. Our small daughter called the girls *manañg* meaning "sister," and they loved her as well. They were caregivers to Karla; ironed, washed, and cooked in tandem with Marjorie, and they shared our table at meals. Today we correspond with some, while we have lost contact with others.

Alfredo Della completed his training and served as a dentist for five years in the Philippines. Now he does Computer Assisted Design for the automobile industry in Detroit. Purissa sold real estate. Brigit is the Administrator of the Benguet Provincial College across from Epiphany Mission in La Trinidad, a suburb of Baguio. Our dear Margaret was killed by a *jeepney* near her market stall at La Trinidad Open Market. We grieve her loss. Cyril Buking once earned the title "Mr. Baguio of 1960" for his level of physical fitness. On Christmas of 1976, he surfaced off a submarine to visit our home on Guam as a Chief Petty Officer in the U.S. Navy. These young people of whom we have knowledge matured to raise and educate fine families of their own.

———◦◦◦———

The Cathedral of the Philippine Episcopal Church in Manila was destroyed by bombardment in World War II, but raised in the new capital suburb, Quezon City, during my first years in the Philippines. It was named for Saint Mary and Saint John to commemorate how Jesus, from His Cross, commended Mary and John each to the other's care. The message intended to be conveyed by those who named the cathedral's patrons in years past is that Jesus likewise commended the people of the Philippines and the Americans among them each into the other's care. Such a reciprocity of affection and nurture commissioned by Our Blessed Lord in the midst of His Sacrifice, describes our experience as missionaries in the Philippines. These people cared for us even as we cared for them.

—PSALM 104:27f (1979 *Book of Common Prayer* TRANSL. PS. 104:28f); ST. JOHN 19:25b-27

The Saving Cross

apañgan is a rise in the middle of a round valley, high in the Cordilleras Mountains of Luzon. The geography resembles the crown of a cowboy hat, with wide brims which stretch as the bottom of a circular bowl reaching to the base of the surrounding mountains. This natural spectacle once provided a place for a short landing strip on top of the flat surface of this small mesa. During the height of Filipino resistance one-and-a-half decades before, light American planes would quickly land and leave in order to deliver supplies to the Filipino Scouts hiding within territory occupied by the Imperial Japanese Army. This location claimed visibility for miles around, allowing for observation of any ambush menace to arriving aircraft as well as to Scouts encamped in the surrounding valley below. It was in the mountains on the northwest rim of this valley that General Tomoyuki Yamashita surrendered his Fourteenth Imperial Army.

I was a new priest circuit rider on a team with Filipino clergy and catechists, the American Priest-in-Charge, and a remarkable lady missionary. Along with my pastoral responsibilities, it was my task to provide Father Pañgwi, the resident Vicar, with a new structure for Saint Andrew's Church. Elsie Sharp, long-time church worker in these mountains, led me and Marjorie for our first visit to Kapañgan. The famous missionary architect, John van Wei Bergamini had designed church, hospital, school, and convent buildings for Anglican missions throughout China and Japan—as well as our buildings on Cathedral Heights in Quezon City. He had envisioned and drawn plans for the new church. It was to seat about 200, to be traditionally rectangular, with a high roof, to be built of reinforced concrete. The sides of the nave would be composed of steel casement windows to admit ventilating trade winds that crossed from the surrounding lowlands. There would be a steeple over the Sanctuary, topped by a Cross which would be visible throughout the circumference of the valley bowl and to the mountains beyond. The rectory stood at the other end of the abandoned and overgrown runway.

I was to utilize my engineering training to supervise the construction of this church. The site which I have described was several kilometers from the nearest road, some distance across the valley. It could be reached only by often steep and slippery paths and across narrow swinging footbridges, suspended by cables above streams and flooded rice fields. The walkways of these bridges were linear strips of "Martian Matting" left from the abandoned landing field. Parishioners would carry the sacks of cement, reinforcing and girder steel on their backs from the truck road to the hill in the middle of the big valley. This incredible undertaking was completed in nine months, and the new Church of Saint Andrew was dedicated with a great community gathering and Eucharist on Saint Andrew's Day, 1960!

Christians (essentially Episcopalians) were a minority co-existing in the population of an area that was strongly anamistic *pagano*. Healings were commonly exhorted by witch doctors who guided the families of the sick and dying to sacrifice their livestock: chickens first, then pigs, and in extreme cases, the water buffalo. (The water buffalo or *carabao* also served their owners as tractors in their fields, and each represented an investment of years of savings.) These sacrifices were made to appease supposedly angered deceased ancestors (*anitos*) with proper banquets (called *kaneaos*), and through these ritual appeals, hopefully pacified spirits were besought to bring an end to current misfortunes. Should a death occur, the corpse of a dead family member would be strapped in a chair and smoked for days and nights of veneration and propitiation (not for preservation) before burial.

The people tried to live in accord with the natural elements, but in reality their existence was permeated by countless taboos and governed by fear of almost everything.

Kapañgan and the surrounding valley were plagued by lightning strikes. The angry *anitos* would visit offending families by a bolt of burning fire from the skies. A grass house would burn instantly. Children, family members, and animals would be killed. Sacrifices would have to be made to signify repentance for unknown crimes against their undetermined wills. Judgment was swift, sudden, and final.

Father Pañgwi lived among his fellow Igorot neighbors and wanted a better and happier life for them. He told them that Jesus was a loving Savior, and that through His Crucifixion and Resurrection, He had taken unto Himself the Sin of the World and made God's forgiveness available to all who were repentant and who asked for it. As Father Pañgwi sat among the Old Men and sipped the ceremonial *Ta-poey* with them as the glass went around the circle, he would tell them how God loved them, that He did not punish or correct people the way they believed the *anitos* did, and that Jesus came to protect them from every fear. But still pagan practices prevailed.

Incorporated into the design of the new church, majestically dominating the valley spread out below it in all directions, was a copper cable that was brazed to the Cross on top of its steeple. This cable was firmly anchored at its lower end to the ground below. Thus that Cross of Christ, so visible to the Faithful and to the superstitious alike, was indeed a lightning rod, as well as a symbol of the Savior. The frequent lightning storms came and went as they had before. But now, for miles around, the people saw the lightning come only to the Cross instead of to their homes, fields, and families. To the superstitious and primitive pagans, however, it was powerful medicine and greater magic than they had ever witnessed before throughout the generations of those who lived in the shadow of Kapañgan.

You can believe that Father Pañgwi now made the best of it. "Did I not tell you?" the *Padi* (Christian Priest) would tell them. "Our God loves you, and He sent His Son to the Cross to protect you from everything that you fear."

And so He did. And so He does for us all, even those who live in the great valley today that surrounds the Church of Saint Andrew, Kapañgan.

—HEBREWS 9:13f

The Ooloog

Marjorie and I travelled a day's journey northward in the Cordilleras Mountain Range to visit the Bontoc and the Western Bontoc Tribes. We wanted to understand more of the backgrounds of the people who were migrating south to the region where I served. Resurreciòn Boteñgan, younger brother of the Easter School Assistant Principal, was our escort. A driver from the Dañg-wa Tranco (bus line) brought us safely through cliff-hanging roads in a Chevrolet sedan.

We stopped at Bontoc "Central," the capital of the subprovince, to visit All Saints' Mission and missionaries Fr. Richard and Betty Over, friends from Berkeley. Then we proceeded further east to see the Banawe Rice Terraces. Retracing our path, we crossed over the Chico River in its canyon at Bontoc and headed up the mountains to the west for our next stop at Sagada, the largest overseas mission complex of the American Episcopal Church. Here we visited Father (later Bishop) George Harris, his wife Mary Jane, Filipino clergy and teachers, Saint Mary's High School, the Filipina and American Sisters at Saint Mary's Convent and the Orphanage, Saint Theodore's Hospital and the medical team there. Westward again beyond Sagada, our tour took us to neighboring Besao and Saint Benedict's Mission.

It was here that I asked "Rex," our escort, who was originally from Besao, "What is that?" I was pointing to a "long house" with a grass roof located fairly near the great stone church. He explained to us that this was a *pagano* (pagan) Ooloog. He proceeded to tell us that this dormitory was part of the pagan ritual of marriage. Young girls just reaching puberty were consigned to the Ooloog. When a young male reached a similar age, he was sent to sleep in the Ooloog with each girl for a short time. When one became pregnant, it would be revealed that the ancestors, the *anitos*, had selected his mate. The Christian Mission was teaching differently, he explained! Children raised in that pagan culture do have "a village to be raised by," but a pagan village raises its future generations in a haunting and ever present fear of the presumed determinations of ancestoral generations of the past. Christ would liberate all people in all ages to grow in love and freedom. The mountain people are destined to find their way into modern life (I use these words instead of "civilization"), but if not prepared for a changing world, they are destined to face it in unprepared and chaotic ways.

Reflecting upon the Ooloog and the pagan traditions of mating, I am tempted to compare it to the common methods by which relationships are being established more and more in America today. Marriages with consideration for God's selection and thoughtful Christian preparation are becoming rare, thus the institution of marriage is becoming more transitory. With cultural expectations of instant gratification, economics and tax laws that seem unfavorable to traditional marriage, and a generation so predominately raised by single and divorced parents, commitments for life may appear unusual or, at the extreme, frightening. Sociologists have warned that "living together" does not prepare couples for marriage commitments. Prominent persons whose lives are heralded as life-models in our media have rarely provided a model for lasting marriage, and all too often they succumb to the pressures of public life in less than healthy lifestyles. The permanence of marriage and the joy to be found in its responsibilities are being sadly eclipsed. Children become the victims, one way or another.

As a parish priest and as a military chaplain, I experienced increasing difficulty finding couples who were patiently interested in preparing for a lifetime together through premarital counseling, or whose faith was strong enough to take the Vows of Holy Matrimony with farsight. But for those who see beyond "a pretty church setting" to what that Church stands for, unions seem to have greater chances of lasting "for better, for worse; for richer for poorer; in sickness and in health; until death us do part; according to God's holy ordinance." It is thrilling for the pastor requiring such standards to find they are truly valued by a couple seeking marriage in the midst of the glitter of the anticipated event. It is always worth the sometimes unpopular and unpleasant effort of trying to convince those intending to marry to consider the necessity of such solemn considerations.

The efforts of Christians in the Cordilleras Mountains of Luzon to bring marriage out of the pagan Ooloog into the Sacrament of Holy Matrimony is really no different than the ministry that commonly confronts clergy who would officiate at marriages of couples anywhere today. Bringing people to Christ involves inviting Jesus to their weddings in such a way that they will share the totality of their future lives with Him.

—Apocrypha Book of TOBIT 8:5b–8; ST. JOHN 2:1f; EPHESIANS 3:14–21; 5:21–33

A Little Child Shall Lead Them

*T*hat calendars did not seem important in these mountains became evident to me when baptisms were requested and a birthday had to be supplied for the records. I gave October 19th to many, after guessing the appropriate year to assign, because it was my birthday to give to those who needed one for the records. In the 35 preaching outstations and chapels served by the Epiphany Mission circuit riders, it was Sunday whenever the priest got there. In the isolated barrios, one day passed just like another. However, in the camps of the mines owned by Europeans, Sunday was observed with cessation of work underground, and Sunday was "church day" in and near Baguio City as well. In the barrio of Antamok Trail, the Lord's Day of sacred celebration was Tuesday morning.

The Christians gathered in the early morning hour of six in the Della Family's home, which was surrounded by avocado trees on the downward slope of the hill. The offering was partly "in kind," and the produce in the basket that was offered on the Altar at the Mass was then taken by the priest to the open markets in Baguio. Here it was exchanged with the vendors for cash that was properly accounted, then sent to the diocese. Avocados were commonly used to fatten pigs, and when it was revealed in casual conversation that avocados were a delicacy "in America," the Faithful were amused that Americans ate pig food. When the following Tuesday offering included a large bushel basket of avocados to please my strange appetite, I had to explain diplomatically that this fruit would bring little or nothing at the market, and that the offering did not go to me or to my family.

Each Tuesday morning, Juanita Tabkaw was among the gathering of Christian worshippers, who were surrounded in the barrio by a pagan population. Juanita was twelve years old or younger. Her parents were animists; her mother's arms were entirely tattooed in the pattern designed to ward off evil spirits. But Juanita had been allowed to make the choice to become a Christian.

One Tuesday I learned that Juanita was not feeling well. Later in the week, when passing by on the way to other outstations beyond "Trail," I checked on her condition and learned from neighbors that Juanita's jaw was swelling in a strange way. The witch doctor was "making sacrifice" of the chickens. The following Tuesday I begged members of the congregation to appeal to the Tabkaws to let me take Juanita to the hospital in Baguio City. Since the road up to the city was paved, I was able to drive the mission Chevrolet to this barrio, and I was getting very concerned about the advancing illness of this beautiful child.

Word came back that many in the region believed that it would be a grievous offense to the ancestors (the *anitos*) if Juanita were to be taken from the boundaries of the ancestral home. If *anitos* became angry because Juanita had left them, they would surely place upon this little girl a mortal hex. Juanita would *not* see a physician!

The next Tuesday, what had evidently begun with an abscessed molar had developed into a very painful swelling of the jaw and neck. Juanita was definitely in severe distress! The chapel parishioners warned that should the child die in the hospital, there might be a hostile reaction by the pagans because of the belief that it would have been caused by her having been taken from the enraged *anitos*. In spite of that, I ran the gauntlet and was able to provoke a last resort consent from her family to transport Juanita to Baguio and to the hospital there to see a doctor.

My first conversation with the physician revealed that Juanita's infected tooth had advanced into meningitis, and that she was in critical condition. A week later it was my sad task to convey to her parents in the barrio that Juanita had succumbed to her condition. I returned to Antamok Trail to report the news to Mr. and Mrs. Tabkaw, and, if I survived the wrath of the community, to offer a Requiem for their daughter. On the door stoop of their house, the witch doctor had just cut the throat of a chicken and was "making sacrifice" to the spirits of the ancestors. I wondered if I would be next! (The newspapers in the States had just six months previously reported the beheading of Christian missionaries by another tribe on the eastern slopes of those mountains.) Head-axes were still carried symbolically in the war dances of the people among whom we lived and ministered, traditional reminders of a not too distant past.

It was with great sorrow that I crossed the threshold of the Tabkaw's thatched hut that day in my white cassock to deliver the sad news. But it was also with some feelings of risk to my personal safety and concern that I might have enraged pagan barrio-mates of the Christians against them.

I stood before the squatting mother in the refuge of her dark room, as her husband stood back in the shadows. I was flanked with only one of the more courageous Christians, acting as my translator. I spoke slowly, and I am sure my tears revealed my genuine love for her and her daughter as I attempted to explain to Juanita's mother what had transpired. The witch doctor listened from the doorway, probably eagerly waiting to spread the news. Mrs. Tabkaw did not move as she sat long in silence. Then I knelt on the dirt floor before her, awaiting her response and what might have been my fate as well.

Finally, yet very slowly through the translator, came her reply. "I understand. I know you wanted to help. I want to be baptized and become a Christian for my Juanita." In that moment of surprise, I thanked God that He had sent me to Antamok Trail.

Later that morning in the house of Mr. Della, the Christians gathered, while the witch doctor on the doorstep busied himself killing another chicken. Inside I was offering to the mourners the Body of Christ to whom the body and soul of Juanita had been entrusted. I concluded with these words: "Remember thy servant Juanita, O Lord, according to the favor which Thou bearest unto Thy People...."

—St. John 11:32–36; Acts 19:17b–20; Revelation 7:2f

How the Infant Inspired Saint Joseph

Dañg-wa Tranco buses were covered flatbed trucks with benches. Sometimes there would be a goat in the baggage rack on the roof, or a pregnant sow in the rack under the bed of the vehicle. These buses, jammed with life, would wind their way along precarious roads through the Mountain Province. In some places where narrow roads were cut into the sides of cliffs, one of the rear dual wheels would virtually spin out in midair. During our time, narrow Bailey Bridges were the only spans over steep river gorges on the Kennon Road as it ascended to Baguio. These unsupported bridges, also used on other major mountain roads, were perhaps intended for single crossings by fighting vehicles. They were left behind in the later 1940s by the U.S. Army

Corps of Engineers. Dañg-wa drivers often found it amusing to frighten any foreigners on board by rushing their vehicle onto these spans in such a way as to cause the bridge to bounce when the bus reached the center of the span.

The Dañg-wa Tranco route from Baguio City's 4,500-foot elevation to the Benguet Consolidated Mine at Balatoc was downhill most of the way. As it approached Balatoc, it descended the canyon wall at the wide end of the deep valley, skirting the precipice. Once in the floor of the canyon, we passed the mine offices and the mine tunnel entrance. There the conveyance would drop some passengers, then whine loudly as it climbed the steep road that twisted back and forth among the two- and three-story family bunkhouses, regaining at least another 500 feet of elevation as it crawled up the narrowing canyon to the end of the line.

When the bus unloaded there at six o'clock in the cold mornings, the priest would gather his mass kit and begin his hike another 20 minutes up the narrowing canyon where a road could never go. Upward, first passing more bunkhouses, then across a long swinging bridge suspended over a rushing torrent from one side of the crevasse to the rock wall on the other, the climb would continue. The rest of the ascent was along a narrow pathway carved as a ledge, and often threatened from above and below by rock slides. High above on the cliffs, or clinging to the sides of the canyon, were the shacks of other Igorot miners and their families who valued their way of life so highly that they would rather live so suspended than to crowd into one of those bunkhouses below, filled with charcoal cooking smoke and too far from banana trees or room for a piggery. After all, these people who had left their various tribal areas farther north in the Cordilleras Mountains with its terraced rice fields and where self-reliance was learned and prized, were reluctant to give up their customary ways altogether. The familiarity of woven *barong* (banana tree fiber) walls, thatched roofs, and bamboo flooring on stilts to shelter the animals below, gave comfort to these geographic-industrial refugees from their tribal roots.

To approach Saint Elizabeth's School, one passed intrusively through the interior of two family huts that straddled the path, precariously sharing the cliff-side ledge. Then the walker proceeded under the stream side of the school building, where pillars supported that side of the two-story structure that clung for support to the rising canyon wall on its other side. The trail ended in the playground that was on a level plane close to the canyon's apex in what was called an *acupan,* meaning "pocket." Hence, this place was called Acupan.

Each Thursday morning was like a scene from a motion picture, and I would have to pinch myself to believe I was really in the picture. As I would get off the bus and start up the hill, children would stream down from the bunkhouses and farther up the path from the shacks among the banana trees on the sides of the canyon, and they would fall in behind me. We would sing "This old man, he played one..." and "I sing a song of the Saints of God" as our procession climbed the narrow ascent in the early, and sometimes cold and foggy mornings, or even in a torrential rain. Arsenio, the retarded teenaged head Acolyte, would lead the joyful parade. Part of the fun for the children was to wait for *Padi* to reach a point of no return on the long footbridge suspended over the stream and canyon, then to start it swinging back and forth laterally, perhaps to test his faith.

Upon arrival at the playground, I was always greeted by Josefa Suyayen, Principal of Saint Elizabeth's School. This dear lady, who spent her life hobbling on two uncorrected club feet, would greet me with a container of drinking water she had fetched and boiled "to keep the missionary in good health." It was routine to expect, suspended in the precious fluid, an occasional unidentifiable ingredient that had escaped her well-meaning attention.

The school and church bell would then ring to announce my arrival and to summon the Faithful to the Holy Mysteries and joys of worship. Its peal resounded and echoed throughout the canyon below and to its summits above. This bell, suspended from an arch welded of steel pipes, like most of the church bells in these mountains, was in fact the nose of a 500-pound dud bomb, dropped somewhere nearby during World War II. Such a bomb had long since donated its explosive contents to some fishermen.

All the pupils and other communicants would then follow Josefa and me up the exterior stairs on the mountain side of the structure to the second floor assembly area, where the Altar had been carefully prepared.

Soon the 250 students, some parents, and other parishioners would be assembled, and the *Missa de Angelis* would be entoned. Their traditions of worship, long practiced in the Episcopal Church missions to the north, had become integral to their way of life, and had come down from the interior tribal areas with them to the mine camps in the southern part of the Cordilleras Mountain Range.

After the Mass, all would gather in the playground to sing the current national anthem, salute the ensign of the proud Republic of the Philippines, as students smartly hauled its flag to the top of the flagpole, then receive announcements from the faculty before class.

On those very rare occasions when prominent guests were present, the parents of the P.T.A. would present native dances with *gongzas* (handheld gongs of sequential rhythmic pitches), spears, balsa-like wood shields, and head-axes. The men would be dressed in G-strings, and the women in *tapis* skirts, all of which were woven in the colors of the individual tribe from which each had come south to work and live at the mine.

When the school day began, I would take up my pack, and in the white cassock which priests always wore on such visitations, I would walk down the path and road below, visiting families in the bunkhouses and huts as I went. Once I was allowed to visit the miners (without my white cassock!) at their work deep in the tunnels of the gold mine, where, in the intense heat, they wore only the G-string. These men had come directly from the Stone Age in their tribal areas, and remarkably they now worked with diamond drills and fairly modern machinery to extract high grade gold ore from those subterranean caverns. Their reward at that time was the peso equivalent to one U.S. dollar a day, and deadly black lung disease before reaching middle age.

If I were to hike without interruption and without riding the bus from the end of the road into the wide-end floor of the canyon below (where the headquarters of the mine and much of the labor population also resided), it would have taken most of an hour. I explained this to Teodora Apacway, a very active Communicant and member of the P.T.A., when she approached me on Palm Sunday of 1960 as a representative of many of the mine families. Her concern was that some of the people from Balatoc at the bottom of the canyon were afraid or unable to walk up to the school at Acupan for the Mass. Some mothers carried their babies up the hazardous walking trail above the end of the road, even in the monsoons. Others, aware of the risks, felt separated from the worship of the church because of the hike and the weather. For the sake of their infants, would I "be pleased to hold a service" in the tin-roofed, one-room union building beside the road at the bottom of the grade in central Balatoc on Easter Day?

The reasonable nature of her request was very evident to me, and had been for some time. The agenda behind the scenes which placed me in a bind was that the American missionary-in-charge, who had ministered to those mountain outstations for a number of years, was on furlough in the United States. He was technically my boss, and I was a relative newcomer. He had given the order that in his absence absolutely no new work was to be established. I presumed that this was because our team was stretched too thinly as it was, and I was pleased to conform to his wishes. On the other hand, I was concerned about the safety of the devout from Balatoc who joined our Thursday early morning processions, rain or shine, and my neglect of those who felt they could not.

Teodora countered my every excuse with a reasonable answer, and even though I refused to reveal the hidden agenda that restrained me, she offered point blank: "And Father Charles is on furlough and we need to celebrate Easter." I admitted nothing, but made this proposal. "After the Mass at Acupan on Maundy Thursday this week, I will walk down to the union building at Balatoc. If it takes less than 20 minutes, I will celebrate an Easter service there. But after Acupan and Balatoc I have two congregations to serve on Easter Day as well, so I must be fair to the others." On behalf of the people of Balatoc, she agreed to this. I thought this was a safe dodge, but I had underestimated Igorot ingenuity and the determination of dear Mrs. Apacway. Little did I suspect an ambush was in the offing.

I did as I promised. After the celebration at Acupan and my brisk downhill march, when I arrived at the miners' union building that Maundy Thurdsay morning, I was greeted by a gathering of as many as 175, mostly mothers who held infants in their arms. Teodora was there smiling, and asking if they could have Holy Communion. "After all, Father, it is Maundy Thursday!" "But I do not have Altar Bread for all of you," I explained. "Never mind, Father," said she. "We got 'bisquites' (crackers) from the company store." So we gathered inside, with an overflow on the porch and under the banana trees, and I did what I believed anyone would most probably have done were they a priest in my situation. I felt very much like Saint Peter did when his conscience from the past ordered him not to eat certain meat, but the vision he received from the Holy Spirit told him to "kill and eat" without restriction.

After a very happy event, Teodora was on the steps of the union hall again pleading the case of Easter. "I do not want to seem ungrateful for today, but you will come on Easter after Acupan to say Mass for us, won't you? You must come for the babies and their parents," Teodora pleaded, holding up one of the newborns, "...for the infant, Father! ...for the infant!"

How could I resist? I set aside the orders from my absent supervisor, and just prayed that my bishop would accept my reasoning. So, even though it had taken me a little over 40 minutes to walk down the canyon slope from Acupan, I agreed, explaining that with the many communicants at Acupan I would probably be very late, and that I would have to hurry off to other congregations. When I got back home in Baguio I wrote a note of explanation to Bishop Ogilby in Manila, knowing there would be no time to obtain his consent or refusal before Sunday.

When I had communicated over 250 at Saint Elizabeth's School, Acupan on Easter Sunday, I walked swiftly down to Balatoc. It was already afternoon and very hot. I was greeted by over 200 there who had reportedly awaited my arrival in a tropical sun for over four hours. We had ten baptisms and two marriages, as well as the Eucharist. I then rushed on to offer Easter Communion at two additional remote mission outstations. It was a thrilling, although exhausting, day of celebration of the Resurrection, one that I will never forget. In the following weeks, Saint Joseph's Chapel was formally organized at the union building in Balatoc, a sister congregation to Saint Elizabeth's at the school in Acupan.

The last news I have received, 37 years later, was that the Benguet Consolidated Mining Company had shut down at Balatoc, either because the once rich veins had been exhausted or because the price of the precious metals had decreased. The management of the school at Acupan was taken over by the Philippine government, but the church is allowed to continue the Mass there for the community. Many families have stayed in the canyon, while some have left. Many of the wives and children remained there while husbands and fathers returned to the ancestral farms and rice fields in the Mountain Province, or had gone to cities in order to provide for their families. Such mid-life separations are common in Igorot marriages. (I think it is a form of birth control.)

The Diocese of North Central Philippines has assigned a full-time woman priest to Saint Joseph's, Balatoc. The "union hall" has been given to the Church, where services are held, children catechized, and from where pastoral ministry and visitations are conducted. Volunteer builders, mostly composed of the women of the mission, have carried gravel up from the riverbed, have mixed concrete, and are acquiring lumber for the enlargement of the chapel and the annexation of rooms for a small vicarage. Slightly over half the funds for construction came from the now indigenous diocese, and the other half was provided by a significant contribution from the Hwang family in California.

Judy Keh Hwang was a high school student at Saint Stephen's High School in Manila, where I would serve next. Judy, a graduate pharmacist, is now a business woman in the Los Angeles area. She has her own family, loves the Church, and, with her husband Song Hwang, saw this as an opportunity to help. It is my understanding that Saint Joseph's Mission has become one of the strongest congregations in the Philippine Episcopal Church, ministering to the many families that live in and near the Balatoc canyon.

When Father Charles returned to take charge of the Epiphany Mission and Outstations in December, I was promptly reassigned to Manila "because of my Chinese language training." In the words of the 18th century English poet, William Cowper:*

"God moves in a mysterious way His wonders to perform:...
Deep in unfathomable mines, with never failing skill,
He treasures up His bright designs, and works His sovereign will."

—ST. MATTHEW 18:1–5; ST. JOHN 6:3–12,14;
ACTS 11:7ff; I CORINTHIANS 11:23–26

---

* From *The Hymnal 1982,* No. 677 (portions of stanzas 1 and 2), Copyright by Church Pension Fund. New York: Church Publishing Incorporated. Words by William Cowper, 1731–1800. Used by permission.

CHAPTER FIVE

In Manila's Chinese Community

A Dream Comes True the Hard Way

*D*uring high school years, I had a part-time, after class job at Glaser Brothers Distributors in Oakland's Chinatown. It was there that I befriended several Chinese children as they passed by our loading dock on their way home from "China School"—which met after the normal public school day. I bought a copy of a small Chinese dictionary from one of them. I still treasure it! Several years later at Stanford University, I purchased Shau Wing Chan's *Elementary Chinese* text, and I studied it when I should have been doing my physics or mathematics, or reading the history of Western Civilization. During the latter half of the 1940s, China's tragic history was unfolding across the Pacific, and China and the Chinese people were in the hearts of many of us living on the Western seaboard. They took up permanent residence in my heart as well.

Marjorie and I received news early in 1959 that we had been accepted as Appointed Missionaries by the Domestic and Foreign Missionary Society of the Episcopal Church. Later that year I would go to Seabury House in Greenwich, Connecticut for indoctrination and initial missionary training. Marjorie decided not to accompany me, because she was preparing for the birth of our first child, and Karla Nancy would have to be at least five months old before her inoculation series could be completed for travel overseas. Since China was closed to us at this time in history, we were assigned to the Philippines.

These were the exciting "heydays" of the missionary efforts of the Episcopal Church, when major overseas ministries were centralized under the sponsorship of the national church headquarters—rather than primarily being delegated to various missionary societies, each having their own agendas and sources of support. When I expressed an interest in taking an intensive first year Chinese language class at Stanford University that summer and demonstrated high motivation to do so, the Church headquarters granted my request and sponsored my studies. During the summer of 1959, I commuted on weekends to Berkeley and maintained a full weekend schedule at the Church of the Good Shepherd.

As I related in the previous chapter, my first placement in the Philippine Episcopal Church was at Easter School and the Epiphany Mission Outstations. During that year of living in Baguio, the Igorot people won our hearts completely. My daily routine included a pre-dawn boarding at the Dañg-wa bus station in the bitter cold, accompanied by a cacophony of squealing pigs, bleating goats, clucking chickens, and dogs howling in distress from bamboo cages. They seemed to suspect their destiny as they were loaded for delivery to satisfy the culinary delights of dwellers in remote barrios. I loved what I was doing and felt completely loved by the people among whom I lived and served. When Father Charles Matlock, Priest-in-Charge, returned from furlough in the United States, the need for a chaplain at the Chinese school and parish in Manila was identified, and I was transferred by the American missionary bishop to Saint Stephen's High School in Manila.

Three of our young Igorot helpers, now very much a part of our family, moved with us. Our new temporary home was across the city from the school in a building owned by the Church in the Ermita District. Our apartment was a quarter of the second story of a former orphanage. The front half of the building, having been gutted by a 500-pound bomb a decade-and-a-half before, was just an enclosed shell. A replacement galvanized metal roof protected the entire structure from the weather.

Below us was the residence of Miss Ada Clarke, a veteran missionary who ran the Episcopal Bookstore, and who was known by some of her customers with limited English as "Miss Eight O'clock." She watched over the College Women's Dormitory, which at the time occupied the rest of the downstairs.

Our small kitchen upstairs was across the stairwell from our quarters, and was thinly partitioned to separate its facilities from the "water closet" of the apartment occupied by a Filipino mission employee and his family in the other half of the habitable second floor area.

Through all of this, little Karla was able to continue her close associations with our host population. One day she excitedly rushed upstairs from Miss Clarke's kitchen with widened eyes to report to us on the meal Miss Clarke's maid and cook was consuming. "Mommy, Mommy," she exclaimed, "Felicia is eating the fishey's face!"

Later in the year we would use the bombed out area of the big house (airless in the tropic heat) to receive the contents of U.S. Navy barges: thousands of "outdated" school textbooks from California which were provided by the AID Mission of the United States Government. It was here that Marjorie and I sorted the books by grade and subject, and distributed them to the many provincial mission schools according to their needs expressed in replies to our survey.

The bishop offered us a comfortable residence on the Cathedral Heights compound where thirty-one other missionary residences encircled the Cathedral of Saint Mary and Saint John (then under construction), Saint Andrew's Theological Seminary, Saint Luke's Hospital and Nursing School, the Diocesan Offices, and an area planned for the future Trinity College. This was a nicely groomed park. We stated that if we were going to work in the slums, we wanted to live in the slums with those we were to serve. Marjorie admitted to me that she had restrained herself from commenting: "All that is needed at Cathedral Heights is a commissary and a hairdresser, then they could close the gates and never know they had left the United States!" Smiles were exchanged instead.

The bishop graciously directed J. van Wei Bergamini, the mission architect, to design a house for us on the Saint Stephen's High School compound. After several years and the construction of the new high school, we moved where we had asked to live—with the people we would serve. The residence was spacious and comfortable, quite nice for that area of the city. Unfortunately, it did distinguish us as privileged foreigners. After our time in the Philippines, the structure became alternately a Home Economics facility, the enlarged Christian

Student Center, then the school library—continuing on the campus as an asset to the school and the students. The house was recently demolished to make way for a swimming pool, demonstrating that the mission school had become affluent under local sponsorship.

I came to the school initially as Assistant Chaplain, serving at the direction of Father Samuel Wu. He later departed for the Diocese of Hong Kong, leaving me in charge. I also assisted the Rector of Saint Stephen's Parish Church, then using the large old Saint Luke's Hospital Chapel next to the high school and prior to the construction of a huge new church building.

The Reverend Hsi Jen Wei had served there many years. His brother had been the Dean of the Nanking Theological College prior to his reported execution by Communist soldiers in the street within sight of his family. Father Wei was ably assisted by his older Lay Reader Assistant, Mr. Tan Tiao Lin. This strong gentleman was to play a major role in my development as my mentor in the language, culture, and the philosophies of his people. It was he who served as the major influence in the fulfillment of my dreams to live and labor among the Chinese. He often said that during the Japanese occupation of China and at the risk of his life, he listened to the *Voice of America* for news reports on his shortwave radio. It was hidden in his wood stove with the metal stove pipe chimney serving as its aerial.

The Chinese community in Manila was, for the most part, encompassed in a Binondo District tenement ghetto bordered on the west by the notorious Tondo squatter slums. Two dialects were commonly used in homes by the elders and by the children among themselves: either Amoy or Cantonese. Mandarin was the teaching language, used half-days in the upper elementary grades and in the high school classes. English was the *lingua franca* for common communications, and was the teaching language for the other half-day of instruction in the school. Tagalog was increasingly required by the Philippines Department of Education.

The students grew up using most of these languages routinely. Mr. Tan taught me Mandarin daily and with great patience. Using the Chinese phonetic called "Chu Yin Fu Hao" (Zhuyin Fuhao), he insisted that I learn to use my tongue and teeth to make the unique Chinese sounds that express the language, and with strict observance of the tones required. I must admit that I made some very embarrassing errors in public, but they were met with the understanding of an appreciative audience. There were times when I would be able to understand a conversation in which I could have been involved, had Mandarin been used by those who knew it. But voices would switch to Amoy—thus excluding me—until I was no longer thought of as an outsider.

Even as a missionary priest, I had to wait for a level of comfort to be achieved with this host population. This was an adjustment required of Marjorie and me, and we had to learn to allow for it after our time with the Igorots who had accepted us immediately. It took about four years for Marjorie and me to find a more complete acceptance with the Manila Chinese, but, when it came, it was with a permanence and sincerity that were indelible. My formal Chinese education would continue at Stanford in the Second Year intensive summer course during our 1964 furlough.

My primary responsibility was with the school chaplaincy. At that time, the elementary school campus was complete with classroom buildings, a residence for three missionary ladies, and a play yard with basketball hoops. This was across the alley from the former location of Saint Luke's Hospital, Nursing School, and the Chapel that would become the Pro-Cathedral after the war. The hospital had been used by the Japanese military during their occupation. I had heard that some medical personnel from our Saint Luke's Hospital in Tokyo had served in this hospital in Manila during "Japanese time." The hospital itself had been destroyed before our arrival in Manila, but the old Saint Luke's Nursing School and nurses' dormitory, a three-story rickety wooden structure, was still standing at the back of the compound. It was left for the purpose of temporarily housing high school classes on the first two floors. The residence of a Chinese faculty member was on the third floor (without any fire escape). In the back of that building there was a Quonset hut that was elevated on bricks piled above the level of the flood waters that filled that area in rainy season—and which sometimes invaded the ground floor of the old Nurses' School. Behind the walls of both campuses (topped with broken glass chips) was an *estero,* or open sewer, covered almost completely with squatters' huts on stilts above the stench. Free land for these dwellers was at a premium, and there were no taxes for living in such locations.

Saint Stephen's High School was founded by Saint Stephen's Mission on July 22, 1917, by its Rector and Chinese members of the church. Before the war, it had been Saint Stephen's Girls School. When I arrived in December 1960, the initial elementary academic program had expanded to include a two-year kindergarten, a Chinese high school, and an English high school. The combined student body was about 4,000.

Miss Constance B. Bolderston was the over-all principal of both the elementary and the high School. She had come from Junction City, Oregon to the Philippines in the early 1940s as a teaching missionary. During "Japanese time" she, along with Bishop and Mrs. Binsted and Ada Clarke, were confined at the prison camp on the campus of Santo Tomàs University. I had heard that some of the Japanese prison guards had been baptized by Bishop Binsted when he was Bishop of Tohoku, before he was translated to the Philippines in 1940. These missionaries were assisted in surviving their long captivity because these Christian soldiers secretly provided them with food. Emerging from liberation, Miss Bolderston undertook the task of rebuilding the girls' school, beginning in an old theater that once stood near the present site of the two neighboring Saint Stephen's compounds. Under her leadership, the school became coeducational.

Miss Bolderston's pioneering efforts were joined by those of Miss Bernice Jansen, formerly a missionary in Japan. On her way to furlough from Japan in 1941, travelling westward, the ship on which she was a passenger was sunk in the Atlantic by a torpedo attack by a German U-boat. Although injured in the lifeboat rescue, this saved her from the rigors of being a prisoner in Japan throughout the duration of the war, and probably saved her life!

Another who joined Miss Bolderston in the rebuilding of the Chinese school was Miss Gwendolyn Cooper from Loo, Cornwall, England. She had been raised on the campus of (Anglican) Saint John's University, Shanghai, by parents who pioneered the construction and the leadership of that remarkable institution that made contributions to China and to her people that would outlast even the Cultural Revolution. Pearl Buck was one of her childhood playmates. Miss Ang Siu Cham and Mrs. Yao Lim Nga Siu, female Chinese educators, assumed positions as principals of the elementary and of the high school respectively.

Ministering with these heroine-Christian visionaries, who influenced literally thousands of lives, was an unforgettable privilege. Likewise, my life and ministry were greatly enriched by serving with Father Wei and Mr. Tan at Saint Stephen's Parish, at times with Father Sham Hon San at nearby Saint Peter's (Cantonese) Parish, and with Father Wu before he left. These were the saints who provided the foundation upon which my ministry, and Marjorie's share in it with me, would build during our remaining years in the Philippines.

—Acts 16:9f

Our School Hymn

Alex, or more exactly Alexander O. Chua Wei Lin, is a Saint Stephen's High School graduate, a former leader of Saint Stephen's Christian Student Center activities and summer retreats, and an Acolyte. He sent me by e-mail from his Toronto book store the text of the Saint Stephen's School Hymn.

We build our school on Thee, O Lord,
To Thee we bring our common need;
The loving heart, the faithful word,
The tender thought, the kindly deed.

We work together in Thy sight,
We live together in Thy love;
Guide thou our faltering steps aright,
And lift our thoughts to heaven above.
Hold Thou each hand to keep it just,
Touch thou our lips and make them pure;
If Thou art with us, Lord, we must
Be faithful friends and comrades sure.

We change, but thou art still the same,
The same good Master, Teacher, Friend;
We change, but, Lord, we bear Thy Name,
To journey with Thee to the end.
Amen.

—PSALM 150

Great Procession of the Trustees, Faculty, and Student Body around the rubble remaining of Saint Luke's Hospital for the groundbreaking for the new Saint Stephen's High School Building. David Ch'ua is Crucifer. (Page 136)

Saint Stephen's Christian Student Center Membership Card. (Page 137)

High School Building under construction. Hod carriers climbed bamboo ladders to deliver the concrete. (Page 136)

Saint Stephen's High School building from the interior courtyard. (Page 136)

From the SSHS 80th Annual Album, 1917–1997

From the SSHS 80th Annual Album, 1917–1997

Saint Stephen's High School building exterior. (Page 136)

Small Chapel of Christian Martyrs of China located in the new High School Building, built partly by students. (Pages 138 & 139)

The Acolyte Guild of Saint Stephen's High School visits the Chaplain and *Patrol Squadron 40* at USNAS Sangley Point, Cavite, Philippines - September 28, 1962. (Page 143)

The Acolyte Guild of Saint Stephen's High School visits the Chaplain on board the carrier USS *Enterprise* on her maiden voyage visit to Naval Station Subic Bay, Philippines - Fall, 1963. (Page 143)

Allegiance was pleged to both the Republic of the Philippines and the Republic of China (Taiwan), by 4,000 students each morning assembled at the Elementary and High Schools when the Author was their Chaplain. (Page 145)

Building in Two Dimensions:
Outward and Physical, Inward and Spiritual

*O*ne of my first assignments at Saint Stephen's High School (the name of a school always reflecting its highest grade) was to hold weekday services for the high school grades in the old, dark, thick-walled Saint Luke's Hospital Chapel. It had been the Pro-Cathedral as well, temporarily replacing the downtown Cathedral of Saint Mary and Saint John that had been destroyed in the Battle of Manila. However, when I had arrived, it was used and named as Saint Stephen's Parish Church.

Mandatory worship experiences were not well received by many of the adolescent students, although they were required as part of the school curriculum. The majority had been sent to the school by non-Christian elders for the superior education and Chinese immersion they would receive, rather than for a Christian education. It would take time to win the hearts and the interest of these teenage students. I had the added task of bridging the language and culture gap with them, because they were used to seeing Americans and clergy mostly from a distance. Providing relevant homilies with object lessons and a more informal atmosphere in the church, walking down the center aisle to address the students hiding in the back who might be reading or otherwise amusing themselves in the anticipation of the next school activity, eventually stimulated increased involvement and interest.

With a student body of 4,000, buildings were urgently needed. Many of the high school classes met in the old three-story wooden structure that had served as the nursing school, and which was structurally questionable and a threat in case of fire. A Quonset hut used for high school classrooms became isolated when monsoons flooded the west side of the campus. Funds were raised in the Chinese community for an appropriate share in the construction of a four-story high school building with a rooftop recreation area. It would have exterior sheltered passageways open to the central courtyard to access the rooms on the four levels of the three wings of the "U-shaped" structure. The front of the building was to face an alley which the city had promised would be enlarged into a thoroughfare, a boulevard which never materialized. To the west of the high school compound, over a wall topped by shards of broken glass, was an *estero* or open sewer-canal topped by squatter families' huts previously described. (These persons migrate to the city from the provinces to seek work.)

The construction of the new high school took 13 months. It could have taken much less time, but the construction committee discovered that the ready-mix concrete being used in the building of neighboring multi-storied apartment complexes did not meet compression strength tests at the University of the Philippines School of Engineering. It was decided that we would mix our own concrete in a single rotary drum cement mixer. The mix was carried by balance boards on the shoulders of hod carriers. They climbed bamboo scaffolding and laboriously poured the concrete into the forms as the building very gradually took shape and rose heavenward.

This decision, which was viewed in the community as quaint, proved itself when the 1967 earthquakes leveled several of the nearby apartment towers, and resulted in many deaths. In one apartment building, a Saint Stephen's Elementary School student was unearthed after 93 hours of entombment in the rubble that had crushed the rest of her family. A school office suffered one small crack that was corrected with a cosmetic patch of plaster. I am proud to say that my wife Marjorie fulfilled her role of auditing every bag of nails, every sack of cement, every tool, and all other such building supplies, thus protecting our project from the rampant fraud that plagued the construction industry there.

Two adjustments were made in the original plans to accommodate this missionary. Two chaplain offices were designed adjoining the lobby which formed the ground floor main entrance to the high school, flanked also by the administration and finance offices. At my request, these two offices were not partitioned, so as to remain one long room. A chaplaincy staff person would sit at a desk at the end of the room adjacent to what was to be a broom closet. The broom closet, then, became the Chaplain's Office. The double room was designated as the Saint Stephen's Christian Student Center. It was equipped with magazines and books of Christian content in both Chinese and English, and with familiar Chinese games and other popular table top recreational devices. This was available to the students during recess, noon break, and after school. The "Center" became the locus for the organizing of the Summer Conference, Boy Scouts, Girl's Friendly Society, the (Junior) Altar Guild, prayer groups, and the Acolyte Guild—which was to grow to almost 90 students.

Saint Stephen's Christian Student Center became a popular "hang out" for students designed to appeal to most levels of interest and involvement. The ticket for admission was simple and singular. To use the Center, one had to possess a membership card—which was free of charge. That card had the name of the student and both grade and section printed on it—in Chinese on one side and in English on the other. While the student was using the Center, his or her card had to be placed on the receptionist's desk (where the Chaplain was quietly memorizing each student during his or her stay in the Center).

To obtain this valued SSCSC Membership Card, there was only one requirement. The student had to be interviewed by the Chaplain in his office. This was an informal chat, which was designed to mutually introduce student and chaplain to each other. Chinese students commonly distanced themselves from foreigners and from those perceived to be in authority, so this interview required some motivation by the student to overcome a culturally expected timidity. Likewise, this American priest-chaplain had the "double hurdle" of culture and clergy to jump in order to be a true pastor to these Chinese young people. The coveted Saint Stephen's Student Center Membership Card helped to overcome such separations, as did the Center itself. There was even a resistance from the Chinese High School Principal, Mrs. Yao. She had the signs designating the various offices and facilities in the new high school building written in both Chinese and English, but prepared the Chaplain's signs in English only. In a quite heated discussion I insisted that they be changed.

From where did this idea of a Student Center come? It came from a chapter in the history of the early Anglican Church Mission as it advanced up the Yangtze River Valley in the early Twentieth Century. The chapels that were constructed for Christian worship by eager missionaries were commonly empty of those for whom they were intended. Learning from this experience, they dispersed into the villages, lived in rooms among the population, and held "open house" for those bold enough to visit and for those who, in casual conversation, might inquire about the Christian Faith. These rented rooms were called "Christian Tea Houses," and it was here that effective evangelism began by gradually establishing personal relationships between the missionaries and the local people.

The Christian Student Center at Saint Stephen's High School was my "Tea House." Out of it blossomed many Christian activities that crossed class lines, many opportunities for service, and many precious friendships. This also stimulated new enthusiasm for school chapel services in which students found new leadership functions. They learned to participate as Acolytes, lectors who read the Scriptures, ushers, and in the work of an Altar Guild. The Acolytes and the Junior Altar Guild expanded to function in the two neighboring Chinese parishes (Amoy speaking at Saint Stephen's; Cantonese at Saint Peter's; with Mandarin used at both).

The second alteration that I made in the original high school construction plans was the creation on the second floor, among the classrooms but over the lobby, of a "Chapel of the Holy Martyrs of China." The name complied with the Church Calendar feast day of June 2nd, on which the commemoration of the Martyrs of China and the Martyrs of Lyon share the day (even though the former seems to have fallen from recent Ordo Calendars). The purpose of this Chapel was to accommodate class-sized worship, small group religious discussions and instructions, to encourage individual meditation close to where most of student life was spent. It also provided a Sanctuary where the Junior Altar Guild and the Acolytes could function. The name of the chapel served to remind the school community that Christianity was not new to the Chinese people and their history. Many who served at the school altar then became involved in parish churches with better understanding, and, for some, with eager excitement. Voluntary prayer groups were organized among students who made use of the completed chapel, and a small keyboard (in the days where such were not common) was acquired from Hong Kong so that several music students, such as Ingrid Chang and Grace Wee, could accompany the singing of hymns. A project to transpose some of the canticles, chants, and even the sequence hymn for the Stations of the Cross, into Chinese musical settings, was begun.

Resistance to this project came from an unexpected source. Some of the teachers and some parents objected to the fact that students were becoming involved in interior construction tasks in the development of the chapel. Although such were within their capabilities and their abilities to learn, a fear had to be addressed that the school would prepare children for manual rather than managerial vocations. Some subtle reminders were offered in defense of this project by the Chaplain and by Miss Wong Yok Wing, the Director of Christian Education, who had joined the team in 1963. Many of these pupils had families in the Mainland of China, and if they were there during this time, they would probably be learning to build railroads instead of going to school. Further, if they had no homeland or current citizenship, they would have to emigrate in order to progress in any profession. In other lands, manual arts could be a precious advantage for survival. Indeed, nothing dangerous was involved in the decoration of the small chapel. Thus, the Chapel of Holy Martyrs of China found its home in the school, and in the hearts of many students who are now alumni of the school.

The finishing touch and climax to the creation of the chapel came when the Blessed Sacrament was brought there and placed in the Ambry. This repository for the Reserved Sacrament is for the immediate availability of the Holy Communion for the distressed or for the sick and the dying. There was no other Ambry or Tabernacle for the Reserved Sacrament on the Church and School compound. This Ambry was fashioned of mahogany, replicating the one crafted for the Sanctuary of the Mission of the Good Shepherd in Berkeley by Mr. George Pascoe. "The Real Presence" of Jesus had come to reside in the heart of the new Saint Stephen's High School.

—⁓—

I would be extremely remiss were I not to pay tribute to Father Samuel Wu and his dear wife Anna (who later preferred the English name Edita). Father Wu was a son of the local community and a university graduate, who had earned his theological degree in New York City at the General Theological Seminary of the Episcopal Church. He had been Chaplain for some time prior to my sudden arrival on the scene, and he was alert to the needs of the students in a very traditional religious program. He graciously served as my guide through an adjustment to ministry in his culture that might otherwise have been a minefield of errors for me. Both of us were young clergy. His wife taught piano and was a fine accompanist. They encouraged my initiatives in ways that made them productive by means of quiet and patient suggestions. My year with them, before they moved to the Parish of the Good Shepherd in Kowloon and eventually to Saint John's Cathedral in the Diocese of Hong Kong, was an apprenticeship that was essential to my future at the school and in the parish. This also provided time for students and teachers to learn to trust this American priest, and Father Wu and Anna expedited this by a kind and genuine demonstration of friendship for me and Marjorie.

The most significant thing which I inherited from Father Wu and from the traditions of the school was the annual Summer Conference that was traditionally held at Easter School, where I had been previously assigned. Most of these young students lived in crowded quarters in what I would describe as a ghetto. Parents were unwilling to permit their family members to leave the immediate area, even to visit some of the public recreation parks and popular resort facilities. This restriction was out of the realistic fear that they would be harmed by prejudiced Filipinos or subjected to demands of extortion in roadblocks by members of the National Police Constabulary (which I had occasion to interrupt).

Thus, there was an enforced isolation—which was only broken for a project under the direct supervision of the mission school with oversight along the highway provided by recognized ecclesiastical authority. Going up to the cool fresh air of the mountain resort city of Baguio and to the expanses of pine trees and green grasses was a refreshing change and a coveted and inspiring opportunity for the participants. As I recall, well over a hundred high school students boarded buses for the long ride up, followed by a happy time which included a great deal of learning about the Christian Faith and the Church— over a week together with their peers and the school chaplains and staff.

One of the most remarkable aspects of this annual Summer Christian Conference was what went on to prepare for it. The Chaplaincy Staff provided the content of the worship and teaching, but the business of the conference was the task of the students themselves. Each year a committee was organized, officers elected, and duties and responsibilities for the financing, contracting, food services, and recreation were parceled out and accepted with great efficiency. They carefully selected fellow students who would make mature use of the conference—not in ways that would keep the group an ingrown clique. Volunteers from the school faculty were recruited. Students made appointments and visited alumni, company presidents, and people of influence (predominantly Chinese) in the community with predetermined expectations of what they would be contributing to the budget of the Summer Christian Conference. This was a demonstration of initiative on the part of these young Christians that astounded me. This annual event and the prolonged preparations for it provided perhaps the greatest opportunity for fellowship and Christian education at the high school level. It was eagerly anticipated by students at the elementary school, still too young to be included, and this provided a foundation and a student network upon which additional activities then could be developed.

Soon after Father Wu left for Hong Kong, a wonderful surprise arrived in the person of Miss Wong Yok Wing (now Mrs. Lawrence Cheung), an alumna of Saint Stephen's School and of Philippine Women's University. She had been advancing her Vocation at the Union Theological Seminary in New York City, where she earned her Master of Religious Education degree. Yok Wing, who uses the English name Yvonne where she now lives in British Columbia, was a most invaluable addition to the school and to the Chaplaincy. She understood what I was seeking to do, and was able to apply cultural relevance to such developments. In many ways she was my advisor and my mentor.

Yok Wing had grown up in Hong Kong and in Manila's Binondo District, and at Saint Stephen's School. After university graduation in Manila, then having done her postgraduate training in the United States, she knew the difficulties of bridging the cultures of East and West in ways that Chinese girls and boys face in the Philippines. She became a close confidante to these young students, and encouraged them to participate in the activities of the Christian Student Center. She taught in the Christian Education Department, and was especially effective with the girls in the Christian student activities. Most importantly, Yok Wing was a mature model of personal development for students to seek and to follow.

Alicia Lee (now Mrs. Victory Go of Temple, Texas)—a former student of mine at the school, and a Saint Stephen's and Philippine Women's University graduate—joined Yok Wing on the Chaplaincy staff during my furlough months in 1964. A woman teacher, Lim Ong Sui Hong, taught Christian studies and Sunday School in the Elementary School chaplaincy. Alicia began that year on the Baguio summer student conference faculty, and remained to serve with me on my return from the United States. After my departure for Viet Nam, she followed Wong Yok Wing in her position when Yok Wing married then-Seminarian Lawrence Cheung in June 1966. They left for Taiwan, where he would transfer from Saint Andrew's Seminary in Manila to complete his theological degree at Tainan Theological Seminary.

Jacob Ching (Alberto) had been a most enthusiastic student leader, and after his graduation he joined the school Chaplaincy for a brief period. Jacob went on to earn his Ph.D. degree in Psychology, and presently resides in Xiamen in the Peoples' Republic of China.

Father Magdaleno Bacagan, the Filipino priest whom I had recruited and who had served briefly with the Chaplaincy, had not returned from Taiwan. He went there enthusiastically under Church sponsorship (which I initiated), to learn the Amoy dialect used in the homes of the majority of our students.

—⟋⟋⟋—

Small interest groups were high on our list of priorities. Acolyte Guild for the boys, and Altar Guild for the girls (in the gender specific traditions of those times) gained the interest of the students. New skills related to these activities were employed in support of the school chapel services, and were gradually incorporated into the liturgical life of the two neighboring Chinese Episcopal and other Christian congregations. I initiated an annual excursion for the Acolytes to American military bases in the Philippines. These became a very popular incentive. On the third such trip, 90 of these youths were guests of the Navy Chaplain aboard the USS *Enterprise* on its first deployment and initial port visit at the Subic Bay Naval Complex.

A Girls' Friendly Society, developed with the aid of Wong Yok Wing, used older students as mentors. With the resources of that international organization, with which we were able to network, programs were planned and executed. Soon, our GFS girls were sending representatives from among their number to attend annual international conferences in interesting places like Japan and Australia. Leong Hing Hwa was employed on the school fiscal staff. He was an enthusiastic supporter and *friend* of the school chaplaincy as well as being an active member of Saint Peter's (Cantonese) Parish. He organized a Camera Club through the student center, which became very popular with students.

A troop of the "Boy Scouts of China in the Philippines" soon gained a membership of 75, with such a volunteer and enthusiastic leader of stature as Professor Lim Giok Khun. I encouraged the Scouts to be trained in sensible rescue procedures that could be mobilized when the frequent tenement fires terrorized the district surrounding our school and parish. The Scouts would know their neighbors and the dialects they used, thus would be able to know whether the people they were helping escape the firetrap residences and shops were legitimate families in need of help, or looters on missions of self-enrichment.

Bars and grillwork were fixed to windows on the first two stories to protect from burglars, but frequently they lacked functional escape ports, which made difficult and frequently impossible ways of escape from flames and smoke. It was a very helpless feeling to watch people being incinerated as they pressed helplessly against metal window grills inside upper floor apartments. We have seen such horrors in the night while standing beside firemen holding charged hoses that were flushing Chinatown's gutters awaiting thousand peso cash bribes for each hose (no checks or securities, please!) before directing their water where it might help.

Indeed, the school's Christian program was intended to contribute to the local parishes, not compete with them. For the curriculum of the teachers in the Department of Christian Education, translations adapted from such classics as *Faith and Practice* by Bishop Frank Wilson and similar sources were taught to augment the Biblical curriculum with theology, church history and customs. Confirmation Classes evolved from the school chapel services and the activities of the Christian Student Center. These classes developed into a twice-a-year series of twelve 90-minute sessions after school hours. They had to be limited to an attendance of 85 because of the capacity of the classrooms. From those attending these classes, many came to receive Holy Baptism and Confirmation. These were not just rites of passage, but were expressions of sincere and genuine conversions.

The problems that were encountered in this enterprise were truly reminiscent of the New Testament Church, and solutions to such problems required careful review of the Acts of the Apostles. For example, children of Buddhist parents and grandparents were expected to offer fruit and incense to their ancestors on home shrine-altars on certain occasions. A refusal to be present would be misinterpreted as disrespect for family and heritage, thus provoking intense emotional resistance and family indignation. In this case, when advising new Christians, we followed the advice of Saint Paul (in I Corinthians 8) with remarkable results. The intentions of the one who made the offering would take precedence.

Another matter that was encountered caused delays and family resistance for girls desiring to receive Holy Baptism. This was the parents' expectation of selecting their daughter's marriage partner. Should a prosperous potential groom emerge, a non-Christian might object to her attending church rather than remaining at home serving him and the children. Many girls were withheld from becoming Christians until matrimonial plans were absolutely certain.

This became dramatically evident to me when Ellen, a high school student who had attended the school Confirmation Class series for a third time and who had joined the parish youth choir, sat weeping in the choir pews while her classmates went to the Altar Rail to receive Holy Communion. This reached the limits of my patience, and as I was experiencing both frustration and compassion following a Sunday Eucharist, we had a chat. Her dilemma was that she wanted to "honor her father and mother" in accordance with the Commandments, but she felt Called to be a Christian and to participate in the Sacraments. "Your *Heavenly* Father must be respected as well," I dared to suggest. With that, we walked to the new high school building's second floor chapel, and, with one or two "secret witnesses" present, the water that was already prepared in anticipation was blessed and poured upon this dear young lady. The following Sunday, her first Holy Communion was a time for smiling and reunion with her friends at the Altar Rail, and an experience of welcome with Christ, the Host of the Celebration as well.

Now an adult with her own family, I still hear from her fairly often. Perhaps she can imagine the tears of joy that still moisten my cheeks as I recall her struggle and her courage in the midst of this cultural and spiritual dilemma.

Each school day in the assembly yard at the Elementary School compound and beside the old nursing school dormitory (later in the main yard enclosed by the wings of the new high school), two flags were raised and saluted, two national anthems were sung in their appropriate language, and allegiance was pledged by our thousands of students. These flags and anthems were those of the Republic of the Philippines and of the Republic of China. Many of these students had come to the Philippines, with or without their families, escaping from Communism and Mainland China. There was no room for them on already overcrowded Taiwan, and citizenship in the Philippines—the key to practicing any profession in the country—was financially far beyond the grasp of most immigrants. "Filipino First" was the hew and cry of the time, and the slogan of many a protest among the host population smarting with the memories of centuries of colonialism first under Spanish, then under American rule, as well as temporarily under the Japanese military. Chinese immigrant extended families demonstrate their ability to operate business cooperatives which aggressively accumulate comparative opulence. This perpetuates an unfortunate cultural stereotype.

Commonly throughout Southeast Asia, there is a jealousy-motivated negative mind-set that still renders the Overseas Chinese objects of discrimination. Thus, the *Hua Ch'iao* ("Blossoming Bridge" to other lands) are, in a sense, people with a homeland, although many are temporarily without a country. The incongruity of our students' pledging of allegiance to a nation which had no room for them, and simultaneously to a nation that had a deep-seated animosity toward them, never dared any expression. But, I am sure, this was secretly acknowledged in the minds of young and old alike. However, this was a population who needed any port in an international political storm.

One of my main objectives with students, a foundation for my preaching and teaching, was to declare that somewhere in the world there was a piece of earth upon which each of our students could stand tall in the knowledge that they belonged, and that soil—whether in the host country or elsewhere—belonged to God their Heavenly Father. As His Children, their immediate task was to believe in their future, and in a Savior who would open doors to the future usefulness of each of His Own. This required strong faith in the lives of these children so that they could make use of their education and aim at what God would be Calling them to do with their lives—even though they could not envision where the journey might take them or how it might develop for them as individuals. I saw families live like rats in multistory wooden tenements serviced by open sewers, potential victims of fire, thieves, and threats to their health in that Tondo/Binondo area, so that their children could study and eventually have a chance to attend Harvard or Oxford or the University of the Philippines.

During one of the years that we served in Manila, the majority of the honor graduates from Santo Tomàs University School of Medicine were graduates of Saint Stephen's School. Many of them would never be allowed to practice medicine in the Philippines. "God needs you; you are His Child, and He has prepared a very special place for you! Have that faith." This creed undergirded most of the activities I led during my chaplaincy at Saint Stephen's High School.

How I wish every American student could attend a school in Southeast Asia, even for a week, to observe the struggles of students to learn and to better themselves! Our mission schools are head-and-shoulders above any others, to the point that there is strong competition to enter them and to remain as pupils. The squandering of youth in modern America is all too common in our age of affluence. The patience and discipline that my daughter Karla (the first Caucasian child ever to attend) learned over four decades ago at Saint Stephen's School molded her life in ways that defy description. There she studied full days in three languages—with homework—from ages 4 through 6. We never bothered to tell her that children in America did not do such things at her age! In their homeland, her parents probably would have been accused of child abuse! The sacrifices the families in Binondo made, and continue to make for their children, is also beyond the belief of the Westerner.

—DEUTERONOMY 4:9; I KINGS 8:6,54ff; EPHESIANS 2:19–22

The Mountain Orchid

*O*ur baby daughter Karla Nancy began her life in the Philippines at five months of age. Her first year was spent in Baguio City with Igorot playmates, but she really did much of her growing up in Manila and at Saint Stephen's School. We left the Philippines when she was seven. By then, she was fluent in six languages, not realizing that this was unusual.

When as a toddler she would accompany her mother shopping in the open markets in Baguio, she was the object of loving curiosity. Igorot shoppers and vendors alike would surround her and attempt to touch her fair skin. The child would panic in fright. This, however, became controlled when Marjorie became comfortable with the interest of the people, thus relieving her own anxieties. The child, sensing her mother's ease, responded in kind.

After the move to Manila, again the little blond child was a subject of inquisitiveness by those around her. When she was pursued, her timidity—no longer on the level of panic—would cause her to move away. However, if one seeking affectionate contact would just walk away, pretending to ignore her, she would then return to approach them with a smile.

When the time came for her to receive a Chinese name for entry into the records of Saint Stephen's School, I approached my mentor and scholarly advisor, Mr. Tan. After a short moment of thought, his decision was made, and the result was reported. The Chinese name in her case would be a close transliteration of the English name, whereas for a Chinese child, an English name was normally an unofficial approximation of the Chinese name already given. Mr. Tan spoke. "Her name is K'o Lan!" (柯蘭). This sounded very much like "Karla Nancy" to his ear. He continued: "K'o is a branch, like that of a tree. But this would be heavier than the branch or stem of a flower. This indicates 'strength.' The Lan Flower is the Mountain Orchid that blooms in the high elevations of inland China. When one goes to smell the fragrance of the Mountain Orchid, one cannot detect a scent. But when one walks away from that flower, the beautiful smell follows and catches up with the one seeking it."

This is how Tan Tiao Lin gave our daughter her Chinese name, and she and her parents have treasured it ever since.

—ST. LUKE 1:62–64

Meet Mister Tan

B eside the former hospital chapel being used as Saint Stephen's Parish Church and for high school chapel services, stood an old two-story Spanish-era building with four-foot thick stuccoed masonry walls and tiled roofing. The rectory was an upstairs apartment with a wrought-iron decorated balcony over the first floor entrance to the building. My office, before the high school was built, was in the bowels of this massive building, and my chamber had all of the charm of a cell in a medieval dungeon.

The portal to the ground floor entrance resembled the mouth of a cave. Behind the heavy doors and barred and iron shuttered windows was a tile-floored entry room. This was the lair of the Saint Stephen's Parish Secretary and Lay Reader, Tan Tiao Lin. A native of a small town in the Fukien (Fujian) Province of China, he became a Christian at an early age when he was a student in a mission school. Tan Tiao Lin came to Manila in 1947 at the invitation of Saint Stephen's Church to join its pastoral staff. This octogenarian of great stature and erect physique could always be found from sun up behind his desk in the cavern just described. Mr. Tan was a dedicated scholar, disciplined in his study and knowledge of Holy Scripture, and the translator of the *Book of Common Prayer* for local Chinese use. His delivery of the appointed lessons each Sunday was both inspired and authoritative, and he was given to helping the then-rector, Fr. Wei Hsi Jen, by frequently preaching the Sunday sermon.

Without charge, Mr. Tan volunteered to teach me to read the Sunday Epistle and Gospel and to celebrate the Eucharist in Mandarin, using Chinese phonetics as an aid to vocal delivery. I gained new and wonderfully enlightened understandings of the appointed texts, as we struggled with the translations during my one-hour or more lessons each morning at his desk. These lessons continued promptly and without fail, because if I was to study with Mr. Tan, I would share his discipline. When we spent hours translating single passages from the liturgy or from the Bible from one language to another, it replicated my seminary experience of exploring them in Hebrew and in Koiné Greek. We traced how scriptural truths had passed through the minds of Chinese Christian scholars, and Mr. Tan made comparisons with how they were viewed by other Oriental religions and philosophies. In this process I was finding yet deeper meanings than I had known before. I am not implying syncretism, but broader experience and application. Mr. Tan worshipped Jesus as his Savior, but he loved Confucius.

A task I contemplated while studying with Mr. Tan, for example, was having the *Four Books of Confucius* bound together with the New Testament, because I believed they represented a genuine pre-Christian experience in the history of the Chinese people. Confucius taught one to have strong morality and dignity. His teachings had been explored, even memorized, by Chinese who were mature in their own culture. "Do not do unto others what you do not wish them to do unto you," may be the Golden Rule in negative terms, but this is truly a precursor of Christian teaching. One can appreciate the annual celebration of Confucius' birthday. It is called "Teachers' Day," and on this Chinese school holiday it is traditional for student classes to entertain their teachers. The relationship of respect of student for teacher taught by Confucius is sacrosanct. In my "senior years," I am lifted by the loving contacts I receive from many of my former Saint Stephen's School students who have kept contact with me over four decades.

This Christian scholar, Mr. Tan, so saturated with his ancient culture as well, brought new applications of Christian living to me. One example of this I have never forgotten. It all occurred one Monday morning, when I arrived at the desk of Mr. Tan with disturbed thoughts. In response to his astute reading of my body language, I blurted: "It's Mr. Yu!" (Mr. Yu was a senior member of the parish, perhaps a patron.) I complained that Mr. Yu regularly attended the 6:30 A.M. Sunday Mass. Instead of observing a fasting communion, he would consume copious quantities of garlic before coming to the early church service, and he would sit in the front pew as an expression of his enthusiasm. Thus, he was first at the Altar Rail, and first to receive the consecrated Sacrament from the chalice—leaving behind a slight aroma as a reminder of his early morning snack. After communing, Mr. Yu would express his satisfaction in traditional style by trumpeting a belch so loud that it seemed to rattle the stained glass windows in the cavernous old church. Having vented my disturbed feelings, I turned to Mr. Tan, expecting him to offer some solution or perhaps to intercede regarding the matter. Mr. Tan applied Taoist philosophy to the matter, as he shrugged his shoulders, and, with palms up, said ever so quietly: "That's his way." In other words, let Mr. Yu be, because: "That's his way."

Mr. Tan's calm ways of handling things may have offered patience as a solution where no great harm was being done. But more than that, this large and powerful man was the embodiment of Christian kindness which would have meant less had it come from weakness. Yet, I also learned the contribution of Taoism (with its emphasis on conforming to "the Way★ of nature") to Christian life and thought in the Orient. To my knowledge, nothing may have changed in the methods of praise offered by Mr. Yu, but something changed in me by the rationale offered by my saintly elder.

I came for my Mandarin lesson the day after a devastating night fire that burned 23 blocks of tenement housing and street-level shops surrounding our school compound. It had tragic results for very many of our neighbors. We had not yet moved to our residence at the school, but Marjorie and I had spent much of the night observing the holocaust, chaos, and panic in the dark streets—feeling helpless and frightened for the victims, but not knowing who or how to help. But the morning after—with many buildings still smoking and in ruins—Mr. Tan was, true to form, there at his desk to receive me! Evidently, about 2 A.M. the night before in his second floor room, he was awakened by the noises outside. He opened his eyes to see the brilliant flickering orange which he recognized as flames nearby and across the street. Still in his nightshirt, he searched without electricity for the possessions that were most important to him at the time—his Bible and the notes he had written for his sermon the following Sunday. With them, he slowly descended the narrow staircase to the street, walked the two blocks to the church, lay down on one of the pews, and resumed his sleep. In the morning he returned to his tenement—still standing as he thought it would be. Yes, there it was, surrounded on three sides by burned wrecks. He climbed the stairs, changed into his day clothes, and returned to his post—the desk at the church office in the compound.

I was still shaken by the experience of the night before, even though I still lived across town at the time. When I asked Mr. Tan how he had fared during the night, he calmly began our lesson without hesitation. "Today we will learn the word for *miracle*," he said. "When we speak of miracle, we use the characters *Shen* (2nd tone) *chi* (4th tone). *Shen chi* means 'God's footprints,' because when we see a miracle we know that God has passed this way."

In our five-and-a-half years together, I learned so much more than language and Bible translation. Tan Tiao Lin was a miracle in my life, because through him I knew that God had passed my way. When I left Manila, Mr. Tan accepted a reclining chair as my simple gift for his room. In no way could I ever repay him for what he had given to me. The chair would make life easier for his body, as his former strength was showing signs of aging. During the ten years after I left for Viet Nam, his physical health did gradually fail. Yet with a vigorous spirit and resilient faith, I was told that he asked the Lord to let him die on Easter Day. On April 10, 1977 at three o'clock in the afternoon, his final prayer was answered.

—ACTS 9:26f

★Tao means "the Way," or a roadway, or path.

Building Bridges

*E*very culture has its language, and that language both conveys and interprets that culture. Languages change, and even have alterations when the culture for which they speak experiences changes. There are many kinds of cultures, each with its unique language. There are languages for each of the military services, for medicine and psychotherapy, for the law, for "the streets," for the hard of hearing, and for various ecclesiastical settings. Likewise, there are languages for various nationalities and for the subcultures of those, as well. For example, until one can "speak Navy," one cannot communicate well with sailors. Until one can speak Spanish, there are places in California where one cannot communicate very well. Obviously, in the ministry in the Philippines we encountered Tagalog, Ilocano and its Igorot subculture, and three dialects of Chinese. Our baby daughter learned and used them all with her friends, then in school, in her first seven years of life—the prime time for such learning. As an adult, I had to focus on one language, and rely on translators or limited English (where it was understood) in order to communicate. My choice, even before going overseas, was to study Mandarin Chinese.

The work of the ministry is to build bridges—bridges of understanding upon which avenues of love can become smooth and solid. In order to build such bridges across the borders and barriers of culture, language proficiency is essential to the spanning effort. Foreign language study for adults learning a second language is more difficult than having had the more natural experience of being a native speaker, but the effort is usually appreciated by members of the host culture. It has been said that the greatest form of flattery is imitation. Indeed, learning the language of the people one serves is usually met with appreciation by them, and with gracious forgiveness for errors made.

The people in the Mountain Province had a long history of friendship and acceptance of Americans that predated team efforts for their survival in what is called "Japanese times," and English has been taught as a second language to the children of the last two or three generations. The Chinese immigrants in Manila were far more culturally isolated and therefore slower to accept "Westerners," even those struggling to learn their language. I encountered some hesitancy to accept my efforts in the beginning, but with gradual acceptance came the rewarding experience of better communication and greater mutual trust. As a student of Chinese, I was increasingly enriched by learning the culture which the language conveyed. Culture and language are indisputably married. Each human is an incarnation of his culture, and presents himself to the world through language.

Although it did not involve a problem of spoken language, I was amused by a high school student's test paper which reflected how Philippine history had influenced her learning of new material. In the religious education instruction at Saint Stephen's School in Manila, at this particular time, we were studying the Christian/Church Year. The quiz question was: "What is the second meaning of the season of Advent?" The proper or desired response would approximate the following:

"This season prepares us: 1.) for the coming of the Christmas celebration of the birth of Jesus, and 2.) for the coming again of Jesus at the end of time." One young girl wrote on her paper: "In the Bible, Jesus said: 'I shall return!'" I gave her a good grade, but marked in red pencil on her paper which was returned to her: "You have the idea right, but those are the words of Douglas MacArthur!"

Of course, understanding requires bridges which support two-way traffic. Frequently, the minister is the one initiating the contact. In order to identify him/herself as an interested friend, one finds that learning culture and language is often a lonely task, and one can feel at first like an "intruder." People of both cultures (where mutual motivation to communicate is present) each have their needs to learn a second means of expression.

When we were building the Chapel of Holy Martyrs in the new high school building, one of the student volunteer leaders on that project, Jacob Ching (Alberto), came into my office with what seemed to be an urgent problem. Somewhat out of breath, he blurted out something about "the crustaceans." I listened for a few sentences, patiently trying to understand what crustaceans had to do with the chapel project. Finally, not wanting to offend, I asked him to sit down beside me at my desk. I wrote out what I heard him saying, and explained that this was a shellfish. "Oh no!" he exclaimed. "Cross Stations!" We both shared a hearty laugh. With a common mind, communication is always possible.

I received even greater patience and "benefits of the doubt" than I may ever know, as I struggled with my homiletical efforts before the huge congregations at Saint Stephen's Parish. Of course I relied heavily on Mr. Tan as I made my advance preparations. It still required the courage to risk making mistakes. I will never know to this day the mistakes I made in public as I attempted to communicate the Gospel. Thus I acknowledge with deep gratitude the forgiveness of the church members and of my fellow clergy as I mustered the courage to speak Mandarin from the pulpit. Only Mr. Tan would tell me the truth in my Monday classes following Sunday efforts, but even those times were sparse, because I suspect he wished to spare my ego so as to encourage future efforts.

One mistake that became evident to me occurred on a Saturday morning when I was addressing a group of Sunday School Teachers. I need to explain that to qualify as a Sunday School Teacher in the culture of that time and place, one needed to be female and at least 70 years of age, or look like it. I was expounding on teaching methods in what I hoped would be my best Chinese. When calling attention to a matter, I intended to say, in Chinese, that this matter was very important. *Hen yao t'ien!* literally means "Very much want (to make) a point!" But what came out of my mouth was *Ken hsiao pien!* which means literally: "with urination!" I noticed some quiet surprise as I continued, but never a comment. It was with chagrin that I later realized my error and their kind forgiveness.

Glossologia or the "Gift of Tongues" (see I Corinthians 14) did not come automatically or spontaneously to me. Some may have been endowed with this Gift of the Spirit, I do not doubt. But I have had to gain many things the hard way, of which language is but one. I reflect on the difficult journey into the American culture so many immigrants have had to make, and I have gained a new respect for them. I would add that pioneering in a second language is done best with an audience that is allied with you and which is long suffering, because an antagonistic audience would "slay the messenger." Also, so that one does not "slay oneself," it is *essential* to develop the ability to forgive oneself, pick oneself up off the floors of humiliation, and begin once again.

—GENESIS 11:1-9; JUDGES 12:6; COMPARE ACTS 2:6

There is No Bridling of the Spirit

We had moved from the bombed out former orphanage building on Taft Avenue in the Ermita district into a new two-story residence on the school compound. According to our request, we were able to live by the school in Tondo. Over the wall to the west of our house was an *estero* (open sewer). Fortunately the house was positioned so as to capture the prevailing winds, so when front door and sliding door to the back porch were opened, the wind provided us with natural air conditioning. The direction of the wind determined whether or not our ventilation brought with it the fragrance of the *estero*. When we returned from the furlough that followed our first four years in the Philippines, our four-year-old Karla donned the violet skirt and white uniform blouse of a Saint Stephen's Elementary student, and only had to cross the high school campus and the alley beyond it to attend all day kindergarten classes taught in Amoy. Like many of her four-year-old classmates, she would return home for a snack after classes in the late afternoon, then go to Mrs. Lin Yu Ping for Mandarin tutoring. Her homework had to be done after dinner.

Living on the compound, I was now available to the school and to Saint Stephen's Parish at any time of night or day. The house was very comfortable for us, and it was a splendid addition to the compound. Staff duplex apartments were added next to it.

The janitors, maintenance personnel and their families, were primarily Igorots from the Episcopal Missions in the Mountain Province of Luzon, and they lived either on the school compound or nearby. Because they were loyal Church people living at some distance from the Cathedral or downtown Trinity Parish, they needed a place to worship in Ilocano or in English. When the Chapel of Holy Martyrs was established on the second floor of the new high school building, we organized the Emmanuel Mission for the Filipino community in the area. It met at the Chapel for worship and fellowship on Sunday afternoons, a time when I could be available. I named the congregation for my first church at Terminous, California, and after the original name of my father's home parish in Fairbury, Nebraska. This newly organized Mission was well attended, deeply appreciated, and provided a meeting place not only for familiar worship, but also for social activities based upon the customs and traditions of the places from which the worshippers had come. Tribal dances and *Christian kaneo* potluck suppers were occasional joyful mission events. (*Kaneo* is the name for a pagan sacrificial feast in the Mountain Province, but we "baptized" the term.)

I approached Bishop Lyman C. Ogilby requesting a Filipino assistant priest. The chaplaincy-related activity level was rapidly escalating, and Miss Wong and I did not want to miss the opportunities that were unfolding. Further, I would need coverage for furlough and a second six-week Chinese language full-immersion study opportunity that the Episcopal Church was again making available to me at Stanford University. This would be the Second Year Chinese course, similar to the China House live-in summer course I had taken in 1959, some months prior to leaving California.

The Reverend Magdaleno K. Bacagan had expressed an interest in the proposed position, and the bishop was agreeable to appointing him prior to my temporary absence. He became popular with the students, and I hoped that Miss Wong would have good support while I was away. Things were going well for the Chaplaincy at Saint Stephen's Elementary and High School. Father Bacagan could serve as the Vicar of the Emmanuel Mission during my furlough, and share or keep that responsiblity on my return. He accepted the position at Saint Stephen's High School and Emmanuel Mission, much to my delight.

Upon returning from furlough, I began to encourage Father Bacagan to take more of the leadership role in the chaplaincy. This was in tune with the policies growing in the missionary diocese designed to shift toward indigenous initiative to decrease dependency on what had been a colonial church, and it was clearly in preparation for the eventual autonomy of the Philippine Episcopal Church. My approach was gradual, but on return to the school I discussed with Father Bacagan the goal of his assuming the official position of Chaplain and of my being his assistant.

I encountered some resistance from him, even after he had the responsibility of the work during my furlough-study leave. Further, feeling gratitude for his service while I was away, I sought a grant that would enable him to learn Amoy in a total immersion situation in Taiwan. This would prepare him for greater service in both the school and in Saint Stephen's Parish, and this found favor with the bishop. Father Bacagan seemed thrilled! With the understanding and agreement of all involved, a suitable training arrangement was made for a period of six months, to be hosted by the Diocese of Taiwan.

When six months had passed and we needed his return, Father Bacagan had arranged independently with the bishop to extend his time on Taiwan for a year. At the end of the year, by the same action he was extended for 18 months, rather than continuing his tutoring locally. It was becoming obvious to me that his return could not be expected "on my watch." I was disappointed to have been "left out of the loop."

———

One of the many preaching engagements I had on furlough in the United States was at the Parish of Holy Innocents in Corte Madera, California. The then-Rector and my beloved friend Father Tod Ewald and I had discussed the potentials for the ministry at Saint Stephen's School. He surprised both me and his congregation that Sunday by asking them at the Eucharist if they would like to provide me with a Chinese typewriter. When he succeeded in clarifying that he was indeed not joking, and that there was such a thing, the funds for this purchase were raised instantly at the Offertory that Sunday.

On the return voyage from furlough, Marjorie, 4-year-old Karla and I booked passage on the freighter *China Bear*. I had made advanced arrangements for a Chinese typewriter to be delivered to the ship through Ch'ung Chi (Anglican Church) University in Hong Kong when we made a port visit there. Jacob, David, and Alex, among others, wanted to print a Christian "news sheet" to be distributed throughout the school and surrounding neighborhoods. When I brought the machine to the school and it was uncrated, the students at the

Student Center and I enjoyed figuring out how to operate it. It was a great asset to the school and to the chaplaincy, and with it our "Good News" paper began publication in one of the storage closets in the high school building. Enthusiasm for Christian service was growing among the students.

—〰—

Several years after furlough, Jacob Ch'ing (Alberto) came to me with a request from some of the Student Center "gang." They were asking for permission and support for the conduct of Sidewalk Sunday School classes for the street children on Ong Pin Street. This street was, at the time, the locus of prostitution, and these children came from questionable parentage. They could be easily gathered on a street corner on a Saturday or Sunday. Our students wanted to teach them about Jesus. The project made sense to me, and I shared it with the School "veteran" Missionary-Principal, Constance B. Bolderston.

I was not aware that this idea alarmed her, and in her private conference with Bishop Ogilby, it was decided that I was "to confine (my) ministry to inside the walls of the elementary and high school compounds." As a young zealous minister who had received his undergraduate training at the Methodist College of the Pacific, I truly thought (in the words of the Reverend John Wesley) that "the world was my parish!" When that mandate to desist was delivered, I was shocked, and I felt genuinely heartbroken. I grieved that I had evidently led these students into a blatantly blind street. I would have to try to bridle their spirits, and felt in my heart that I would be attempting to bridle the Holy Spirit as well. This directive was delivered to me in the form of an order, and its confirmation devastated me. I felt both sad and angry that I had been moving openly in obvious directions, not secret ones, and I earnestly believed the projects shared by chaplain and students were not only exciting, but commendable and "of the Lord."

—〰—

In 1963, I had been invited to join the U. S. Naval Reserve by Chaplain Warren H. Johnson at Sangley Point Naval Air Station, across the bay from Manila. The Navy Chaplains at the Subic Bay Naval Base were quick to contact me to express their agreement. As they shifted their priorities with the acceleration of warfare in Viet Nam, they were in need of help with routine ministries and counseling. Additional military ships and aircraft squadrons had been transferred to their bases, and many of the combat wounded were being treated at military hospitals in the Philippines and being routed through them to the United States.

I was accepted into the Chaplain Corps as a Lieutenant (junior grade) in the Naval Reserve in December of that year. After that, I used my Fridays off duty at the school to do "cockpit counseling" in uniform on the flight line at Sangley Point. With the encouragement of newly befriended Chaplain John W. Berger, circuit rider with composite Service Squadron 3, I spent my first two-week summer vacation period on "Active Duty for Training" under his supervision, providing chaplain services for fleet units at Subic Bay.

A second two-week "ACDUTRA," a year later, was spent augmenting the chaplaincy at the Subic base. The closer I got to the needs of those in the military, the more aware I became of the suffering in Viet Nam of Asians, Americans, and their allies, and the more I felt the need to express my care for them. The only experience I had had with the involvement of the United States in war was as a youth on the home front during World War II. The Korean conflict had taken many of my friends to the front, while I was exempted as a divinity student. I had joined the Coast Guard Reserve as a gesture of allegiance, and I made a solemn vow that I would serve my country in uniform if ever needed—but as a priest. From the perspective of living in the Philippines, isolated from the American news media, I truly thought that my country had mobilized in support of the war against totalitarian communism in Viet Nam; that my government had rationed butter and gasoline and called out the reserves! (It was several years later that I learned that neither had been done, and I was shocked at the realization.)

I was able to observe a calming of a volatile political situation in the

Philippines, which I believed to be the result of the stand the United States was taking in a country so very near. It made a great difference in stabilizing the domestic scene in the Philippines: quelling resistance movements, reducing crime and labor unrest—especially bringing to an end the terrible garbage strikes.

Marjorie and I had invested six-and-a-half years in the Philippine Episcopal Church. We were excited to have had the opportunity, but we still felt the pain of leaving our beloved Good Shepherd Mission congregation in West Berkeley. Then, there was the time and expense to others involved in the study of Chinese, both on the part of the Episcopal Church and in the daily tutoring given by Mr. Tan. I had come overseas with the sincere intention of spending the rest of my ministry in Asia, but I felt that I was facing a brick wall by being restricted to a ministry exclusively within the school. Further, that brick wall had been placed before me by the very people to whom I would have turned for friendly understanding and defense if ever faced with a problem like this from any other source. I had taken positive steps to share my visions for the school ministry and to prepare others to do what I had been doing there. I felt torn by the dilemma, so I turned to the Lord with a sense of urgency. I felt I was with my Savior in the Garden of Gethsemane. I prayed, asking whether or not my work in the Philippines had run its course, and to discern what His priorities for me were at the time.

His answer came like the "Man from Macedonia" in the vision to Saint Paul (Acts 16:9). "Come over (to Viet Nam) and help us!" I felt the great burden of the war that was there, and the pain of those involved on both sides. I felt Called once again to follow the Master into the unknown as His priest. Certainly He had been with me in my frustrations in the Mission. I felt His guidance with the same strength that I had felt it as a boy when I was unknowingly in the path of that runaway truck in North Hollywood. I knew that with the Lord, there could be nothing wasted! With the Lord, there could be no "blind streets."

I went immediately to the United States Embassy in downtown Manila and talked with the Naval Attaché. If I remember his response exactly, it was: "If you're stupid enough to want to go to Viet Nam, I guess we're stupid enough to send you! Welcome aboard!" The rest of the arrangements were somewhat automatic because I was already a commissioned Chaplain in the Naval Reserve. In order to clear myself with the Episcopal Church as my "endorsing agent" with the navy, I would have to be diplomatic with the Bishop of the Philippines. Our conversation went like this.

Bishop Ogilby: "Your contract is for another year or so. You can't quit."

Lester: "Americans and Asians are bleeding and dying in Viet Nam, and I feel Called to go there."

Bishop: "How can you go there from here?"

Lester: "With your permission, I joined the Naval Reserve several years ago. I just volunteered, and they have called me to Active Duty." What I should have added, though I refrained from saying, was that my Calling could not be confined to the walls of a school compound topped by shards of broken glass! Father Bacagan could now return to Manila and be the school chaplain that he had agreed to be, and for which he had been well trained.

—ECCLESIASTES 3:1; ST. JOHN 3:8

Some Hindsight Thoughts on Missionary Forethought

*T*he golden lotus (the symbol of Buddhism) flourishes in the swamps, cesspools, and *esteros* of Asia. Lotus blossoms rise above the stagnation to provide a beauty of loveliness. In like manner, Buddhism has inspired generations to lift their heads above desolation and devastation in search of exaltation and hope. But the lotus does not drain the swamp. Likewise, Buddhism does not compel changes that would end the cyclical causes of floods, famines, epidemics, and deteriorating living conditions. It has given courage to millions over centuries to survive, while ignoring worldly needs. Buddhism promises Nirvana and the extinction of self, rather than mandating self-respect that demands betterments in ways that the activism of Christianity requires. Communists have called religion "the opiate of the people." Christianity is the very antithesis of that claim, because it is concerned for the present as well as for the future, for this world as well as for heaven. In Chapter 4, I made my case for the introduction of scientific medical care by Christian missionaries, as opposed to the lethal magic of paganism in the Mountain Province of Luzon. Christianity requires selective change, be it at home or abroad.

Historians and sociologists are fond of reminding us that missionaries through the ages have blindly usurped the individuality of peoples whom they evangelized, often resulting in "cultural" conversions. (For example: putting blouses on native women as a moral imperative; teaching European literacy, while shaming native heritages; using the church as an instrument of colonization.)

Woven throughout the stories of foreign missions presented here, however, there is demonstrated a respect for the culture and language of host peoples and a genuine effort to experience their various heritages with them as our interpreters. I have learned from and been enriched by those with whom I have shared life, without declining to assert the potential contributions and saving grace of the Christian message. Marjorie and I struggled to affirm the principle that the communication of the Gospel must begin with relationships built upon respect. I learned much from the ministry in the Dakotas of the Clark family, who loved the Sioux and spent their lives immersed in that culture and language, while not denying their own unique identity as missionaries. I went to Asia because I love the Asian people. I went because I knew that God had put that love in my heart, and He Called me and prepared me as an American Episcopal Priest to go west to serve. My wife agreed wholeheartedly with this truth.

As I reflect upon my years in the overseas mission, I detect some ways in which the missionary endeavors of the Church misfired. I believe there was a political hope underlying the spiritual objectives of our American Mission in the Philippines. It was certainly included in my dreams, and there was nothing essentially wrong with it. This was the hope that through worship, the building of churches, schools, colleges, nursing schools, and hospitals, and the provision of scholarships for promising aspirants, we were contributing to the building of a new generation with strong Christian integrity. I think we did! However, it was our hope that this generation of Christians would find their way into the politics and professions of their homeland, and lead it, through their influence, into better times. Historically, this proved to be too restrictive an objective for our efforts. In our passion to bring Christ to a host people or to reinforce the evangelism of prior generations of Christian stewards, we brought educational and material improvements and spiritual enrichment for service to the nation as well as for the benefit of individual recipients.

The marriage of these efforts in the minds of the recipients, however, caused many of them to seek our way of living as intergral to our way of believing. We missionaries could retreat to our homeland and the comforts we demonstrated as expatriates, which we eventually did. This inspired many of them to follow us—even in anticipation of our departures—rather than to pioneer in the building of their homeland. The large degree to which the emigration of this identified population has occurred seems to demonstrate that our Mission was entrapped in elements of old colonialism. What has been the effect of this?

Some few years ago I was sent a roster of the Asian congregation which gathers monthly for Episcopal worship in New York City. They come together from various cities in the Northeast. I am glad that they have brought with them to the United States and Canada the Faith they were taught, and which they shared with their parents in the barrios. I add with gusto that it is also good that they come together to share Christ and many aspects of their lives as they acclimate and settle on this continent. We need them to be missionaries to us in America! I only hope that they have experienced at least a portion of the loving welcome that consistently surrounded us during our six-and-a-half years in their land—both in the Mountain Province and in Manila.

But I would be remiss if I were not to admit that when I received this list of members of this congregation, even though I recognized most of them, I felt some disappointment. What caught me by surprise was that the *majority* of the names on that church roster were those of the offspring of Igorot Episcopal Clergy, plus adult sons and daughters of prominent Church leaders I knew when they were children, and/or former recipients of church-provided education and scholarships. This list seemed to represent a *majority* of "the cream of the crop"—young church people who were recognized as leaders during "my time in the field." They were fostered because of their obvious potential.

In a republic that was in such great and obvious need of unselfish leadership, a nation which we missionaries loved so dearly, advantages were liberally distributed by the Mission. Admittedly, in these benevolent efforts, there was some degree of a hope of building within the citizenry a stronger and more ethical top echelon for local and national government—not just in the Church, but also in education, and in the many professions that provide, and could improve, the infrastructure of that Christian country. I ask rhetorically (and perhaps unfairly): "What percentage of those we had identified as leaders have remained in their homeland to contribute as prophets to their people?"

Certainly what the Mission contributed were gifts, and gifts are not gifts if there are conditions or expectations attached. All humans must have the right to find their own way for themselves and for their posterity in life and in the world. That is the essence of freedom! However, many of my contemporary missionaries shared the hope that we were inspiring Christian leadership among those who claimed the Philippines as their homeland. Likewise, we made every effort to encourage those who were unwelcome there (and destined to emigrate) to prepare themselves to grow and to contribute in another land. Was this a selfish hope? I have no immediate answer to this question. This, however, is "the missionary dilemma."

Who now tends to the doors of the local church? The Episcopal Church did a good job of inspiring and educating Filipino clergy. These church leaders who were "raised up" while we were there have performed well, as the Church achieved its national, if not total financial, autonomy. But, in the words of the Psalmist, "Who guards the gates of the city?" That is, who has been raised by the Episcopal Church to lead the nation and its professions? I am no longer close enough to the local media to know. The existence of our fine Saint Andrew's Seminary prepared future clergy to minister in their own land, and only a notable few left for other countries. Would fewer of the other well-educated cadre have left the country if there had been more graduate study opportunities available in the Philippines or made available in other neighboring Asian countries rather than in the United States? I believe so.

When I was a chaplain in the Viet Nam Mekong Delta, I observed the indigenous Protestant Church routinely controlling its own administrative destiny, calling for missionaries only where and when, in the judgment of the host Church, they were especially needed.

Certainly, the Christian and Missionary Alliance demonstrated great foresight in the ways they planted their missions. Indeed, this prepared them well for wartime, when they had to be "on their own." They developed self-reliance and self-respect among their laity, their congregations, and their clergy. This was how the Anglican Church survived World War II in Japan, and how it has survived to contribute in the amalgamated Protestant Church today in the People's Republic of China. I pray that this is the kind of lay, as well as clergy leadership our Church schools now are determined to develop. I trust that at Saint Stephen's, the school faculty still guides, and the alumni continue to perpetuate the grooming of Christian ethical and prophetic leadership. I know this will reflect in future generations in the land where they remain, or where they resettle, to become today's "Blossoming Bridge" (*Hua Ch'iao*).

As I reflect upon where people have gone to settle and to serve, I know that the nation-building aspirations of missionaries, mine included, were too narrow. Rather, the Church's mission must be to develop Christian people for God's glory and His purposes throughout this world and beyond the Age. Did not Hugh Hamilton send us off as we left Good Shepherd, Berkeley, with the unforgettable challenge: "Why can't you just stay home and mind your own business?" That was our first personal encounter with "the missionary dilemma." In response, we had to be obedient to John Wesley's affirmation: "The world is my parish!" Every Disciple must evaluate his/her personal Call as to where to go, how to develop, and in what ways to serve. But I would be remiss if I were not to bring this conflict of hopes for a nation as well as for her people to light for inspection and critique.

Now that Episcopal "Appointed Missionaries" have all left the Philippines and have "gone home," we can legitimately survey what difference the three Philippine dioceses are inspiring in that land. Perhaps both the Episcopal "Foreign and Domestic Missionary Society" and its beneficiaries were caught up in currents of past colonialism, both parties lacking sufficient wisdom and strength by which to resist its tides. I question whether or not we inspired a prophetic generation or just perpetuated a paternalistic mind-set. Did we leave too early under the guise of having established a strong indigenous ministry, or in premature response to intimidating local cries for independence? Did we American missionaries retreat from this land with the impatient desire to retire to our more comfortable homeland, substituting financial support instead? Has the Presiding Bishop's Fund for World Relief (now known as "Episcopal Relief and Development") become an easier substitute for sending Appointed Missionaries to build personal relationships as the primary way of communicating the Gospel of the loving Savior?*

Only history can give us these answers, but I am committed to asking these questions for the sake of posterity and the future of Church Missions.

There is great cause for rejoicing that people have found Jesus Christ and are determined to follow Him in His holy Church, wherever they might be! Likewise, Marjorie and I shall always be deeply grateful for the sponsorship of the Episcopal Church to minister in the Philippines during the great missionary era of the last century.

—St. Luke 19:41f, 45f; Hebrews 11:1–3

---

* When Marjorie and I served as Appointed Missionaries for the Domestic and Foreign Missionary Society of the Episcopal Church (1960–1966), it was my understanding that there were 325 serving in that capacity. As of December 2001, 49 Appointed Missionaries are in the field receiving the direct support of the Episcopal Church in the U.S.A. 105 Episcopalians serve independent missionary societies, and 58 serve in the field as volunteers for the Church. We are sincerely grateful to have had the opportunity to be missionaries when our Church was able to send us.

CHAPTER 6

With Marines in Viet Nam

Ministry in Uniform

I have devoted some chapters to my experiences in the Chaplain Corps of the U. S. Navy: one chapter devoted to combat ministry with the Marines, one with the riverine forces in the Mekong Delta, another with combat medical battalions, and others in ministry to the fleet and at shore facilities. I have included these experiences in this book for several reasons. First and foremost, people in uniform are ordinary people, perhaps called to service life primarily by their nation, yet also perhaps as their personal Call from Higher Authority. The terrible decisions to summon our country to arms must be made rarely by presidents and their advisors, but the answer to that call has been made once and for all by those who raise their hand to swear an oath of allegiance to serve in our armed forces. Ministry to them and to their family members has broad relevance to evangelism and pastoral care both in times of peace and in times of war.

Secondly, and unfortunately, we live in an age which has been plagued with sagas of brushfire conflicts in many places on the globe. The names of these places we often learn to recognize only after thousands of troops have been sent there to help. With these troops go their chaplains, many of whom have never before experienced armed conflict. I believe there are lessons to be shared from my experiences in Viet Nam and in the fleet which promise to be beneficial to chaplains in their deployed ministries, and which could prove to be lifesaving both for them and for others. Further, if through these stories, military personnel and civilian citizens gain an additional understanding of their chaplains, this would be a benefit that would please me greatly. The stories I relate may have been preserved in no other way, with the exception of several paragraphs in Keith Nolan's book, *Operation Buffalo*.*

Although I believe there to be historical value in this material, my primary purpose is not autobiographical. However, I have no other way of relating experiences that may have value in regard to ministers in uniform other than couching these events in true personal episodes. I hope that this will make interesting reading, as well as providing a means of teaching what is not available in seminary, and which may be beyond description in the curricula of the Chaplain Schools of the various armed services.

I have placed these chapters in the middle of my book, because the experiences related herein (with direct or implied lessons intended for clergy) came in the middle of my life in the Sacred Ministry. I dare say that my training and exercise of priestly and pastoral ministry in the Navy and Marine Corps added substantially to my personal Vocation and to my maturity for a return to ministry in the civilian setting.

—◊◊◊—

The first half of my year with the Third and First Marine Divisions was spent in two Field Medical Battalions. In 1997, thirty physicians, surgeons, oral surgeons, anesthesiologists, dentists and a brother chaplain, who had served together in these incredible combat field hospitals, came from all over the country to gather at Camp Pendleton. We laughed and cried as we relived our experiences from thirty years before. We shared where our lives had gone from there. Our rapport was instantaneous, as though we served together but the day or the week before. My basic contribution to the program of this reunion was to read aloud before the assemblage the section of this writing that follows in Chapter 9 in the vignette "On Saint Michael's Team," under the title: "Third Medical Battalion, Third Marine Division, Da Nang, Viet Nam, 1966."

This gathering proved to all of us the importance of preserving these memories and valuing what we did, how we helped, how we grew personally and professionally. If anything of lasting value could ever have come out of the sweaty hell that was the Field Medical Battalion—in addition to benefits for the patients we helped to restore as best we could—it would be in the ways that we have contributed to the advancement of our professions in the years since—ways which resulted from our experiences in Viet Nam. We learned a lot, we learned it quickly, and we learned it the hard way! I have positioned my stories about being the chaplain to *Charlie Med* and *Alpha Med* in the chapter entitled "Hospital Chaplaincies," rather than after the two following chapters which deal with ministry in the direct line of fire.

I dared to record these stories in the face of painful memories of my post-Viet Nam rejections by some civilian brother and sister clergy who espoused pacifist convictions. However, I tenaciously hold to the conviction that there is value to be found for others in the records that follow.

Gravestones and memorials have no audible voices to enlighten a current age, even though they stand in silent witness to allegiance, and, in many cases, to human bravery. It is my hope that these chapters will give voice to many Viet Nam veterans who have been otherwise silenced. I wish to give expression on behalf of those who might have been able to bequeath greater effectiveness to future clergy in settings of both war and peace. I wish to speak for those who paid a supreme sacrifice, and for those who have survived, but with haunting memories about which they are either unwilling or are not yet ready to speak.

—JOSHUA 24:26f

---

* Keith William Nolan, *Operation Buffalo: USMC Fight for the DMZ*. Novato, CA: Presidio Press, 1991.

The Marks of a Pastor

I was a boarding student at the Harvard School during the 1943–1944 academic year. After the completion of eighth grade, I returned to my Oakland home in June 1944 to continue my college preparatory studies at the A-to-Zed School in Berkeley.

During my year at Harvard, Mr. Hamilton was the Principal, but the President and episcopal visitor was the Right Reverend Robert B. Gooden, Suffragan Bishop of Los Angeles. We always ate better at lunch during his Thursday visits. I loved the school and its military life, but it had been expensive for my parents to board and educate me there, even for the year. I had seen the good bishop from my pew and on occasion I had served him at the Altar, but always at a respectful distance, or so it seemed to me. When I left the school at age 13, although I remembered him with affection, I did not know whether we would meet again. Twenty-two years later I would learn where I truly fit in his life and ministry.

It was the first weekend of October of 1966 and I had just completed the courses at the Navy Chaplains' (orientation) School at Newport, Rhode Island, and the Field Medical Service School (training for combat) at Camp Pendleton, California. I was to have three days to be with my wife, our daughter and our newborn son; then I would be off to Travis Air Force Base to board a chartered plane for "the bad place" far to the west.

Marjorie was living temporarily with her two sisters on a remote street in Richmond, California. On a dreary Saturday afternoon I was doing my best to contribute to the dear ladies who had provided refuge for my family until an appropriate apartment could be found. Thus, dressed in my jeans and a dirty sweatshirt, I was pushing an old lawn mower. A shiny black Buick sedan pulled up at the curb, and a dignified lady stepped from behind the wheel, came over to the sidewalk, and inquired, "Are you Father Westling?" With genuine surprise, I replied, "Yes."

She responded to my puzzled expression by saying, "I am Bishop Gooden's daughter. He is ninety-three years old, but he insisted that I drive him from Glendale (almost 800 miles roundtrip) so that he could bless you before your departure for Viet Nam."

She helped him from the car, and we entered the living room of my sister-in-law's modest home. There we knelt as a family before this humble servant of God to receive God's Blessing. "You are one of my boys," Bishop Gooden said. "You have always been in my prayers as I have watched you grow. And whether you live or die, you will always be safe in the Hands of the Savior."

With that, he returned to the sedan, which set off for Glendale.

Bishop Gooden's blessing and his words of faith followed me as allies of God's Guardian Angels through those frightening nights and days of death and war. It was my good fortune to have survived to serve again, and to attend his 100th birthday celebration at Saint Mark's Church in Glendale seven years later. It is my understanding that he died shortly after his 101st birthday, and soon after preaching his last sermon.

—St. John 10:14f

Fitting In

$\mathcal{I}$ had completed a half-tour with Third and First Medical Battalions (in that order). I had my "in-country" physical and dental examinations. Seeing all the gold crowns in my mouth, the Dental Officer commented: "You won't be hard to identify," which I accepted as questionably reassuring. I had learned the three basic expectations of serving with Marine Infantry: "Your feet will get wet; your pay will get screwed up, and your fellow Marines will always take care of you." I was now ready to be a chaplain with the "grunts."

I was reassigned to the Third Battalion of the Ninth Marine Regiment

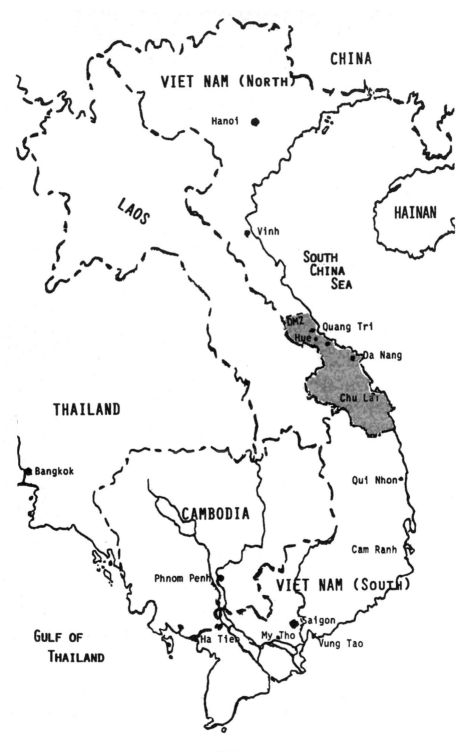

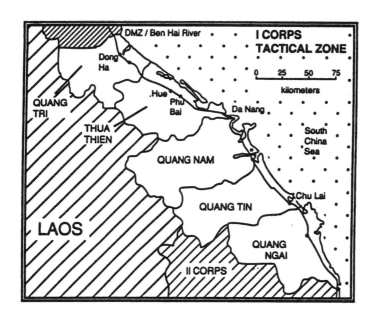

I CORPS
TACTICAL ZONE

DMZ / Ben Hai River

Dong Ha

QUANG TRI

THUA THIEN

.Hue Phu Bai

Da Nang

QUANG NAM

QUANG TIN

Chu Lai

QUANG NGAI

LAOS

II CORPS

South China Sea

0   25   50   75
kilometers

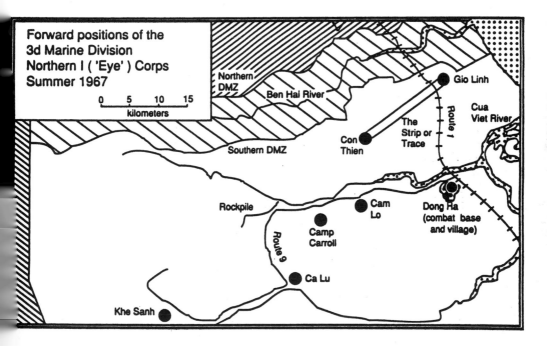

Forward positions of the
3d Marine Division
Northern I ('Eye') Corps
Summer 1967

0   5   10   15
kilometers

Northern DMZ

Ben Hai River

Southern DMZ

Gio Linh

Cua Viet River

Route 1

Con Thien

The Strip or Trace

Rockpile

Cam Lo

Dong Ha
(combat base
and village)

Camp Carroll

Route 9

Ca Lu

Khe Sanh

Two maps of I Corp are from *Operation Buffalo: USMC Flight for the DMZ* by Keith
William Nolan. Novato, California: Presidio Press, 1964. Permission to use these maps
has been granted by the publisher.

(3/9), which had companies dispersed in such garden spots as Khe Sanh (to the southwest of Camp Carroll), and firebases slightly south of the Ben Hai River in the Demilitarized Zone (D.M.Z.) at Con Thien (to the north of Cam Lo) and Gio Linh (under construction northeast of Dong Ha). A ten-mile-long wide strip had been plowed bare of vegetation just south of the "border" with North Viet Nam between Con Thien on the west, and Gio Linh on the east. I would see much of the "Strip," or be getting my bearings in relation to it, during many operations through much of the rest of my time in-country.

I was flown north over Highway Route #1 from Da Nang to Dong Ha, then driven by "Mighty Mite"—the light-weight low-profile, easily deployed Marine equivalent of a Jeep—west on Route #9. We travelled about a third of the way to Khe Sanh, then south a short distance up a hill on a dirt road to where 3/9 was in bivouac. My destination was Camp Carroll, the rear encampment for Marine 9th Regiment's three reinforced infantry battalions. I was told this was within a "fairly secure" perimeter, encircled with foxholes and machine guns with their appointed fields of fire, but still vulnerable to mortar and ground attacks. It was our battalion's temporary rear echelon, and our "home away from home" where we returned between search and destroy missions or other offensives. While rotating there, elements of Marine battalions provided perimeter security for the firebase. From this location, the Army's 175 mm "Long Tom" artillery were hurling their shells over 20 miles toward targets north of the D.M.Z. I was assigned to a tent on the hill with other battalion officers, and when a 175 mm shell was fired overhead, it actually sucked the tent canvas up from the frame-poles in their wake. These projectiles sounded like fast moving freight trains going past very close at hand.

When I arrived, I knew that I was relieving Chaplain "Macho," who was proud of his physical prowess and was a self-styled Marine's Marine Chaplain. He was at least six years younger than I was at 36. (I was duly aware that I was probably twice as old as the average Marine in this battalion of 1,200.) Chaplain "Macho" was so attached to "his Marines," that he left prior to my arrival without debriefing me—probably unable to accept the fact that another chaplain could replace him. On arrival, I found the Executive Officer of 3/9 in his tent. When I reported for duty, he asked me abruptly: "Can you run nine miles?" He added: "Because if you can't, I don't want you in my Battalion!"

I knew that I would be "taking out the garbage" for a while, as the new kid on the block. With limited control over my anxiety upon entering a totally new experience, I mustered the courage to respond to him: "No, I probably can't run nine miles. But I can do other things, which you are going to find out. I was ordered here, and I will serve you and your battalion well, sir!" He cautioned me to remember that every Marine is basically an 0311 (infantry rifleman). Then, with obvious reluctance, he directed me to the Adjutant's tent to check in. I was greeted by the Marines there in a more positive manner. Secretly, I was thanking God for Field Medical Service School at Camp Pendleton, where I was introduced to "the Green Machine" (the USMC). Thus, I knew what to expect.

Every chaplain was assigned a Marine enlisted assistant, this being long before the creation and training of the Navy's "Religious Program Specialist" rating. The young man who had been newly assigned to me had distinguished himself by several glaring errors, the most recent of which was filling the fuel tank of a Mighty Mite with Diesel fuel rather than with gasoline. His errors continued in his short time with me. At my request he was replaced, but with another "loser."

The initial message of "unwelcome" I received from the Executive Officer was being reinforced. If I was to accomplish my mission, I would have to confront this issue. A Chaplain's Clerk must be his bodyguard, his supply clerk, and his field secretary. I revisited the Executive Officer with the request that the games stop. "I need a dependable Clerk," I said. "Well, what are your criteria?" he demanded. In reply I stated: "I have three requirements for a Clerk. He has to be able to shoot straight; he has to be able to dig deep, and I want the biggest thief in the battalion!" "Then Chaplain, you are obviously better qualified to pick him than I am," he said, as he directed me to the personnel files in the Adjutant's tent to look for myself. I thanked him and left. After a day or so, with the efficient help of the enlisted staff, I came up with the file of Corporal John Ray Phillips, the son of missionary parents in the Canary Islands, who spoke and wrote fluent Spanish. With many Mexicans and Puerto Ricans in the battalion, I knew that I had a winner! Our logistic problem was that he was then with "Mike Company" on Khe Sanh, and had to be summoned to the rear. When he appeared, I had only begun to feel the depth of my gratitude for having made the right choice of this strong, young, blond Marine. When news came soon thereafter that his entire Fire Team of five men had been overrun and killed the day after his departure, I believe there were unexpressed reciprocal feelings, although they must have been mixed with the grief of having lost his buddies.

John was with me through thick and thin on every mission, and I never lacked for supplies, because he knew incredible "acquisition procedures" and seemed to have friends in every quarter. John excelled as a C-rations chef, and was able to prepare from those little brown cans such delicacies as sloppy joes, various soups, and angel food cake with chocolate icing. He taught me how to use a thimbleful of C-4 explosive to provide heat for disposable tin-can cook stoves. He was able to write letters in Spanish on behalf of many of our troops—especially the bereavement letters that were the responsibility of my "office."

I had three reinforced companies to serve, and we travelled by dangerous roads or by helicopter to the firebases at Con Thien and Gio Linh, and to the one (to be constructed soon after my arrival) at "C-2" to the north of Cam Lo, halfway to Con Thien. All these places were under heavy enemy bombardment from the north. At the fire bases, I held religious services, counseled, and baptized in bunkers. On operations, we gathered in open fields with perimeter surveillance deployed, or I would distribute Holy Communion crawling from foxhole to foxhole.

Corporal Phillips and I went on company- and battalion-sized search and destroy missions. We dug foxholes at dusk, and filled them every morning before moving on, so the enemy could not use them. John almost succeeded in making an "0311" Marine out of this chaplain. Routinely we cleared battlefields of the dead and wounded—often under fire. We identified casualties in a team with the Medical Corpsmen—and where evacuation tags were not available, we marked names on bodies with grease pencil and kept records in a pocket-size notebook. On several occasions, these chaplain's records were the only source of such information preserved in the chaos of combat—for which the Marine Corps was officially grateful.

Back at Camp Carroll, I was approached by the Army Artillery Executive Officer with the request for me to provide an Easter worship service for his troops in their area, and perhaps at other times when we were "in the rear" and when his personnel were not operationally free to be far from their guns. Of course I agreed, but with the proviso that his baker (in their well established cook tent) provide me with a regular supply of cookies to distribute after dark to the Marines that were manning foxholes on the perimeter. The deal was sealed in cookie dough! This gave me an excuse to make "the rounds" of my troops at night, to cement good-neighbor relations with the Army, and to praise the Lord as well.

—◦◦◦—

July 2, 1967 came on a Sunday, and it was warm and sunny with a pleasant breeze. We had barely returned to Camp Carroll from a June operation. The battalion had just settled in, and we had enjoyed a day of mess-tent hot meals. I had arranged for the Catholic Chaplain to come from Regiment for Mass, and we cleared one of the abandoned dry fallow rice fields adjacent to our battalion's rear area for his service. I took another dry field for a service of Holy Communion, just across the dirt road from where his Mass was to be offered. These small square fields were separated from one another by the usual low border of raised dirt to trap the rain in monsoon season. Additionally, on this high ground, "walls" of trees had been planted on these low berms to act as wind breaks. These flat protected areas were ideal for church gatherings. With altars made of ammunition boxes and with the contents of our chaplain's kits (plus some American Marine ingenuity), our outdoor cathedrals were prepared for this Christian celebration of an American Independence Day far from our homeland and the families we represented. These divine services were very well attended that day. The First and Second Battalions of our regiment were in the field, and it was our chance to "kick back" and refresh ourselves.

After mid-morning worship and a good noon meal, a familiar but very unexpected command was shouted through the tented encampment. "Saddle up! Saddle up!" Rumor quickly followed that First Battalion (1/9) had walked into an ambush by no less than seven battalions of North Vietnamese Regulars in the very early morning darkness northeast of Con Thien. They had been cut up badly (thereafter being known by the unfortunate title: "The Walking Dead"). We had just minutes to grab our 782 gear (field pack equipment), and form up to march down the hill to board the Chinook helicopters that were approaching. Every heart was pumping hard; every mouth was dry. We knew that our brief R&R at Camp Carroll was a mirage that had quickly vanished, and that we were back to war "big time." We were "sparrow hawked," that is, dropped into the middle of a battle, disembarking from the rear ramp of the helos and fanning out so as to avoid or confuse direct incoming small arms fire.

Operation Buffalo was a fierce five-day battle which is the subject of Keith William Nolan's book by that name.* The media reported a five-day total body count of 1,200! News reporters arrived at the Command Post (CP) north of "The Strip" just prior to an artillery pounding that may have been touched off by their helo's arrival and departure. They approached our new Commanding Officer, then-Major Willard J. Woodring, USMC, and asked for a statement. He asked them to get their notebooks and prepare to copy exactly what he had to say. When they were ready, he pointed to the freshly dug foxhole at their feet, and said: "I dug that. That hole is mine! When we get incoming fire any minute now, if you are in there ahead of me, I will treat you like the enemy. Go dig your own! That is the end of my statement." I wanted to cheer!

My own first encounter with the media was on this operation. I was giving last rites to a dying Marine. Suddenly, I looked up into the "eyes and ears of the world," a television camera. The reporter thrust a microphone in my face, with the statement: "Say that a little louder, Padre, so the folks back home can hear." What I said into that microphone could not have been broadcast back home, neither are the words suitable for reporting here!

Getting the wounded and the dead loaded in helicopters at the Landing Zone (LZ) was a tricky business. Corporal Phillips and I gathered and identified them, as did the Hospital Corpsmen. But the incoming choppers first had to off-load ammunition, supplies, and water before there would be room for evacuations. Incoming aircraft would give enemy artillery and mortars the location of the LZ, so things had to be done fast. Sometimes they would just have to make their drops from the air and turn away without touching the ground. We would routinely use our own bodies to shield from incoming fire the living who were left behind, because we were wearing flak jackets and those of many of the wounded had been cut off or discarded in the administration of emergency treatment in the field. From time to time Corporal Phillips and I needed to hide under tanks to accomplish our mission of retrieving casualties and ministering to them.

Somehow in conducting our work, we got separated from the first elements of our battalion that had returned to Camp Carroll when relieved by the Battalion Landing Team (1/3) of the 9th Marine Amphibious Brigade. They had been helo-lifted from the USS *Okinawa* offshore, and they were a welcome sight when they approached westward on foot up the cleared "Strip."★★

When, with a small group, John and I walked up the dusty road from the dry rice patty LZ near Camp Carroll, we were greeted by many with surprise and affection as though we were heroes. We were mystified by this reception as we approached the camp. Our greens were shredded and bloodstained, and we were filthy, but we assumed that our condition was no different from that of any others. However, it seems that on July 4th, John and I had been reported Killed in Action. When I heard this, I recalled the quotation from Mark Twain's cable from Europe to the Associated Press: "The reports of my death are greatly exaggerated!" My immediate thought, however, was to get connected in some way to a MARS radio telephone to notify my family. Friends in the Adjutant's tent again came to the rescue. After some delay, the voice of my 7-year-old Karla came on the line. She had been instructed by the operator how to handle the call, and how to say "Over." She explained, "Mommy is out shopping." I gave her the exact time and date, bid her write them down, and I told her that it was important to tell her mother that I was very much okay. She handled the assignment well. However, the feared report was never delivered to Marjorie at the apartment.

The Executive Officer, who had remained in camp while we "sparrow hawked" into the middle of battle, and who had shunned me upon my arrival for duty, laid out his own newly starched set of greens and bid me use his "shower" (overhead bucket of water). From that moment on, life was different for me with 3/9, but this was a sad way to have won one's place in a command.

At last I "fit in." Evidence of this came a few weeks after we had returned to Camp Carroll from Operation Buffalo. I had Church Call announced, and again had arranged for the Catholic Chaplain to travel up from Regimental Headquarters in Dong Ha to celebrate Mass on one field while I would gather the others for Protestant worship on another. As I made the rounds of the camp, I observed the troops furiously preparing for an inspection. I went to the tent of the First Sergeant to inquire if there would be a conflict. He said that he had allowed a half hour for worship, and that he had "called away" a rifle inspection to follow. I acknowledged that both evolutions were important, but that with worship being voluntary and the time allotted being much too short, we were both confronting a dilemma. I further suggested (assured now of the support of the command) that one of us was likely to be leaving the battalion soon if this matter were not resolved to my satisfaction. As a good Marine, he understood my drift. I left the resolution of the potential conflict up to him as "Top" Sergeant.

As I awaited Church Call in a big tent at the time allocated for my services, I heard the battalion forming up outside. Next, the voice of the First Sergeant called out the command: "Battalion, 'Ten-shun!... Catholics, Right Face! Double-time March!" Obviously that is not the way worship musters are to be conducted in the military, but at least I knew that the First Sergeant had exercised his authority, and that I, at last, was able to exercise mine.

Several months after "Buffalo" on a Wednesday morning, a call on my field telephone at Camp Carroll summoned me to the tent. It was the Division Chaplain calling from Phu Bai. I could tell by the tone of his voice that he was very upset, and I assumed correctly that he was upset *with me.* "I got your weekly report, and you failed to have services on Sunday. I want to know why not!" I responded: "Captain, sir, we were in heavy combat Sunday, so I held field services on Monday. This will be reflected on next week's report." To my shock, he growled, "That's no excuse!" and hung up.

Now I was of an older generation than most other junior chaplains; I was not a child of the post World War II era, and I had been isolated from my culture as a missionary among Asians for almost seven years. I had not adjusted my thought patterns to the current age, so I never owned a bumper sticker with the logo: "Challenge Authority!" In short, I was raised to respect my elders, and, as a Lieutenant, the Division Chaplain was decidedly my elder. Thus, at first I examined myself and prepared to feel guilty for having failed to fulfill the expectations of my boss. But something snapped in the process! I learned a very important lesson for someone in his late 30s, yet still naive. Sometimes, even if rarely, the boss *can* be wrong.

This stung my memory, but I slept well that night. In spite of the opposition I had encountered, I felt confident that I belonged in the ministry to which I had been assigned by the Navy and Marine Corps, and I felt an inward joy that I was carrying out the "Orders" of my Lord.

—DANIEL 6:19–23

---

* Keith William Nolan. *Operation Buffalo: USMC Fight for the DMZ,* Novato, CA: Presidio Press, 1991, p. 43.
** Nolan, op. cit., p. 185.

Surviving

During a previous operation, some weeks before Operation Buffalo, our battalion had stopped for the night near a grove of trees. The Battalion Surgeon (Navy Medical Officer physician assigned to a Marine Corps battalion) had refused to go into the field during operations, so my Clerk and I usually dug our holes and set up near the Corpsmen. We often answered calls for help together. Trees could offer shade from the afternoon sun or limited shelter from rain, but it was not good to camp too close to them because incoming mortar rounds or an artillery shell might ricochet off a tree, sending shrapnel in a shower of lethal pellets in that area. In this case, however, one of our Corpsmen set up in the shadow of a tree, a bit too near to it, at dusk.

We were all in the process of consuming our "evening meal" of C-rations as the sun set. Suddenly we received several volleys of incoming 60 millimeter mortar or RPG rocket rounds, and we all hit the foxholes in the dark. I heard "Doc" cry out, "I've been hit, and I'm bleeding." "Where are you hit?" I shouted back. "In the butt," he replied. "We're coming," I reassured him. Corporal Phillips and I crawled over to his hole to offer emergency assistance. It seems that our neighbor consumed his C-ration meals with the traditional adjunct of the Tabasco hot sauce that most Marines carry in their packs. Shrapnel evidently had hit the little bottle which was standing beside his foxhole, and a sharp shard of glass and some of the red contents from the exploded container were propelled into the part of "Doc's" posterior that protruded slightly above the summit of his hiding place. In the dark, the sharp splinter of glass felt like the sting of a hot piece of metal, and the hot sauce felt like blood to the victim. Our hasty examination in the dark from the edge of his foxhole determined that the wound was not mortal, but this assured our lifesaving Hospital Corpsman of continuous ribbing for a good while to come.

The battalion had been in the field several weeks, and it would be twenty-nine days before we would see one of those portable shower rigs again. After one has been without a shower for over four days, the "super stink point" would be passed, and no one would seem to mind. When the monsoon rains poured down, we stripped, reached for the soap, and enjoyed the luxury of a cleansing. In the field, a foxhole had to be dug every night in any kind of terrain, and each morning before "Saddle Up!" was the command, we would have to fill them with our garbage, some soil and rocks. This was not only to prevent a following enemy from having the protection of our holes (as previously stated), but also so that the cleaned bivouac area would demonstrate that our unit was very well disciplined. Where old C-ration containers, trash, and toilet paper were left on the ground by some troops, the North Viet Nam Army would follow them to engage such a unit in battle. They would read the condition of a previous encampment as evidence of the lack of military acumen.

For some reason, which later became evident to us, it was past noon and we had not yet moved out of our night encampment. At about two o'clock in the blazing hot afternoon, a helicopter arrived, and a Marine General stepped out of it to review our companies. In his starched greens and highly shined boots, he stopped briefly at each foxhole to ask the trooper: "How's it going, Marine?" The standard answer was returned with the salute: "Fine, sir!" When he came to one corner of our perimeter, he stopped beside a young machine gunner who was using his steel helmet to bail out of his foxhole the mud and water left from the last night's rain. He was hot and tired like the others. This Lance Corporal from Oakland High School in California had one "cauliflower ear" and a misshapen nose, giving evidence that he had been a boxer, perhaps both in the ring and outside it. His greens were torn, he had a severe head cold with a runny nose, and he was caked with the mud. The General looked down at him, and routinely asked: "How's it going, Marine?" With a bit of hesitation, the machine gunner looked up from his hole beyond the shiny boots into the face of the General and replied: "You've got to be shittin' me!" With that, and to his credit, the General sat down on the side of the foxhole. In a prolonged chat, the General learned to listen to his young warrior.

We got a very late start that afternoon, which placed us in jeopardy. As we started to ascend Hill-22 in twilight, suddenly the North Vietnamese Regulars on the high ground attacked from ambush positions in the vegetation, cutting off one of our rifle companies from the other two. I was hiding behind a stump across a small clearing from the inclined path that was in our line of march up the forested hill. Corporal Phillips must have gone ahead, because we joined up shortly after.

Huddled with me was a young Marine Sergeant. Blue-green tracers (mark of the enemy, because ours are red) came from the opposing hill, blocking our advance. When one is in combat, trust the expert! Neither rank nor age count. The young Marine pointed right at the last burst of tracers, and said: "Go on the count of three!" And I said "Yes, sir!" And on the count of three the firing hesitated (probably to reload) and we just made it across the clearing to the underbrush-lined path beyond it. A second later the stump that had shielded us took a heavy direct hit, and splinters flew in all directions. The Sergeant knew what to expect! Welded in my mind was the thought that my son was nine months old on this very night, and I hoped that I would see him again one fine day.

The night turned dark and ugly. People were yelling commands. We lined up twenty-two of our wounded along the narrow jungle path, only to have the enemy "walk" 60 millimeter mortars down it in a straight line, and kill them one-by-one. By this time, it was pitch black. The tall grass and bushes crowded the sides of the path, and enemy soldiers were jumping out and killing our Marines at point-blank range, then disappearing back into the dark brush. My purpose for relating this follows. This is the only time in my life that I have locked and loaded a weapon in my own defense. In two years of combat I never carried a sidearm except for that night. Corporal Phillips joked that he carried two pistols and his M-16 rifle, and he was always beside me. This night he threw me a pistol and shouted, "Use it if you have to!" I took it.

There are two reasons why chaplains are not to carry weapons. The first is well known. It is to comply with the Geneva convention of the International Red Cross. These protocols are established to protect every chaplain, should one become a Prisoner of War. If one chaplain is armed, no others can be considered noncombatants. Noncombatants may not be released by an enemy, but they are allowed to function in humanitarian endeavors which could be of value to other prisoners. The second reason chaplains should be unarmed is a reason that I perceived in Viet Nam. (There were a few chaplains who joined the "noncombatant" medical corpsmen and battalion surgeons in carrying sidearms.) The Marines considered armed chaplains to be cowards, believing it was the Marines' duty to protect their chaplains. In turn, Marines expected their chaplains to trust their protection, freeing chaplains for the performance of valued ministerial tasks on their behalf.

"Puff, the Magic Dragon" was the nickname given to AC-119 aircraft that were equipped with Gatling guns. They could come in close, and in seconds cover with hot lead an area the size of a football field. The hail from Puff's bullets came so close that dark night that the dust they kicked up covered my face. Somehow we made it to the top of the hill. A small observation airplane was shot down into the trees next to us. The pilot was killed. To avoid a grenade, I dove into a foxhole with such force that I "rearranged" my nasal septum. I spent the next 30 years breathing out of one nostril.

We spent the next day evacuating our casualties, with Corporal Phillips and I recording the names and comforting the wounded. We dug in there. A helicopter arrived to deliver our new Commanding Officer, then-Major Willard J. Woodring, USMC, and to take away the Lieutenant Colonel who was then relieved in the field—we assumed for cause.

Late that afternoon, while others watched our perimeter, many gathered cautiously near a group of foxholes for Evening Prayer. The trees and brush on the edges of the clearing were still smoldering from napalm dropped in close air support the night before, as well as from the other expended ordinance. In my brief homily, I reminded the Marines of the lessons taught to prepare us for combat, especially of the one entitled: "Night Noises." We learned to be alert to the snapping of twigs, to whistles that could be signals, and to sounds that a boot makes on the jungle floor. I told them to be alert. But I reminded them that there were night noises that also were friendly and

God-given: wind in the trees, birds chirping, rain falling, and sounds of streams. My point was that not everything in the world is hostile or threatening, that we were also surrounded by the loving Savior and His many Angels. I added that there were places where the peace for which we were struggling could be enjoyed. I asked them not to forget God's goodness and human kindness in the midst of smoking battlefields and the evacuation of friends who had dedicated their lives to making this a better world.

As Battalion Chaplain, I was one of the first of the staff that the new Commanding Officer wanted to talk with, and to whom he wanted his policies known. This came as a bit of a welcomed surprise to me. This Ozark Baptist outdoorsman, whose career in the Corps started in Boot Camp as a Private, was soon revealed as a delight to this Episcopal priest. Although he said nothing about it, I am sure that he recognized that I was in the field with his Marines, not in the rear with his Battalion Surgeon. In a private chat with me, he said that when he was at Camp Pendleton, he could pray for himself, "but out here and before I meet with my Company Commanders each morning, I expect you to pray with me privately, maybe out behind some trees." He went on with these memorable words: "No amount of schooling or military training can prepare a man to hold in his hands the precious lives of twelve hundred others. I have got to have God's help on this job." Here was a leader that I could respect, follow, and to whose battalion I could be a greater asset.

Living in the midst of all this carnage and danger endowed me with the importance of maintaining a positive attitude. Marines in harm's way survive best if they are realistic, but also have a sense of humor. Infantry Marines (called by various names, such as "Grunts" or "Snuffies") taught me how to keep my heart up and my head down. At the cry of "Incoming!!!," when one must jump into the nearest hole or hide behind the nearest berm or rock, usually the voice of a Marine could be heard yelling over the din: "Another grand and glorious opportunity to serve," or "Every day's a holiday, every meal's a banquet," or "One good deal after another!" Corporal Phillip's favorite was: "It's good for your career!" This ability to see the best in a scenario, or to make a joke out of something so bad that one cannot redeem it, is a gift that the Grunts gave me, one that I pray I shall never lose.

I believe being a morale officer is a must for every minister, whether in the military or in civilian life. It was this operation on Hill 22 that I call "my watershed for survival." Everything that came after it, even "Operation Buffalo," seemed tolerable because my faith had been so strengthened by this experience. Christ is the Author of Miracles and the ultimate Victor for good in all things. As Bishop Gooden told me before I left for the Marines and Viet Nam, "Whether you live or die, you will always be safe in the Hands of the Savior."

—PSALM 23:4; *Apocrypha* SONG OF THE THREE 1f,26–29

Some Notes on R&R

The Department of Defense established a program called Rest and Recreation (R&R), which provided relief for service members operating in areas of hostilities. They were given a brief vacation leave, with free transportation to selected sites of interest. For those in Viet Nam, these places were famous exotic cities on the Pacific rim. The most popular R&R sites for personnel who desired to meet a spouse and/or other family members for a brief reunion were places like Hawaii, Japan, or Hong Kong. Of course, the expense of family travel had to be borne by the individuals, rather than by the government.

My experience with this program brought to light some issues I believe to be worthy of comment. This program influenced military families during the war in Viet Nam, and it also exposed some issues regarding military families that experience other separations due to lengthy, sometimes hazardous, deployments. They would also have relevance if this program or an equivalent would be replicated in future wartime or "peacekeeping" situations.

Of course, for the service member, the anticipation of travel away from the grime and blood provided something to anticipate that was not as remote as the days yet to be marked off on the "Short-Timer's Calendar"—time remaining to the end of one's tour of duty and departure for home. For single personnel, R&R was "Party Time!" I think many wives were pleased with the prospect of an R&R reunion, because they missed their husbands, because it was a well-known and accepted chance for a change from children or from employment (neighbors, relatives, and employers willingly helped), and it was a chance for travel. Some wives admitted that they would rather enjoy a vacation with their husbands than to imagine them in "one of those Asian ports" in a possible liaison with a local prostitute.

This program was quite positive in design, and it provided a great lift to morale in a time of war. Yet, I want to share the decisions Marjorie and I made in regard to our own use of R&R on the occasion of two combat tours of duty, and how we applied what we learned from the experience.

Eligibility for R&R was determined by the longevity of one's time "in country." Because R&R was obviously a popular privilege, we had to "wait in line" for it. Therefore, it was usually granted when the service member, irrespective of rate or rank, was three-quarters of the way through his tour of duty. My time with the Marine Infantry had substantially advanced when it became my turn for R&R. I was tired. The stress of combat turns off only slowly. We met in Hawaii. Marjorie brought with her, according to plan, our eight-year-old daughter (who had been her mother's assistant and frequent babysitter), and I was truly glad to see them both. This arrangement was typical for many of the couples and families who shared the R&R experience.

Our time together was difficult. The first reason for this was that I was too exhausted to enjoy the intimacy of our time together. I was still "coming down" from being in the field. By the end of the year of duty I had lost 42 pounds, and a good portion of that loss was evidently apparent at the time of our reunion. Secondly, there were many loving and caring inquiries, such as: "What was it like?" and "What do you do out there?" I was in a quandary as to how to answer, and what details to share. We tried to walk on the beach.

We tried to go to a movie. We tried to visit a mall. I was still trying to settle traumatic thoughts, while being a good companion to my precious and supportive family members. This made me impatient, sometimes silent, irritable, and certainly unlike the "hero" whose image was in the photographs displayed at the apartment in California. In a short week it was all over, and it was back to work and school for them, back to war for me.

I truly believe that many of the men who greeted their wives on R&R answered those questions about what they did in the war. All of us needed to unload and share our all-too-recent memories. I think that when the terrors of war, or perceptions of it, were shared with unprepared loved ones, it could have set in motion the anticipation that their man was not going to return alive. There is an accepted process initially researched in 1971 at the University of Minnesota Center for Death Education and Research by Robert and Julie Fulton with caregivers for terminal patients.★ They called it "Anticipatory Grief Work." Their study brought to light what follows.

We know that when a loss occurs, certain things are triggered in the emotional makeup of the care-provider or loved one. Grief is the turning loose of a relationship, or the reframing of it in intangible ways. The closer the relationship, the more intense the "grief work" of relinquishing or reframing it may be. Elisabeth Kubler-Ross and other researchers have written a great deal about the emotional adjustments that occur involuntarily in the lives of survivors who mourn a death. Grieving is work, a process that can be a prolonged journey from denial through anger to acceptance. The Minnesota research revealed that even when an important loss is *anticipated,* some grief reactions set themselves in place involuntarily in advance of the expected loss. The unconscious mind says to itself: "I don't think he will survive." In the case of the man in the war, "I don't believe he is coming home alive, therefore I must prepare myself for the shock." Such thoughts are demonstrations of the safety valve of the psyche. If this idea is not brought to the attention of the conscious mind of the waiting loved one(s) through frank discussions, in time it can become surprisingly irreversible. By that, I mean that it is not possible to relate to one as living after his (imagined or actual) death has been psychologically accepted as having occurred. I believe it was this process that played a major role in the divorces sadly experienced by over half of our Prisoners of War who returned from North Viet Nam.

A concerned and coached pastor might have asked of Marjorie after her return from our R&R reunion, "Do you think he is not coming home?" This kind of intervention can break the grief cycle in the unconscious mind. But no one knew, or would dare to broach such an issue, and I am sure no one knew that our week in the "Paradise of the Pacific" was not all that it was expected to be.

When it came time to consider making arrangements for R&R during my second Viet Nam tour of duty, Marjorie and I both agreed that I would visit friends in Manila at Saint Stephen's School and Church where we had served, and Marjorie would be quite content with the letters and photographs I would be sending. "Go, do your job and get it over with. Then when you're home, you *will be home!*" my wife said. This arrangement was better for both of us. When I returned home from the Mekong Delta three years after my first tour of duty in Viet Nam began, there was no doubt in anyone's mind that I was not only home, but very much alive!

—St. John 11:11, 43f; 20:2, 8

*Lester Leon Westling, Jr. "Manual for Ministry to Prisoner of War Returnees and their Families in the Long-term Readjustment Period." San Anselmo, CA, 1974. (This unpublished Doctor of Ministry dissertation is available in the library archives of the Naval Postgraduate School, Monterey, CA and the San Francisco Theological Seminary, San Anselmo, CA. Chapter 6, entitled, "The Returnee and His Family: Re-entry and Reunion," cites the following references in regard to "Anticipatory Grief":

Robert Fulton, "Death, Grief and Recuperation." *Omega* (I–February 1970), pp. 23-28.

Robert Fulton and Julia Fulton, "A Psychosocial Aspect of Terminal Care." *Omega* (II–May 1971), pp. 91-100.

Elizabeth Kubler-Ross, *On Death and Dying.* New York: The MacMillan Company, 1972, p. 169.

Staying Alive

*O*n August 31, 1967, 25-year-old Lieutenant (junior grade) Dave Carey's A-4E Skyhawk was shot down over North Viet Nam. (He retired from his career as a Navy Captain.) Dave had deployed in June of that year in USS *Oriskany*. He returned from captivity as a Prisoner of War in March of 1973. His experiences are related in his recent book: *The Ways We Choose: Lessons for Life from a POW's Experience.*★

During the five-and-a-half years he and his fiancée were involuntarily separated, they kept each other "alive," awaiting their eventual marriage, which occurred May 5, 1973.

I knew and admired Karen during this time when I was one of the staff chaplains at Naval Air Station, Alameda, California. When I first met her, she was not even permitted to enter the gates of the Air Station from which the carrier *Oriskany* had deployed, because she was not a Navy Dependent. NAS was just a few blocks from her apartment. But with the aid of an understanding Recreation Officer, Karen was issued a "Gold Card" for the use of the Officers' Club. She never learned that what she believed to be a usual courtesy for others was really a unique one for her.

We conversed frequently about Dave, especially during those dark and uncertain days when there could be no correspondence, or even any assurance that he was alive.

Eventually I was given the enormous honor of officiating at the marriage of the couple when he returned, and after they were truly ready to share their future lives as well as the past. There is much more to their story, but it is not my story to tell.

I have included this narrative at this juncture in my text, because I want to share one of the most potent examples of a self-appointed instrument by which "Anticipatory Grief Work" was constantly interrupted during the uncertainties of this long separation. It did not originate between them with that intent, but it worked for them because of the words that were often rehearsed by both when they were apart.

It was what Karen introduced to me as "Their Song."

The original English lyric of the theme from "Mondo Cane" was written by Norman Newell. Dave and Karen repeated the words to "More" like a creed. I believe this song served as an instrument to preserve their love to its fulfillment, where many other relationships—even in marriage—failed prior to the release of the Prisoners of War.

The words served to bring freedom to their minds while torture, prison, an ocean and enormous uncertainties kept them apart. The song kept Dave alive in Karen's mind, and kept Karen alive in Dave's thoughts in prison.

Each stanza speaks in support of their commitment, but I believe "Their Song" served to interrupt "Anticipatory Grief Work." Thus, I believe these words written perhaps as just theme music ended up having an enormous effect on this couple by preventing an involuntary severing of their hope for a future life together. Of special interest to this theory are the words of the last stanza.★★

"Longer than always is a long long time,
But far beyond forever you'll be mine.
I know I never lived before, and my heart is very sure
No one else could love you more."

—SONG OF SOLOMON 2:8–12; 3:1–4; ACTS 5:17–21a

★ Dave Carey, *The Ways We Choose: Lessons for Life from a POW's Experience.* Wilsonville, Oregon: BookPartners, 2000.
★★ This lyric is quoted under the "Fair Use" provision of the U.S. Copyright Act of 1976.

Homecoming

hen I was a 17-year-old oiler on the troop transport USAT *General Simon B. Buckner* out of Fort Mason, Embarkation Port of San Francisco, we took elements of the First Cavalry to Inchon, Korea (Jin Sen, as it was then known). In Inchon Bay, the transport ship loaded aboard the companies of soldiers that had been relieved and were returning to the United States. After a two-week eastward voyage, I watched them debark on the West Coast. Those groups returned as units. During that time at sea, they had time to debrief each other in the many huddled and casual conversations that I observed in the berthing holds and on deck. Time was a friend to them, as we plied the seas on that slow boat from the Orient.

It is true that war had not yet begun in Korea, but we knew by such unfriendly acts as the sudden cessation of hydroelectric power from the north and by voices of the diplomats, that tensions were high. I believe there was little difference between the way troops were returned from Korea in 1948 and the way troops were transported homeward from the front during World War II—a war that had so recently ended. They returned *slowly*, and they returned *together*. For the most part, fresh troops went overseas *with* their fighting units; likewise, survivors returned *with* their fighting units. Another difference was that our fighting men returning from World War II were greeted with cheers of welcome, which became progressively muted (or worse) for the returnees of subsequent conflicts. Certainly, in these respects, the experiences of participants in the Viet Nam conflict were indeed very different.

Corporal John Phillips, my Marine Clerk, and I were under heavy artillery fire on the southern slopes of firebase Con Thien on the DMZ, together with the chaplain I was taking there to be my replacement. I got sudden word from a radioman hugging the ground nearby that I was to board the inbound chopper, which was at that moment almost in sight. The shelling lifted briefly; the helo made its approach to drop mail and filled water cans. I was on board with my pack and all of my belongings that I could gather quickly. There had been no time for goodbyes. We were airborne instantaneously. I was handed endorsed orders on the ground in Da Nang, walked briskly across the terminal and airstrip and onto the "big bird" amid a hundred or so strangers in the green uniforms of our several services. We had only one thing in common: all had finished their year someplace in the combat zone. The heavy airplane door closed, and the Boeing 707 raced down the runway, then turned sharply upward to what seemed to the passengers like a vertical climb, in order to avoid small arms fire that might come from the village at the end of the runway. When the noise of the thump from beneath the fuselage told us the wheels were in flight position, a great unison shout of celebration erupted from all the passengers, acknowledging that Viet Nam was undeniably behind us (at least physically). But during the rest of the flight a strange silence prevailed in the cabin as each man kept quietly to himself.

My point is precisely this: most who were assigned to combat units "in-country" went as individual replacements, and were returned swiftly as individuals, as well. We returned without time to debrief or to adjust, although at the time no one complained about getting back home quickly. The logistics were efficient, but we returned without comrades to listen to us, devoid of an audience to appreciate what we had endured or to applaud our families for the uncertainties they had faced and the support they had given. Imagine, just 18 hours after I was extracted from combat and separated from my devoted Marine Clerk and the officers and men of my battalion, I was standing on the tarmac at Travis Air Force Base in California greeting my wife Marjorie, our eight-year-old daughter Karla—who had obviously missed me greatly, and our one-year-old son Lester III—to whom I was yet a photographed stranger at best, an intruder at worst.

Following a spousal reunion, what might be the usual symbol of a family gathering at home after a long absence? Typically it would be the family meal. After a year of C-rations, this would be a long awaited treat that would exceed every expectation. I was ordered to rest while the commotion in the kitchen was producing tantalizing smells. Then came the long-expected moment. When I entered the dinette, dinner was served. "Where do I sit?" I asked—as the newcomer in my own apartment home. "Oops!" came the reply. There were chairs and place settings for just three. I had yet to make a place for myself in the family routine. Daughter Karla ran to get another plate, and Marjorie and I moved in another chair. They had adjustments to make in their routine as well.

During the week following my return, I drove the short distance south to Redwood City to make a sentimental pilgrimage to the Church of Saint Peter where I was ordained priest, and to kneel in the quiet of the Chapel there where I had given my First Blessings to my Godmother, to members of my family, and to the congregation. I went there alone to give thanks for my ministry in Viet Nam and for my preservation. I was in the old service dress khaki uniform, because my civilian clothes were at the tailor's shop. They hung awkwardly on my body that had returned 42 pounds lighter.

When I was leaving the chapel, walking across the courtyard between the church and parish hall, a dear lady who had served on the Altar Guild when I was curate there, saw me and approached. With an air of delighted surprise, she blurted out: "I remember you! You used to be Father Westling." I embraced her with a "bear hug" and replied: "I still am, Honey; you better believe it!" Yes, I was truly home at last.

However, there was still some unfinished business to which I needed to attend. Marjorie and I took several short trips to visit and to comfort families of Marines I had known who had died in battle near me.

Typical of these was a stop in the Southern California home of the mother of a Second Lieutenant who had served well as a good Marine Officer, a kind gentleman, a man of faith, whom I had selected to be the Protestant Lay Leader for his company. "Andy," a tall and slender Platoon Commander, died directing his men during a fire fight, and I had grieved his loss for some months. Marjorie and I consoled his mother, and then, with her permission, we opened his bedroom door. Behind it we found everything untouched, exactly as it had been when he left. With her approval, we opened the blinds and windows to let in the sunshine and a fresh breeze from the ocean. We loaded his clothing and uniforms that were still hanging in the closet, and took them to Camp Pendleton's Thrift Shop. "Andy's" mother was grateful for our visit, and so was

I. This was one of those experiences that were important to me as a part of coming home. Such visits moved us all into the future.

———《《《———

Viet Nam taught us many lessons as participants, as observers, and as a nation. We have heeded some of these lessons better than others. Our medical people and emergency responders have incorporated many of the lessons of this war into new strategies for treating and evacuating victims of trauma and the handling of mass casualties. The field of psychology gained a new understanding of posttraumatic stress, and protocols for its debriefing and treatment. We did a much better job with our POW Returnees than was done after World War II and Korea. But most of these lessons have been learned *after the fact* of the experiences so many of us shared in combat and which our families and close friends lived vicariously through our letters, our R&R experiences, and in the long-term readjustments in reunions following war. Our nation has developed perhaps the most efficient methods of managing the strategies and logistics of war. However, the most efficient means of "managing" the *major instruments* of warfare—the people who must go and fight—has proven to be an emotional disaster.

On the international level, our diplomats have failed to discern the logic of Asia that cost us lives and temporarily crippled our nation. I can best illustrate my point through a parable.

There is a Chinese proverb that begs the question: "How does one slay a dragon?" The answer is: "Go find another dragon and introduce them to each other." China successfully introduced us to the North Koreans, then to those who defeated the French in Viet Nam. The conflicts that ensued hurt us and hurt our opponents. These conflicts divided us and devastated our economy. However, our hidden rival enhanced his world position and prospered in the world market. We are in desperate need of improving our understanding of China. The "Middle Kingdom" has exercised its unique wisdom, self-discipline, and patience throughout the last half century, while observing the dragons at war. One fears what one does not understand, and no true and lasting peace can have fear as its foundation. Fear of the unknown is the objective of terrorism, and this psychological weapon has been well employed in all of the conflicts by the "inscrutable East" against the West.

I returned from Viet Nam to a nation that had failed to "read the tea leaves," placing our creature comforts and greed for fossil fuels ahead of forethought, returning to the blind streets that have brought us sadness and pain in the past. It took the attacks on America on September 11, 2001, to unite the American people (and much of the world beyond our borders) in a rally of patriotism to a degree unimaginable in the last four decades of the previous century.

However, a call is still needed for the prophets among us to see, to speak, and to be heard. This writing is a sincere attempt to emerge from the sadness and pain of the battlefields to offer a prophetic cry for a realistic peace.

—EZEKIEL 37:1–14

The Chaplain rides a tank near "The Rock Pile" in the D.M.Z. - Summer, 1967 (Page 178)

CHAPTER SEVEN

With the Brown Water Navy

On the Mark, Get Set

While I was on duty at the National Naval Medical Center in Bethesda, Maryland, a directive was circulated from the Chief of Chaplains. I had only been at NNMC about a year at the time, covering wards filled with combat casualties, with occasional pastoral visits to Members of Congress and to the Presidential Suite. The Chief of Chaplains was asking for volunteers among chaplains who had already completed a tour in Viet Nam, who would be willing to accept orders for a second tour of duty there. He stated that he was at the point of ordering others who were less than willing to go, and would rather seek volunteers. Whether it was survivor guilt or the Call of the Lord or a combination of these, I was confronted with a burning urge to respond. After several sleepless nights, I shared the reason for my unrest with Marjorie. After some thought, she replied characteristically: "Do what you have to do." She added parenthetically (and with a smile): "But with two children here in diapers, I think you want to go back to war because you are a coward."

My experiences with the Field Medical Battalion and with Marine infantry on my first tour restricted me from close contact with the Vietnamese people. In the Da Nang area, they had their own medical facilities, and on the DMZ, the civilian population had been resettled to keep them out of harm's way (and to keep us from the threat of "turncoats"). A major factor in my initial goal of going to Viet Nam from my missionary work in the Orient was to minister to all of the populations that were experiencing the pain of war. For this reason, should I return to that troubled country, I wanted a position in which I would have helpful contact with the host people.

By appointment, I visited Navy Chief of Chaplains, Rear Admiral James W. Kelley, in his office at the Bureau of Naval Personnel on the Virginia side of Washington. In our interview, I suggested that I would be willing to accept Orders to return to Viet Nam, but that I had some conditions I would like to discuss in advance. In a most friendly manner, he inferred that "one does not make deals with Admirals." Yet he was willing to hear what I had to say. I explained that I had lived in the Orient and had a deep appreciation of its people and its culture, and that I had Chinese language capability. I stated that I would volunteer to return for duty in Viet Nam if I could have some Vietnamese language training at the Defense Language Institute—with the prospect of placement in a geographic area where I would have contact with Asian people as well as with our military forces. Chaplain Kelley thought for a moment, then said, "And what do you plan to do if I do not give you what you ask?" I explained that I had only three months left on my commissioning contract, and that I would resign and seek a return to the mission field. He promised to think about it.

The following week I received Orders detaching me from NNMC after 14 months of service there, to three months of temporary duty under instruction at the Defense Language Institute (West Coast Branch) at the Presidio of Monterey, California. Following this, I was to report to Naval Support Activity, Saigon for duty. I smiled, assuming that the Chief of Chaplains now shared my vision. I hoped that the Admiral was smiling also. I knew he was pulling for me, because we were setting a new precedent: one that had added importance to ministry to Vietnamese people as well as to our own. Marjorie would have our nine-year-old daughter Karla with her for comfort and support, but Karla's brother and sister were still toddlers. At the time, the paper shopping bags in the Navy Commissaries had a printed logo on them to the effect that being a Navy Wife was one of the biggest jobs in the service. Likewise, in any field of service, a married Minister who is without a supportive wife is destined to fail.

We relocated to a small house in El Cerrito in the East Bay Area, which had been a friendly place for the waiting family during my duty with the Third Marine Division. I rented a motel-cottage in Carmel near the language school for my study headquarters, and on the weekends I drove to and from home at night, while listening to tape-recorded language practice lessons. The course was twelve weeks in length, and as an officer I was given leadership of a class of twelve enlisted Marines who were being groomed as translators prior to flying over to join their units.

Knowing that I had served with Marines in combat, these young men were interested in my experiences and tips for their future. Marines on an Army Base are a challenge, as I soon found out. When others had deserted the post for the afternoon or on weekends, "my charges" formed up for P.T. (physical training). This consisted of forced runs up and down the steep roads of the Presidio, while calling cadence. At the lower portion of the base, making a turn to run again up the hill, the Marines passed by the Army Base Military Police headquarters. "Sound off! One, Two! Wish I had a low I.Q.; I could be in the Army too!" would be repeated at least four times within hearing range of those inside. After several such probes, an MP sedan with red lights "pulled over" the jogging squad and demanded that the person in charge surrender. When that person was taken to the stockade, following the best POW training, the next in seniority took charge, and the run continued. With the next pass, the unison cry was: "Wish I had a low I.Q.; I could be an MP too!" With each cycle up and down the hill, the next in command was captured. These Marines had declared war on the Army. The following morning, it fell to me to plead with the Provost Marshal and to make certain promises about repentance and reforms, thereby gaining freedom for the squad, and enabling their return to class.

Kitchen Police (K.P.) duties rotated through the language classes, and my squad took their turns. Shortly after the jogging encounter, when these Marines were running the dishwashers and had their hands in the after-dinner garbage, it happened that an Army Private came through the galley with certain demands. He was dressed in his "Class A" uniform, complete with highly polished boots, a uniform "pogy rope" (braid indicating a special detail) over one shoulder and various insignia and ribbons ablaze. As he stood in the midst of the sweating Marines, everyone stopped and stared at him. (I need to explain here that it is an informal Marine custom to make a minimum display of one's uniform. A Marine must be sharp, but the bigger the hero, the less the ostentation.) In the silence, someone shouted: "God, you're beeeautiful!" The food fight that followed resulted in a return to the brig, and again I had to deal with the authorities on behalf of my Vietnamese language class.

—ᔕᔕᔕ—

After returning from one of my weekend home visits, I was listening to the radio news report while I was shaving and readying for class. The reporter related that a man was apparently drowning in the undertow at Carmel beach on Sunday, when a group of Marines formed a human chain into the surf, with the lead man swimming beyond it to complete the rescue. I knew at once that this must be my bunch. So it was. I congratulated them, and wrote them up for a military recognition. At last their bravery had been directed in a useful manner! I was told later in Viet Nam that because of this incident, one of these Marines had received the Navy and Marine Corps Medal, and two were decorated with the U. S. Coast Guard Silver Lifesaving Medal.

These twelve Marines that I had "inherited" were my rooting section as I was theirs. At our graduation, an Army Major received a Letter of Commendation for having the highest academic score, when soon after the ceremony it was revealed that I had bested him by a fraction of a percent. This matter was adjusted to the satisfaction of my fans. However, as I left the ceremony, six "side boys" flanked either side of my passage from the assembly hall. This was their touching salute to our twelve tumultuous weeks together. They then gathered around me, and the senior enlisted man presented to me a set of Gunnery Sergeant chevrons in recognition of my leadership. I have that "Gunny" insignia right next to my Bronze Star Medal as one of the highest awards I shall ever have received.

Why have I taken so much space to tell this pre-war story and to occupy the reader with such material? It is because, as a chaplain–minister, I learned a few lessons from this experience.

First, Marines do their best when they have a designated enemy to oppose. Similarly, should any congregation choose to oppose something, let it be identified as a genuine source of Evil. This will keep the members from struggling over trivia.

Second, when a minister sees acts that are deserving of recognition, initiatives need to be taken to see that due recognition is given. I learned this by hindsight. I wrote only one medal for heroic actions I witnessed during my first year in Viet Nam, whereas I would write nineteen citations during my second year of combat duty. We need to act in the civilian realm in similar ways, when we see laudable deeds done. The more we "accentuate the positive," the less contention we will have with negatives.

Third, I learned to appreciate unexpected blessings. When I had requested language school, I never imagined that God's Call would also include the initially unwanted experience of adopting twelve "sons" for twelve weeks. However, this experience became one of the most joyous relationships of my life. I pray these young men survived the war and returned to raise young people of their own.

—ACTS 13:2ff; II TIMOTHY 4:11

(explaining the geography of Chapter 7)

Major cities and military installations are labeled in capital letters. Those designated by number or in lower case letters are villages, small encampments, or areas not otherwise indicated on the map. Locations are listed in this Legend approximately in the order they are described in the text.

SG	SAIGON	BH	BEN HOA
TSN	TAN SON NHUT AIR BASE		
NB	NHA BE / NAVAL SUPPORT ACTIVITY, SAIGON (HEADQUARTERS)		
RSSZ	Rung Sat (Capital) Special Zone		
VT	VUNG TAO	TA	TAN AN
VL	VINH LONG	SD	SA DEC
1.	An Long	1a.	Tram Chim (No Village)
TC	TAN CHAU		
CD	CHAU DOC (CHAU PHU)		
2.	Tinh Bien	3.	Vinh Gia
HT	HA TIEN		
4.	An Toi (on Phuoc Quoc Island)		
DD	Duong Dong (on Phuoc Quoc Island)		
5.	Kien Luong (Cement Plant and air field)		
BT	BINH THUY / NAVAL AIR BASE		
CT	CAN THO / ARMY BASE	LX	LONG XUYEN
RG	RACH GIA	SF	"SEA FLOAT"
MT	MY THO	6.	Cho Gao
DT	DONG TAM / 9th INFANTRY HEADQUARTERS		
BTR	BEN TRE		
PP	PHNOM PENH, CAMBODIA		
7.	Neak Luong & Highway 1 (&4) River Crossing (ferry was sunk)		

—•—•—•—• National Boundary with Cambodia

– – – – – Boundary with III Corps (to the north of IV Corps)

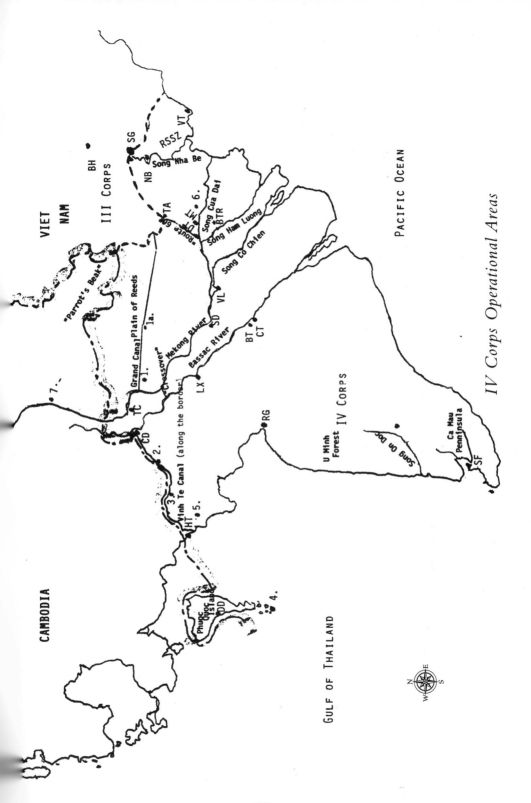

IV Corps Operational Areas

VIET NAM

III Corps

BH

SG
RSSZ
VT
NB
Song Nha Be

PACIFIC OCEAN

6.
TA
MT
Song Cua Dai
BTR
Song Ham Luong
Song Co Chien
"Route 4a"

"Parrot's Beak"
Grand Canal
Plain of Reeds
1a.
1.
"Crossover"
Mekong River
VL
SD
Bassac River
BT
CT
LX

7.
TC
CD
2.
Vinh Te Canal (along the border)
3.
HT
5.

RG
U Minh Forest
IV CORPS
Song On Doc
Ca Mau Peninsula
SF

CAMBODIA

Phuoc Quoc Island
DD
4.

GULF OF THAILAND

207

Shaded area in Viet Nam was IV Corps during the War

CHINA

VIET NAM (NORTH)

Hanoi •

LAOS

HAINAN

Vinh •

SOUTH
CHINA
SEA

DMZ • Quang Tri
Hue •
• Da Nang

Chu Lai

THAILAND

Qui Nhon •

• Bangkok

CAMBODIA

Cam Ranh

Phnom Penh •

VIET NAM (SOUTH)

Saigon •
Ha Tien My Tho
Vung Tao

GULF OF
THAILAND

On the Road Again

After a night in Nha Be, the headquarters of the Naval Support Activity, Saigon—and the day before the terrorist bombing of the billet where I spent the night—I was flown to Vinh Long, up the Mekong River about a fourth of the way to the Cambodian border. There followed a long bumpy Jeep ride to the NSA Detachment at Sa Dec. A River Patrol Boat (PBR) squadron was housed there in the middle of a then peaceful village. This was to be my home base for most of the year to come.

Before the dust cleared from the wake of our arriving Jeep, and before I managed to get out of the vehicle, an officer approached carrying baggage. He said, as he prepared to board the conveyance: "You're my relief." Gesturing behind him, he added: "The river is out that way." He was gone as fast as I had arrived. That was the only briefing I was to receive to acknowledge my arrival and to prepare me for the giant task ahead. Fortunately, the Officer-in-Charge, Navy Lieutenant Ploeger, was most hospitable, and he and his staff would become not only colleagues but instantly good friends as well.

I understood that my assignment was to provide chaplain services for the principal Navy assets on the river, with the exception of the major operating base at Binh Thuy. It had resident Navy chaplain assets and accessability to the two Army Chaplains at the Can Tho complex nearby. Thus, my initial assigned "parish" was to include four NSA shoreside detachments at mini-bases, three large support barges, and three reconfigured LSTs. The bases were those at Sa Dec, Chau Doc, My Tho, and Dong Tam. The three "Yard Repair Barges, Medium" were the YRBM-16, YRBM-20 and the YRBM-21. They had two enclosed decks above the main deck, and they were propelled short distances by small stern pusher-barges to avoid mortar targeting. The three LSTs were the USS *Hunterdon County* (LST-838), USS *Garrett County* (LST-786), and the USS *Jennings County* (LST-846). These afloat assets were on the Mekong and the Bassac Rivers, and all were redesigned especially for the support of river patrol craft and helicopters. Each had floatation piers or spars rigged perpendicular to the vessel for one or two squadrons of PBRs and "Heavy" (armored) River Assault Squadron boats.

All of these LSTs and YRBMs were equipped to be afloat home bases to Navy close air support "Seawolf" helicopter detachments of the HA(L)-3 Squadron, and had landing pads with parking for two helos on the "roof." Some of the support vessels had alongside a "beer barge" with a recreation club house on it (thus avoiding the prohibition of alcoholic beverages on board U.S. Navy ships and the danger of liberty ashore). Naval Support Activity Detachments ashore had machine shops and complete boat repair facilities. The "base" ships and barges had complete repair shops for both boats and helos, plus messing and berthing for all hands. This gave me ten small support bases and floating platforms to cover as circuit rider—for a start. Shore facilities were subject to mortar, rocket, and artillery fire, sometimes as often as every night. The assets in the middle of the rivers were *relatively* safe if they moved at dusk. The living on the support ships and barges was relatively comfortable, compared to patrol life on the canals and for Army advisors in the Vietnamese villages.

The more common fast craft in our Brown Water Fleet were the River Patrol Boats (PBRs). These Mark I and Mark II models were 5-man boats with lightweight, yet vulnerable, fiberglass hulls. They were powered by Jacuzzi pump-jets rather than propellers, so as not to foul in the flotsom or trash in the shallow canals.

The work horses of "the heavies" (River Assault Squadrons of the Mobile Riverine Forces) included the Armored Troop Carriers, called "Tango Boats." These were Medium Landing Craft (LCMs) with a helo pad for an "LZ" welded on top. The name "Tango" indicated they were used mainly for the transport of troops of the 9th Army Infantry or Navy SEALs making insertions into the jungle. These Mobile Riverine Forces (MRF) Squadrons also included Monitors (armored boats, platforms for a canon); Zippo Boats (armored, having a napalm nozzle); and a few "Charlie Boats" (armored command and control boats or CCBs), which were located forward to coordinate the action out on the canals.

CÙNG ĐỒNG-BÀO Ở DỌC THEO SÔNG :

CHÍNH-PHỦ VIỆT-NAM CÔNG-HÒA ĐEM CÁC TÀU TUẦN TỚI
VÙNG NÀY ĐỂ BẢO-VỆ ĐỒNG-BÀO VÀ ĐỂ NGĂN-CHẶN BỌN VIỆT-
CÔNG ÉP BUỘC ĐỒNG-BÀO ĐÓNG THUẾ CHO CHÚNG.

VẬY ĐỒNG-BÀO HÃY GIÚP ĐỠ NHỮNG TÀU NÀY BẰNG CÁCH
CHỈ CHỖ BỌN VIỆT-CỘNG THÂU-THUẾ VÀ NỚI CHÔN DẤU VŨ-KHÍ
CỦA CHÚNG. NẾU TIN-TỨC ĐÓ CHÍNH XÁC ĐỒNG-BÀO SẼ ĐƯỢC
TRỌNG THƯỞNG.

Chieu Hoi ("safe to return to your home") Safe Conduct Pass of the "Open Arms"
Program, which invited Viet Cong to safe amnesty if they would surrender. Those who did
were slaughtered when U.S. Forces left. These leaflets were dropped from Navy "Seawolf"
and Army flights over IV Corps. The boat shown is a PBR (Patrol Boat, River), a familiar
sight on the rivers and in the jungle canals of IV Corps. (Pages 210 & 236)

USS *Benewah* (APB-35) with "Tango" and PBR craft nested at barge alongside. (Page 210)

"Seawolf" landing on the flight deck amidships on USS *Jennings County* (LST-846) (Page 234)

"Tango" Assault Boat leaves USS *Benewah* (APB-35) for night patrol. (Page 223)

MEMORANDUM

11 December 1969

From: Chaplain Westling

To: Commanding Officers/Officers-in-Charge concerned

Subj: General Worship Services on Christmas Eve

1. Plans are in progress to provide a brief general Christmas service for each unit that would welcome this across Operations Tran Hung Dao and Barrier Reef   on 24 December – Christmas Eve. Air transportation is to be provided for the Chaplain which will allow brief stops according to a schedule which will be worked out after the desires of units are surveyed. It is requested that you advise SNAKEING ONE NINE if you desire such services at your location.

2. In order to expedite the time limitations so that all requesting units may be visited, it is requested that Commands expedite rigging for Church in a suitable place in advance of arrival, and assemble all interested personnel when word of approach to your location is passed.

3. In many locations this will be the only opportunity for worship on Christmas. For this reason, the service will consist of carol-singing and a brief order of worship at which any of your personnel who want to observe Christmas should feel welcome and included. Effort will be made to arrive in the morning, afternoon, or evening when the maximum number would be off patrol if practical in planning the travel route. It is hoped that shop work might be re-scheduled to accomodate the visit, however.

4. This plan is offered in the hope that Commanders will find this effort helpful in fulfilling their responsibilities for the spiritual welfare and morale of their commands. A longer pastoral visit by your Chaplains will follow Christmas as soon as time permits.

L. L. WESTLING, JR.

Memorandum arranging multiple Christmas services throughout "The Circuit". (Page 236)

Holy Communion on the helo pad of a "Tango" boat on the Mekong River at Neak Luong, Cambodia, celebrating the Great Rescue - May 17, 1970. (Page 246)

These boats were heavier and slower because of their protective steel hulls and sides. The "bar armor" around the personnel areas was composed of a cage of metal bars spaced a foot from the external walls of the boat. This "bar armor" was designed to detonate incoming Rocket Propelled Grenades (RPGs) and mortar rounds before they could penetrate the side of the boat and explode in its interior. Units of River Assault Squadrons 13 and 15 operated in the areas I would be serving. Occasionally one of the larger Swift Boats would come up the rivers from coastal off-shore "Operation Market Time" or in support of "Seafloat" in the U Minh Forest, to patrol the rivers and enter canals in high water periods. When upriver, they would find temporary homes at piers at NSA shore Detachments or beside the larger mother vessels.

Later in my tour, the 4-man very high speed out-drive Strike Assault Boats (STABS) joined our Brown Water fleet under the command of Commander J. Kirk Ferguson. "On step," they could hydroplane. Their fast reaction capability made them especially suited for clandestine SEAL insertions. But they came in-country at a time when the strategy of the war in IV Corps was changing to one of defensive interdictions and ambush "Guard Posts" along the canals. These fiberglass STAB boats were designed for speed and surprise offensives, not for defensive tactics. Lacking any canopy protection, they were too vulnerable for sitting and waiting to be engaged.

Canal Mine Sweeper boats and their remotely controlled "sleds" were also part of our inland "flotilla." The men who manned and fought all these craft and those who labored to support them in a dangerous environment constituted an enormous potential "parish," and I could only imagine, at first view, what a huge pastoral challenge it would be.

As I made my first rounds, it seemed best to use Sa Dec as my mid-point and place to spend a day or two preparing sermons and readying myself for the next venture up and down the rivers. Even with a brief stop between "rounds," I was able to perceive more clearly what was needed, and in what locations I could provide a more comprehensive ministry and presence among the population I was to serve.

This stopover proved to be of great value as the ministry developed. Every day revealed new challenges, and I was soon to learn that mind and body needed an occasional rest, however brief. I also learned that I would miss many of the troops on the rivers and canals if I restricted myself to the support ships, barges, and bases. Those at the support facilities had their needs and deserved the ministry of worship and counsel, but I would have to go where the boats went and share the lives and hazards of the sailors who manned them in order to serve them, as well.

Chaplain Commander Ralph Caldwell at the Naval Support Activity, Saigon headquarters in Nha Be had given me a free hand to develop this ministry, and, with his trust and logistic support, I was able to use my own judgment as though I were on independent duty. I did not have to look over my shoulder, worrying about what my boss might be thinking. I simply submitted reports when I could.

During my first visitations and introductions throughout my original "circuit," I surveyed the field. It was the time for decisions regarding the development of my objectives for what was to come. I cannot emphasize enough that a minister in any situation needs to have a vision of the direction for his or her ministry. Such a vision needs to take into account two factors.

First, any vision will develop as the journey proceeds, much like a mirage lifts with advancement down the road.

Second, and of greatest importance, a vision for ministry is gradually revealed through ongoing consultation with the Lord and with the people to be served. So, in my prayers, clearer goals developed and expanded as I pursued them. I was given to understand that there were men who might never see a chaplain nor attend religious services, because their duties on watch or in the field might not coincide with the chaplain's visit. I would have to tour the spaces on board, as well as to get out on the water, in the jungle, and in the rice patties, in order to be knowledgeable and creative in this ministry. Not only were Navy sailors deployed on patrols on the rivers and canals, but there were Army Advisory Teams, groups of a dozen men located in isolated Vietnamese villages living in houses or tents. We were all on the same team, and they would be included on my proposed route. They rarely, if ever, saw visitors of any kind.

Several months later, I added to my "circuit" pastoral visits on board USS *Benewah* (APB-35), USS *Colleton* (APB-36) and USS *Satyr* (ARL-23) south below Dong Tam Army Base in the Ham Luong River near Ben Tre (Truc Giang). Then I found a regular welcome on board the repair ship USS *Askari* (ARL-30), usually in the area of Long Xuyen on the Bassac River. These major vessels had no assigned chaplain for worship or counseling ministries.

There were chaplains available and doing good and courageous work on either side of the "corridor" in the middle of IV Corps to which I had been assigned. Therefore, it would be necessary to project a circuit along the Mekong and Bassac Rivers and along the Cambodian border westward as far as to Ha Tien on the Gulf of Thailand. There was no need for me to cross the Gulf to assets at An Thoi on Phu Quoc Island. Navy Chaplains flew there from Binh Thuy. Further, I would not duplicate the ministry of chaplains in "the Parrot's Beak" beyond Tram Chim, halfway eastward from the Mekong on the Grand Canal into the Plain of Reeds. The area beyond this was called "Operation Giant Slingshot" and was being served by courageous Navy Chaplains.

Southwest of Binh Thuy, in the area of the dangerous Ca Mau Peninsula, other Navy Chaplains rotated to minister to personnel on "Operation Sea Float." Nha Be was headquarters for the Naval Support Activity, Saigon (NSA), and it possessed chaplain resources who covered the "Rung Sac Special Zone" at the lower end of the river delta. My expanding circuit would have to be manageable as to an effective length of time within which regular visits could be expected by the units served. However, my chosen route still covered over one-third of IV Corps, a geographic area of approximately ten percent of South Viet Nam.

Thus, I had defined my territory and had a vision to pursue. (Maps and a legend are provided on pages 206 to 208 to enable the reader to follow this narration.) I record this geographic information here for the sake of preserving its history, as well as to describe the rightful demands of this ministry. My route would roughly resemble a giant figure "9," and require about three weeks for a given cycle. Adhering to this visitation route would define my year of ministry in the rivers.

From "home base" at Sa Dec, I would proceed up the Mekong River to the YRBM anchored near the An Long mouth of the "Grand Canal." After circulating with personnel and having services on board, I would find a PBR ride a third of the way east on that canal to Tram Chim. This is where the PBR Squadron on canal duty slept and rested on their boats during daylight, in tropic heat and during monsoon deluges. (Modern wars are fought mostly at night.) Tram Chim was the location of an Army Advisory Team. These dozen soldiers resided in a tent on the berm that was the levee separating rice patties from the canal. I would meet the personnel, go on ambush with the PBRs, and hold a Communion Service for Navy and Army personnel, preferably in the afternoon before night patrol, but sometimes afterward in the morning if so requested. This was to be my pattern for ministry, to be replicated on the canals in my self-appointed area of responsibility. Also, in the An Long area on the Mekong, I would provide a pastoral visitation on board an LST when one might be there near the YRBM, plus a visit to the Army Advisory Team up river at Tan Chau on the west side of the river—when I could get transportation.

From this upper Mekong area (near the Cambodia border), I would transit over to the Bassac River by either Seawolf helo or by PBR via "the Crossover" that connected the rivers not far to the south. In the vicinity of Chau Doc, there were usually two YRBMs in the river. On occasion, an LST support ship would be anchored there in the Bassac. All would merit thorough chaplain visitations.

Parenthetically, I wish to insert information about the LSTs that supported operations in IV Corps. At least two of the LSTs would be in the upper rivers where needed. The third LST "in my parish" was usually stationed in the Gulf of Thailand. It would alternate between a station off the south coast, providing air support for "Seafloat" and boat units in the Ca Mau Peninsula, and a station just off Ha Tien in support of Vinh Te Canal operations. When that ship was stationed off the beach at Ha Tien, I would fly to it for a chaplain visitation.

The LST in the Vam Co Tay and Vam Co Dong Rivers was served by chaplains of "Operation Giant Slingshot," thus beyond my area.

Returning to a description of the circuit I was following, from the area of Chau Doc, I would transit west on the Vinh Te Canal along the Cambodian border. This canal was the scene of fierce fighting, because it stood as a narrow barrier against intruders. The North Viet Nam "Transportation Companies," frequently composed of fierce female warriors, were constantly seeking to cross the canal our boats were guarding to carry munitions and supplies south toward the U Minh Forest on the Ca Mau Peninsula.

Along the Vinh Te Canal I would visit boat squadrons for services, spending the night on patrol with them, and "daisy chaining" further down the canal to the next squadron in the morning for a repeat of this routine with the next bunch of boats. Mobile Riverine "Tango Boat" squadrons as well as PBR squadrons operated here, but with deeper drafts these heavier boats would have to leave the Vinh Te Canal during the annual dry season to return with the next monsoons.

As in the other border canals, all boats would take up night ambush positions, with each boat separated roughly a kilometer (called a "klick") from the units on either side of it, to provide an interdiction fence. These defensive ambush positions were called "Waterborne Guard Posts." These boats were always on alert for surprise attacks. If the enemy could eliminate one boat and crew, they would have time to rush across the waterway barrier in the dark with their loads and reinforcements, to head south before neighboring crews could react. Of course there were radio communications and Seawolf helos at the ready—if the attacked boat crew lived to call for help.

There was an Army Advisory Team at Tinh Bien that lived in buildings about a third of the way down the Vinh Te Canal. One of the rotating PBR squadrons rested there during days, standing out in ambushes each night. Tinh Bien had been overrun by enemy "zappers" more than once. They invited me to "over-night" with them and to have services there when "on my rounds," which I was pleased to do.

Another third of the way down the canal to the west, before the waterway joined a river and turned from west to south toward Ha Tien, was a place called Vinh Gia (properly pronounced "Vin Yah"). This was destined to become my second home, because I spent much time at this place. Here was a small tented Navy detachment and the "Charlie Boat" (CCB), one of the heavy armored river boats which was a communications center for command and control of the border operations.

The Area Commander, Lieutenant Commander Michael Brian Connelly, heartily welcomed my presence, and participated enthusiastically in religious services. He provided crucial suggestions as to how I could best serve in a ministry to his personnel and to the PBR and "Tango" Boat squadrons that were operating out of Vinh Gia.

This place was the nerve center for resistance to interdiction along the border, known to be a great threat to the NVA supply units. Thus, it was quite vulnerable to attack. When we returned from PBR and Tango Boat ambushes along the canal in the mornings, it was not uncommon to see enemy bodies being extricated from the surrounding perimeter barbed wire by men stationed at Vinh Gia.

It was here that I came in contact with Chinese "Nung" mercenaries who ran the air boats. These "sleds," armed with a 60 caliber machine gun at the front, were powered by large pusher fans like those used in the Florida Everglades. Known as the Air Boat Company (Detachment A-404), they came to patrol this area around Vinh Gia in the season when the rice fields were flooded. They were employed by Company "D," 5th Special Forces (Airborne), of the Army's First Special Forces. These "Green Berets" were only too happy to make use of my Chinese language skills when I was at Vinh Gia to communicate with these troops.

My next stop would be Ha Tien, a Naval Support Activity tactical support detachment (mini-base) and home to a PBR Squadron—with an LST usually within sight offshore in the Gulf of Thailand. At this beautiful shoreside location, one could sit on the beach and watch local artisans fashion jewelry from the shells of the huge tortoises that were native to this area. At Ha Tien I provided services, counseling, and a pastoral presence for NSA personnel and the PBR squadron operating from there. From Ha Tien I either rode a boat or flew by Seawolf to provide chaplain services on the support LST, if it was anchored in the area.

Soon I was to discover an Army Advisory Group of 12 soldiers south of Ha Tien near a big cement plant and an air strip at Kien Luong. The air strip was used for a refueling station for our "Seawolf" helicopters. The Army Advisors requested regular visits on my route. I would get there from Ha Tien by a helo in need of fuel.

Each visit included gathering the 12 soldiers at the dinner table for an evening communion and I would spend the night at the team house. The next day I would await the sound of the Australian C-121—that delivered the "AvGas"—which I would ride, if I could get on board. The trick was to successfully dodge the 55-gallon gasoline barrels as they rolled wildly out of the plane's lowered aft ramp and danced unpredictably onto the runway pavement. All this occurred while the plane was turning around and racing its engines, preparing to make a fast getaway from the threat of incoming rockets that were frequently attracted by the plane's presence.

The Australians would usually transport me south along the Bassac River to the place where their flight originated, the U.S. Navy air base at Binh Thuy. From there I would head a short distance upstream to Long Xuyen for a visit to the repair ship USS *Asakari* (ARL-30), anchored nearby in the river. The Protestant Pastor in Long Xuyen had hopes of building a school, and I explained to the crew our joint project in Sa Dec.

From Long Xuyen it was hard to find a ride back to Sa Dec, there being no connecting patrol routes because this area was very peaceful. The Cao Dai religious sect controlled this portion of the river, and they were strongly anti-communist. However, when I had success, by radio, begging a helo to pick me up, I would return to my "home base" at Sac Dec. It was then time to write a new sermon and ready myself for the next leg of my route, which would be downstream.

My Tho was quite a large town compared to the places where I visited near the Cambodian border. The NSA Detachment repair shops were on the beach near the PBR piers, but an old concrete hotel in town had been leased to double as a berthing facility and as a bar/club. The substantial building served as a shelter from big incoming rockets.

Before Church Call, I would make the rounds of the piers and the PBRs, the repair shops, and the berthing areas. I spent time talking to people and renewing friendships. The crew's lounge was on the ground floor of the hotel, the only place I thought I could gather a group safely. The chaplain had to sweep up the beer cans from the night before, to make room for services and prior to setting up the Altar on the bar.

In the town of My Tho, the Protestant Pastor and his wife became my good friends, and again I encouraged his congregation's plans for a school that would serve both documented and undocumented children. I was frequently invited to share lunch at his parsonage. (I fear that his welcome for Americans may have brought him a sad fate a few years later, when U. S. Forces suddenly left.)

During subsequent visitations to My Tho, riding with PBR patrols, I was to discover the contested Cho Gao Canal to the south (which the patrol sailors called "Indian Country"). I never had time or the opportunity to ride the other identified threat north of Dong Tam, a canal that was carved eastward as straight as a board from its mouth on the Mekong, which the sailors called "Route 66."

After My Tho, I would thumb a ride on one of the Army "Six by" trucks that plowed up and down the broad military highway a few miles northward from My Tho to my next stop, Dong Tam.

This "parish call" would be to Navy personnel at the NSA Detachment on the major U.S. Army Base that served as headquarters for the Second Brigade of the 9th Infantry. These soldiers were the ones that routinely made jungle insertions from our boats. The Dong Tam base was pummeled with heavy mortars and artillery nightly, forcing us from sleep to hit the foxholes and bunkers frequently. The Army was planning to vacate this huge target. The YRBM-17 was rather permanently moored off the river alongside an inlet pier. It was used for its machine shops, berthing and storage. I did not mention it earlier because it was not organized as a separate NSA Detachment, as were the other support barges in the rivers.

With the Army pullout being planned and then in progress, the Navy had consolidated its personnel in one corner of the post near the YRBM-17, while the Army downsized rapidly. I had a hand in "scrounging" sacred items from the large Quonset Chapel that was abandoned in the middle of the acreage to furnish a smaller Quonset chapel for Navy personnel in their area.

Down another of the Delta outlets of the Mekong River also south of My Tho and Dong Tam, I soon discovered and included in my growing circuit three major support vessels and the Mobile Riverine Forces they were supporting. The USS *Benewah* (APB-35) and USS *Colleton* (APB-36), two converted LSTs supporting the Tango Boats, and the USS *Satyr* (ARL-23) their primary repair ship.

Unlike the other LST and YRBM Navy grey support vessels, these ships were painted dark jungle green like all the smaller assault craft. The armored "Tangos" they supported inserted soldiers from Dong Tam along the canals near Ben Tre where fierce offensive fighting often took place. The crews of these boats and the soldiers they carried to battle suffered many casualties. Chaplain visitations with these units were most welcomed and well utilized! Later in my tour of duty, with command encouragement, I would shift my "seabag home" from Sa Dec to a stateroom in the USS *Benewah*.

After these downriver visitations and services, it would be time again to go back upriver to Sa Dec to prepare for my next rounds, then head north and upstream once again. This cycle would repeat like a kaleidoscope, with each trip its own unique experience. This routine would continue throughout the year of chaplaincy duties on the Delta and along the Viet Nam border with Cambodia.

How did I get from place to place? I just put my thumb up in good old American fashion. Frequently it was by "Seawolf" combat patrol or by PBR or Tango Boat, or by "daisy chaining" down a canal in order to transfer to a boat of the squadron in the neighboring operating area. Sometimes it was by Boston Whaler motor boat. The Army Caribou (airplanes) and Army helo

Warrant Officer pilots and crews were always very helpful. They knew that I was adopting their small isolated units, acting as their chaplain. Rarely, I travelled by Jeep. People didn't like the roads "down river" because there were explosives unpredictably buried in them, and there were few roads elsewhere in IV Corps, transport being mostly by waterway. We had to sweep canals for mines, and our boat patrols were smart to leave for night posts at unpredictable times in order to avoid ambushes.

I recall spending the afternoon of my 39th birthday in a motor boat on the Vinh Te Canal. There were no other assets available to take me from the YRBM in the Bassac River near Chau Doc to my next stopover at Tinh Bien. A sailor volunteered to take me where I was going in a Boston Whaler.

The sound of the outboard motor called attention to us as we made our way down the canal. The trees canopied the channel and thick vegetation shrouded the banks. It was a risky transit, the cost of keeping to a schedule on which the many units I served could depend. We said little to each other, yet we knew we were both frightened. I would arrange for him to return with the boat in tow with the next PBR rotation to the YRBM.

Although it was difficult to keep up the pace as my number of calls escalated, I was able to keep fairly consistently to a schedule of three weeks for the complete "cycle" so that the troops could plan on the time of my return. In some places, I was the only one they saw from beyond their own perimeter. Needless to say, advance radio messages from a helo or a patrol craft indicating "Chaplain Whiskey approaching" (using the phonetic code for the "W" initial letter of my name) was universally welcomed, which was enormously gratifying to me. It made the risks well worthwhile.

My three-week circuit included regular chaplain visits, Holy Communion services and counseling of personnel at scattered combat units and squadrons—both major and small commands, including YRBMs, LSTs, Naval Support Activity shore facilities and Advance Tactical Bases, Tango Boat Assault Squadrons, PBR Squadrons, Navy Attack Helicopter Squadron Detachments (Seawolfs), Army Advisory Groups, the STAB Boat Squadron, and any others I could find.

On occasion I served SEAL and Marine Reconnaissance Teams, and an occasional U. S. Marine Advisor and his Vietnamese Marines that I would find in the field. I served as translator for Chinese "Nung" Mercenaries who fought the noisy airboats south of Vinh Gia when the rice fields were flooded.

Ministering to these brave young men who fought in IV Corps on the canals, on rivers and in the jungles was a most humbling experience. I saw 19-year-old Petty Officer boat captains call in air strikes and troop movements, making combat decisions that few senior officers would ever have to make in their careers. The Lord had protected me. He kept me safe, and I was grateful.

Field Medical Service School at Camp Pendleton and my first year in-country with the Marines in 1966-67 had taught me scores of lessons and trained my instincts in ways that undoubtedly saved my life on many occasions during this second combat tour. I knew that the most vulnerable times in combat were when one first arrived and just before leaving: when just learning how to conduct oneself under fire and how to handle one's fear, and when one had grown tired and perhaps careless. Thus, I paced myself at these times, and I intervened to get sailors off final patrols when I thought, from observing them, that they could be a liability to themselves and/or to others.

My initial "parish" had increased from 10 units to 65 almost immediately, an increase of 650 percent! Had there not been a war in process with all its pain and sadness, I would say that this was a ministry beyond imagination both in need and in response. But the needs were usually sad ones. Like any ministry, it began with a vision. And from such initial seeds, huge trees have been known to grow.

When I departed the USS *Jennings County* in the Gulf of Thailand off Ha Tien for the last time to head for Tan Son Nhut Air Base and the big "freedom bird," the flight back home, there was genuine sadness in my heart. I was leaving behind so many people with whom so much of life and death had been shared.

I climbed down the rope Bo'sun's Ladder suspended over the side of the LST to a waiting PBR in the tossing sea below. As I was making my departure, I heard the Boatswain's Pipe over the 1.MC (ship's P.A. system) for all to hear: "Chaplain, United States Navy, departing." I was being "piped over the side," a distinct Navy honor. I wept unashamedly all the way to shore. This was my parish. These were my brothers. We had been in Harm's Way together, while we shared a vision of world peace and of home. I would miss them! I still do!

—ST. MATTHEW 9:35-37; I THESSALONIANS 5:16–25

Summer Turnover in the Vinh Te Canal

It's hard to go back to Vinh Gia
  Where dust flies along the shore,
And there's echoes of the Tango Boats
  Lined up once by the score.

It's hard to see the purple sun
  Seek refuge in the night,
While remembering lines of smoky boats
  That journeyed to the fight,

And men who waited by the bank
  For twig or branch to break—
Or sudden pain or death instead
  If they should act too late.

It's hard to go back to Vinh Gia,
  Tho' the seasons seem the same,
Brave voices of last November
  Were drowned in monsoon's rain.

But we remember Vinh Gia
  And the lessons that it taught,
And tho' we change and go away,
  May it not all be for naught.

—28 May 1970

Providence Means that God Plans Ahead

God knows where He would like to take us. When we have followed His Call and then look back on where we have been, it is awesome to trace how His Providence has acted in our lives and in the lives of others He has touched through us.

When I recollect my journey in the past, what may look to others as aimless meanderings seems to me as a carefully calculated and guided adventure in which each experience prepared for the next one, or for ones thereafter. In order to demonstrate this, I have invited the reader to accompany me on many travels in this book. A list in sequential order would include Church military school at a young age, years in engineering college, work in the engine rooms of merchant ships, studies in Asian languages, living and serving in the Orient, and having a marriage and a family. I even marvel at how well the Navy trained me at Field Medical Service School at Camp Pendleton prior to sending me into combat chaplain duty with Marine Infantry—before returning me to Viet Nam.

All of these experiences were crowned by my theological studies and my Vocation as a priest. I can acclaim joyfully God's continuing plan for me, and therefore I can perceive God's Hand gently guiding others into His future hopes for them. Even amidst gruesome memories of battle, I know that God was always grooming me for the next step He wanted me to take for Him, even though I had no idea what or where it might be—in this life or in the next. I know quite personally that "with God, there are no blind streets!"

I am not inferring that God wanted this war. I am saying that, given the war, God had consistently prepared me for the next ministry, which was to be with these military men with their boats and engines, in danger and grieving, in an Asian land. The big word in all this is "minister." God gave me tools and prepared me to stand beside these men as their chaplain, and, even from a distance, to understand their families. I now can see how He went about this for years in advance of this tour of duty in South Viet Nam!—I was here to serve for Him.

As a missionary, I had been chaplain to a school of Chinese children. Education in Asia was (and is) a matter of great importance to me. I believe that people fight because they lack the "big picture." Thus, to develop and improve education is to encourage peace. I was particularly intrigued and excited about a proposal of the congregation in Sa Dec. The children of the Viet Cong had no proper government papers, and without such certification to identify them as loyalists, they were "invisible." These children were not eligible to attend the government-sponsored public schools.

Although the Sa Dec Protestant congregation had a small school, conditions were primitive and books were nonexistent. The pastor and his congregation wanted to reach out to children who would be deprived of an education because of politics. They explained to me that they hoped that educating the children of the enemy would help bring peace in the midst of war.

A Chinese contractor was located, and the men of the Sa Dec Detachment of the U.S. Navy Construction Battalion (SeaBees) agreed to help with this plan. It was my role to use my capabilities in the three languages to coordinate the construction of a three-story concrete school building. I hope it still stands in that village, and I hope that pastor was not martyred for his friendship with us, as many were. With this strategy in mind, I provided support directly for the pastor in My Tho to build a similar school, and indirectly through the crew of the USS *Askari*, I encouraged the building of a third church school in Long Xuyen.

Another of God's plans came about in a surprising way. Halfway down the An Long Canal at a small tent on the rice field berm was an Army Advisory Team of 12 soldiers. This was the gathering point and daylight resting place for the PBR crews that patrolled that canal or set up along it in ambush mostly at night. Later, they were joined by patrol crews of the new

Strike Assault ("STAB") Boats. At remote Tram Chim, Holy Communion was provided for the sailors and for the Army Advisory Team. I noticed that one of the crewmen always was attentive to my needs and volunteered to set up some ammunition boxes for my Altar. However, he never attended the sermon or worship services. I took him aside quietly to ask how I could respond to his kindness and be a good chaplain for him. He explained that he was Jewish, and, although he respected my ministry, he could not include himself in Christian worship. I expressed my gratitude for his honest response. I asked him to guide me patiently in ways that I could include him by providing for his special needs and those of other Jewish men who might be scattered throughout the Delta.

On returning to the USS *Hunterdon County* (LST-838), which was then the support ship for this operational area, I began a search through personnel records for someone who claimed the Jewish Faith. I needed someone who might be willing to provide my roving ministry with support for Jewish personnel for whom I would now be looking on my rounds.

I discovered that the Communications and Assistant Operations Officer on board, Ensign Arnold E. Resnicoff, seemed to be a likely candidate. When I presented him with my plan and asked if he would serve as Jewish Lay Leader for his ship and for this developing ministry, he reacted with humble surprise, stating that he believed himself to be totally unprepared for this responsibility. I responded that I had read in his records that he had spent a year in Kibbutz Kfar Glickson south of Haifa in Israel, and that he must have background in his Faith and in the Hebrew language. I further emphasized that there were men out on the firing line who needed their Faith to guide them in life and possibly in death. With hesitation, he agreed.

Together we set in motion his liaison with the Jewish Welfare Board to guide him, and for provision of devotional materials, Scriptures, prayer books, and greeting cards for the Jewish holidays for the men to send home to their loved ones at appropriate times. We also asked for selected canned Kosher foods that could be utilized in the field, and for "solo Seder Kits" for Passover.

Our program developed in wonderful ways. I would send message requests for Jewish supplies from far-flung installations around IV Corps that had radio or teletype capabilities. "Arnie" responded with requested materials on hand, and he continued to order supplies from the JWB. He would send the requested supplies to a Jewish sailor or soldier on a boat, ship, base, or in a remote camp. At times he would give me small items to carry in my backpack for delivery during my rounds. He often wrote greetings to Jewish men and to some of their families.

The USS *Hunterdon County* was a primary support ship for the refugee rescue operation into Cambodia by our Mobile Riverine Forces in the early Fall of 1970. The ship's mission was to wait on the Viet Nam side of the Cambodian border for our return from the 21.5-mile limit on incursion across the border.

After returning from this successful operation, my year was drawing to a close, and it was time to make my final rounds and to say goodbye. I boarded now Lieutenant (junior grade) Resnicoff's ship, and stopped by his stateroom to rejoice with him in what we had been able to do together. I wanted to thank him for his inspired support. In a moment of quiet, he spoke of how his father had always wanted him to become a Rabbi. He stated that he had a year or more remaining on his contract to the Navy, but he owned that his father's hopes for him had become his own hopes as well. He wanted to enter the rabbinate.

Arnie requested orders to Russian language school, and then spent a year applying that training in the naval intelligence community. Following that, he honored me by requesting that I endorse him for the Jewish Theological Seminary in New York City. He shared with me the experience of becoming an Ensign in the Navy Theological Student Program—what it was like to exchange his hard earned gold Lieutenant stripes (on the brink of promotion to Lieutenant Commander) for the single stripe of a probationary Ensign.

However, this time the Tablets of the Law, the insignia of his Faith, replaced the star of a Line Officer above them. Chaplain Resnicoff has not only fulfilled the dreams of his late father and his own Calling, but as a Rabbi he has blended theological scholarship and wisdom with the pastoral priority of ministry to people of every Faith.

As Rabbi and Navy Chaplain, even when we were separated by oceans and continents, he continued to be my guide on matters Jewish, which enabled me to include Jewish personnel in my chaplaincy in appropriate ways. With him as my inspiration and guide, I was able to organize at least a dozen lay-led Jewish congregations afloat and ashore and to insure that High Holidays were celebrated with reverence.

With this as a pattern, during my 1983 to 1985 duty as chaplain for the USS *Carl Vinson* Battle Group, I was able to implement a comprehensive multi-faith ministry that included religious expression not only for Christians and Jews, but also for Islamic and Mormon personnel in very specific ways.

All these innovations were indirectly motivated by Arnie's insistence that no one who wished to exercise his or her religion in the military be forgotten, but rather that they be accommodated and encouraged in every way possible. His publication: "Prayers that Hurt: Public Prayer in Interfaith Settings" has been frequently reprinted, and it gives valid instructions to both religious majorities and minorities on how to respect each other's sensitivities and avoid being exclusive in practical uncompromising ways when offering corporate prayer for public gatherings.★

Chaplain Arnold Resnicoff was at the site when a terrorist truck bomb demolished our Marine's billet in Beirut, searching the rubble for the victims—living and deceased. In 1986, he was sent to Reykjavik, Iceland to lead Yom Kippur services during the United States-U.S.S.R. Summit. In 1999, he was a guest with others at the White House to dine with our President. He served throughout the eastern hemisphere as the Command Chaplain to the Joint European Command. From this tour of duty at times of serious international tension and conflict, Arnie wrote kaleidoscope-like letters from Germany, Belgium, Lebanon, Zimbabwe, Kosovo and Israel, where he was demonstrating God's care by his presence, and where he participated in diplomatic missions. He gathered for training and program development chaplains of many Faiths from his own American Armed Forces and from the armed forces of nations of Europe, Africa, and the Middle East. He promoted peace by aiding pioneering chaplaincies in developing nations in ways yet unheralded in a worldwide sphere. Arnold Resnicoff retired from his final duties in the Office of the Chief of Navy Chaplains as a Captain in the Chaplain Corps with thirty years of naval service. He is now the National Director of Interreligious Affairs for the American Jewish Committee. All this began with Arnie's response to the need to include a single Jewish sailor in a PBR out on the An Long Canal.

—◦◦◦—

I believe God has all things in His Providential Plan! Often, He just waits patiently for us to do our part.

—I SAMUEL 18:3–5; I CHRONICLES 29:10–13;
ST. MATTHEW 10:29–31; ST. JOHN 1:47–51

★ A. E. Resnicoff, CHC, USN. "Prayers that Hurt: Public Prayer in Interfaith Settings." *Military Chaplains Review,* Winter 1987, pp. 30-40.

How the Seawolf Saved Christmas ... and Easter

Commander Walter B. Lester, Jr., Commanding Officer of Helicopter Composite Squadron Seven (HC-7), invited me to give the Invocation at the Disestablishment of his squadron on June 30, 1975. As I stood on the landing strip of the Naval Auxiliary Landing Field in Imperial Beach, California, I was wonderfully aware that I was surrounded by many old friends who had transitioned from the former Helicopter Attack (Light) Squadron Three [HA(L)3]. Among them was the C.O., whom I had known previously as the "Skipper" of HA(L)-3's Detachment 8. That squadron had been the U.S. Navy's only attack helicopter squadron in history.

When I first met them six years earlier in Viet Nam, it was in detachments dispersed throughout my "circuit" in the Delta. They were all *volunteer* aviators and door gunners, and their mission was to provide immediate close air support for the PBRs and SEALs, especially when the sailors on the ground were outgunned and outnumbered. They initially flew Huey "Bravo" models that had been cast off by the Army, but by the time I "left country" they had graduated through various and successively improved versions to the more powerful "November" models. They proudly called themselves the "Seawolf" Squadron.

My prayer at the Disestablishment of HC-7 acknowledged thankfully that the need for us in Viet Nam was over. As we stood together readying for the upcoming formation, sights and sounds of the past filled our heads, and stories were swapped recalling memories of HA(L)-3 and risky dust-offs that saved many lives—including mine.

For us, Viet Nam was over, or was it? As I stood on that quiet flight line in my dress uniform, I could still hear the whack-whack of the rotor blades as they cut the tall bamboo on the side of the An Long Canal in the early morning darkness, while the "Seawolf" helo lifted me off the top of a beached Tango Boat under attack. These guys were skilled—yet crazy! Standing on the skids, hugging the rocket pod that night as the helo fought the elements to rise, I thought: "if we all go down I would feel completely responsible." But once we were "off the deck" and I was seated inside, the aircraft commander yelled back to me: "No sweat, Padre!" *He* knew what he was doing. For me, the memory was a lasting one indeed, to say the least.

Because I was only too familiar with the risks that had to be taken by the "Seawolf" crews, my prayers for them were continuous. When boarding a helicopter on the flight deck of an LST, a YRBM, or from a Landing Zone (LZ, called a "Dust Off") in the field, it was often necessary to pass to the far side of the aircraft to enter. One never crosses behind the spinning tail rotor, always passing in front of the helo. It was my practice to bless the pilots and crew as I passed before the noisy aircraft as it was turning up. I did this by making the Sign of the Cross toward the pilots, where they could see this through their windshield as I rushed to board their flight. This became an understood ritual, and this identified me from among the other passengers in jungle greens with packs.

One moment that stood out in my mind occurred when boarding on one of the YRBMs. As I signed my blessing in sight of the "Seawolf" pilots, one of them returned my Sign of the Cross by tracing the Star of David with his free hand, in reply. By that, I knew I was in good hands with "one of Arnie's boys" (or, as we said, a member of the Tribe) at the controls.

I remembered that one crew with whom I flew on patrol the night before had taken automatic weapons fire that ripped up the radio console between the two pilots. They felt compelled to show me how to reach over from a back seat and use the collective to bring the aircraft down to a soft landing if those in the front seats no longer could.

I remembered then-Lieutenant Henry "Pete" Freas in the pilot seat laughing heartily when he allowed me to try to hover his aircraft over the Chau Doc airstrip. That helo danced a jig while I was attempting to keep it steady. I was even more impressed with the skill required to fly one of those things, especially with the accuracy of those Naval Aviators who could land one on a postage stamp or hover over a bum boat in the canal while inspecting its cargo. Pete explained that one never put the full weight of the aircraft on the landing pad atop an ATC ("Tango Boat"), always hovering with the skids on the deck. Those boats could never take the full load.

Pete had his picture taken for his Christmas card, literally armed to the teeth. He was standing in the door of his "Seawolf" helo, one foot on the rocket pod, bandoleers of bullets over each shoulder, an M-16 rifle in one hand and a rocket launcher in the other, grenades on his belt, pistols in his holsters, and a bayonet knife between his lips. Below the photograph, his season's greeting sarcastically expressed the tension that we all were feeling with the words: "Peace on earth, Good will to men!"

Yes, Christmas! My reveries meandered there at Imperial Beach five years after I had left Viet Nam, as we waited for formalities to begin. In the stories we exchanged at the reception that followed, we discussed unusual Holy Days that we had shared in IV Corps. I recalled how I had approached Lieutenant Commander Lester, Fire Team Leader of HA(L)-3 Detachment Eight, and Lieutenant Commander Kirk Walsh, Fire Leader of Detachment Three, and perhaps other Seawolf Officers I cannot now remember, with a proposal for Christmas 1969. "Put it in writing, and let's make it happen!" was their immediate response. "How remarkable!" I thought to myself. How deeply grateful I am for the bond I felt and still feel with these combat airmen.

With the help of the "Seawolf" helo assigned for Christmas Eve and Christmas Day, I was able to conduct a total of 18 religious services in as many ships, boat gatherings, and Advisory Groups throughout IV Corps. Each service began with *a capella* singing of well-known first verses of a few carols, included a brief homily and Communion for all hands, and each service took no more than 20 minutes! I brought the Altar furnishings with me, and had them so staged that they were almost instantly in place on landing. Radio messages ahead instructed "congregations" on board ships and the big barges to be in the mess hall or crew's lounge in front of a table, and for a sentry to guide me to them with dispatch. Those in the field were instructed to gather in a circle around several ammo boxes stacked to serve as the Altar. I allowed myself exactly five minutes to set up, and five minutes to return to the waiting aircraft.

While field services were being conducted, the helo and crew would fly around the perimeter, door gunners at the ready, to assure the safety of the gathered group. Total time for each stop was thirty minutes, and because we kept the schedule, had the troops muster ahead, and planned our route much like I made my three-week circuit, ten services were held on the day before Christmas, and eight on Christmas Day!

Some of the Hueys were equipped with psychological warfare (PsyOps) loud speakers aimed at the ground. These systems were used to play tape recordings in Vietnamese addressing people on the ground, urging the benefits of surrendering, and offering a bounty for weapons. These PsyOps broadcasts were conducted mostly at night. I had asked Marjorie to send me cassette tapes of recorded familiar Christmas carols which could be used in the

PsyOps tape players. After sunset on Christmas Eve 1969, we flew over the canals where the Waterborne Guard Posts (patrol boats hidden in ambush under the forest canopy along the shore) were on station—not giving away individual positions, of course. But with the aid of the speakers, we "went caroling" over most of the Delta and along the canals on the Cambodian border. Someone reported this to the *Navy Times,* which ran a short article on it. Thus we knew it was heard, appreciated, and, hopefully, brought to many reassurance that the Christ Child had come to this world for them and that *He knew* where they were.

We replicated this project of providing multiple services the following Easter Day. Because the day before Easter, Easter Even, was not commonly understood as a time for services, we confined our "rounds" just to Easter Sunday, getting a very early start. Still, with the essential "Seawolf" support, we were able to provide fourteen short services from dawn to dusk.

When we arrived at the Army Advisory Team at Kien Luong, the young Officer-in-Charge greeted me exclaiming: "Padre, we have already had our Easter Sunrise service." "How so?" I asked with surprise. "Come, I'll show you." In the small house the team occupied, where the back bedroom once stood, there was just a gaping rocket hole. "We were lucky!" the 2nd Lieutenant said. "Only one wounded. He was evacuated, but he will be okay."

I knew the team must have been upset. Still they requested that we proceed with Holy Communion around their dinner table as usual, and as I left we wished each other and the helo crew a good Easter. Our prayer was that from many sad tombs, God would raise with His Christ a new and transfigured world.

—Joshua 3:14–17; St. Luke 2:13f

Christmas in the Delta

The Holy Child is with us here
    To guard our souls in times of fear;
To keep us right in times of cheer:
    —He knows us.

In Bethlehem's humble cow-barn lay,
    Or was it Vinh Gia or Cai Be?
He came amongst us all to say:
    —He loves us.

He worked with hand and tool and plow,
    He walked through dust, He rowed a scow;
He braves our dangers even now.
    —He's with us.

He prayed at night, forgave the hate;
    He knew our strain, but saved our fate.
If we but choose, it's never late.
    —He'll cheer us.

And so it's Christmas far away;
    Yet Christ is also here today
On guard-post watch, in engine bay:
    —He's near us.

—CHRISTMAS 1969

Children Missing in Action

T he forgotten ones in any war are the children. Many are orphaned, some rejected, some simply lost. I had been so pleased with the Orphanage of the (Episcopal) Sisters of Saint Mary the Virgin in Sagada, Philippines and with several of their "graduates" (displaced from World War II) who shared our home in their teens during our missionary years.

I soon included in my My Tho visitations occasional calls on the Protestant Pastor, sharing his hopes to build a school. I also visited the Roman Catholic Sisters' Orphanage there. This was a huge old facility. The large rooms were filled with row upon row of cribs of crying infants, who had been lost or abandoned in the overwhelming seizures that had taken possession of their country. Their cries personified the terrors of a people being torn apart.

On my chaplaincy rounds, I was always looking for suitable mature fellows whom I thought might make good adoptive parents. Engineman Chief Bill LaRue on the YRBM-20 was quite interested. We made plans to catch a helo to Saigon to explore the matter with the Navy and with Vietnamese authorities. Except for the eighteen-hour stopovers when entering and leaving the country, this was my only trip to the city of bright lights.

We arrived at the Continental Hotel on Tu Du Street by taxi. The driver had inquired of us if we wanted girls, and we declined. A doorman helped us unload our small bags from the car, and asked: "Want girls?" "No thank you," we responded simultaneously. We checked in at the desk, but not before the clerk inquired: "Want girls?" Losing patience, we responded in the negative, but with greater forcefulness than we had before. The same question was posed by the elevator operator, and by the bell hop. By the time we reached our modest room and closed the door with sighs of relief, we felt we had been under attack by the image that Americans in field uniforms seemed to have acquired in Saigon.

Just as we had opened our bags, there came a knock on the door. I opened it to a scrub woman with a wet mop over her shoulder. "Want girls?"

she asked. "No, damn it! No!" I exclaimed. Demonstrating her knowledge of English, she replied: "Oh... queer, huh?" I slammed the door in her face.

As it turned out, the red tape for adopting a child was wound too tight and piled too high for any such prospect for Chief LeRue. Thus, our stay in the big city was brief and for this business only.

It was some time before I ventured into the adoption arena again. I had other duties to which to attend to keep my schedule on the Delta and along the border. It did happen again, quite by surprise.

I was riding in the cab of a large "six by" Army truck, northbound, on the wide heavily trafficked military highway from My Tho toward the huge Army complex at Dong Tam and the Naval Support Activity Detachment there. I spotted something beside the road, and ordered the driver to stop. I intuitively felt the need to investigate. I got down from the truck, walked back and recovered a small box containing the tiny, living body of an infant perhaps three days old. I retrieved my gear from the truck, thumbed a ride back south to the My Tho Orphanage, and delivered this child to the Sisters. They helped me identify him as of Black and Vietnamese parentage, and, asking my consent, said: "Let us call him *Lester*." I approved. I made visits to the orphanage every three weeks on my stopovers in My Tho. As we prayed for this child, obviously rejected by a mother amidst a very race-prejudiced population, perhaps of an unknowing American soldier father, Lester prospered! Now I was on the search again for proper parents. I felt a strong affection for my new namesake, but I was also aware that I was committed to a wanderer's life as a chaplain in the Navy, and that Marjorie, with three small children at home, had her hands full.

As the infant thrived, I found a senior petty officer upriver who readily discussed this matter with his wife in the States. The couple was childless and wanted this child. The sailor was Black, and his wife was Filipina. They believed the mixed race of the child meant that he was destined to be theirs. I was excited on receiving their news, and shared my excitement with the Sisters when I got to My Tho. However, their news was disappointing. After a check with the Viet Nam equivalent of our departments of social services, the national law of their land—not a rule of the Sisters to my knowledge—was against us. What could be an impediment to this perfect and loving solution for little Lester?

The prospective parents were Protestant Christians, and the Orphanage (therefore considered to be current parents of their charges) were Roman Catholic. In Asia, these Faiths are not considered denominations of the same Christianity, but separate religions altogether. The law of Viet Nam prohibits without exception the adoption of children by parents of another religion. What a very sad state of affairs! A phrase in the *Book of Common Prayer* refers to "our unhappy divisions," and that term had no greater impact than it did on the life of this child, his hopeful prospective parents, and upon this heartbroken chaplain. I am fearful even to speculate upon the fate of this tiny, unwanted infant whom I found in a shoe box along a truck highway in South Viet Nam.

I will never forget this child and the sorry world into which he was born. However, my sadness was somewhat eased when my niece Leslie and her husband Joe Hagedorn returned in the summer of 1999 from Southern China with their newly-adopted daughter Lulu. She was 10 months old at the time, and had survived in the orphanage at Xin Hui near Guangzhou (Canton) City. She had been found as a baby on the streets of the town when she was about eight days old. Too many little girls in China face what little Lester might have had to endure (if he survived), except for the absence of laws that would exclude loving parents from acclaiming them as their very own. I guess that is progress on a very slow road to peace.

—EXODUS 2:1–6; ST. MATTHEW 19:13f;
ST. MARK 9:36f, 10:13–16

There's a War Going On!

*L*ong before Indochina was colonized, Viet Nam was the highly contested landbridge between East Asia and India. Thus, this region was the frequent battlefield of foreigners who wished to control the trade route to the south. The very name "Viet Nam" means "the bridge (to the) south." Centuries of warfare jaded past generations to the inevitability of war in their land. This could be observed in the lives of aged farmers who plowed behind their water buffalo oblivious to artillery shells being lofted high over their heads. Old concrete signs still display Vietnamese titles and messages in Chinese characters, and currently Vietnamese is written in a phonetic system dictated by the French.

During my tour with the Marines, one time we established a temporary company-size camp in Quang Tri Province. I was there when our commander attempted to explain our presence to a local farmer. I witnessed how this Vietnamese struggled to believe that we were there to protect his harvest, instead of demanding a large portion of it to feed our troops.

Bridges are there to be walked on, yet with a new generation came the detonation of a chaotic explosion that had been latent in the emotions of the people of Viet Nam over countless past centuries. Visitors had always been intruders. How could these people tell the difference between friend and foe? Was it intimidating threats from the opposition, confusion, expediency, or sincere commitment that motivated many of the peasantry to act like our friends in the daylight, yet be our lethal adversaries in the dark?

I have described how and why our patrol boats stationed themselves at night along the north bank of the "Grand Canal" out of An Long and along the Vinh Te Canal in defensive positions called Waterborne Guard Posts. This was also happening in other canals and along the rivers' edges in many other places throughout IV Corps. However, it is quite another thing to take the reader out on one of those ambushes. Sleeping under the blazing tropical sun in daytime and standing watches at night was routine for the PBR, "Tango" Boat, and STAB crews during the periods they were "on the river" (meaning on patrol). This was what duty consisted of for one's year "in country." As an example, I will describe below what this was like for a typical PBR crew along the Cambodian border.

Each PBR had a crew of five. The bow of the boat was nuzzled in the mud against the north bank vegetation and under the cover of the jungle canopy. The dark green—almost black—color of the boats made them virtually invisible in the dark. When there was no moon, one maintained one's orientation by being seated in the forward gun tub with triggers at hand, by holding on to the controls of the boat or the radio mike, or by bracing oneself on part of the boat itself. Quiet was strictly maintained, with whispering kept to a minimum and for urgencies alone. Rarely the muted radio would report movement suspected by one of the other boats dispersed a "klick" apart, hiding at intervals along the canal. All members of the crew would listen intently for any movement in the underbrush, the snapping of a twig, a foot-fall near the bank, or anything out of the ordinary. Everyone would be on alert, sitting or standing like statues steeled against the threat of a lobbed hand grenade or the *whooshing* sound of an RPG (Rocket Propelled Grenade) flying out of nowhere. In the cold night air, bodies were poised to kill or be killed, frozen not so much against the chill as by the tenseness required to stay alert and alive and for mutual protection.

Each boat was equipped with a hand-held "Starlight Scope" which could turn a night field into a greenish-colored virtual day for the user. The Sailors would hand it off to one another to scan the surroundings, and for the diversion it provided. If it detected figures approaching from either side of the canal (but more likely from the Cambodian side), the Boat Captain would whisper map coordinates into the mike. This would inform the Squadron Commander in his boat, the other boats of the squadron, and the Area Commander in the "Charlie" Boat (CCB). But silence was kept with everyone at the ready until something or someone was in range of fire. Then all hell would break loose. If a large number of attackers were observed approaching, the boat would suddenly back out into the stream with the twin .50 calibers pouring hot lead from the forward gun tub in the direction of the assault. Every crewman would be firing, and neighboring boats would rush from hiding to assist—if ordered by radio to do so, so as to avoid a diversion. A patrolling "Seawolf" would be called in for an air strike, or the helos would be scrambled from a mother ship or barge.

It is not hard to understand why people in combat bond quickly, and usually that bond endures for a lifetime—certainly the memories do!

When I went on patrol, I stood watch with the others. With only five sets of eyes scanning for intruders and five sets of ears listening for them, another present to help was always welcome. One night when I rode one of the boats out of Vinh Gia, there was no moonlight to break the darkness. We all stood alert in our ambush position, watching and listening intently. I was standing on the steel engine cover aft of the canopy that shelters the boat's controls, yet forward of the rear gunner. Suddenly at my feet with a metallic clank something fell into the boat. The 19-year-old boat captain screamed "Grenade!" and fell on it to save my life and the life of his crew! Although we all wore flak jackets, he was willing to be blown to bits for us.

I wrote this Sailor up for the nation's highest honor, the Congressional Medal of Honor. In doing so, I should not have told the truth, and I chastise myself to this day that I did. When I returned to Sa Dec where I wrote my reports and sermons, I submitted the following words for his citation: "While serving as Boat Captain on Waterborne Guard Post in the darkness of the night, without thought for his own life and intending to save his crew, he spontaneously threw himself on a live *catfish.*" I never got a response of any kind from Saigon on that one. Good heavens! He was willing to give his life for mine and for the others. I should have lied to get him the recognition he deserved.

———

From May 9 to 18, 1970, the "Tango Boats" of River Assault Squadron Fifteen commanded by then-Lieutenant Commander Kennedy "J" Rhea, along with elements of River Assault Squadron Thirteen, received Orders to join Assault Task Force 211. ATF 211 provided escorts for five or six Viet Nam Navy LSTs summoned up the Mekong River to Phnom Penh, Cambodia, to rescue Vietnamese and ethnic Chinese refugees.

This was the first time Americans had clearance to enter Cambodia, and it came at the same time that our President had ordered limited operations inside the border with Laos to challenge the threats and supply lines along the Ho Chi Minh Trail to the west. These were areas that supported the enemy— but where we had not been allowed to reciprocate! However, our forces were forbidden to go beyond 21.5 miles into Cambodia. For us, that meant that our boats halted at a sunken ferry, the Mekong River crossing of Highway 1, at the village of Neak Luong. I stood with Commander Rhea and other dignitaries as we waited on shore in the village for a meeting with the Cambodia military commander. He arrived in a small helicopter. He addressed our group and made it very clear that Cambodia was a neutral nation, and, in the exact words conveyed by the translator: "My people want no part in your terrible war." Then he took his leave as quickly as he had come.

Why had we come into his "neutral nation?" Why were the LSTs manned by Vietnamese sailors transiting beyond that point in the wide river where we in U.S. Navy Mobile Riverine escort boats were obliged to wait for them to return down river? The evidence came floating by us, and lined some areas on the river's edge. *Life* magazine and CBS news reporters were there in that remote village to record and photograph this very sad story. Vietnamese and Chinese who lived and did business in Cambodia, and especially in the area of the capital city, were being slaughtered by soldiers and members of the Khmer Rouge in acts of racial and political "cleansing." Bodies of those our Task Force could not rescue floated by our boats, and we watched as packs of wild dogs devoured their remains along the shore.

An approximately fifteen-mile-wide corridor on the Cambodian side of the border we had been guarding from the Viet Nam side was controlled by

North Vietnamese forces, blocking the way of escape for refugees. We expected to be attacked by NVA land forces, rockets, or by artillery every inch of the way as we proceeded up the river—and on return, but evidently the string of big gray warships, for which we were a reaction force, served to intimidate the surrounding enemy. The expected attacks did not materialize.

The days and nights we stayed out in the big river after the LSTs proceeded on their own seemed to last forever. We awaited anxiously the results of their rescue operation amidst floating grim reminders of why they went beyond where we were ordered to stop. Then slowly downstream they came. Only two or three rockets had been fired at them during their transit beyond Neak Luong to Phnom Penh without our escorts. The big ships were loaded to the gunnels with people—reported by the media to be one hundred thousand refugees of all ages, children, adults, and old people alike. I am sure they had with them limited possessions, sewing machines, and just what they could carry.

A shout arose spontaneously from all our "Tango Boat" crews, and Commander Rhea ordered the boats together for a brief Communion service in thanksgiving for the success of the operation. Then we turned south to escort the slow heavily laden ships downstream through the enemy controlled corridor to safety.

I shall never forget Ken Rhea, his Executive Officer and their sailors for their desire to offer Eucharist to the Lord right where we were—on those "Tangos" gathered together in the middle of the Mekong in Cambodia. I shall always remember that sunny afternoon and the sight of those ships as they passed by with their human cargo.

———

At Phu Quoc Island in the Gulf of Thailand a short flight offshore from Ha Tien, we had Navy people and a support ship, but this was covered by other chaplains and was beyond my area of responsibility. However, I learned about the fishermen who sailed out of the Village of Duong Dong there in the early morning hours to make their daily catch.

As they passed the jetty and into the gulf that was given to sudden tempests with heavy seas, they viewed a statue of the Blessed Virgin blessing them, and they prayed for a safe trip and good fishing. On each side of the bows of these fishing boats, great eyes are painted. These eyes are there to scare away mythical denizens and evil spirits that could threaten their boats. So, if the blessing of the holy Saint or that of her Savior Son would not be sufficient protection, "the eyes would have it!"

Yes, there are very few atheists in foxholes or in river patrol boats, in combat aircraft or in ships-of-the-line that are at war. Some of us came home, and some of us did not. I held many memorial services on the ships, boats and berms of Viet Nam.

My prayer is that the Faith that we once shared in harm's way will have proven so sufficiently strong that it will have had lasting effects in our future voyages after we sailed away. Painted eyes on the sides of a junk "just in case," or equivalent talismans or superstitions acceptable in *our* culture are not required to protect us in times of peril or fear—if one's relationship with the Lord is strong. Christian worship is offered out of thanksgiving, not as payment in advance as a persuasion for God's favor. We already have that for the chosing at all times and in all places, in death as well as in life. This I know.

—St. Matthew 14:27–33; St. John 15:13–17;
Hebrews 13:12-16

CHAPTER EIGHT

Navy Ministry After Combat

After Action Report

Regardless of uncertain developments in the war itself, when I returned in May of 1970 after my second tour of duty in Viet Nam, I had the feeling that I had completed my work there as priest and chaplain. I did not have such a feeling of completion after the first tour of duty there. Perhaps this was because at the end of my first combat tour I went directly from the D.M.Z. to the hospital, where I was surrounded by combat casualties and immersed in their needs. Perhaps it was survivor-guilt. Perhaps it was the desire to fulfill a more positive mission with the Vietnamese people. Perhaps it was all of the above in combination. In any case, the Lord had Called me back to Viet Nam, and I had gone. And my second homecoming was accompanied by a feeling of satisfaction that, for me, the war was over and it was time to move on. Home at last!

There is always a reality that confronts one when moving from one world to another. Some call it "culture shock." After six-and-a-half years in the Philippines, two years in Viet Nam, and 14 months in a very preoccupying hospital ministry, I had been rather isolated from my own country in the cultures of Asia and of the military. I would be in for some unexpected surprises in the struggle to achieve an adjustment to my homecoming return to America.

It was expected upon this return that I would arrive on a specified scheduled flight. However, things got juggled in Saigon, and suddenly I had a chance to leave country two days ahead of my scheduled flight. It took me a split second to accept this opportunity, and just as suddenly, I was crowded into a seat of a Braniff chartered 707 racing down a runway at Tan Son Nhut.

My mind tingled as a plot evolved during the long flight. I would pick up my daughter from her fourth grade class at school, and we would surprise her mother at the apartment with an unscheduled arrival. I did not telephone home for a ride. The bus to the Oakland Army Base left Travis Air Force Base immediately after my flight arrived, and the driver let me out on San Pablo Avenue in El Cerrito about four blocks from the school that sunny morning. Karla was summoned to the Principal's Office, and we held hands and sang the song we had invented, "Up and down, and around and around," as we skipped merrily the few blocks that were the last leg of my year-long journey back to my front door.

At last I was home! We opened the door. Karla exclaimed: "Surprise!" Busily vacuuming the house, Marjorie had her hair in pin curls and was clad in a housecoat. She looked at me and said: "Well! If you were only a day later, I would have been ready."

—ECCLESIASTES 3:4f, 8

Welcome Aboard!

Following a month's leave, I reported for duty at the Naval Air Station in Alameda. I was the fifth chaplain assigned, but there were only offices for four. I was given a room in the Sunday School Building a block away from the chapel complex, because I was assigned the leadership responsibility for Protestant Christian Education. Later, with the rotation of one of the other chaplains to another duty station, I was given one of the regular chaplain's offices—but this was symbolic of things to come.

After two years of duty in which life and death were the concerns of each day and night, and fourteen months of hospital duty which gave proof to the urgency of those concerns, it became increasingly obvious to me that the chaplains at NAS Alameda were preoccupied with trivia and politics, to the detriment of the reasons for which the Chaplain Corps existed. This tour of duty would stand in stark contrast to the ministry in Viet Nam.

I was permitted to hold an Episcopal Communion service in the small chapel on Wednesday evenings, but if I would do more than preach on Sunday mornings, it would have to comply with the Baptist rites of the two Protestant Chaplains senior to me. In this regard, it was interesting to me that I was the only chaplain willing to conduct immersion baptisms, using the Baptistry Pool at a nearby Baptist Church. (Few Episcopalians know that this means of baptism is given a place of preference in the rubrics of the *Book of Common Prayer*.) I knew that the restrictions that confronted me in the Protestant Chapel program at NAS included blatant violations of the policies and the motto of the Chaplain Corps: "Cooperation without Compromise." But I was also aware that I was still adjusting from war, and, initially, I wanted to serve amicably on the team as best I could.

The Protestant Chaplain second senior to me on the staff had responsibilities for the decoration of the Main Chapel. In preparation for Christmas season, he *sternly ordered* me to arrange for the delivery of three dozen poinsettias and their placement at the unused Altar Rail and below the lectern and pulpit. I was glad to do this, and executed the order promptly.

After returning from two years of combat, I was rather amused by and partly smarting from the impersonal use of the chain of command to get things done. I felt that all that was necessary would have been a polite request, to which I would have complied. Nonetheless, the flowers were delivered and placed as commanded, without comment. Each day thereafter, this chaplain would pass by the open door of my office (now in the chaplains' complex) grumbling that no one would help him, as he carried water to those thirty-six poinsettia plants across the lawn in the Main Station Chapel. He never requested (or ordered) help. He just complained for all to hear. After they were finally removed at the close of the season, he rudely questioned me as to why I had not helped him. I responded that I had other responsibilities, and that he had not asked me for help. He grumbled again as he went on his way. I would have told him, if he had asked, that the plants that I had rented for him were all made of plastic, thus, irrigation and the guilt he tried to displace on me and others were entirely unnecessary.

—⁓—

As a priest of the Episcopal Diocese of California and a participant in the local gathering of Episcopal clergy called "The Clericus," I thought it would be polite to invite this group of twenty or so to a dinner at the Officers' Club as my guests. After dinner I proposed to show them a film, prepared by the Navy Chaplain Corps, which explained what chaplains did in combat and in the fleet. This motion picture was a 20-minute recruiting effort at a time when the Navy was very much in need of chaplains. The dinner was well attended, but the film met with cat calls and "boo" responses, which caught this host quite by surprise. This costly gesture had been offered as a courtesy and in friendship. It was also an attempt to explain my work in ministry to my colleagues. But the pacifist attitudes of my fellow clergy left me feeling rejected—if not despised.

—⁓—

The next story requires a brief digression to another time and place, to give some background that may enhance a better understanding of my dedication to Martin Luther King, Jr., and my motivation for supporting Navy and civilian commemorative events in his honor.

I was overseas during the great civil rights protests that began dramatic movement for equality for minorities in the United States. The overt segregation I witnessed while I was a Midshipman at the U.S. Merchant Marine Cadet School in Mississippi in 1948 and as a student at Tulane University in New Orleans in 1949-50, and the covert segregation we fought against when at Good Shepherd Mission in Berkeley, California, had been challenged during our absence from the country by many champions and martyrs.

While serving on the chaplaincy staff at the National Naval Medical Center in Bethesda, Maryland, I received my first installment of lessons in recent American history that would only receive my full attention after my return from the Mekong Delta.

In the late winter and spring of 1968, Dr. King proposed to lead a "Poor People's March" on Washington, D.C. The clergy of my denomination were divided about this— some very supportive, some staunchly opposed. The Very Reverend Francis B. Sayres, Dean of the National (Episcopal) Cathedral of Saint Peter and Saint Paul, called for a meeting of the clergy of the Diocese of Washington in the crypt of the cathedral to discuss this diversity and search for a common reception for the march. In an attempt to break a stalemate at that meeting, I suggested that Dr. King be invited to take the pulpit of the cathedral to explain his objectives. This was met with a consensus by the assembled clergy, and Dr. King accepted this offer.

The lengthy sermon he gave on March 31st, the Fifth Sunday in Lent 1968, was his last Sunday sermon. He was killed the following Thursday. From our suburban street, Marjorie and I watched smoke fill the sky as the rage in reaction to Dr. King's death and frustration over the March moved people to destroy properties around 14th Street in Washington. Had we been in Manila, we would have been on the fire lines rescuing the innocent. We felt completely helpless, but there was not a thing that we could do but pray. I have always been deeply saddened that Dr. King's prophetic voice was silenced, but grateful that I had a small hand in bringing him to the pulpit of the National Cathedral in our last opportunity to hear his message. I am dedicated to preserving his mission and memory.

—*ᐁᐁ*—

January 15, 1971, the birthday of the late Reverend Dr. Martin Luther King, Jr., was an observance of growing prominence in the United States. Some representatives of the military community at NAS Alameda and civilian workers from the Naval Aircraft Rework Facility (NARF) approached me about having a commemoration of the event in the chapel. I agreed, and, having informed the Command Chaplain of this interest, I proceeded to help develop a plan for the service. One person would read a poem, another would sing King's favorite hymn, "Precious Lord," and I was to participate. We projected an hour-long noonday service on the Monday date of his birth.

When word was passed of this service, the Navy Commanding Officer of NARF, a tenant command on the Air Station, demanded that it not take place. "I would have to lose work time from a huge roster of personnel, and that would cost the government thousands of dollars," I was told. I asked that the Command Chaplain respond through the chain-of-command that this would occur during the lunch period; further, that happy workers would be better workers, and that the government would ultimately win from their investment of interest in their people. The Naval Air Station Commanding Officer remained neutral. The other chaplains gave me no support whatsoever.

On the Wednesday before King's birthday, the illuminated reader boards at the entrances to the base announced the service for noon the following Monday. The "fat was in the fire," and "the world" seemed to be against me. But some lovely folks wanted this memorial, and I thought they had a right to it. Assuming NAS Command's approval (without being told "No!" when all echelons had been properly informed) it *would* take place.

On the very next day, an ALNAV (All Navy message) was received at every Navy and Marine Corps command throughout the world, ordering a commemoration of Martin Luther King's birthday. The message specified that appropriate memorial services would be held. We were ready! None of the other chaplains attended. They walked by the door on their way to the Officer's Club for drinks and lunch. But 1,100 others came to crowd the chapel and the lawns outside.

Some years later, a State of California Assemblyman by the name of Elihu Harris passed a bill that proclaimed King's Birthday a statewide holiday. He later became Mayor of Oakland. Elihu had been a Sunday School "scholar" and an Acolyte as a boy during my tenure as Vicar of the Church of the Good Shepherd in West Berkeley. We were still on the same track!

—St. Matthew 13:57

How the Flight Line Ministry Came to Be at NAS

The chaplains who went to the Officers' Club that Monday in January 1971 were observing a sinister daily ritual. Two things were understood in our department. First, the Command Chaplain, a Roman Catholic Priest and Captain in the Navy Chaplain Corps, had an alcohol problem. Second, the next in line to head the department, a Protestant Chaplain Commander, would have enjoyed succeeding him.

Their daily noonday errand took them to the bar before lunch, where at least three other chaplains would take turns buying drinks for the senior. I was astonished at this intrigue, which was openly discussed in staff meetings when the Command Chaplain was absent. The scheme eventually yielded the desired results, in that the "number two" chaplain really controlled the department, leaving the Command Chaplain as a benign but dependent figurehead. After I had left the command, it was reported that our alcoholic senior, while serving on a promotion selection board in Washington, suffered a case of delirium tremors and was transferred to a rehabilitation center.

I wanted no part of this plot. I saw it as evil, and certainly unworthy of our Calling. As the junior in rank on the staff, I correctly assumed that my lines for communicating any protest were blocked. I refused to lunch with the others.

With the invitation and to the delight of the Electronic Countermeasures Air Wing (VAQW-13) Commander and the C.O. of the Transport Squadron (VR-30) housed in the two main hangars on the flight line, I decided to relocate. The VAQ Squadrons were deploying Detachments on carriers and flying over Viet Nam at the time, and I felt a vital kinship with them. I emptied my desk into several shopping bags, and, with the titular approval of the Command Chaplain, I moved my office to a room over the "tin-benders" shop in the middle of Hangar 40. One of the enlisted personnel proudly installed a sign of his own devising over my new door at the top of the outside stairs: "CHAPLIN." I kept this marker in place as long as I occupied the space. (If that word were ever to have been spelled correctly, I would not have thought that I was in the U.S. Navy.)

As often as possible, I would be present at morning personnel musters, rotating through the six squadrons, where I was expected to offer a morning prayer. I would then make the rounds of the shops, offices, and hangars. I had other duties on the base as well, such as the Sunday School, but the hangars were where I felt the most valued, and where most of the counseling and confidences were shared.

For example, Commanding Officers expected my presence in their offices privately to plea bargain for an errant sailor after a Captain's Mast, when they knew the punishment they had meted out had been too severe. When one of their sailors was in trouble with civil authorities or had a problem at home, they knew I would follow up promptly as a pastor, and that I would keep them informed. Occasionally I would occupy the third seat on an A-3 training flight, and I took leave to make a cross-country flight with one of the skippers who needed his hours in the aircraft. He ferried me, so that I would attend a December 1971 reunion at the Naval Academy of officers with whom I had served in the Mekong Delta.

—JEREMIAH 23:23-32; ST. MATTHEW 4:10f; ST. MARK 4:3-9

Addiction on Our Watch:
Fact or Fantasy?

*I*t was evident in these opening years of the 1970s in Alameda that the Haight-Ashbury district in San Francisco and Berkeley were magnets for young service men and women on liberty. The Air Station command was in strict denial that there existed any problem with drug abuse on NAS Alameda. However, Electronic Countermeasures Air Wing 13 squadrons and Transport Squadron 30, which were the primary organizations to which I was ministering on the flight line, were quite alert to the narcotics problem.

One sailor returning from liberty walked into a spinning airplane propeller. Shortly thereafter, a toddler in enlisted housing, the child of one of the squadron families, drank from a glass mistakenly believing it to contain water—but which held mescaline instead. After a prolonged yet successful struggle to keep that child alive, and following a toxicology report, a Captain's Mast was held and disciplinary action was initiated following civil action.

The VAQ Wing Commander approached me and pleaded for help with the escalating problem of substance abuse among military personnel and their families. Together with the Human Resources Management Center on base, we created what was a pioneering effort in the Navy—an in-patient alcohol and drug rehabilitation facility at NAS Alameda. I took a two-week training-certification course, held at Mills College in Oakland, which was given by a team from the National Institute of Mental Health in Bethesda, Maryland.

Our treatment unit, headed by a junior commissioned officer and two very able petty officers, provided a 30-day diversion program followed by a client evaluation. We then recommended either return to duty, discharge, or (in rare cases) additional treatment.

I recall vividly, during an evaluation interview following treatment, the response of one sailor to the panel. I asked him: "Now that you are off heroin, what do you do instead?" In all innocence, he responded promptly: "Oh, I screw alot." This sailor had really come a long way, but we had contributed all that we could to the betterment of his life. Obviously, in his case, the task was not complete, but we had to understand that progress is to be attained one step at a time. He went back to the fleet, and we had to be satisfied with commending him prayerfully into the Lord's Hands for further development.

—ST. MARK 1:27

Christ or Comfortable Career?

The air wing and squadrons were considered tenant commands. Although I was loaned to them informally, I was still under the Naval Air Station Command and answerable to the "non-functioning" Command Chaplain.

In this situation, as I suggested before, influence came up, rather than down the chain-of-command. Evaluation of our project to curb addictions had to pass through my chaplain superiors whose influence was having a deleterious effect on the alcoholic Command Chaplain. At Fitness Report time, my report was written in the Chaplain's Office as unsatisfactory and sent up the chain to the base commander, where it received "rubber stamped" approval. Simultaneous Fitness Reports were sent independently by the four squadron commanders and forwarded through the Air Wing Commander. There was a movement to quash my next orders to graduate school instruction. However, the Orders had been confirmed, and I left NAS shortly thereafter for my year of study.

I was in a moral dilemma in that command, but I never doubted the righteousness of my stand. I kept plowing forward against adversity as I would have against an enemy in armed combat. In the midst of this, the parish where I had been Seminarian Intern, then a year later had served as Curate (as a deacon and newly ordained priest), honored me with a definite invitation to become their rector.

Marjorie and I were disillusioned with the Navy at this point, and we envisioned my having a position where our family would always be together, and where my children would always have easy access to their father. This prospect was very appealing! We were the guests of the Vestry of Saint Peter's Parish in Redwood City, and at this meeting actually accepted their offer to serve there.

On returning home that night, neither of us slept a wink. On the one hand we were loved and respected in that parish, and our life there would have been much easier. On the other hand, we were in the midst of a battle with Satan, and I knew I had not finished a hard job I felt I had been Called to complete. We could not turn away from it. I called the next day, to the surprise and disappointment of all involved, and reversed our decision. It was one of the hardest things I have ever had to do in the support of my conscience, my God, and "my Navy."

—◦◦◦◦—

I began the process of appealing to the Board for the Correction of Naval Records, petitioning to have expunged from my records in Washington the evaluations written by the NAS Chaplain and signed by the Commanding Officer of the base. These records determine eligibility for promotion and retention in the Naval Service.

As a first requirement, I travelled to pay a courtesy call on the then-retired former Air Station Commanding Officer at his home. I informed him that I would be appealing his evaluation, and gave him opportunity to submit a corrected report. He curtly refused, but at least I could check that task off the list required for the appeal.

Former aircraft squadron commanders (one an Admiral selectee) and the Air Wing Commander, were well aware of the situation at the Naval Air Station, and they were grateful for the support I had provided them. Every one of them provided strong correspondence in my favor—as did other officers who were familiar with my work. After the year of postgraduate study and during my tour of duty at the San Diego Naval Training Center, the Commander selection list was published. My name was not on it. The findings of the Board for the Correction of Naval Records were not yet complete. This agonizing process of appeal would take over four years!

Months after settling in the Department of Defense Housing, Finegayan, Guam, at 3:30 in the early morning, the telephone at our bedside awakened us with a start. It was a female voice who identified herself as a secretary in the Office of the Secretary of the Navy in Washington, D.C. The findings were out. My appeal was *upheld!*

This ended a four-year heart-wrenching struggle for me and for my family. My integrity had been recognized. I was—at that instant—a Commander in the Chaplain Corps of the United States Navy! I was not considered to have been "passed over," the lady reported. According to her, the Secretary of the Navy had said: "That chaplain *was right!,*" and asked that he convey his apologies for what I had endured. The Navy was apologizing to me!

The following day I was the honored guest of the Submarine Squadron Commodore in his Stateroom. The Commanding Officer of the tender USS *Proteus,* in which I was embarked, and several of the submarine commanding officers I served, were present. Marjorie pinned the new silver oak leaves on my uniform, and there was a round of applause. But in my heart and mind this was no ordinary promotion. This was a moral victory in a crusade for Christ. I believe that the Chaplain Corps and the entire United States Navy had won that battle, as well.

After the ceremony my mind was spinning, so I noticed nothing out of the ordinary when I left the ship. I escorted Marjorie to our car on the dock; then I returned to the ship, ascending the officer's gangway. At the brow, as usual, I turned to salute the National Ensign. But then the Quarterdeck was called to attention to acknowledge the approach of a senior officer. I stood aside and went to a brace awaiting such a personage. The Officer of the Deck walked from his post quietly to my side and whispered: "Sir, that is for you!" I came aboard to a smiling assemblage. What a day that was in the life of a chaplain!

—I Samuel 17:37, 45, 50; St. Matthew 5:1–14

Of Peace, War, and Freedom

*M*y interlude between two combat tours was as a chaplain on the staff of the National Naval Medical Center in Bethesda. This was when I first became aware of the political climate in the United States concerning the Viet Nam War; but it made little impact on me. I was preoccupied with ministering to combat casualties, patients and their families, and counseling medical personnel who were anxious about the possibility of being ordered to Viet Nam. I was too busy to deal with political debates outside the hospital setting.

As a pastor, the first time I was really confronted with the diversity of convictions over the war was when I had completed my tour in the Mekong Delta and had returned to California for duty at the Alameda Naval Air Station.

The Navy had changed its requirements regarding Conscientious Objectors, by which such a claim by a service member no longer resulted in an automatic discharge. In some ways these changes eased the ability to attain Conscientious Objector status. There were several additional categories by which some could be assigned to noncombatant duties, which could include medical corpsmen billets with the Marine Corps or with in-shore patrol boat squadrons, which were still potentially hazardous.

To complicate matters, this Air Station was just across the bay from the Haight-Ashbury "hippie ghetto," and just south of the University of California at Berkeley, which were hotbeds of political agitation at the time. All the Bay Area cities sprouted pacifist counseling centers, and many of the churches joined that parade.

Suddenly I found myself drowning in claims for the new status by service members, most of whom had been well coached. Having just returned from two combat tours for which I had volunteered, I had to get my own mind straight on this very human issue. I had to transcend any internal conflicts of my own that might impede pleas for justice by those I had been ordained and commissioned to serve. I had gone to Viet Nam as a priest, and I believed God had Called me there to care for those in the midst of the conflict, not to bless war. I loved Asia and I held no enmity toward any of the people of Asia. But when one is on a battlefield, within gun range of its shores, or in the air above it, enemies fade into causes when one is striving to stay alive.

No citizen of our country who voted and paid taxes was exempt from responsibility for this fight, and even as a "noncombatant," neither was I. At the time I thought that those who left the United States over this issue, intending not to return, were perhaps the only protestors who acted with consistency. However, without a doubt, our body-politic was failing to listen to our people, with the predictable result that many became angry and out of patience.

Although I believed at first that our involvement was truly a "rescue mission," I also knew from history that we were mired in issues that were ancient and far beyond our control. I came to believe that both sides in this conflict were pawns in a contest for dominance between East and West.

Having returned from two years of armed conflict and having put hundreds of young Americans in body bags, I had to deal with my own emotions. Intellectually I could accept the fact that if we were fighting for freedom for the Vietnamese people, then our own people should enjoy the freedom to express their convictions as well. I had to get this message from my head into my heart!

The new regulations delegated chaplains as primary evaluators of the religious and ethical convictions of applicants, to sort out the *conscientious* objectors from the *unconscientious* objectors. The issue here was that the fakes were not being fair to the true ones, and the true Conscientious Objectors needed me to defend their rights. As an instrument of freedom, *I had to have my mind straight on this matter,* so that I could be objective and fair for each person I would interview.

Voluminous documentation was required in the case of each applicant, and multiple personal references were required. I spent hours pouring over the new directives, and more hours studying the doctrines and the latitudes allowed by various denominations. Each applicant's papers had to be examined with a clear heart and an open mind.

For example, one applicant, a Member of the Church of Jesus Christ of Latter Day Saints, wanted out of the Navy on *religious* grounds (moral grounds were also acceptable). I confirmed my research with his Bishop. There is no provision for this status in that Church, which requires of its Members patriotic attitudes and lauds those who serve in the military. I gave his bid a negative endorsement. I may have learned more about his faith than he had in the process.

I believed profoundly that the sacrifices we were making in Southeast Asia were for the defense of freedom there. Therefore, it was up to me to guard that freedom at home as though I were on a crusade. As a decorated Viet Nam veteran, I became an expert counselor of Conscientious Objector applicants, leaving no stone unturned to examine and guide them in righteous directions in their appeals. I saw my efforts as a tribute to those who served on all the battlefields of our country's history.

— ST. LUKE 6:35f; COLOSSIANS 3:12–17

Getting to Know You

I had returned twice from Viet Nam to an awaiting family. I left on my first tour when my son, Lester III, had just entered the world. Each day apart from him, I watched the calendar and wondered about how he was growing. For example, my reflections were still fresh of the night when he was exactly nine months old, during which we assaulted Hill 22 in darkness. The companies of our battalion were separated by the enemy in a hail of blue-green tracers, incoming mortar rounds killed 23 of our wounded, and grenades came at us—like the one that gave me pain and a Purple Heart.

I celebrated his first birthday in the adjutant's tent at Cam Lo. Some

Marines, hearing me talk about my son, surprised me by fabricating a birthday cake of their collected individual C-ration pound cakes pressed together with one Vietnamese candle in the center of it. Raucous voices were lifted in strains of "Happy Birthday to you"—baby boy in a photograph.

When I returned from that time with Marine Infantry, he was still a toddler, and my stay was not long. But after I came back from the Mekong Delta, when I really came to live "at his house," for a while he must have wondered who I was and what I was doing there with his mother and big sister.

A parent who must be away from his wife and children involuntarily for an extended period of time not only longs for them, but hungers deeply for their affection and expressions of it. When I returned the second time, Lester was four. Fathers who exist mostly in photographs are ideal, because they never intrude or offend. They just stand there erect, witnessing what everyone else is doing. But the photograph came to life, and this time my son was old enough to see the idol fall.

It became specific one night when he had been acting up, and I was destined to become "the bad guy" as the parent appointed to administer the discipline. As I recall, his day ended abruptly with a spanking and by being put to bed. In his anger and tears he cried out as I left his darkened room: "I love you, *but I don't like you!*" My heart ached at the price I had to pay that night for doing "what had to be done"—my share of what Marjorie had been required to do alone for most of his first few years of life. After a while, the crying subsided and he became calm. I tiptoed back into his room, knelt down, and quietly kissed his forehead. After a moment of silence, he conceded: "Now I love you and I like you."

I have always remembered that step in our reunion process, and, with it, the wisdom of childhood. If the difference between "loving" and "liking" were more commonly recognized in our culture, there would be fewer family heartbreaks, separations, and divorces, and there would be more lasting friendships in this world. To allow oneself the luxury of not having to like everything in those we love is to exercise a flexibility in relationships that can make them more realistic and more accepting.

My son had seen photographs of his father in greens, helmet, and flak jacket, in the jungle and riding on tanks. Now assigned to the Naval Air Station in Alameda, I came home from the chaplain's office at the base in service dress blues or tropical white uniform. On Sundays I was usually to be seen in clerical suit and collar. In December of 1971, I flew in an A-3 with Commander Bardecki, the Commanding Officer of VAQ-135, on a cross-country high altitude flight. Marjorie picked me up at the flight line. I was still in my flight gear, carrying my parachute bag and my aviator's helmet (decorated with squadron insignia). I was tired after the long haul, and I was glad to cross the threshold of our home in El Cerrito. As I entered the house, Lester came running, and when he saw me he was obviously startled. In all sincerity and almost frightened, he looked up at me and asked: "Who are you today, Daddy?"

―――――

In the spring of 1976, we were living in San Diego on Narragansett Street on the very summit of the Point Loma ridge. Young Lester was nine years old. We agreed to take an extended bicycle ride together on one of those sunny Saturday afternoons when the refreshing wind swept up from Ocean Beach, a day just right for such an outing. From the location of our house, we could ride the western half-length of Point Loma's crest, mostly up hill on Catalina Boulevard, with a termination point at the Cabrillo Monument. Then we could enjoy the pleasure of coasting downhill all the way home. The alternative for the ride was to coast through a circuitous route of a cross-hatch of residential streets on the ocean side of the hill, all downward into Ocean Beach. Then we could bike across the park on flat land into Mission Beach, traverse the long paved beach walk, and return.

I presented the first route to my son. As I reflect on it, my comfort with it must have been based upon the Puritan work ethic which I inherited from my hard-working parents. Namely, if we pedal uphill to the monument on the way out, then we would have *earned* the pleasure of coasting home on the way back. My youngster strongly disagreed. He advocated the route of coast now, pay later. I argued that once we had expended all our efforts riding to the bottom of the hill then across to Mission Beach and back, we (I) would be too tired to pull up the long steep Narragansett Street to our house at the end of the ride. He won the debate. We coasted back and forth along the sloping streets on the Ocean Beach side of Point Loma. Then we zoomed across the flat parkway into Mission Beach to the north. The beach walkway was a delight on that sunny, windy day, and the hot dogs we consumed on a vendor's bench at our chosen turnaround were delicious adjuncts to the excursion we shared. I must confess, however, that the climb back up the long hill had dominated my thoughts throughout the ride, not just as we turned homeward.

Finally we reached Ocean Beach and the bottom of the forbidding climb. A rest stop at a gas station was in order. I was panting from pedaling fast enough to keep up with my boy, and I welcomed a recess before tackling the incline that was now in sight and our next objective. "Gimme a dime, please Daddy. Gimme a dime?" he asked. Thinking he was going to buy candy (which a dime could do in those days!), I shelled out the ten-cent coin. He returned from his brief errand smiling. "What's up?" I asked. "Well, I just called home, and Mom will be right down with the station wagon to pick us up, and the bikes too." "Smarty!" I responded. The little guy had won again.

This is not just an illustration of the generation gap, but of a gap that can widen when a father is absent from his family—either geographically or due to a preoccupation with his endeavors. Certainly this represents a hazard to a pastor's family, even when the church is nearby. Somehow during my career through the years that demanded some absences and many departures, the "little Man-of-the-House" became more competitor than buddy. It is a father's expectation and his fondest hope that his children will surpass him in every way. Such succession provides him with assurance that his life has had meaning, and that he has left the world a better place than it was when he entered it.

My son Lester and his family have made their home in the interior of Alaska, where he has found joy and the freedom of an unlimited frontier.

He delivered one of his children in his home without the aid of midwife or maternity ward. I rejoice in the fact that he truly is a better father than I ever was. He rarely writes or calls, but paid us a visit on Mother's Day in May of 2000.

The chill thaws gradually as our years advance in number. He has his own life now, his own growing family, and a developing career. I miss him very much, and I am very proud of him. I think he would like to teach me to take more risks and to live more by my wits. I would like to teach him to live more cautiously and to plan more for the future. I think we are both right. His wife told us that even after growing up in the Church, he had found the Lord "in his own way." I am glad that he has. Indeed, if we are to meet the Lord it has to be that way, because that must be uniquely personal for each of us.

No one can put the pages back on our calendars after the years have passed. As I think of my son, I shall always long for him to be close, just as I did on his first birthday. I hear his searching words echo in my soul: "Who are you today, Daddy?" And once again I hear a small boy say: "Now I love and I like you." I do pray that those words still ring true. Both my son and I are victims of Viet Nam and my absence in the fleet. The bonding in early and formative years evidently never developed as it might have. When on shore, I watched my young catcher on the Little League fields, but I was not there to teach him to walk or to shave. He reached out to surrogates to fill such voids in his life.

The wakeful night I spent discerning with Marjorie that God was Calling us to remain in the Navy Chaplain Corps and fight for its integrity, rather than to accept the loving invitation of Saint Peter's Parish in Redwood City (just across the street from Sequoia High School where my children would have attended), still haunts me. However, the alternate choice could have had the same result. Even if I had been rector of a local parish, I could have been so involved with the lives of others that my own family would have become emotionally neglected.

I am aware of what my absences cost my family, but I am also sure in my heart that we agreed to accept the Greatest Commission of all: "Follow Me."

Of all of the sacrifices involved in answering God's Call to ministry and of all of the wounds of war, longing for my son has been the most lasting and painful for me.

—Genesis 22:1–18; St. Matthew 19:29; St. Luke 2:34f

Unfinished Business

My experiences at the Naval Air Station, Alameda caused me to view politics in ministry much as I had the enemy in Viet Nam—lethal. But I was also aware that there were matters in my own life that needed resolving after two years in the combat arena.

During two visits to my adult daughter Karla who lives in the Washington, D.C. area, I had refused her invitations to view the Viet Nam Memorial Wall. On my third visit, she literally made me go there with her. I traced names on the wall like Swigart, Anderson, and some others who had been friends during each tour "in-country." It was a gut-wrenching experience for me, but Karla knew it was something I had delayed too long.

The second symptom which signalled that I needed to settle things was an abiding feeling of guilt that I had left Corporal John Ray Phillips, the Marine Clerk who had served with me with such loyalty during my time with the infantry, on the slopes of Con Thien without so much as a chance to thank him and say goodbye. Every attempt to locate him through the military failed after he had left the Marine Corps. The only identification I had for him was his full name and his old service number given before Social Security Numbers were used as military serial numbers. (A civilian search located him in November of 2000.)

At home, I had much to learn to be a father to three children, two of whom were really new to me upon my return, as well as to be a more appreciative and patient husband to the wife I loved so dearly. These needs are all too typical for returning veterans. The only observable residual I had retained from combat was a startle reaction that was triggered when I was awakened from a nap or sleep. If I were disturbed at such a time, my instantly jumping to my feet was disconcerting to the children.

—〰〰〰—

The Navy granted my request for a tour of "Duty under Instruction." Under the supervision of the Naval Postgraduate School in Monterey, I was assigned to the course I had requested at the San Francisco (Presbyterian) Theological Seminary in San Anselmo, California. I pursued a Master of Arts Degree in Pastoral Psychology, with adjunct study at the Family Therapy Institute of Marin and an internship at McAuley Neuropsychiatric Institute of Saint Mary's Medical Center in San Francisco.

I have always held the conviction that a minister must also be a professional when it comes to counseling, because lives of individuals and entire families can depend on what transpires in the counseling room or in the pastor's office. Therefore, as a clergyman, I felt the need of solid education in that field and an awareness of the standards required of those licensed in this profession—even though, as a minister, I was exempt from the oversight of the State or from having to answer to the standards of any professional counseling association.

As I studied psychotherapy and family systems and I practiced counseling in my internship, simultaneously I was gaining new self-understanding and healing from unresolved stresses of war. I assimilated the lessons of this year like a starving soul who had been granted a horn of plenty.

My greatest learning for clinical practice was that of being immediately in touch with my feelings when dealing with counseling clients. In combat, one learns to defer feelings in order to act on the moment. To be overcome by feelings would be a great liability under fire. Posttraumatic stress develops from delaying or denying one's emotional reactions to an encounter with danger or to witnessing one without the ability to resolve it in one's mind. But in order to survive under fire, a soldier must deal with his reactions to threats and traumatic experiences only after the danger has subsided. Some never do, so the stress only intensifies in the unconscious mind.

In stark contrast to this, I learned that a counselor or psychotherapist must know his or her feelings in response to the client in an interview—at the very moment of the interaction with the one being counseled. The ability of the minister/counselor to know what is going on in his/her own *simultaneous* emotional responses to the client yields clues that can be "read" and explored. These clues may interpret the behavior of the counselee to the counselor. This is a major instrument of the therapeutic process. It took me almost two years to make the adjustment from delaying the perception of my emotions, as was necessary in combat, to recognizing them at the instant I was experiencing them.

The Navy allowed me an extension of studies through the summer months that followed the awarding of the Master's Degree. This, plus previous practicum courses I had taken, allowed me to complete the residency course requirements for the Doctor of Ministry Degree. Following some additional studies and the completion and acceptance of an original Dissertation/Project, which took another year, I was awarded this degree as well.

Prior to attending postgraduate school (but in preparation for my plan to do doctoral research on the family reunions of prisoners of war and their homecomings) I attended the Navy's Survival, Evasion, Resistance and Escape (SERE) school—"evasion of capture and POW prep school."

In order to attend this training on a voluntary basis, my previous command required that I do it on regular leave. This experience was arranged for me by Commander Russell E. McJunkin, Jr., Director of the Survival Training Department, Fleet Aviation Specialized Operational Training Group, Pacific. He fully understood my motivation, and he acknowledged that I was surely the first to undergo this training *on leave*. Thus, my entire Master studies were aimed in the direction of my reseach in regard to our prayed-for POW returns.

My second goal for additional education was to continue my pursuit of understanding my own country and overcoming the reverse cultural shock I was experiencing after returning from years overseas as a missionary and as a chaplain. I had lived in the Philippines for six-and-a-half years and in Viet Nam for two. My only visits to the United States were given to language studies during missionary days and to 14 months of hospital ministry with little awareness or involvement outside it.

When at NAS Alameda, I encountered a youth culture and new political struggles that were initially mystifying to me. I had to understand my own country so that I could minister to her people—especially her young people. Thus, while in postgraduate studies, I elected courses in contemporary developments in matters such as race relations, drug and alcohol rehabilitation, and "New Age" spirituality and meditation. I even sat "zazen" with young commuters in three-piece suits at a Marin County Buddhist monastery—in my search more for an understanding of the temporal than for the eternal.

Patricia Jones, Licensed Clinical Social Worker (LCSW), had been my supervisor at the McAuley Institute in San Francisco. By special arrangement with the seminary and with her gracious acceptance, she became my Graduate Advisor for the preparation of the doctoral dissertation. I chose a topic which was timely and never previously attempted. In addition to learning acquired in the academic curriculum, I would be able to apply the lessons I had learned from combat, from being an absent father and husband, and from my life in Asia, to help others.

My next duty would be in San Diego where I would be expected to contribute to the Navy what I had learned in postgraduate studies. During that year I shared and learned a great deal from a voluntary liaison with the joint services Center for Prisoner of War Studies on Point Loma, in addition to my primary duties at the Naval Training Center and its counseling programs. My informal association with the Center for POW Studies was made possible by the Director, John A. Plag, Ph.D., of the Navy Medical Neuropsychiatric Research Unit in San Diego, and by Captain Hamilton I.

McCubbin, D.S.W., of the Army Medical Service Corps. My studies and my contribution were prior to and in preparation for "Operation Homecoming."

The topic of my dissertation was: "Manual for Ministry to Prisoner of War Returnees and their Families in the Long-term Readjustment Period." The Manual was a practical 72-page compilation of suggestions for the professionals who would be advising these reuniting families, and it included problems to expect and ways to help. The Manual was designed for easy reading and ready reference without footnotes. The dissertation that accompanied the Manual was 183 pages of heavily documented reasons for every detail presented in the Manual. Bound copies were placed in the library archives of the Navy Postgraduate School and of the San Francisco Theological Seminary. It was stated that this was the first time theological-based pastoral contributions had been made to POW research! The ministry of God has relevance to all of life, and into every journey taken by His Children.

—◊◊◊—

When I graduated from the seminary with the Master of Arts in Pastoral Psychology in June of 1973, some of the other graduates appeared in skeleton costumes, protesting the war in Viet Nam. One would be crazy to like war, but as a veteran who volunteered to serve his country in a priestly way, I found this to be inappropriate behavior for the seminary's graduation ceremony. I resolved that rather than appearing in clerical garb when I completed my doctorate, I would do it differently than at the awarding of my Master's Degree. A year later, when I received my doctoral hood, it was over my dress white uniform adorned with full medals. I wanted the seminarians and the professors to know that I was indeed a minister, a Minister in Uniform—proud to be in the uniform of his country.

—EZRA 5:15f; 6:16; ROMANS 8:35–39

Therapy is Ministry, and Ministry is Therapy

*I*n Biblical (*Koine* or "common") Greek, the word "therapy" is properly translated into English as "to serve, to minister, to worship" and "to heal, cure, restore to health."★

That is what Jesus did, and what He sent His ordained followers into the world to do in His Name. The Navy had given me an education to develop my skills in counseling and therapy. I benefited greatly from this, and I trust my ministry has benefited as well.

Following my year in postgraduate studies, I was excited to be sent to the Naval Training Center (NTC) in San Diego to contribute the expertise I had gained. This once-massive educational complex included boot camp and the technical training schools for those who qualified for one of a great variety of jobs beyond initial navy orientation. NTC personnel included not only the transient Recruits and those under additional instruction, but also instructors, administrators, and those of some tenant commands.

My initial assignment was to relieve Chaplain Philip Jerauld at the "Contact Center." This counseling center had a three-fold mission as a drop-in for students and staff: to provide counsel and advice in matters of race relations and conflict, to address drug and alcohol problems, and to offer individual and family counseling. It was my task to develop the latter area, and to provide supervision and training for the twenty-one enlisted counselors in the other two divisions. A Lieutenant (junior grade) was the administrator, and a Civil Service secretary was the receptionist and provided office support.

Because of my identified subspecialty as a professional in the counseling field, I was in demand for special projects for the Recruit Training Command, Service School Command, and the Administrative Command. For example, I was able to research and correct causes which had led to courts–martial for some Company Commanders for maltreatment of Recruits.

It was here at NTC and in the Contact Center that I was able to exercise new counseling skills. Lieutenant Commander Arthur D. Garfein, M.D.,

Medical Corps, Center Psychiatrist, consented to be a consultant and my supervisor for the purpose of licensing with the State of California. I learned a great deal from him, and I was able to qualify for the 3000 hours of supervised counseling required prior to applying for examinations for a State of California professional license as Marriage, Family and Child Counselor (now known as Marriage and Family Therapist).

The San Diego branch of the California School of Professional Psychology assigned advanced students to perform internships with me. All of them were experienced in the field of psychology and had Master's Degrees. Most were in their final year of studies for the degree of Doctor of Psychology. We tackled difficult and often deployment-related problems in conjoint family sessions. Because those who were sent by the school were women, we commonly used male-female co-therapy teams to do the counseling. We enjoyed great popularity throughout the entire San Diego military complex, and some prospective clients were obliged to place themselves on our waiting list.

I established a training conference which I had hoped to conduct annually. Initial contact through the School of Nursing, Department of Psychiatry of the University of Nevada, Reno, was made with the late Virginia M. Satir of Palo Alto, California. She collaborated with me for a period of two years, and she was the primary presenter at the first conference held on the sound stage of the tenant Naval Radio and Television Production Command at the Naval Training Center.

Virginia worked several days with selected Navy families to demonstrate her methods before some eighty military psychiatrists, psychologists, physicians and chaplains. I was transferred before the second planned conference could take place.

My work was delightful as a professional supervisor for the senior petty officers who served as counselors at the Contact Center. These persons had a sense of mission, they were effective in their desire to help those who came to them for discussion or for help, and they knew the areas in which they were assigned to function. We held "Grand Rounds" once a week, during which cases were discussed in a closed-door confidential session. During these sessions we all helped each other.

I recall an inquiry during "Grand Rounds" when one of our stocky bearded petty officer counselors disclosed that a young sailor was constantly seeking assistance at unscheduled times, such as lunch hour or after closing time. As the counselor related this and questioned how he might better handle the situation, the rest of the crew remained quiet. Suddenly, a light of recognition came to him. After a moment of awkward silence, the man blurted out: "My God, I think he has 'a thing' for me." After group laughter, in a serious manner we tackled how that student-sailor might be questioned, helped, and advised.

The Contact Center had advisory responsibilities for the several commands in the area of race relations. By now, the celebration of the Birthday of the Reverend Dr. Martin Luther King, Jr. had become an All-Navy evolution. We designed an event which would begin at the Recruit Training Command (RTC) with a muster on the "grinder" (parade field). Then, with our staff and volunteers from Service School Command (SSC), we would hold a march through SSC streets to the Technical Training Building. There, King's "Letter from a Birmingham Jail" was to be read. A large picture of Dr. King would be carried at the head of the marchers by four sailors: one Asian, one Hispanic, one Black and one Caucasian— demonstrating that King's dream included all of us.

The Reverend Ralph Abernathy agreed to come and address a memorial service when the march arrived at South Chapel. There has been a growing trend in the military (and throughout the country) to make Dr. King's Day celebrations essentially Black events. This is to be resisted because, when this occurs, these events become segregated, neutralizing King's dream for America.

Everything planned for the January 1974 event proceeded as planned except for the assembly of the Recruits and Staff at the Recruit Training Command. The RTC Commanding Officer refused to allow his recruits to be mustered for the occasion, and expressed the view that he was opposed to the day's program.

I was aware of King's objections to the Viet Nam War. However, I believed that we were fighting there for freedom of conscience for people in America as well as in Asia. I loved Dr. King and what he stood for, and I was influential in his giving his last sermon from the pulpit of the National Cathedral, as related previously. I also respected the Commanding Officer of the Recruit Training Command, even though I did not agree with him on this matter. What to do?

I strolled over to the massive main RTC galley, gathered "the Brothers" who were staff cooks, and we had a back room chat. Somehow there was a change in the menu for all the Recruits at lunch on Dr. King's Birthday. Black-eyed peas and collard greens fulfilled the vegetable requirement, and I think chitterlings were available on the steam table, along with other protein alternatives. My staff ate their lunch there before the march. The Commanding Officer did not. But every Recruit had a reminder of the one for whom that day was dedicated!

Standing the chaplain-watch one night for the Naval Training Center, I had a telephone call from RTC. It was rare that emergency messages were delivered to Recruits after Taps, but the Command Duty Officer was willing to make an exception in this case, and it was less than an hour after "lights out."

The little brother of a Recruit had been killed while playing in the driveway of his parents' rural home. The boy had been crushed by a piece of farm equipment. This Recruit's Chief Petty Officer Company Commander knew that these brothers were very close. If they would send the Recruit to the Chaplain's Office, would I deliver the Red Cross message so that Emergency Leave could be expedited without delay until morning? Of course I agreed to do so, and soon thereafter the young man reported to me. I had him sit down, and in my best pastoral way prepared him to receive the tragic news. When, with some hesitation, I revealed to him the death of his little brother, the Recruit sat still a moment, his eyes "rolled back in his head," and he spoke "in tongues" for some minutes.

Not having experienced such a charismatic religious experience, I had always been skeptical of the glossolalia phenomenon. Finally, he returned to his presence with me. I asked him if he had understood what I had told him. "Yes sir," he said quite calmly. "You told me that my little brother is with Jesus," he added. Then he asked immediately: "Are you all right, Chaplain? Are you all right?" We then arranged for his flight home. From that moment on, I have never questioned the validity of speaking in tongues nor the unselfish motivation of those who claim this Gift.

———

The "Family Concern Unit" was receiving so much traffic that I had to expand into the back rooms of South Chapel. Thus, it became independent of the "Contact Center." Submariners from the base at Point Loma brought families for our interventions, but due to the demands for our services, we had to refuse would-be clients from other facilities in the San Diego area.

Our day began early with individual and family clients. In the evenings, I conducted Pre-Marriage Seminars for groups of Recruits who were planning to marry their girlfriends on Recruit Leave before heading to the fleet or to classes at various service schools. Many young Recruits were naive and inexperienced in regard to the responsibilities of family building, so these seminars became important to the eventual happiness of the service member and also important for his retention in the Navy.

The number of interns simultaneously engaged with us from the California School of Professional Psychology swelled to three.** A public affairs Naval Reserve Officer,*** whose civilian position was as a high school teacher and who held a Marriage, Family and Child Counselor license, spent his two-week summer duties two years in a row with us at the Family Concern Unit, participating in our co-therapy teams. It was obvious that an enormous need in the military setting had been uncovered, and that we were "bailing with a small bucket."

Shortly after the beginning of 1976, it was perceived by the Navy Department that the human resources management emphasis, created in response to adjustments required of many in the wake of Viet Nam, had escalated out of proportion. I heard it said, with tongue in cheek, that there was one counselor for every three sailors.

The Navy Counselor rating now was to be directed more toward career counseling, and there was a cry for a drastic reduction in Human Resources Management Detachment and other counselor billets. Projects like the NTC Contact Center and the Family Concern Unit were in jeopardy. The Chief of Chaplains feared that chaplain billets would be lost if chaplains were identified as "counselors."

Around March of 1976 he issued a directive that chaplains would not be identified as counselors, and my boss, Chaplain William Cohill, had to comply and terminate the Family Concern Unit and my identification with it. He expressed his sincere regrets at the termination of the ministerial service we had been performing, and he arranged for me to be awarded the Navy and Marine Corps Achievement Medal for my efforts. But from April through June, my date of rotation, I would go home at the end of the work day like everyone else. I spent some evenings as a therapist working with holocaust survivors referred to me by the (civilian) Jewish Community Center. The closing of the Family Concern Unit was a very sad day for me.

A few weeks after the closing of the unit and the dispersing of the wonderful Intern Therapists, I had a telephone call from Army Chaplain (Lieutenant Colonel) William M. Nagata of the Army Human Resources Division. He headed Army Community Services. His organization had just completed a multi-million dollar center at Fort Ord, California, and he had done much to expedite family counseling for his branch of the military service. He had visited our back room at NTC's South Chapel, and was greatly impressed by our efforts and accomplishments. "Please come and make a joint presentation with me at the Omni Hotel in Norfolk in May. I want the 500 people that will be assembled there to know about the millions of dollars we are spending to erect and staff facilities to help Army families, and I want them to know what you are doing in a back room in San Diego without a budget. I think we can affect some changes!"

The conference was co-sponsored by Family Service of Travellers' Aid, Army Community Service, and the Fifth Naval District. Knowing that the prohibitions from the Chief of Chaplains might contradict his idealism, I dared to join Chaplain Nagata in Norfolk. I knew that once again I was "running the gauntlet" for a cause greater than my career. I believed that God wanted a change in the unofficial acceptance of the traditional adage: "If the Navy/Marine Corps wanted you to have a family, it would have been issued in your seabag." I knew from my own deployments in Viet Nam and the effect they had on my family, and I knew from clients who came pouring in to South Chapel during the weekdays, that Navy families and Marine Corps families needed available help to cope with hardships of military life. Further, these adjustments not only involved just the service member, but all whose lives were touched by him or her.

The spontaneous positive reaction of the concerned professionals and volunteers present at the Norfolk Conference was what Colonel Nagata had expected. The Chief of Chaplains sent a Captain from his staff to monitor our presentation. Although no direct connection could ever be traced, I got immediate orders to Guam. Thus I was unable to participate in or to observe the birth of the Navy's instrument for counseling outreach, although I had experienced some of its labor pains.

It took a second annual conference a year later to confirm and formulate the design for the Navy Family Service Centers, and another year to initiate construction and staffing. But, from an unbudgeted program in a back room in the Naval Training Center South Chapel grew the Family Service Centers that now exist on Navy and Marine Corps bases all over the world. Military families have at last been enfranchised as integral to the sea services of the United States. Professional individual and family therapy now assists thousands, and retention statistics have proven the justification for this program.

Those who sent me to San Diego for a "payback" tour of duty to make use of the skills in which the Navy trained me may have gotten more than they bargained for, but this duty was both exciting and developmental for me. Chaplains have always considered counseling to be one of their major functions, and in many cases they have been the sole resource for such compassion and confidence.

Broken hearts—even broken minds—traditionally have received less understanding than broken arms or legs. Proficiency in counseling is to be coveted by any pastor as a representative of the God of love. In spite of the Chaplain Corps directive that had commanded: "Thou shalt not be identified as a counselor," therapy means ministry, serving, healing, and "ministry is therapy"—by no less than a Dominical Command.

—St. Luke 9:1f; St. John 5:7ff

★ Greek scholars, see St. Matthew 4:23f, 8:16, et.al.; Acts 17:25.

★★ The Psy.D. interns that served in rotation were true professionals and effective therapists. Frances Davidson and Joy Kenyon remained the longest at the Family Concern Unit, serving three semesters at their own requests. I regret failing to recall the names of the others who served so well.

★★★ Lieutenant William Tumbleson, USNR, later declared his Vocation and, after attending seminary, was ordained an Episcopal Deacon and Priest. He became a Navy Chaplain, and later a parish rector. He retired after serving as Chaplain to Hospice in the Cleveland, Ohio area.

On Guam With the Submarine Navy

Finding military housing was a trick on Guam immediately after "Typhoon Pamela" that had wrecked the island. Near Polaris Point, where my ship was tied up, military houses still had frogs jumping inside them in a half inch of receding flood waters. We finally located in Department of Defense "Finegayan" housing, a third of the length of the 35-mile-long (and 2-mile-wide) island from the ship. The house was made of basalt block, with a concrete slab roof. During our stay, it survived winds as high as 175 miles per hour during the typhoons we experienced on Guam, but most of the weather was ideal—indeed a Paradise of the Pacific. However, the road to work was dangerously slippery when wet, because the coral in the aggregate surface grew algae when it rained, and it rained a lot.

The motto of the Navy Family is: "Bloom where you are planted," and that motto kept us going in the adjustments that had to be faced. Our eldest daughter Karla had lived overseas with us before during missionary years in the Philippines. Now her younger brother Lester III and little sister Karen June could boast of such overseas experiences because they had been swimming in Saipan, had played in the jungle, and had attended local schools on the island.

I was assigned to USS *Proteus* (AS-19), a submarine tender (support and repair vessel), and to the staff of the Commander of Submarine Squadron Fifteen. The "Old Pro" was affectionately known as "Building 19" because it only moved away from Polaris Point and off its coffee grounds when a big storm threatened Guam. Having been in Tokyo Bay for the Japanese surrender at the close of World War II, "The Old Lady" *Proteus* was showing her age. Sailors were known to get in trouble intentionally to escape the hot, five-high berthing areas, to sleep ashore in an air-conditioned brig. The ship's mission was to provide any support and repair required by our squadron of deterrent patrol "boats," as well as for all the Attack Submarines in the Western Pacific.

Submarine Squadron Fifteen was composed of seven Polaris Missile armed nuclear-powered strategic patrol submarines, with rotating Blue and Gold Crews. Each of these crews would "buy the boat" for a period of three months. Then they would rotate to Hawaii, where they would have a month of rest, followed by two months of training. I would meet the crews when they returned to Guam, first to spend a month alongside the tender preparing their boat for their next cruise. Then they would embark on a hidden stealth run for two months under the surface. During the cruise, they could receive radio messages by floating an antenna, but they were forbidden to transmit in order not to compromise their location. Should the "red telephone" ring from the White House for the Squadron Commodore aboard the *Proteus*, the boats stood ready to fire at any preassigned huge target. This was the "Cold War" at its peak.

My introduction to the submarine Navy taught me that I was confronting a whole different mind-set. The goal would be how to make it work for the advancement of God's ministry. The majority of the junior officers in the tender were Navy Warrant Officers, "Mustangs" who had advanced through the enlisted rates the hard way. They were expert specialized technicians who could practically rebuild a huge submarine from the keel up if they had to do so. However, their patience with or knowledge of wardroom niceties that were expected of commissioned officers in the Navy were absolutely lacking. Most had served in submarines. The senior officers aboard the tender had to have been in the undersea "silent service" throughout most of their careers. What was new to me with this seasoned population was that many had learned to distance themselves from a target, calculate its range and bearing viewing it through a periscope, then cautiously approach it. This had its social implications, which I called "seeing the world through a periscope."

For example, usually when a chaplain arrives at any command, an interview with the Commanding Officer is expected. During this punctual evolution, the C.O. presents his expectations of the chaplain, and the chaplain presents himself as well. By means of this ritual, information is exchanged, enhancing the effectiveness of future professional assistance. However, in *Proteus,* it was three weeks before this invitation was received.

During this period, which was rather awkward for me, I would inadvertently turn around when walking down a passageway and notice that I was being observed by the skipper from a distance or around a corner. When I did finally stand before the Captain, he asked me abruptly: "Are you one of those Jesus freaks?" I responded immediately (using the vocabulary of a Seaman Recruit): "Sir, yes sir!"

I viewed the submarines just as I had the field units on "circuits" I had served in Viet Nam. Together with the 1,100 embarked in *Proteus*, they were my parish, and I would make every effort to minister to them. Just as in a parish, some individuals are more enjoyable to serve, likewise, some boats proved to be more fun to relate to than others. I never let this have any effect on my presence with them or my ministry to their personnel. It just made it easier in some cases than it was in others. This is an important rule to be observed by a "circuit rider": the chaplain cannot play favorites.

Usually we had no more than two of the squadron submarines alongside the tender at one time, but there were Attack Submarines that would visit Polaris Point, as well. When USS *Hawkbill* (SSN-666) was alongside, I could always anticipate most of the crew at Sunday worship! These Sailors were aware of Revelation 13:18, and eagerly sought God's protection!

The chaplain I relieved in this assignment was an ardent evangelical Christian. Because the *Proteus* and the inner portion of Polaris Point were fenced off as highly guarded security areas, it was not possible for civilians from other church bodies or for missionaries on Guam to enter the ship or its immediate dockside area without security clearances. There being no appropriate place on board for the conduct of worship services in all kinds of weather, and with the Chaplain's Office and stateroom one and the same high on the "O-3" level in Officers' Country, my predecessor had made use of a Quonset hut outside the inner security fence for his chapel.

The congregation of about 30 that I found meeting there on Sundays was over half composed of people from the Christian community "on the beach." The civilian organist, Phyllis Whitney, was the wife of a missionary, who, with her husband, directed a servicemen's center above the Christian Book Store in Agaña. Sailors on duty or restricted to the ship were unable to leave the vessel to attend services. It was also difficult for the submariners to climb up to the tender, cross the ship's quarterdeck, then descend the gangway, and pass through the Marine guards at the gate, in order to reach the chapel on Sundays.

I appropriately modified the formalities of Episcopal worship to accommodate the group, and I employed folk songs in the manner that they had been offered in worship prior to my arrival, but Holy Communion was offered in accordance with my tradition. However, it was made obvious from the start that my predecessor was fondly missed, and the nature of the complaints that were leveled at me from worshippers rather identified their origin. Phyllis, the chapel organist, revealed to me that prayers for my *conversion* had been offered in worship services for about three months before my arrival, when it became known that an Episcopal priest had been identified as the incumbent chaplain's replacement.

Facing a ground swell of disgruntled worshippers, I could see the "handwriting on the wall" and I was convinced that the chapel program as it had been conducted was not reaching its intended audience. I had no alternative plans, but I had the growing conviction that the Lord did.

Therefore, at the sermon time during my third Sunday service (and with the secret collaboration of the loyal lady at the organ), I began this way. "I have known of situations in which congregations have fired their minister. I have never heard of a minister firing his congregation. Therefore, to my knowledge, this is going to be a first. I am a chaplain in the United States Navy, and I have been ordered here to serve the Navy community. Therefore, next Sunday's services will be held on the Mess Decks on board USS *Proteus*. This will be our temporary location until a more suitable place can be found. All of you are welcome to attend, if you have a security clearance. If you are unhappy with this arrangement, please attend one of the many churches on Guam that are readily available to you. I speak to you in the Name of the Father, and of the Son, and of the Holy Spirit. Now, go in peace. Amen." Few remained for the final hymn.

Phyllis, the organist, stayed with me, and we arranged to get her on board. We sang *a capella* for a while, and she was content to receive her small stipend and wait for what might come next. In the meantime, I examined that ship from stem to stern, looking for a suitable chapel, and I found one!

My next task was to woo the command into a plan that I would present in detail. Below the waterline in the fantail of the ship was a large space athwartships (side-to-side) which was used for storage of steel stock of varying lengths. On either side of this space were voids that once had been wing tanks—probably once used as insurance against torpedo attacks. These tanks were located on both sides of the ship, just outboard of the storage area. They had not been filled or used in any way in recent memory. I approached one of the enlisted draftsmen, and with his help, we documented a conversion plan which would make the storage space into a crew's lounge during the week, suitable for chapel on Sundays.

The starboard wing tank would become the ship's first Chaplain's Office that was not in "Officers' Country," but on the contrary would be right below enlisted berthing areas. My office would be in the starboard wing tank forward of the lightening hole in the ship's strut, and a space aft of it, with an access port to the crew's lounge, would be for an enlisted chaplain's assistant and a reception area for the chaplain's office. On the port side, the inner area of the tank would become a ship's library, and the outer area would become a ship's internal radio station. All these facilities were innovations for "the Old Pro" and for her crew.

Because the "homework" had been done, my presentation was found acceptable. Three months later, without paint and with only temporary lighting rigged, we held our first worship service in the old storage area. It was Christmas Eve. The place was filled! There was no turning back. I now had the ship behind me, and I was indeed their chaplain!

Pastoral care was just as varied as it might be in a civilian or in another military setting. The ship put to sea when typhoons threatened the island. At those times, I was left behind to direct what was called "The Yellow Crew," to render assistance to families of ship's company whose quarters might become flooded or damaged by the storm, and to assist those without power. When the high winds approached, windows needed boarding up, and children became frightened and sometimes were stranded at school. I used a special pair of waders for these occasions. I did not like our crew to be called "yellow," because we were the brave ones facing hazards and upset family members, while those on board had moved to sunny waters, and had no boats to repair. Most would be sunbathing, while we battled the elements.

—ᴈᴧᴦ—

I had a midnight telephone call at my quarters one night from the Command Duty Officer. He explained that there was a young sailor from Kansas that was extremely upset, but who refused to reveal why he was so emotional. Of course I would dress and come down to the ship. I sat with this sobbing youth for a time before he would share his plight with me. His revelation was as follows.

He had spent a pleasant evening in Agaña on liberty, but he was faced with the fact that his shipmates had left and that he was stranded (there being no public transportation on Guam). It was dark, and the hour was getting late, so he thumbed a ride, which is commonly the way to transit the island. After several miles in the passenger seat with the single male driver, he felt the man's hand on his leg. "What did you do?" I asked. "I screamed and got out of the car as soon as I could!" he replied.

Then the young sailor from Kansas asked a question that he dared let no other hear: "Is it catching, Chaplain? Oh my God! Is it catching?" This farm boy from America's heartland feared that he might been exposed to homosexuality, and that it was a condition that he might have caught. In order to be of help to this sailor, I had to refrain from showing my surprise at his naiveté. Rather, I had to focus on the fact that this young man was genuinely in fear—almost to the state of panic. I was able to calm him through reassurance, and with a patience that he knew he would not find elsewhere. Is that not what chaplains are for?

—ᴈᴧᴦ—

It was noon. An urgent call came from one of the submarines docked on the Point. The Weapons Officer had locked himself in his stateroom on the boat and was trashing it. We could hear noises of glass breaking and a typewriter being hurled at the bulkhead. The tremendous stress these men face had finally crushed him. Both of two keys on such a boat are required to launch missiles. One is locked in the safe of the Commanding Officer, the other is held in the Weapons Officer's safe. Somehow I was able to "talk him down." He unlocked the door, and admitted me. Those on board followed my counsel that everyone treat him calmly and with dignity. He was taken to the Naval Hospital.

I am sure our world was in no danger, but this case serves to illustrate how human resources can be exhausted by the pressures individuals must bear to defend our country. I am sure that his career in the Navy was over, and all of the education required to qualify for his job could no longer be employed.

—◦◦◦—

A sailor from one of the submarines came to my new office next to the Crew's Lounge in the tender. The problem he addressed was a claim of claustrophobia. In response to my probing, because the interior of these boats was spacious enough for a crew of 175, he stated that being under the water was the source of his anxiety. He denied panic attacks, just an abiding discomfort with being under water. I asked him about his present state of mind, and he said he was quite comfortable. I asked where he thought he was, and he answered casually that he was in the Chaplain's Office on the tender. Then I reminded him that the converted wing tank where we were talking was perhaps two decks below the surface of Agaña Bay. His claim did not prove to be valid. Obviously there were other matters on his mind. But I understand that after we cleared the air and dealt with other issues that were of concern to him, he returned to his boat and served well.

—◦◦◦—

When the Polaris Submarines put to sea for their two months without surfacing or transmitting messages, Lay Readers were designated for both Protestants and Roman Catholics. They gathered volunteer worshippers on

Sundays for Church Call. Proper arrangements were made for the Roman Catholic Lay Leaders to have been trained and designated as Lay Eucharistic Ministers, and they distributed Holy Communion (in the "one kind"—only the Consecrated Bread). The Reserved Sacrament in a pyx was kept in the safe of one of the senior officers on board.

I became aware that there were Protestants on those cruises who would like to receive Holy Communion regularly, but no procedure existed for this. In correspondence with the Episcopal Bishop of Hawaii, with copies to the Bishop for the Armed Forces in New York, I requested that we have Episcopalians in these crews, who could be properly identified, trained at Saint George's Parish in Pearl City during their three months in rotation off the boat in Hawaii. I proposed that they be authorized to take and administer the Reserved Sacrament on patrols from Guam to sailors who had been baptized. The Right Reverend Edmond L. Browning, the then-Bishop of Hawaii, approved the plan.

With the training support of the clergy at Saint George's Parish, we were able to provide Holy Communion for all Christians on those long and isolated submarine patrols. I completed last minute instructions before the boats left Guam, and I consecrated the Hosts for the cruise at a Sunday Protestant departure service on the tender.

Suddenly faced with the need to purchase seven very expensive gold-washed Sterling silver pyxes, I ended up buying seven cans of Planter's Peanuts with the plastic lids and a can of gold spray paint for the outsides of these. Obviously I emptied and sterilized the containers, and found that they made decent carriers for the precious Body of Christ. My rationale against possible cries of sacrilege (even those that originated in my own conscience) was that "Jesus was born in a cow-barn cave, and from that vantage point He acted to save us all."

When Bishop Browning was translated from the Diocese of Hawaii to be the Presiding Bishop of the Episcopal Church, he evidently nationalized for his entire Church the Lay Eucharistic Minister program, which began on the boats of Submarine Squadron Fifteen.

One of the submarines entered the harbor after dark to pick me up for a portion of the cruise. These boats are painted black without any hull number displayed in white. A Russian trawler stationed itself in international waters, but close enough for surveillance of our submarines. With electronic sound equipment, they were attempting to identify the undersea sounds of each boat's propulsion equipment (called the boat's "signature") to match with an identification of the name and number of each vessel. It was all part of the "cat and mouse" game we were in called "The Cold War."

I was conveyed in a liberty boat out into the black of night toward the mouth of Agaña Bay, but the trick was for my small craft and the submarine to locate each other in the darkness without breaking radio silence. Several times I had the coxswain stop the engines, and in the silence I yelled out the words of the Passing of the Peace from the liturgy: "The Peace of the Lord be always with you!" Following the third try, an answer came back across the choppy water through the darkness: "And also with you!"

We had found each other in the night, and I was reunited with another part of my undersea parish. I found myself most welcome on these boats. I was not viewed "through a periscope" any longer, and I even got my turn on the bow planes (under close supervision).

Before I left the squadron, the Commodore awarded me the Submarine Deterrent Patrol Pin. I was only the second chaplain in the history of the Navy to receive one, and the only one, at the time, worn by a chaplain on active duty.

When my time arrived for rotation, the Navy Orders read that I was to report to "Naval Submarine Base, Idaho Falls, Idaho." I knew of no large bodies of water in that part of the world, but I was aware of the nuclear prototype some distance from that city, where our operators received an essential part of their training. I telephoned Father Bob Noble, rector of Saint John's Episcopal Church in Idaho Falls. He was overjoyed that an old friend would be coming "to take care of the Navy." He reported that the stress level among trainees was very high, and that he had spent a great deal of his time counseling commuters to that Naval Facility, irrespective of their religious affiliations.

Marjorie left Guam ahead of me to meet our relatives in the Bay Area. We ordered a station wagon, and it was ready for delivery to us in Reno, where we could pick it up on our way to the new duty station. Before I could leave Guam, the orders were suddenly cancelled! I learned "through sources" that when Admiral Rickover heard that the Chaplain Corps was ordering one of its own to one of "his" nuclear training facilities, he would have none of it. My guess is that the Admiral (whom no authority dared to cross at the time) feared that a chaplain might dilute the discipline necessary for the production of the supermen and superminds that he required.

My mind reflected on that submarine Weapons Officer in port on Guam, whose human needs had been repressed for too long and whose pain suddenly caught up with him. Dispatch Orders diverted me to the Naval Weapons Station, Concord, California. I would be close to my aging father in Oakland, who, during my time on Guam, had lost both my mother and his own eyesight. The "Divine Detailer" was again busy overriding the Personnel Detailers of the Navy in Washington.

—EXODUS 14:21f; DEUTERONOMY 30:4f, 11–14; JONAH 2:3, 9

Praise the Lord, and ...

I did not pass the ammunition, but throughout my next two tours of duty I would be ministering on a daily basis to those who did.

———•∿∿•———

Naval Weapons Station, Concord, California

Duty at the Naval Weapons Station (NWS), Concord was not considered to be career enhancing. The chaplain I relieved explained that he spent most of his time dictating books to his secretary. Although he claimed to have passed by the chapel on Sunday mornings, there was no evidence that there had been services conducted there during his three-year presence.

The station boasted of the largest Marine Barracks in the continental United States, but at first glance the place seemed to empty out on weekends except for the duty section and the reaction force. The base included 13,000 acres of grasslands with covered storage bunkers, munitions rework facilities, and piers where the Navy Ammunition Ships of Commander Service Squadron Three loaded and discharged cargoes. All civilian vessels handling dry explosive cargoes in the Bay Area were obliged to load or discharge there too, under the watchful eyes of U.S. Coast Guard inspectors. Vivid reminders of the need for restrictions could be seen between the main base and the waterfront several miles away.

The town of Port Chicago once stood there—before two Liberty Ships at the piers exploded during munitions loading operations on July 17, 1944. Steel fragments of the ships were hurled for miles. Three hundred twenty Black sailor stevedores were killed and three hundred ninety others were injured. Street curbs lined with trees and stop signs still stood among the weeds in a fenced-off area. Civilian housing structures were either demolished or moved to the base side of a hill outside the explosive arc in a small settlement which adopted the name of its former Sacramento Northern electric interurban train station: "Clyde."

At the Naval Weapons Station during my ministry there, the three hundred Civil Service employees kept normal work hours, working alongside sailors, doing many of the same tasks with at least twice the pay.

I remember arriving for the first time at my Chaplain's Office. I climbed a dark flight of stairs to the second floor of an old wooden barracks building. At the top of the stairs I was met by the Chaplain's Secretary, a crusty former World

War II veteran WAVE Yeoman First Class. She snarled upon seeing me approach: "Get this straight! I don't make coffee for chaplains!" The juxtaposition of civilians and sailors outside the administration offices produced constant tension that the Command seemed to ignore. Further, my presence posed a threat to the Commanding Officer, whose wife remained in the C.O.'s house on base while he escorted the civilian Women's Program Coordinator around the base "on business," but in an obvious display of affection—which eventually culminated in his divorce.

As a chaplain, my distress over this challenged the Skipper. I knew that leaders live in "glass houses," and that the influence of leadership "rolls down hill." I knew that a disproportionate percentage of the single Navy Women who worked on the tugs at our piers were becoming pregnant.

In preparation for establishing a viable religious program on base and for the Naval Housing area, Marjorie and I spent hours cleaning the half of an old building that had been used for worship.

One afternoon when we were washing windows and evicting the wheat weevils that had taken up residence in the hymn books, a Chief Petty Officer in civilian clothing dropped in to inquire: "Do you do weddings?" I replied, "I do windows." Our relationship developed, and the couple was counseled and had the first wedding on "my watch" in that chapel. Very soon Sunday worship attracted a small, regular congregation, and more single personnel from the barracks joined.

A Roman Catholic priest from nearby North Pittsburg, California had visited the base, and he now ventured to come for regular Masses and received a stipend as an Auxiliary Chaplain.

Rumors were heard that with the departure of the chaplain at the Naval Communications Station (NCS) in Stockton, the religious program there would be defunct. I started commuting to Stockton on Mondays, held a Bible Study in the old (and occasionally flooded) chapel, invited the Roman Catholic Diocese to send a priest on Saturdays for Mass, and struggled to prove that a chapel program was viable there as well. Victory was acclaimed when the Navy sent a replacement for the NCS Chaplain. With his leadership, a new on-base chapel near the family housing area was constructed over the next few years.

———◦◦◦———

Obviously I enjoyed ministering to the Marines at NWS, who at the time were still "guarding the Navy's gates," somewhat unhappy that this duty did not match the pictures in recruiting posters. The ribbons on my uniform gave me credence with them. I accepted their admiration in the service of advancing God's Ministry, in accordance with the slogan: "If it works, don't knock it!"

In nearby Martinez was the headquarters of an organization whose objectives were to provide aid and comfort to the families of incarcerated persons. "Friends Outside" runs daycare centers at major prisons throughout California, and provides a change of clothing for a visitor who might have appeared wearing prison colors of blue (in some places, khaki), which is against the rules.

This organization has a history of providing helpful social work-related interventions with their clients. It is not uncommon for a parent to be arrested in front of the children, perhaps even during a meal. This often develops in the children of prisoners feelings of hostility toward people in uniform, sentiments which can lead to negative attitudes and self-defeating behavior as these children mature.

With the help of all concerned, we gathered some of the children identified by "Friends Outside." The Marines arranged to pass them through Security onto the base, and a game of basketball in the gymnasium ensued. This was followed by some entertainment and ice cream. It was good for both populations—the kids and the Marines.

The Lieutenant Colonel who commanded the Marine Barracks became a close friend, and he recognized that I was having a positive influence on his personnel. When I heard that the Marine Club was scheduled to have topless female entertainers on Saturday nights, I was in his office like a shot. He anticipated what was on my mind, and he had prepared "his defense." I countered his claims by reminding him that I believed that his career in the Corps would be on the line over this issue. In our "dialogue" behind his closed doors, I further reminded him that our fence line and gates were subjected to constant demonstrations from anti-war protestors, and that any negative information would add fuel to their agitations. Certainly, the moral controversy that would be generated by the topless entertainers in *his club* would spread swiftly to the Commandant in Washington.

I could see that my tenacity and his "Leatherneck" determination were challenging our friendship at the moment, and I gave voice to my regret. But I told him that the influence this would have on his young men could not justify what popularity he would gain in this case. "How would the media learn of what we do inside the fence?" he asked. "Colonel, there are no secrets in this town." "They'll never know," he objected. "Then, and with regret, I guess I'll have to call and tell them," I confessed.

The projected entertainment was cancelled. It was "touch and go" for a while, but in the long run, this strengthened our relationship. He came to realize that I may have saved his standing in the Corps, as well having defended what would prove eventually helpful to the young people under his command.

—◦◦◦—

I had the opportunity to help a young Petty Officer and his new wife who resided in base housing. His first wife was a proven addict, but she was given the custody of their three children. He wanted this reversed for the care and safety of his youngsters. We went to court, his objective was achieved, and his children were overjoyed to be reunited with their father and their stepmother. Their financial resources were drained with attorney and court costs. Yet the couple and the children wanted to express their gratitude to me for my persistence and encouragement in achieving this outcome.

They went to a beach in San Francisco, picked up driftwood, and, with some hemp and two small wooden balls from one of their toys for the eyes, they spent the day weaving for me a two-foot macrame owl, with the name

"Noah" printed on one of the driftwood pieces. "Noah" had survived the flood, and so had they! That owl will always occupy space on one of the walls in my office or at home, reminding me of a family that will always occupy a prominent place in my heart.

———⁓———

The structure of the old base chapel would soon have been condemned for public assembly without major renovation. Although I was approaching the end of my time there, I had a design and location planned for a multi-purpose chapel structure. It would face the main road as it approached the Administration Building, and it would be closer to on-base housing. The plan was approved and included in the Navy budget for the station.

The Commanding Officer procrastinated, and I could tell that if action were not taken before my departure, there would be no new and suitable chapel. The term: "damning with faint praise" is a familiar expression in the Navy. It means that a project or a person is given positive mention so mildly that advancement is unlikely—but not so strong that an appeal may be justified. Popular support was behind the chapel construction, so the project could not be criticized. But the delays in readying for the construction told a negative message, and my rotation date was imminent.

Again turning to the community for leverage, I suggested a groundbreaking ceremony for the chapel. No objections were voiced from the Quarterdeck. I set the date, issued internal correspondence, and when no negative comments where received, I set about inviting the Navy Chaplains from neighboring installations, as well as local clergy, to the affair. With shovels spray-painted gold, a brief and published homily, and prayers offered by clergy of several faith groups, ground was broken for the Naval Weapons Station Base Chapel. There was no turning back. Until the base was "down-sized," that structure continued to witness to the fact that the U.S. Navy belongs to our "one nation *under God.*"

—◦◦◦—

I found that there were only two options for the chaplain to take at the Naval Weapons Station at that time in its history. One had either to do as little as possible so as not to "rock the boat"—which was the choice my predecessor had taken—or to swim against the tide. Either way would have been difficult for me, but I chose the latter and less happy option.

Although not always obvious, I have found this to be the choice that confronts almost everyone in almost any place in the active ministry: the role of the prophet, or the role of the puppet.

It is true that not every battle must be won to achieve ultimate victory, but Christ Calls His servants to serve, not to run and hide. This is because we have the assurance that, from His Cross, the Savior has already triumphed in everything that really matters.

—ST. MATTHEW 25:14-27; ACTS 19:23–27, 35f

—◦◦◦—

Commander Service Squadron Three

My next assignment was to a new billet on the staff of the Commodore who commanded the eight ammunition ships that supported the Pacific Fleet. This made sense, because these were the ships that loaded their cargo and discharged retrograde★ from the fleets and overseas at the Naval Weapons Station. Many of the personnel that deployed in those ships lived in the Weapons Station Naval Housing, where I had organized Sunday Schools and where I had been a frequent visitor. The squadron staff headquarters were at the southern tip of Mare Island next to Vallejo, California, where the Weapons Station had begun many years before. The "AE" (Auxiliary carrying Explosives) vessels were big ships, although they did not qualify as "deep draft" for purposes of mariners' qualifications for naval promotion. These ships are named for volcanoes or gods of fire, and I became familiar with the motto oft-quoted by crew members: "If it goes up, we'll never hear it!"

I reported to the Commodore as the first chaplain to serve in this squadron, and I was given a nice office with a window with view of the mouth of the Napa River. It would be my job to establish a chaplaincy and circuit rider program for the squadron, and to keep the Executive Officer informed.

These ships normally deployed in a Battle Group and received services of chaplains embarked in the carrier or in surrounding ships by means of "holy helo." It would be a while before I would establish a program that would justify the support of a Religious Program Specialist, the enlisted rating that, by this time, had been established to provide assistants for Navy chaplains. However, the wait was well worth it.

When Religious Program Specialist First Class Gray came into my life, I received a gift too joyous to describe. This tall and lanky Black man was full of humor and professionalism. He was supporting his wife's educational ambitions in her studies at Grambling State University in Louisiana, a location which required some long-distance commuting for her. He was always on time, seemingly having anticipated my every need, and he was an accurate advisor to me on personnel issues.

I flourished as a circuit rider, always giving equal attention to each ship. Of course some were more supportive and accepting of ministry than others, and therefore more pleasant to visit and to help. This was usually a reflection of the attitude of the Commanding Officer/Executive Officer team.

My initial efforts were focused on in-port visitations and the provision of Sunday services for the duty sections and for any who were on board. Our ships docked at Mare Island, Oakland Naval Supply Center, Naval Air Station Alameda, and at Naval Weapons Station, Concord, for loading and unloading. Rarely, one would tie up at a pier in San Francisco for extended repairs by shipyard technicians. When we went to ships on the weekend in Oakland or Alameda, Petty Officer Gray would meet me at the Hilltop Mall parking lot in Richmond, and I would pick him up, coming directly from Concord. If the Commanding Officer or the Executive Officer was on board, I would head to his stateroom first for a conference, while Petty Officer Gray would circulate through the berthing spaces, rally crew members, and start setting up "for Church" in a Mess Hall or Crew's Lounge. If we had several ships in port, we would include as many as we could in a prearranged schedule. It got so that one could sense the mood of a ship just crossing the Quarterdeck, by the demeanor and attitude of those on watch.

―――≈∂∂∂≈―――

One of God's great saints became a partner with me in this ministry. The late Bob Oliver was a leader in the Gideon Camp of Vallejo, and he had a special place in his heart for sailors. Prior to the deployment of the Ammunition Ships, Bob and I would visit on board with cartons of small New Testaments and some complete Bibles. These gifts represented expensive contributions from the Vallejo Gideons. I arranged for a brief ceremony in the Captain's Cabin, during which the ship's designated Roman Catholic and Protestant Lay Leaders received the boxes of Bibles, and at which the Commanding Officer was presented a Bible bound in leather. Bob had the C.O.'s name and rank imprinted in gold on the cover. Often these books would be used in reenlistment ceremonies, but we hoped that the captain would read his for spiritual enrichment as well. Bob and I would plan these visits over lunch at the Mare Island Officers' Club, which Bob insisted on hosting.

The spiritual strength of Bob Oliver made a special mark on my life and ministry, especially regarding the event of one of our prearranged ship visitations before deployment.

In this case, I drove Bob and the heavy boxes of books to the Naval Supply Center piers in Oakland. It was a cold and rainy day, and Bob proudly carried the imprinted Bible for the ship's Commanding Officer. When we arrived and made the long climb up the gangway carrying the first increment of our load, we were met with blank stares from the Officer of the Deck. The Commanding Officer had gone ashore; the Lay Leaders were not informed.

The Executive Officer passed us on his way over the side, only acknowledging us in passing. With some help, we took the boxes to the Executive Officer's cabin, and placed the special gift Bible on the CO's desk. I was dismayed, to say the least, that the captain seemed to have missed our appointment.

When we returned to the car on the pier, I apologized profusely for our having been ignored, and how the generosity of the Gideons and this time and financial support in supplying the Bibles seemed to have been shunned. Bob's response was immediate and genuine. "Those books are God's Scriptures. Now that they are on board, the Savior will do his work through them. We have done our part. Do not worry." Bob's *investment* was in his Lord. I shall never forget this man of faith, nor his humble Gideon brothers.

—◦〜◦—

Chaplain John W. Berger, my old friend from my Naval Reserve days in the Philippines, was now the Command Chaplain for Service Group One headquartered at Naval Supply Center Oakland. His organization was parent to the squadron of AEs that I was serving, and both of our organizations' ships deployed with the Battle Groups. His supply ships carried "the beans" (the groceries and repair parts), while mine carried "the bullets" (ammunition). He organized a network of wives whose husbands deployed for significant periods.

These volunteer "Ombudsmen" had to be carefully screened, then trained for the tasks of providing emotional support and referrals for their peers in all kinds of situations "while hubby was away." This effective program handled every concern. There were needs for comfort and encouragement, and companionship needed to be expressed when a spouse might feel overwhelmed by loneliness. There were rare threats of suicide, which required calmness, skill, and maturity to handle and to refer. Most contacts were made by telephone, some by home visits, some with the assistance of a chaplain. Ombudsmen knew when referrals were appropriate, and they often made their own follow-ups.

This program reduced in great measure the number of emergency leaves that could threaten the mission of an entire division on a ship—even the effectiveness of the ship itself. In the quarterly "Ombudsman School," I conducted the "Deep Waters" course, which taught how to identify psychiatric emergencies and how to promptly and effectively refer them. Each geographic county area of the home port (from San José and Oakland to Pittsburg and Marin County) ideally had an Ombudsman for each deploying ship. The Ammunition Ships I served were very well represented, with my office as coordinator, and I was available to my Ombudsmen as their advisor around the clock.

I composed a program to reduce the stress I identified in families when the ships returned from deployments (which then averaged nine months). I called this proposed series, "Pre-Reunion Seminars" with the subtitle: "It's All in the Navy Family." The content was gleaned from my Prisoner of War family research, adjusted to my observations from pastoral ministry with families in Naval Housing and with the returning officers and sailors themselves. My perceptions included my own experiences when I returned from Viet Nam.

This program had two increments. One was a 2-hour seminar designed for groups of twenty-five, to be held on board ships returning from deployments. These seminars were to be given throughout the ships for personnel who had families at home or who were anticipating marriage on return. The first group was to be held with the Wardroom Officers and with the Commanding Officer present. The second would be held in the Chief's Mess, followed by several others for the enlisted population. That way the leaders would be fully aware of what would be given to their troops. They would not only be able to make personal use of the learning they might receive, but would also be able to act as "Sea Daddy" to their sailors and answer questions they might have.

The subjects covered returning to homes with new babies and children a year older than they were on departure, communication and active listening, problem solving, anger management, and sexual reunions. The increment for the wives was to be held simultaneously at home port. These meetings covered similar subjects, and were adjusted to the reunion with the returning sailor from the perspective of the awaiting spouse and family.

My Commodore was interested, but no commitment was made to implement the Pre-Reunion Seminars. One of the principal detractors of this program, a Command Master Chief on one of the squadron ships, returned from deployment to a house emptied of all his family and contents except for a note from his wife explaining that a divorce was in process. Tragic consequences resulted in his case, and this moved the Commodore to summon me and to order me to go to the fleet and execute this program. The Commanding Officers of the ships reporting to him would be required to submit attendance reports by message.

The Human Resources Management Detachment at NAS Alameda had several Chief and First Class Petty Officers who were experts in personal communications. They were pleased with opportunities to accompany me in rotation and to participate in the conduct of the seminars on board. We put the seminars into action when the next Battle Group transited eastward from Pearl Harbor.

Our team of two joined the support ships of the Battle Group at Pearl Harbor, and presented workshops on board continually until we reached the Bay Area. We strapped our equipment to ourselves when we transferred by helicopter from ship to ship during the six-day steaming from Hawaii to California.

When Chaplain Kenneth Botton received orders to join me in this circuit ministry, he was able to direct the wives' presentations on shore. Later he joined me on the ships as others qualified to accept leadership for the seminars at home port. These proactive seminars reduced post-deployment traumatic problems and counseling load dramatically. To my knowledge, the Pre-Reunion Seminars continue to be presented in the ships of returning Battle Groups in both Atlantic and Pacific Fleets, and are routinely conducted by chaplains.

Together with a mature woman Nurse Practitioner attached to the Mare Island Clinic, six weeks after a ship's return we offered a Parenting Class series presented in four age-group-related sessions. This was to assist the reunited families in working together to adjust to and understand their growing offspring.

The addition of a second chaplain to Commander Service Squadron Three (ComServRon 3) staff demonstrated that the religious and counseling ministries in these ships (that had previously depended on the larger commands for services) was indeed justified. With RP1 Gray, then-Lieutenant Kenneth Botton and myself, we had a team that ministered together with common purpose.

As I write, before any changes due to the military "drawdown" may have taken its toll, every Ammunition Ship (AE) homeported on both coasts has billeted and serving on board its own chaplain and Religious Program Specialist!

—GENESIS 2:18, 21–25; 8:11f, 20; ISAIAH 55:10f

★ Various munitions including missiles have a "shelf life," after which, if not expended, must be returned from the fleet or overseas installations to a Naval Weapons Station for reworking or destruction. Retrograde refers to these munitions that were being returned to NWS Concord.

Charlie Chaplain Sails Around the World, and Much More

*I*t was a foggy late February morning in Norfolk, Virginia. I had found my way to a large observation window on the starboard side of the navigation bridge from which I could view the pier instead of the flight deck. What was at that time the largest ship in the world was easing away from its mooring so gradually that it was a few minutes before it was evident that we, rather than the pier, were moving. This would be the maiden deployment for the USS *Carl Vinson* (CVN-70), accompanied by the assigned Air Wing and Battle Group. It was to be for us "around the world in 270 days." As Command Chaplain for the carrier and Staff Chaplain for the Admiral commanding Battle Group "Charlie" of the escort and supply ships and a submarine, I would become known for the next two-and-a-half years through two deployments as the "Charlie Chaplain."

I had just joined the ship from California less than a week before, on a Sunday afternoon. With limited guidance I had found my stateroom, my office, the Officers' Wardroom, and now the bridge. In fact, I had carried my luggage and boxes of books to their new home that afternoon without assistance or so much as a "Captain, welcome aboard!"

The "plank-owner" Chaplain, who had seen the vessel through construction and sea-trials, had been preoccupied with escorting the retiring Chief of Chaplains on board and in Washington, and it was obvious to most who the most likely candidate for the Chief's successor would be. I would have to forage for myself as far as a briefing was concerned. The two assistant chaplains would soon be introducing me to what would be the biggest ministerial job I would ever hold.

Christian Worship on Board

The modest pre-deployment schedule of worship services and religious events would have to be revised for sea, especially with the arrival of the Air Wing, which swelled the population of our floating metropolis to 6,500. I was told that the galleys routinely then would be serving 1,900 meals each day, with four sittings to provide for around-the-clock shifts. Yet, "man cannot live by bread alone."

The Roman Catholic Chaplain on board would have complete responsibility for the programs of that faith group, and the Protestant Chaplain and I would share responsibility for the rest of the Christian events. As Command Chaplain, to the best of my ability, I would see that provisions were made for other faith groups represented on the ship and in the Battle Group. But, at the very least, this would be a crushing load for the chaplains alone.

Five Religious Program Specialists under the management of a Chief Petty Officer would provide administrative support and correspondence, and, for the most part, they proved to be an excellent team. Soon I would become acquainted with sailors who would tell me that they had been Ordained in their denominations or that they had served as Sunday School teachers or deacons in their home churches. I selected and mobilized many of them into a cadre of Lay Leaders for the ship. They organized prayer and Bible study groups for interested sailors in their shifts, either in the Ship's Chapel or in their work spaces. By the time we had crossed the Atlantic, the Command Religious Program included thirty-five scheduled events each week that were dispersed throughout the ship and around the clock.

Small services, with an attendance of less than forty, could be accommodated in the Ship's Chapel. The large Sunday Services, with average attendances of two hundred (one each for Roman Catholic and Protestant services), were held in the ship's forecastle in the bow immediately under the flight deck. Flight schedules could not always be halted on Sundays in operational areas, but for the most part we were spared the crashes of the catapults and the deafening blasts of after-burners every three minutes as necessary to launch the required number of flights for a given exercise.

The religious furnishings, folding chairs, Altar, portable organ, and Sacred Vessels were stored in secure walk-in lockers along the port side. Astride the portable Altar, where it was placed forward of the congregation, were the two Hawes Pipes. These openings to the sea far below conveyed the anchor chains on both sides of the carrier's bow through the skin of the ship. The giant horizontal capstans of the windlasses that hauled the anchors up by their chains, then dropped the chain links into the chain lockers below the deck, were also in the forecastle. But the capstans were aft of the open space where services and other ceremonial events could be held. The windlasses, obviously, were not in use when the ship was at sea. The boatswain's crew kept this space brightly painted and immaculate. This provided the only covered place for the assembly of large groups that was not subject to sudden demand for operations—like the hangar deck was.

Even though this forecastle space was high above the water line in calm seas, during storms even the carrier, a stable "platform" for the storage and launching of aircraft, would plow through tons of water that opposed her headway. At such times, the rough sea forced waves up the Hawes Pipes, distributing one or two inches of water in the Altar area. During heavy seaways on Sunday mornings, two Religious Program Specialists would be stationed on either side of the portable Communion Table armed with large mops, poised to swab the area where worshippers would present themselves to receive Holy Communion. This successfully kept worshippers from slipping in the incoming seawater.

The motto of the Navy Chaplain Corps is "Cooperation without Compromise." At times during my career in the Navy when I was a junior in a chaplaincy staff, my traditions as an Episcopalian had not always been honored. As a Senior Chaplain I defended this pledge vigorously on behalf of my team. There are various schemes used by chaplains who serve together in ecumenical services. This especially impacts worship which involves the administrations of Sacraments, such as Holy Communion and Baptism in the "Protestant" (non-Roman Catholic) camp. In some places, separate services are possible, but in the fleet such opportunities rarely can be staffed among Protestants. The Protestant Chaplains who served with me (one relieving the other) on the carrier were Baptists. To promote the symbolism of unity among those who worshipped the same Lord, I chose not to provide a division in the means of distributing Communion in a single service. With the approval of the other chaplain, we agreed that the chief celebrant would determine the liturgical form and the species used for the elements of the Eucharist. The other chaplain would assist in that form. None objected. So, when the Assistant Chaplain presided, the liturgy was his to determine (within the hour provided by the ship's operational schedule). When I celebrated, a booklet was used which made it easy for worshippers to follow "The Holy Eucharist: Rite II" of the current *Book of Common Prayer*. The first Baptist Chaplain came aboard without supplies for his services, so I opened the catalogues on board and made sure the ship was equipped with trays, individual plastic (disposable) Communion Cups, and the Communion breads he would ordinarily use. The galley provided us with all the canned grape juice we could use. On the other hand, Communion wafer Hosts and wine were administered from Chalices by both of us when I presided. Our congregations did not complain. They were just glad to have Communion so far from home.

Most Episcopalians are not aware that immersion is the first means of administering Baptism mentioned in the rubrics (directions in small print for the conduct of worship) in the *Book of Common Prayer.* I am convinced that both methods of baptizing are quite Biblical, especially considering the shallow areas in the Jordan River where this Sacrament was administered in Jesus' time. I baptized in the canals in Viet Nam, on the beach on Guam, and at NAS Alameda I would respond to requests for Holy Baptism by "full immersion," using the Baptistry of a nearby Baptist Church.

When "pouring" the water is the method used for administering Holy Baptism, it is Navy Custom aboard ship to invert the ship's bell and use it for the font. I did this twice in the USS *Kiska* when I was serving the Ammunition Ships. It was a heavy bell, and it took a great deal of effort to "rig it for Church."

On board the carrier, both the Baptist Chaplain and I responded joyously to many requests for Baptism by immersion. Our first opportunity came when we were making our initial around-the-world voyage. During our port call at Abidjan, capital of the Republic of the Ivory Coast, we utilized the swimming pool of the luxury Ivoire Hotel to initiate twelve sailors and one Marine into the Christian faith. A group of our congregation gathered for prayers and hymn singing during the service, which was witnessed by a gathering crowd of appreciative local people.

On the second deployment in the middle of the Indian Ocean, half of a steel cylindrical container used to transport jet aircraft engines, was emptied for our use. It was laid lengthwise on the hangar deck one Sunday morning. Aviation Boatswain Mates enjoyed filling the container-half with water, using a ready and generous fire hose. The Protestant congregation gathered in the ship's forecastle at the usual time for opening prayers, a Bible reading, and a brief sermon. Then a procession of the congregation followed the Acolyte Cross bearer, filing through berthing compartments and passageways to the hangar deck. Once there, a number of Baptisms were administered by both chaplains, alternating one with another.

Ministry in the Battle Group

A Battle Group is composed of ships of various types who travel in company to provide both offensive and defensive capabilities. A nuclear carrier is self-sustaining as far as fuel is concerned, circling the globe on just pounds of material that require replacement once every two years.

But when it comes to groceries, fuel for the aircraft, and munitions for both the ship and the planes, the carrier can be a hungry hunter. Supply and ammunition ships that steam with the Battle Group can also run resupply errands to nearby friendly ports for the replenishment of other ships. They also require fuel oil, "beans, and bullets."

Our aircraft carrier carried on board eighty-five aircraft configured for a variety of missions which were capable of attack or defense from the air. The destroyers and the cruiser could perform missions both for surface and for subsurface threats, and they have antiaircraft weaponry. Submarines watched us quietly from below. During underway replenishment ("UnRep") evolutions, the carrier and supplying vessels must steam side-by-side at cruising speed, while keeping specified distances from each other during the transfer of cargo by night or day. This is a risky procedure that requires constant vigilance to resist the powerful "Venturi forces" that could suck the ships together.

I had always been on the smaller of the vessels during "UnReps." I had served on most of these counterparts prior to my duty on the carrier. Now from above on the carrier I watched with admiration, as those on the bridges of both ships demonstrated their expert seamanship while lines between the ships suspended transferring loads, hoses throbbed with fuels, and helicopters ferried loaded pallets suspended below them across the separating waters.

—⁓⁓—

As Battle Group "Charlie" Chaplain, it was up to me to coordinate the religious program for these gathered ships underway, some of which rotated with others with similar configuration and mission. The cruiser had a chaplain embarked, and an occasional "circuit rider" would join us from the destroyer squadron, and rarely a chaplain from one of the supply ship squadrons would join the Battle Group.

In order to provide for chaplain presence and services to the smaller vessels and to see that Roman Catholic and Protestant services were provided in rotation throughout the Battle Group, my responsibility was to organize helicopter transfers of all chaplain assets to the various ships. This required knowledge of the constantly shifting obligatory operational schedules that might block the availability of the crew of one or all the ships on a given day. Of course, Sunday was the "target day" for this evolution, because, by tradition (a tradition that made us vulnerable on December 7, 1941), Sunday is usually a day of ease for nonessential tasks and time to accommodate Christian worship. Since the Boatswain Chair is no longer the common conveyance between ships (as well as a means of dunking unsuspecting passengers), this Sunday evolution between the ships has come to be known throughout the Navy as time for the "Holy Helo."

Routinely, on Sunday afternoons at sea, I, together with the other chaplains, suited up, strapped my communion kit to my flight suit, and made ready to board an Antisubmarine Warfare helicopter. In order to board "the small boys," the chaplain would be dangled below the helicopter in a lowering "horse collar" as it hovered over the deck or landing pad of an awaiting ship. Thus, I participated in the schedule which I had planned.

Very soon I learned that when one leaves the stable platform that a carrier provides, to land on a destroyer that rolls twenty-two degrees in routine seas, one had better prepare oneself for the change by taking an adequate and advanced dose of motion sickness prevention medication.

A dampened bath towel spread across a mess deck's table prevents Altar gear and Sacred Vessels from sliding with the heavy movement of a small ship. By bracing oneself athwartships against a mess table, rather than facing fore-and-aft, a celebrant can easily provide Communion and a sermon with little difficulty while underway in all kinds of weather.

Interfaith Ministry at Sea

As in the Mekong Delta, so here it quickly came to my pastoral attention that traditional fleet programs were primarily built around Christian needs. I succeeded in finding good Jewish Lay Readers on board the carrier and in the Air Wing when it was embarked.

Friday evening "Welcoming the Sabbath" services were established in our ship's Chapel, and a printed Torah and (electric) Eternal Light (Ner Temid) were in time located, installed, and appropriately available. I invited Jewish men from the Battle Group ships to come to the carrier once a month on a Friday afternoon, attend our "Kabbalat Shabbat" services, eat a traditional meal (which the galley crew provided in a private messing area), and enjoy the larger ship's amenities, such as ship's stores and good showers. These worshippers would then return to their own commands on Saturday morning. I called this evolution the "Hebrew Helo." I think this was a "first" for the Navy, and I hope this established a precedent for the fleets.

Our first port visit after crossing the Atlantic was Monaco. It was Christian Holy Week, and also Passover. Through our consular offices, Jewish "Church Parties" (the Navy term for groups going to worship centers on shore) were dispatched to synagogues for worship and Seders in Nice, Cannes, and Monte Carlo. With each group went one of our crew who could understand and interpret French. When the Rabbi in Nice looked out over the uniforms that swelled his congregation that night, he asked from his pulpit: "And where are the *Russian* sailors tonight?" On the carrier's second deployment, our Jewish personnel attended Passover in Subic Bay with families gathered in a home.

A Petty Officer who had been raised in Tunisia surfaced about the time we reached Morocco on our Around-the-World (maiden) Cruise, and I was convinced that he was a sincere follower of Mohammed. In Casablanca, we purchased a genuine prayer rug. The Ship's Chapel was then made available on Saturdays for him to build a congregation. A basin was installed in a closet near the chapel for proper pre-worship ablutions, and, with the leadership of this Petty Officer, we formed the first Islamic congregation in the fleet.

While the Hull Technicians were plumbing the closet near to the Chapel entrance, I had connections made for a stacked washer and dryer to be installed later. When this was purchased, it provided our Mormon congregation with facilities for the private care of their special undergarments which devoted members of the Church of Jesus Christ of Latter Day Saints expect to wear. This provision avoided unwelcome comments about this tradition by shipmates who might not understand.

Some Port Visits and Special Events

I did manage to meet the Anglican Church Vicar in Monte Carlo, and we enjoyed a dinner together at a French restaurant. I was wearing my "Tropical White" uniform.

During the meal an elderly lady left a table where she was dining with her husband, came to the table where I was sitting, and embraced me. She kept repeating, "Thank you, thank you, thank you for saving us!" This was a bit of an unnerving surprise, but, according to my comrade, I acted appropriately. It seems that Americans had liberated the couple's prison camp near the close of World War II, but not before their captors had purposely blinded her husband. When this was related to me, I wept during the remainder of that meal.

—◦◦◦—

Holy Week in Monaco was a very busy time for me. On board we held services each day, reflecting its significance in Biblical tradition. On Easter Morning our first service was held on the flight deck, with Monte Carlo across the waters, as a backdrop. This was an ecumenical service with all the chaplains and Christian congregations participating—about 400 in number. Then the normal schedule for services was kept below decks: Mass and Protestant Communion in turn.

Our next flight deck service at sea was on Memorial Day in the Indian Ocean, with our crew mustered topside. During this, the Battle Group ships formed a parade at sea, steaming past us in the opposite direction. Passing Honors were rendered—with crew members in white uniforms lining the rails in silent tribute, while our Admiral and Commanding Officer participated in a ceremonial casting of a large floral memorial wreath into the sea. Where does one get flowers in the middle of the Indian Ocean? A supply ship that recently joined us had transported the wreath in chilled storage from Singapore, then had it sent to us by "UnRep" chopper.

We had a Black choir on board that had organized themselves as "The Voices of Vinson." During a port visit at Perth, Western Australia, following our first deployment's extended stay in the Indian Ocean, "The Voices of Vinson" were looking for a project. We decided to go to the Mall in Perth on a Saturday night and sing hymns for any who might pass by or gather. I, with a number of our congregation, accompanied them to this open area of several blocks of wide cobblestone pedestrian walkways and Victorian shops. Before long, a crowd surrounded us and joined our impromptu concert by singing familiar choruses with us. When the crowd swelled to about several hundred, the police riot squad arrived, thinking that mischief was afoot. Soon they joined in the singing as well.

—◦◦◦—

Part of the diplomatic mission of the "Around-the-World" deployment of the USS *Carl Vinson* was to make contact with royalty and significant personages in nations that we passed. A visit was made by our Commanding

Officer Captain Richard Martin and our Battle Group Commanding Admiral to Prince Rainier III at his palace in Monaco. The Crown Prince of Morocco was entertained on board by a Drill Team demonstration and a parade provided by our Marine Detachment. The presence of our ship with others of Battle Group "Charlie" offshore at Abidjan probably quelled a potential revolution in the Ivory Coast. When we passed South Africa and Singapore, where we could not stop, influential leaders were flown out to the ship and were treated to a luncheon in the Officers' Wardroom and a tour of the ship.

As we approached Hong Kong, a selected group of civic and business leaders were flown out to the carrier at sea in advance of our arrival, as guests of our new Commanding Officer, Captain Thomas Mercer, for a luncheon and tour.

I was seated at a wardroom table for lunch with a group of gentlemen visitors who seemed to have been selected because of limited English conversational proficiency. Several seats to my left was a man in a light blue uniform, but I was unable to see his insignia. I asked him in my best Mandarin what would have been the equivalent of: "Are you one of theirs, or one of ours?" He laughed and replied in perfect English: "I am Colonel Bill Sung, Air Attaché at the U.S. Consulate." I asked if he had ever lived in California, to which he replied in the affirmative. I asked him if he had ever lived in Berkeley. Again he replied that he had. I asked if he had ever lived on Durant near Shattuck Avenue. "Why, yes! How did you know that?" (All this transpired with some polite interruptions to address our seat mates and to talk around those who were between us.) When the opportunity presented itself, I explained that as a teenager, I knew his father, the Reverend Dr. William Z. L. Sung, the former President of Saint John's University, Shanghai, who, after his arrest by the Communists, had been able to immigrate with his family to the United States. Bishop Block (of the Diocese of California) had been able to arrange a position for Dr. Sung to be Chaplain to Asian students in the United States who were also refugees from Communism. I told Colonel Bill Sung that I had been a visitor in his home when we were both boys, and that his father had encouraged my early hopes to study Chinese.

On our next deployment, we met again. I learned that the Colonel had been the pilot that had flown President Richard Nixon to Beijing on his history-making mission. I was an overnight guest in Colonel Sung's penthouse on the side of Victoria Peak. When I arose for breakfast, the Colonel said he had a surprise for me. Seated at the table was his mother, who stood and embraced me, saying: "Lester, I have not seen you since I was at your seminary graduation in 1955." We both shed a few tears of joy.

The Ship's Library

It is not irregular for chaplains at sea to have the management of the Ship's Library assigned as a collateral duty. On this carrier, the Library is physically adjacent to the Ship's Chapel, adding to the convenience of the responsibility. Routine library management was handled by designated Religious Program Specialists, who also kept an eye on the nearby Chapel and its needs. Quiet music was "piped in" to the library by equipment purchased for that purpose.

I believe the library is one of the more desirable collateral duties for chaplains afloat, because the library provides a great opportunity to encourage uplifting activities for the crew both at sea and in ports of call. Further, this duty provides an opportunity for the ship's chaplain to acquire books and materials that are relevant to activities of the Command Religious Program.

When we are at sea for weeks, in some cases for months, we have "a captive audience." This can prove advantageous to both the religious program and for the utilization of the library. Sailors do a lot of thinking at sea. I specially ordered books which were designed to stimulate interest in marriage and family life, and I had special sections for books about our ports of call, and for books of nautical and historical interests. Books about Asia, Europe, and Africa had inviting travel tips for sites of interest. It was my hope to use the library to encourage personnel to explore beyond the "gin mills" near the piers, and to promote individual growth and mature family life as well as positive international relations.

"People Programs"

Roman Catholic Chaplain Oddo and I collaborated on the writing and filming of a television spot in the ship's "studio." It was designed as a deterrent to an epidemic of ill-advised and unprepared marriages of sailors in Subic Bay, Philippines—at the time, our principal naval support base in Asia. Those who visited this port needed to be informed that it was not a good or even typical example of the Philippines.

For business reasons, a large population gravitated to the City of Olongapo just outside the gate, because, when the fleet was in, the Yankee dollars flowed copiously. In ten blocks of the main street, practically every other establishment was either a bar or a brothel. Girls who came to Olongapo from their provincial homes had to accept the fact that this was a one-way trip, because they were rarely found acceptable back where they had been raised. The American image of comparative prosperity was perpetuated in American motion pictures and by the displays of cash from stashes sailors had accumulated after months at sea. It was an explainable dream for the ladies of Olongapo to persuade a lonely and sometimes intoxicated sailor into marriage.

Despite the naval restrictions that required police clearances, testing, group counseling, and other delaying strategies to insure that both parties to an international and intercultural marriage were mature and prepared, there were corrupt means and magistrates who could circumvent these precautionary legalities. Certainly the girls themselves soon became experts in building quick relationships and were knowledgeable of "the system." Time in port was short, but there was also the prospect of making contact with a man on his way out to the Indian Ocean, the Persian Gulf, or on other Western Pacific missions, then, through the mails, arranging a reunion on his return eastward. This was quite an industry, there was no guarantee that these new wives would ever be allowed to enter the United States, and international litigation for financial support and the accompanying broken hearts and promises had for years become a major problem for the sea services.

Our video was used just before the ship hit Subic Bay, as well as prior to other port visits in Asia, and it reduced our personnel problems to a significant degree.

Chaplain Pete Oddo is short, well built, and, in blue chambray and denim, he made a believable "Petty Officer Heartthrob." I acted the part of the Chaplain. When Petty Officer Heartthrob burst in on me, I observed how excited he appeared to be. "I'll bet you're in love," I commented. "How'd you guess?" he wondered. As the interview progressed, the chaplain anticipated the sailor's questions, demonstrating that this man was not "first in that pipeline." "You want to get married!" "How'd you guess?" "What's her name?" "Well, ...they call her Mona." Reluctantly, Petty Officer Heartthrob admits that he cannot remember her last name, that he has never met her family, and that he has not known her very long. He asserts that she must be a "nice girl" because she surely makes him feel good. "I'll bet she does!" responds the chaplain. At the end of the vignette, Petty Officer Heartthrob decides on his own to give this proposed marriage more thought.

—————

From the time we left Asia and headed eastward toward home, the Chaplains and Religious Program Specialists scheduled regular Pre-Reunion Seminars by pre-registration only. (This program was described in the section on the ministry in Ammunition Ships, where it was identified as an outgrowth of the research done to prepare P.O.W. Returnee's Families for "Operation Homecoming.") These seminars were very well received by all rates and ranks on the carrier, and there were waiting lists for each workshop.

After our return from the voyage around the world, and after most families had settled in the San Francisco Bay Area, I spent months organizing and training our Ombudsmen for the next deployment (this program was described previously as well), and several Ombudsmen were established in the counties surrounding the bay and in the Treasure Island

Naval Housing. These women were willing and able to provide family support and referrals when we left again for the Indian Ocean.

The American Red Cross "Military Family Support" emergency message traffic that flowed through my office during our second deployment was reduced from about four thousand to one thousand messages over a similar nine-month period of time. This reduction was due in part to the fact that on the first deployment many of our families were relocating across country from the Norfolk area, whereas on our second deployment most of our families had established themselves near our new home port, and our Ombudsmen were known, trained, and functioning.

Civic Action

With both engineering and missionary experience behind me ("with God there are no 'blind streets'"), and with full knowledge that our continuing mission was as diplomatic as it was military, I set about organizing our logistic and volunteer capabilities for humanitarian service projects at appropriate ports of call. Using the Command and Control Computer on my desk, I formulated various task groups divided into work crews, each with the optimum number for its identified task.

For example, we soon learned that a paint crew of five was best—more got in the way, fewer were not efficient. Task groups were designated, then recruited from volunteers in ship's company by personal skills. We discovered sailors who had a variety of hidden talents and experience as well as those with military occupational skills. Glaziers, electricians, carpenters, painters, machinists and enginemen, pipefitters, landscapers, and plumbers surfaced to offer to help when needed. Men who worked with tiny components and electronics in the "clean rooms" were quite ready to get out in the sun and swing sledgehammers or pound nails for a change. The pipe shop customized designs for children's play yard equipment—slides, swings, climbing ropes, "Jungle Gyms"—that could be prefabricated in pieces to be transported on the liberty boats to be later assembled at an orphanage or school. To my great joy and even surprise, the ship mobilized around the potential of providing civic action projects at ports of call. This motivated some to see more of a country and to meet people where we visited beyond what they might see at pier-side "recreational" spots. This program provided a great lift to morale during our long deployments.

My first move was to send sufficiently ahead of our arrival a message to the U.S. Consulate or Embassy at the next port, informing of our offer to provide a civic action project. I requested by return message the identification and description of an appropriate task that would be possible within our availability timeframe.

Next, I enlisted shoreside cooperation in the ordering and staging of materials at the work site, and the negotiation of expenses—guaranteeing our payments. (Funding these projects from the voluntary contributions of our generous crew was never a problem, and all funds were regularly audited.) If a concrete base was required, it would have to be poured in time so as not to be "green" when we arrived—firm enough to provide foundation for new construction. Once a project was identified, the number and types of work crews were selected, and volunteers were recruited on board (with their duty schedules permitting). Onshore transportation to the site for our men and materials had to be reserved in advance. This scheme was utilized repeatedly, and it served the carrier and the ships of the Battle Group very well during two deployments.

The first project we executed was for the Royal Orphanage at Casablanca. The United States Embassy cooperated with us by means of a great deal of message traffic. They arranged for Moroccan Army trucks to transport us from the liberty boat landing to the three highrise towers and other buildings that housed the orphanage, situated downtown. We brought with us the playground equipment parts to be assembled in place, and our tools. Our ship had to anchor four kilometers offshore, a common requirement for nuclear-powered vessels.

Eighty-five Officers and Enlisted Men were selected from the four hundred who volunteered to help. Evidently an electrical fire four years before our arrival had rendered the facility without power. This disabled the flushing pumps for the sanitary system that served the bath and toilet rooms used daily by the four hundred children who lived there. Extensive rewiring was required. The water pumps had to be rebuilt, and an Engineman held a class for some of the teen residents on the lubrication and maintenance needed to keep the pumps running long after our departure.

A "Scotch" (fire-tube) boiler that provided power before it had become defunct was repaired and placed online with the help of our Boiler Technicians, and with the eager assistance of Moroccan boiler operators. Three floors of bunk-rooms were repainted, and hundreds of broken glass windows in the buildings were replaced with glass the Embassy had arranged to be delivered. One of our task groups assembled and installed a large number of swings, slides, and other playground equipment. All this was completed between our arrival at the site at 8:00 in the morning and 5:00 in the afternoon. The day ended in the play yard with ball games between the orphan-residents and the sailors.

The French press interviewed me, asking if we had come on a crusade to convert people to Christianity. I responded: "We have come to shake your hands in friendship, and to demonstrate that your children are our children as well." We were given good media coverage in both Morocco and Tunisia.

—◦◦◦—

Our next project was at the National Orphanage in Bingerville, Ivory Coast. Painting, and the repair of high voltage electrical supply lines and circuitry were primary efforts here. Electrical work was complicated by the need to replace obsolete French equipment, for which no parts were available. Jury-rigging the required substitutes demanded the skills of a very professional electrician like Ensign Joe Turk.

Our Mess Management Specialists provided a lunch of roast beef sandwiches and cow's milk from the ship. These children had never had either before, and, although the meal was a thrill for most, it proved to be too rich for others—and a learning experience for us. The hot equatorial day ended with children and sailors splashing each other in the facility's wide wading pool.

We painted the interior of the Seventh Day Adventist Orphanage and did some carpentry work for them in Pusan, Korea. Captain Bill Woodman of the Battle Group Admiral's staff and I spent the day setting new toilets and unclogging others in the children's restroom. The caretakers reported that the thirty-five residents lined up each morning to use the only two operational commodes, so this contribution was considered to be a major one by all. The following Christmas I sent that orphanage a gift check for fifty U.S. dollars as a follow-up from our visit. The letter I got back thanked me for the swimming pool, with photographs of the large pit the children had dug and lined with concrete.

—–ᴐᴠᴐᴏ—–

Our final civic action project on the 1983 around-the-world cruise was perhaps our *Opus Maximus*. I had determined, through former missionary connections, that in the mountains of Luzon in a poor area of Baguio City called "Holy Ghost Extension," there was a need for a multipurpose building.

This three-room structure would house a neighborhood health clinic and an elementary school, and it could be used on Sundays and Holy Days for Church services. I designed a three-room building with (a great novelty for the village) flush toilet bathrooms. A cesspool would have to be dug and lined with rock. Our playground equipment would have to be transported and erected, and the structure would be electrified. It would be roofed with galvanized sheets atop the trusses with materials which I knew were available and could be delivered at the site. The area needed to be leveled, and a concrete floor poured in time to support the construction of supports and walls. The basalt block and steel window frames would have to be delivered to the site in advance of our arrival.

All preparations were accomplished through an exchange of messages and the volunteer labor of the two hundred village residents. They joined our Sailors and a few from our on-board Marine Detachment to work together to raise this building and dig the region's first internal sewage system. I coordinated the American and native Igorot working crews, and I had reserved overnight billeting for our men at Camp John Hay, the Air Force R&R Center not far away.

Eighty-five volunteer Sailors and Marines left Subic Bay on two chartered buses at 4:00 A.M., rode through the provinces and up the steep Kinnon Road to the 4,500-foot elevation of the site. Some slept on the way.

We arrived at 8:30 in the morning. After conferences with the local folks, we dispersed our crews to their various tasks, and all started to dig, pound, lift, wire, and plumb. In a single day and six hours of the next one, we had completed our task!

The only things left to be completed by the residents were placing and glazing the steel window frames, because the cement between the supporting concrete blocks was still too wet. Also left for completion by our host craftsmen was the building of the school desks with wood donated by the ship's Jewish congregation. Local carpenters are excellent, and time had run out for us at the site. The school desks and blackboards had to be installed before the government would send a teacher for the school, we were told. Of interest to us was the fact that small children had to walk four kilometers (and, in winter, ford a stream) to attend school, prior to this new building being placed into service in their barrio.

One does not leave the Philippines without accepting the lavish hospitality of a loving and generous people. About 1,500, young and old, gathered with us, some sitting on the roof of the new multipurpose structure, some on the ground and on surrounding hillsides. Sailors and Marines were invited to join in the native dances to the ringing of the "gongzas," and we sang, ate and drank together. Bishop Benito Cabanban of the Philippine Episcopal Church had come from Manila to join the occasion and to greet his returning missionary. Children sang, and our men held them on their laps. This was a most joyous celebration! It was relished by an exhausted group, before buses were boarded at dusk and it all became a precious memory for us. For those at "Holy Ghost Extension," a Public Health Nurse began weekly clinic visits, school started, and the following Easter eighty-five of the new congregation received Holy Confirmation.

———～๑๑๑～———

As our 1983 around-the-world cruise headed eastward from the Indian Ocean toward the Pacific, we visited a rural orphanage on Luzon north of Olongapo. Deserving institutions in that city received assistance routinely from Naval Base personnel and from visiting ships. This more remote facility was targeted for me by the Base Chaplain, and that orphanage was most appreciative of our visit, gifts, and promises of future assistance. Our preplanned visit for Christmastide 1984 during our second deployment benefited from better preparations.

For example, the shoe size of each child had been requested, and the outline of each small foot arrived some months ahead of our arrival. During our second deployment, toys were purchased in Japan, articles of clothing were acquired in Hong Kong, and a plane was dispatched to Korea (on a training flight) with the tracings of many small feet, so that rubber shoes to fit could be purchased for each orphan. When Santa Claus arrived with his motorized "sled," each child received an article of clothing, a pair of shoes in his or her exact size, and also a toy. A big party included Philippine food, and much merrymaking.

Two orphanages in Olongapo City also received simultaneous Christmas 1984 visits from our Santa Claus, with gifts and greetings from the Sailors and Marines of the USS *Carl Vinson*. Not to be outdone, the ship's Executive Officer called away a "Hundred Man Working Party" (non-volunteers) to paint the interior of the Olongapo City Hospital.

The Battle Group Admiral summoned me and directed me to represent him at a social event in Manila at the Hyatt Regency Hotel on December 27th. This was after all of the Christmas religious events had taken place and our children's projects had been completed. After bus travel to Manila, I took a taxi to arrive at the hotel across old Dewey Boulevard from the seawall and Manila Bay. It was here that I was surprisingly greeted by thirty-five of the eighty-five Saint Stephen's School Acolyte Guild of two decades before. They were accompanied by their wives and in some cases their children. Bishop Cabanban presided at this dinner held in my honor, an exciting climax to my final stay in the Philippines. This celebration brought together the old and the new in a demonstration of the maturation and gratitude of those to whom I once ministered and taught when they were of ages similar to those of the children I had just visited in the orphanages.

—◦◦◦—

Two deployments of the USS *Carl Vinson* and Battle Group "Charlie" were missionary journeys for me. It was not all sweetness and light. There were personnel problems, political encounters, and the distasteful situations that we go through in any of the enterprises of life. But whether I was preaching, administering, mingling with aviators in the ready rooms or the Combat Information Center praying for them in their night approaches on the flight deck, I was "at home." Whether I was setting toilets in an orphanage, or being initiated as a "Royal Diamond Shellback" crossing the Equator at zero degrees latitude, zero degrees longitude off the Ivory Coast (getting my khaki backside swatted on the flight deck amid a great sea of denim ones), I was "at home." It was thrilling to be serving the Master in this unusual parish!

When we sailed under the Golden Gate Bridge at the end of our first voyage, I had Bishop Swing of my Diocese of California flown on board to join celebrities on the Admiral's Bridge to watch the fireboats spray and see the pier ends decorated to welcome us. We were being celebrated as we became "San Francisco's Own." There was a double rainbow over the North Bay that day, and my family was on the pier at Naval Air Station Alameda waiting for me. I was truly home at last, the home and family that I missed terribly, but in a sense, as priest and the "Charlie Chaplain," I had been at home all along the way.

—NUMBERS 9:1–5,18; 10:33-36;
ST. MATTHEW 8:19f; JAMES 1:27

Why I Stayed in the Navy

*M*arines in Viet Nam called each other "Animal." This was probably a commentary on the fact that in many ways, while we were in the field, we lived, ate, smelled, hunted, and looked like animals.

Sometime in 1972, when travelling in civilian clothes, I entered the Marine Exchange at Camp Pendleton to make a routine purchase. I was stopped on the steps by a Staff Sergeant, who hailed me by saying: "Chaplain Westling! I remember you!" In the chat that followed he amazed me further when he said, "I remember your sermon of Easter 1967! It had great meaning for me and for the others. Thank you!"

No chaplain expects to be remembered five years after a single service. No minister expects those who hear his sermons to be that retentive. However, this forced me to reflect on what had transpired on the Easter Day he mentioned. I think that sermon was the shortest of my 50 years "in the pulpit."

There were several companies of First Battalion, Fourth Marines (1/4) on the beach at the entrance to the Cua Viet River. Parenthetically, it would be well to add that it is impossible to dig a foxhole in beach sand. I had taken a side trip from the 3rd Medical Battalion at Phu Bai to provide Easter Services for troops in the field, and we set up an "ammo box" Altar in the shade of some palm trees. The Marines formed a semi-circle, and I began the service of Holy Communion. We sang a familiar Easter hymn, the Bible lessons had been read, and I was just starting to preach, when the Marines had to scatter to duck suddenly incoming shells. As they ran to their positions, I yelled after them: "The meaning of Easter is that we are not animals!" I guess they got my point. That Staff Sergeant remembered.

A young Ensign telephoned me from Bahrain Island to ask my advice. I was in California, and this was some time after my Navy retirement. I had known Steve when he was a junior Petty Officer in USS *Carl Vinson*. I had watched him advance rapidly in his rating, I had rejoiced when he was selected by the Navy to complete his college degree as a prelude to the officer commissioning program, and I celebrated with him and his wife when their daughter was born.

I felt honored by his confidence in calling me, and I did my best to answer him appropriately. He called to report that he was having a communications problem with his Commanding Officer. I suggested that he request an appointment to discuss the matter with the C.O. of his small ship. "I did that," he replied. "I stood before him and said that I believed we were having a personality conflict." "Well, what happened?" "The Skipper told me that I was 'the conflict', and that he was 'the personality.' Then he threw me out of his office." I told him that I was sorry, because I knew that he was very respectful, and that he had great potential for the Navy. (He now sells securities in Miami.)

—◈◈◈—

The Reverend Donald Beers came aboard the USS *Carl Vinson* on June 26, 1985, as the official guest of Captain Thomas A. Mercer, our Commanding Officer. Fr. Beers was the Executive Assistant of the Episcopal Bishop for the Armed Forces and the official representative of the Presiding Bishop. He carried with him a plaque for the ship's Commanding Officer's trophy wall.

The ship had been designated a "Jubilee Ministry for Humanitarian Service," an award normally given to model congregations of the Episcopal Church. The recognition was for the major renovations that the ship's personnel had made to orphanages in Africa and Asia during the 1983 and 1984–5 deployments. I trust that the plaque is still treasured on board.

—◈◈◈—

A beautiful circular wall hanging decorates my office. It depicts Christ at prayer in the Garden of Gethsemane. It came some years ago from a young Woman Marine on duty in Korea. I had ministered to her and anointed her with prayers for her healing when she was a patient at the Oakland Naval Hospital, and when the best medical consultants declared she was dying. She recuperated, and, at her plea, was returned to active duty to complete her enlistment. Vanda Baughman now teaches school near Salem, Oregon, and is in the "discernment process," considering attending the General Theological Seminary in New York City in preparation for ordination in the Episcopal Church.

—◦◦◦—

My telephone rang in Redding, California on a bright summer day in June 2001. It was the voice of William Paul Pennell from Oahu. "You baptized me in a bunker at Fire Base C-2 in August 1967, and you sent the information to my home Parish of Saint Mary in Phoenix. I have been searching for you all these years."

We enjoyed several telephone "reunions" after that. He had lost his Baptismal Certificate, so I sent him another to verify the date and place where he became (in the words of his new document) "a Child of God and incorporated into His Holy Church."

—◦◦◦—

So many stories from my years in the military ministry like those above flood my memory like a great tidal wave. Earlier I related why I entered the military. In brief, it was because Asians, Americans, and Allies were bleeding and dying in Viet Nam, and I felt Called by God to be with them as His priest. Then, when that war was over, I believed God wanted me to stay in the Navy Chaplaincy because my job was not finished.

I found the youth of my nation there. I met hundreds who were hungry for answers to life and death questions, and I found those who lacked this quest typically to be in jeopardy. From a distance, leaders and politicians in Washington generally make crucial decisions of peace and war once or twice in their lives. In contrast, those in the military make this grave decision once and for all when they raise their hands and take the oath to defend this nation and the freedoms for which it stands, or, for the lack of which, it would fall.

Whether in the fleet, in the trenches, or "in the rear with the gear," our nation's youth was standing tall in the military. As a combat chaplain, I had seen this all too vividly.

When I looked at the prospect of returning to a domestic parish, I questioned whether or not I would find as rich a field for harvest. Furthermore, from my early and decisive experiences as a chaplain, I knew that the military was a segment of America that was not being well reached by our churches, synagogues and mosques. That was the cognitive part.

Subjectively, through all of this, I heard the Lord's Call. Being an Episcopal parish priest always had been my vision of ultimate fulfillment. As an Anglican Christian in the military, I felt exiled from my familiar liturgical and theological world—rarely understood as being somewhere between the Protestants and the Roman Catholics, but not fitting exactly within either. But this was a price I willingly paid to be a missionary to all the troops, whenever and wherever we were obliged to go. I became a fierce advocate for the expression of religious freedom for both my fellow chaplains and for the laity. Still, I often felt lonely, like an ecclesiastical exile.

After the war, Marjorie and I were offered a golden chance to accept a Call to Saint Peter's, Redwood City, and in 1985 I was a nominee for the episcopacy, although still in the Navy. It was *God's* choosing that compelled me to answer: "Here am I, I must stay where I am."

I had discovered in Viet Nam that there are no blind streets with God. He had used every experience I had in life as a training ground for the next one. We did not know what the future would bring, but we had to accept the fact that Our Blessed Lord knew where He was leading us, and, if we were responsive, He would take us where He would have us go. I knew ships from the bilges and the forecastle to the bridge, and I knew the people who worked in them. Since age sixteen I had been one of them—somewhat unusual preparation for the priesthood. This is how the Lord had led me. So, Marjorie and I had to trust that this was all according to His Purpose.

———

There are people manning our fleets in port and on the high seas who are contemplating the meaning of life and its destiny. As related previously, my last ship, the nuclear carrier USS *Carl Vinson,* had 6,500 embarked when the Air Wing was with us on deployments, and our Battle Group "C" surrounded us with as many as eight other ships at times. That was a parish the average size of which was thirteen thousand. The average age in these crews was about 20! When in our operating area, we had on board one of the largest hospitals and surgeries in much of Asia.

During my two-and-a-half years on board that floating metropolis, there were three suicides at sea. We carried three chaplains, and there were usually one or two chaplains embarked on the other ships. Good Lord, what a challenge! And, ...what a need! God was telling me that there was still a place for me in this chaplaincy.

So I remained in the Navy and Marine Corps ministry, through the good times, and (literally) through hell and high water. In doing so, Marjorie and I committed our children to share this life at ages when they had no idea what we had done either to or for them. But we were in it together, and I pray that the Lord had His Way. We had stayed in the Navy as long as I was fulfilling my priestly and pastoral Vocation.

———

Promotions had obligated me to a desk in a hospital full of the sick and dying. My desk was piled high with reports, fitness evaluations, and too many of my program support specialists at this duty station were unreliable. The chaplains I supervised were fulfilling their pastoral ministries and their answers to the Great Commission, and I felt I was not. The chain of command and military discipline seemed to me to have fallen into disuse in the medical Navy. I said to myself, "I came into this outfit as a priest, and now I am a supervisor, report writer, and baby-sitter for incompetent support personnel. This is no longer my fight. I brought priesthood in, and now it is time to take priesthood out. The Lord is telling me that my work, my ministry here is finished."

On May 1, 1987, I became Rector of All Saints' Episcopal Parish in Redding, California while on "terminal leave" from the Navy. I gave the keynote address at the area Memorial Day exercises at Shasta College on May 31st in dress uniform and full medals—my last day on active duty.

In order to offer this presentation, I waived my Navy Retirement Ceremony with band, flag, and perfunctory medal. I considered this transition to be milestone enough, and I was eager to begin a new chapter in my life and ministry. I was on the road to discovering "life after Navy," which, I confess, I am still travelling.

—◁∿∿▷—

The God who has given us life is the same God who Calls us to our Vocations. The Ordained Ministry is certainly but one of many Vocations that God has in mind for His people. Each of us has his/her own unique Calling, and each one must decide whether or not to respond. God has made us trustees of our years of life here on this earth, and He has also made us trustees of our several unique Vocations. As trustees, each of us has the innate responsibility to utilize the time we have been given to be true to our Calling. I believe each of us is obligated to evaluate how, when, and where we are serving the Master. In our Father's House there are many rooms, and so in our book of life there are many chapters. That book is greater than the sum of its contents.

—PSALM 107:23–32; ST. MARK 6:34;

II CORINTHIANS 6:1–10

CHAPTER NINE

Hospital Chaplaincies

Joining Saint Raphael's Team

*J*esus ordained his pastors (St. Luke 10:9) and his Apostles (St. Mark 3:14f; 6:7, 13) to heal the sick and to cast out devils. The Church, from earliest time, has continued this ministry of healing (including the Sacrament of Holy Unction—the Anointing of the Sick—as specified in James 5:14f). Although the names of angels are rarely identified, some we refer to as archangels are named in both Testaments and in the Apocrypha, and they are distinguished by their function in their presumed leadership of angelic delegates for God.

The three sections that compose this chapter are dedicated to the hospital and healing ministry. Saint Raphael (Tobit 3:17) has been traditionally known as God's agent for healing. Under the patronage of Archangel Raphael, I share my formative and early experiences, with lessons learned. In the name of Saint Michael, archangel warrior for righteousness against Evil, I relate stories derived from my time with Marine Corps Field Medical Battalions under combat conditions. Under the watchful eye of the messenger archangel, Saint Gabriel, I relate subsequent experiences in the hospital and healing ministry (after Viet Nam), which demonstrate greater experience gained in prior ministries. These incidents are told in such a way as to explain how the minister acts on Saint Gabriel's Team as God's messenger.

God has often guided me in ministry through avenues of partnership with physicians, nurses, paramedics, therapists, and in institutions of healing. In relating the events that follow in this chapter, where exact identification seemed inappropriate, I have chosen to substitute pseudonyms where names might help the syntax.

Sequoia Hospital, Redwood City, California, 1955

As a deacon and curate in the nearest parish, I was assigned by the rector to be the Episcopal Visitor at Sequoia Hospital. Several times a week, I would pick up at the admitting office the slips on which entering patients had identified themselves with our denomination or with Eastern Orthodox Churches with whom we shared the Sacraments.

This was my first experience of calling on possibly vulnerable strangers and taking the unwanted risk of intruding where my presence might not be welcomed. The dilemma of what to say and how to enter a closed hospital room door added to my otherwise hidden timidity, and I would stand in the hallway outside each numbered entrance momentarily paralyzed, praying that I would do and say what might be proven helpful to the patient and to his or her relationship with the Church as an agent of healing. I was literally driven to prayer for the courage to initiate each visit as I gradually became at ease with this visitation ministry. Although I was led into a ministry that involved a great deal of hospital ministry, the initial need of prayer remained an integral part of serving on "Saint Raphael's Team" in Christ's ministry of healing.

One bright afternoon, as I was leaving the hospital at the completion of my rounds, I was stopped on the front walkway by one of the ward nurses whom I had come to know in the course of visitations. She was leaving, also at the end of her shift, and she seemed tired. "Father," she summoned. "Why is it that you always leave the hospital whistling and singing?" I replied that I had never thought of it before, but I promised to think about this and provide her with some reason—if I could discover one.

As I proceeded with my duties that day and evening, I pondered her question. Finally I had my answer to a question I was very glad she had asked. It seems that, without thought or plan, I had spontaneously followed a rather predictable route through the wards. I started in the intensive care units, then to the oncology and obviously terminal patients. Then I would proceed to the surgical trauma units, then to orthopedics and internal medicine wards. The last calls I would make, just before leaving, would be to give thanks with the new mothers and to bless their newborn infants.

My answer to that nurse the following day was mutually helpful to both of us. It boiled down to the fact that variety is the spice of a life of service, and that caregivers need to protect themselves emotionally as well as professionally in order to continue to serve and let Christ be the One to save. This is how I had evidently been guided to protect myself while still caring deeply.

The nurses warned me. But she was on my list, so I knocked and cautiously entered Ada's room. The reward I got for my intrusion was having a bed pan and its contents thrown in my direction. Having these hints of her desire to be left alone in her troubles, again I consulted the nursing staff. It seems that Ada had recently learned that she was in advanced stages of cancer, and she was enraged by her loss of energy and the anticipation of her fate. Whoever reached out to her, including the medical staff, would be struck by whatever lightning she could ignite. The task I accepted on the medical team was to do what I could to wear down her anger. I made it a point to crack the door ajar each time on my rounds just to say "Hi." After a week or ten days I dared to enter her room, and daily I inched closer to her bed. Finally we got to the point where we could converse, and then she became open to some ideas and suggestions.

The desired effect was taking place, and Ada was becoming reasonable, and, according to the nursing staff, she was becoming treatable. The weeks stretched on, and her stay in the critical care unit was increasingly justified by her condition.

As she recalled her baptism long before, she accepted Holy Communion, and Holy Unction for healing (whether it be for the strengthening of her body or the preparation of her soul for her promotion into Paradise). In one of our final visits, Ada spoke in the rough whisper that she could muster. What she said gave evidence of the spiritual growth that God had given her through our new relationship; yet I was both surprised and greatly humbled by the gift she gave me.

This very sick lady spoke with hesitation and with great effort in the weakened condition of her body, but what she said came from the newfound strength of her faith. It took some time for Ada to say what she did, and in the presence of her message I listened in awe.

In essence this is what she told me. "You taught me that everything in life needs to be offered to God, either in confession or in tribute. I want to offer you something so that you can help me offer it to God. As a minister, you have seen me change, and I am grateful for that. In response, I offer to you my death, so that you can tell others what happened to me after my anointing. Will you accept my gift?" As one so newly ordained, I was astounded, and it took me a while to respond intelligently. "I will be with you, and I accept your death with a sense of great honor. But as part of the transaction, I want your permission to tell everyone I instruct and prepare for Holy Confirmation in the Church about your gift and how the Sacrament of Healing helped you die. That way I will fulfill the request in your offer to pass along your gift to others." "Deal!" she responded. Soon thereafter Ada died quietly and in the Peace of Christ.

I have included Ada's story in every one of the Confirmation Classes I have taught to young and old alike for over five decades. This is the reason I include this event in this collection of the memoirs that have been most meaningful to me. I pray Ada's story will be helpful to you as well.

Herrick Memorial Hospital, Berkeley, California, 1957

Dr. Paul Morentz was a pioneer. Both Medical Doctor of psychiatry and ordained Lutheran Pastor and professor of pastoral theology at the Pacific Lutheran Theological Seminary, Dr. Morentz created a 6-unit summer course for pastors entitled "Pastor and Patient." It was conducted at Herrick Memorial Hospital for those in the pastoral ministry, and in the late 1950s it was a precursor of what would later become institutionalized as Clinical Pastoral Education.

It was my good fortune to be able to enroll in this summer intern experience while serving nearby Good Shepherd Mission in Berkeley. This course at Herrick Hospital (now absorbed into the Alta Bates Medical Center as its West Campus), included a full orientation to ministry to both patients and staff, with practicum requiring personal contact with both populations.

(Little did I ever imagine that twenty-eight years later I would be administering such a training program on a routine basis for Naval Reserve Chaplains at Naval Hospital Oakland.)

In the course of my participation, my ward visitations took me to the room of a heart patient of mature (but not yet "senior") years. Although I remember her true name vividly, for rhetorical purposes I will call her Mrs. Bloom. In six days of visits, Mrs. Bloom and I became fast friends, and she trusted me with many precious tales and confidences. The following Monday I was transferred to surgical services and pathology, which included rare opportunities to participate "behind the scenes." I had the opportunity to observe a gall bladder surgery. During this, I experienced a predictable psychological identification with the patient on the table to such a degree that when the surgeon called for the scalpel and made his first cut, I felt a paralyzing shock reaction. This was something that forearmed me for things I had to do in Viet Nam.

Following that surgery, I would next gown and assist in pathology at an autopsy. I did well with what was involved here until I dropped a tissue specimen in a glass receiving container of formaldehyde. A little paper label floating in the surface turned over as I inserted the sample of tissue, revealing the name of the deceased printed on it. "Bloom," it said!

I was startled and almost sickened by this revelation that one for whom I had learned to care had not only died, but had been consigned to a postmortem investigation in which I was involved. I was just beginning to understand the life of the physician, the nurse, the therapist, and the technician who could resist the temptation to become jaded in their professions of healing and care giving to persons in need. Although I had been serving in hospital ministry in my previous parish, at Herrick under Dr. Morentz and the medical staff, I was being introduced to the total picture of medical ministry which included patient care, yet which also reached into the heart of the inner world of the caregivers as well. I was just beginning to become an effective hospital minister.

—St. Luke 4:16–23; Acts 3:7–10

On Saint Michael's Team

The Book of Revelation (12:7f) tells us that Saint Michael did battle with Satan. "There was war in heaven." Well, I can attest to the fact that there has been war on earth after Satan was cast out of heavenly places. Christ's crucifixion provided us with ample evidence of this, as well as demonstrating the Source of ultimate victory.

Before battle, one of Abraham Lincoln's generals was reputed to have exclaimed to him: "I hope God is on our side today," to which the president is said to have promptly replied: "I pray we are on God's side." I have always accepted the fact that "war is hell," and, as such, it must be a very *last resort* for humankind. May it always be acknowledged by the participants in war that violent engagement has been entered into as the best of two evils—whatever the other evil may be.

When I was a missionary in Southeast Asia, I observed firsthand the need for reversing the "Domino Theory." This term described how the nations in that part of the world were falling, one by one, under the influence of Communism in both overt and subtle ways.

I remembered the history of how the economic empire building of the Japanese (called "Greater East Asia Co-Prosperity Sphere") was succeeding in the 1930s, but eventually failed when it became overwhelmed by an ambitious Japanese military later in that decade. When I lived in Asia, I observed that this history was being repeated, but this time with China as covert aggressor. Thus I was inclined to accept as a sad necessity American intervention in Viet Nam, and I was not neutral in my support of our military effort.

From where I had been living and ministering, far removed from the American political climate, I thought that when my country sent its armed forces to Viet Nam, this was indicative of a national consensus. The victims of what was a lack of general commitment were our career military personnel, our draftees, and the people of South Viet Nam—who were led to believe that our nation would stand by them to the end in the declared cause our diplomats vowed was ours, too.

I saw the wounded bodies and the dead from both sides of the conflict. I knew of the broken hearts as well, because one of them was mine. I admit my sentiments were not neutral in the beginning, but though my Commission was from the United States Navy, my Calling was from God to minister in that hell for a heavenly cause: to be an instrument of healing. This is why I found myself on Saint Michael's Team.

Third Medical Battalion, Third Marine Division, Da Nang, Viet Nam, 1966

Following Chaplain (Orientation) School in Newport, Rhode Island, I was ordered to the Field Medical Service School at Camp Pendleton, California, where precombat training is given to Hospital Corpsmen, Physicians, Dental Officers, and Chaplains who would be serving with the Fleet Marine Force. All of our group were bound for Viet Nam.

We learned about combat wounds and the dangers of cellulitis, booby traps, how to treat contaminated water for drinking, and what we would wear and carry. We did our 5-mile forced march at night, we slept in tents and in the open, and while encamped our class successfully captured (by stealth) the guidon pennant of our instructors. Some of the medical officer personnel were not happy to be drafted, much less to be "abducted" from their academically and clinically sterile environs. I was almost 37 years of age and a volunteer, while most of my "classmates" were in their 20s. The school was excellent, but nothing could completely prepare us for the year ahead.

Before picking up an infantry battalion on the D.M.Z., I was initially assigned to the "C" Company, 3rd Medical Battalion in Da Nang, known as "Charlie Med," then to Alpha Company in Phu Bai as the Third Division moved farther north. Then I was loaned to the First Marine Division to return south to Freedom Hill near Da Nang with their First Medical Battalion. This was in the "facility" where I had served before with "Charlie Med."

All this translates to a hospital ministry that handled great volumes of trauma and death in hardback tent wards and Quonset hut operating rooms. There was a small tent behind surgery for those rare lulls, where alcohol was dispensed to commissioned staff members—our version of an Officers' Club, known affectionately as "The Recovery Room."

Triage was a covered area adjacent to the helo pad. "Jolly Green" Marine helicopters, Chinooks, Hueys, and the Air Force ambulance with two slanted side-mounted rotors with blades that almost touched the ground on either side (which had to be approached only from the front—we called it "the widow maker"), would arrive in chaotic waves. They would disgorge their muddy, bloody passengers, some on stretchers, some walking, and some in body bags. Hours would go by without a sound. Then an operation or an ambush, or an encampment would be overrun by the enemy, and we would hear the ominous sound of approaching aircraft and could receive as many as 65 casualties in a twenty-minute period.

The first major challenge that confronted me was that of developing a trust relationship with the physicians and paramedics in triage. They needed to know that I had a valid reason for being there, and that I was in a position to support them and their goals as I went about doing the work of priest chaplain. They soon learned that I was on the team, not an obstacle to it.

Corpsmen carried stretchers up the ramp and placed them on sawhorses that paralleled each other on either side of a middle aisle in the tarpaulin covered enclosure. The dead in body bags from the field were taken to an outside area, hidden by a wall of canvas to one side of the ramp to the triage.

I would pass from stretcher to stretcher as they were placed in the triage area, anointing, washing mud off faces, consoling, seeing that those rushed immediately to surgery were anointed and reassured first and quickly. The physicians and corpsmen would make way for this, knowing that I would be but a second. Then I would minister to the others when physicians and the medical staff were not assisting them, rotating from patient to patient while they awaited the doctors.

By soothing prayer, reassuring words, and in some cases casual conversation, one could see a dramatic reduction in anxiety. They had been transported from the terrors of battle where some had lost friends, often in the dark of night, suddenly thrust into what could appear to be an impersonal confusion of our "emergency room"—with people rushing, shouting orders, and performing emergency procedures right next to them. But it was good teamwork, because each of us tending to the wounded knew our role and respected the vital role of the other. This professionalism saved lives, expedited miracles, and developed among the crew unforgettable bonds of friendship.

I recall a time in the triage when a young Marine with a groin wound heard the news that one of his testicles had been destroyed. "Will it work?" he cried out to the doctor. When the physician only said, "I guess so," I added, "Son, you've got two. God gave you a spare tire." This met with the physician's approval, and our patient finally smiled.

Another wounded PFC with shrapnel in his thighs was obviously frightened as he watched a newly arrived doctor (who did not look much older than his adolescent patient) tearing off his clothing to gain access to the wounds. As hands ripped and scissors cut away the Marine's dirty green trousers and under shorts, the surprised and offended doctor confronted his patient and angrily demanded: "How come you shit yourself?" The scared youth replied tearfully: "But sir, we was ambushed!" As I overheard this repartee, I could not restrain a burst of spontaneous laughter that seemed inappropriate to our new doctor, but which set his patient at ease. That response grew to haunt that Medical Officer until his ego adjusted to the fact that his mission was one with that of our patients. However, every time something went wrong around "Charlie Med," someone was often heard to protest mockingly: "But sir, we was ambushed!"

When there would be an appropriate break in the demands of the living, I would rush to the outside yard strewn with body bags, open each, record in my pocket-sized notebook the names and serial numbers of the deceased, administer final prayers for each—for the repose of the dead as well as for the comfort of their surviving families when they would receive the dreaded notification.

Sometimes I would take it upon myself (legally or not) to cleanse wallets of photographs of exploits during staging on Okinawa or on R&R, pictures which might not be pleasing to mothers, wives, or to loved ones back home. All this had to be done frequently by flashlight, and rapidly, before the next helos might set down on our landing pad with a new load of Marines or Soldiers covered with blood and mud.

On one twilight run to the side yard, I hastily unzipped a body bag, and a young Marine (who had evidently been unconscious in the battlefield and had been taken for dead) suddenly sat up and asked: "Where am I?" I was not about to tell him!

—◦◦◦—

When action was heavy and demands great, as triage would empty out a bit, I would assist as allowed in surgery. Our operating rooms were two Quonset huts side by side, accessible from triage and from the wards by ramps covered for protection from occasional heavy monsoon rains. It was in surgery that my hospital internship in Berkeley proved to be of greatest value. It was here that my ministry to staff as well as to patients was exercised far beyond what use I might have been to the procedures of medicine. I think the surgical team was aware of my prayers, silent though they were, ardently being offered for them as I assisted in other ways, as well. Here, as elsewhere in the Medical Battalion, as undeserving an agent for the Divine as I might have been, I stood as a reminder of God's Presence and His compassion that embraced us all in the midst of constant tragedy, trauma, and pain.

Yet our patients ministered to us as well. One picture that remains etched in my memory is that of a man, perhaps in his late twenties or early thirties, on his back on the operating table, with no less than four surgeons working simultaneously on wounds on various parts of his body. His arms were strapped outstretched on boards extending at right angles to the table at the patient's shoulders, with doctors working on each. This sight was reminiscent of the Christ nailed to the Cross on Calvary to save us from enmity and its consequences—a reminder that our pains are His pains as well.

One night I held a man's feet as one of our general surgeons and our oral surgeon together removed a live M-79 propelled grenade from his throat. I know both of these physicians today, and I am constrained from revealing their identities without their permission. But for the sake of this true story, I will preserve the initials of the head of the surgical team involved by the pseudonym Doctor "Joe Carson."

After this patient had returned to the United States and when he had progressed substantially in his rehabilitation, his story was reported in the *Chicago Tribune*. The article about his experience and his progress in recovery was headed by a statement, the sense of which was "I prayed to Jesus Christ, and I was healed." When that newspaper was circulated through the staff, "Joe Carson" stated aloud, "I think he prayed to the wrong J.C.!" Again I was reminded that I was needed where I was, doing what I was doing for both staff and patients, and fulfilling my Vocation as well.

During a night when I was in the Operating Room (if I might dignify our field surgeries with such a title) and a surgery was in process, suddenly the sound of the electric generator began to whine with a progressively lower tone, and we were bathed in darkness. It was at this very moment that the surgeon's scalpel accidentally tipped the aorta and blood gushed in a fine spray out of the open chest cavity. Fortunately I had made it a practice of carrying a pen sized flashlight in my pocket. It was there when we needed it! I clicked it on and pointed it into the surgical field. The physician's gloved and skilled hand seized the punctured vessel. We all had reason to celebrate that night. Although I had always been welcomed there, after that, the presence of the chaplain in surgery seemed to take on new meaning both during operations and in our "Recovery Room" after the fact.

I was loaned for a time to "Alpha Med" in Phu Bai, to the north of Da Nang. The encampment was developing as a "rear" area for an increasing number of infantry battalions, and would later be operational headquarters for the Third Division when the First Marine Division moved north from Chu Lai to Da Nang. Alpha Med was slightly smaller than "C" Med at the time.

Its one surgical Quonset was adjacent to the end of the civilian Vietnamese airstrip, which was also used on occasion by military transport supply planes and combat helicopters. It also served as our MedEvac Landing Zone. I add this for the reader to imagine what it was like for the medical team when a major surgery was in process in the night at times when the sound of incoming mortal rounds could be heard advancing down the airstrip. At first, the insidious "whoump... whoump..." would be faint; then become increasingly louder and louder, as the lethal rounds danced their destructive way progressively closer to the Medical Battalion. Patients in the hardback tented wards, some carrying others, and all other staff would run for revetments and foxholes. Some would jump under cots with mattresses. But where does the surgical team go when before them on the table is an anesthetized patient, the field open, and surgery in process? It did not happen often, but when it did, I observed the Hippocratic Oath heroically kept without question or hesitation. Fortunately the mortars never reached the very end of that runway. If they had, I probably would not be around to write this!

—◈—

Ward visitations were a must, and the Navy hospital ministry stresses that every noncritical patient will receive at least one daily pastoral call. Critical patients will receive more contacts as might be appropriate. The frequency of these visitations develops a closer relationship between chaplain and patient, and assures the patient of the staff's continued concern for his or her welfare. This rule was kept "in country," as well as in large naval hospitals and medical centers elsewhere. This was especially important with our rapidly revolving census—many of the more serious being airlifted out of the combat zone from the Da Nang Air Base when they were sufficiently stabilized for travel—and with our medics preoccupied with constantly new demands. Prayer, the sharing of Scripture, and talk about home was always welcomed.

On the wards, I got so that I could identify a patient's home state, and sometimes even the county, by his speech accent. I escorted Francis Cardinal Spellman, comédienne Martha Raye, and other dignitaries through the wards at "Charlie Med."

On one occasion, when contact with what we called "the world" had been sparse, I persuaded some Navy Nurses to fly in from one of the hospital ships to "Alpha Med" in Phu Bai to inspire the troops. When their visit through the wards was met with a minimum of response, I asked of one of the seemingly more mature patients why there appeared to be a lack of enthusiasm. He rolled over on his cot with his back to me and responded with his head in the pillow: "Ah, round eyes," then continued his nap. The implication was that he had been in Asia so long that American women were boring to him.

Occasionally in the mornings at "Charlie Med," the Commanding General would come down from Division Headquarters on Da Nang's Freedom Hill to pin Purple Heart Medals on postsurgical patients, even in our Intensive Care area or on the X-ray table. His surprise visits were very well received.

Once when escorting him on the wards, as we approached one who would be a recipient of this award, I greeted the Marine with an enthusiastic "Hello, Ted!" "Do you know me?" asked the startled young infantryman. I was able to answer him: "I know we put you to sleep shortly after you got here, so you would not know what happened after that. However, not only do I know you, but last night when your chest was open, I held your heart in my gloved hand!"

A Marine guard dog handler was on our X-ray table receiving his "wound medal" from a colonel from First Division Headquarters, when a photographer from *Look* magazine asked the man's permission to take his picture and to use his story in his publication. The Marine, lying on his back in pain just after surgery, seemed rather abrupt when he replied: "Well, I already gave you permission yesterday!"

It seems that the reporter and his photographer had followed the Marine dog handler and his dog on rounds of storage warehouses on the Da Nang Air Base the day before. Then, after dark, the reporter had come to "Charlie Med" to cover our activities. The Marine had been wounded by a sniper that night, and had come through our triage and surgery after midnight. The magazine team had photographed this Marine, together with others, in both places during progressive stages of treatment, but without recognizing that he was the same man on whom they had reported and photographed the day before. At the morning meeting with the colonel present, the coincidence came as a complete surprise to the newsmen. His story then took on a new twist.

Later, when my wife was sitting in a dentist's waiting room in Berkeley, she opened a copy of *Look*, and casually turned to this story with the "before and after" pictures under the banner: "A Marine's Longest Night."★ As she turned the page to view the center spread photographs of the operating room, she saw not only the Marine on the table and the surgeons at work, but also, to her surprise, her chaplain husband there in the attending surgical team.

—◦◦◦—

What distressed one young trooper more than the wound in his arm was the fact that it had messed up his tattoo. The débridement was completed and he had been written up for the offense of having had an accidental discharge of his own weapon. He was in physical pain. But, after talking with him as a chaplain, I was still convinced that his primary concern was not for his arm or his military record, but for his tattoo. From what I could make of it, it had once had intertwined in its pictorial design the motto: "Born to Lose."

He explained all this by telling me how, when in Infantry Training Regiment at Camp Pendleton after completion of Boot Camp, he and his buddies all went out and got "tacked up." I asked him why he had chosen those words, "Born to Lose." "Well," he answered, "that must be my middle name. I'm always messing up somehow." Here was a Marine who was defeated before he met the enemy, because he really believed that he was a loser. I told him that I was glad his tattoo was destroyed, because I thought that his choice of those words reflected the self-destructive belief that he seemed to be fulfilling. "What can I do about it now?" he asked. I responded: "Get well. Get yourself out of trouble. And if you are into tattoos, get another one that reads: 'Born to Win,' and then live up to it!"

In my ward visitations, I met another Marine whose jaw was wired shut so the break could heal. He would be medevaced to the States, and, when returned to full duty, would probably be ordered back to complete another tour of duty in Viet Nam. It was difficult for him to communicate with me, but between his limited speech and scrawl on paper, I learned his story. First, however, he made me make a pledge of secrecy. He explained that it was his practice, when in the rear area, to turn in early on Saturday night so he would be fresh for early church services on Sunday morning. However, at times like these his buddies usually went looking for a good time at the Enlisted Club at the Da Nang Air Base (or elsewhere, if they could get away with it). In preparation for their celebrations, they made a rumpus in the barracks to taunt "the Christian" who was trying to sleep. One of the revelers came over to his bunk and mockingly, for the benefit of his audience, said twice, "Hey, Christian, do you turn the other cheek?" Not getting a rise out of him, he took the butt of his M-16 and hit him in the jaw. It was not until the next day that his empty bunk gave them a clue that he had been seriously hurt.

When they traced him to "Charlie Med," the perpetrator came anxiously to visit him, and saw that his jaw had been broken and that his jaw was wired shut—and would be for some time. In whispered and frightened voice he asked: "Did you tell? Did you tell?" With this, the patient told me, he wrote on his pad of paper for the other to read: "I turn the other cheek."

As the "big bird" was making its steep descent on its approach to the Da Nang Air Base, an Army Private felt a stinging sensation in his buttocks, and, on moving his hand down past his seat belt, discovered blood. He had received his first bullet wound through the skin of the aircraft, even before standing on Viet Nam's soil. What a welcome! After the intruding round was removed, as well as some débridement of the offended tissue, he was our guest at the field hospital for a week or so, sleeping on his stomach and eating standing up. Then it was bandaged, and with a "see you later" greeting, it was on to the war for him.

A soldier was flown in from the Army Engineers. Tom Long was just that— *long*—much taller than six feet. That may have saved his life as well as saving our staff a lot of work. It seems that Tom was standing on a ladder while building a bunker. He was holding in his mouth some of the tenpenny nails he was driving into the timbers. When the ladder started to give way, there was only one nail left between his lips, and... you've got it... Tom suddenly swallowed the nail!

What to do was the plea of his sergeant who accompanied him on the helo. The diagnosis, coming from a surgeon busy triaging critical combat injuries, frightened me when I overheard it. "Put that soldier to bed and feed him lots of bread! Take an X-ray every morning! ...Next!" The Doc knew best!

The journey of Tom Long's tenpenny nail was followed with interest, and his X-rays became a matter of daily reporting. One morning he went out back to the three-holer to discharge his duty, when "PLINK!" came the echoed sound from the drum filled with chemicals below him. And then it was back to duty for long Tom Long. Someday he may be asked: "What did you do in the war, Grandfather?" Then he may be faced with a decision to tell or not to tell the story about what happened to him as a young soldier at "Charlie Med."

—◆◆◆—

The lesson in all this is similar to that which the nurse at Sequoia Hospital in Redwood City helped me to see some eleven years before. The healing ministry is composed of a wide range of encounters, and the truly caring person finds him/herself continually on an emotional roller coaster. In order to continue to give of oneself without burning out or becoming jaded, one needs to see the joys that balance the sorrows, and to walk in the Presence of Him who is our unlimited resource beyond those of our limited selves. He who experienced Cross and Tomb gives us His Victory. As we assimilate His gifts on a daily basis, there comes reassurance of the significance of life, and the assurance of Life Eternal.

—ST. LUKE 10:30–37; ST. JOHN 19:5; REVELATION 21:2–6

★ J. Robert Moskin and James Hansen. "A Marine's Longest Night" (story of Corporal Andre Williams, USMC), *Look,* May 2, 1967, pages 30–35.

Acting for Saint Gabriel

*S*aint Gabriel was the archangel of proclamation, and the message delivered consistently for God was: "Do not be afraid!" This message, together with the assurance of God's loving favor, came to Mary at the Annunciation (St. Luke 1:30), and Joseph received a similar angelic message of assurance and explanation (in St. Matthew 1:20). "Do not be afraid! It is *good* news!" was proclaimed to the frightened shepherds in the fields that the Savior was at last among us (St. Luke 2:10). Saint Gabriel's message in times of doubt, uncertainty, and fear, permeates the New Testament and comes to each of us through the love and ministry of Christ and His Church.

As a Christian priest, it has been my great honor to act for Saint Gabriel by delivering God's message of encouragement and greater glory to people in need of assimilating it in times of despair, doubt and pain. This vital message was shared in many differing circumstances and crises, but one most evident was in the hospital ministry with the sick and the dying.

National Naval Medical Center, Bethesda, Maryland, 1968

"Stop hurting my patients!" the orthopedic surgeon demanded. "Good heavens, I would never do such a thing!" I countered. "Well, then, stop holding the doors for them."

The orthopedic wings were long open wards filled with combat casualties, many missing limbs. The fire doors in that area of the hospital were heavy, and of course I was obliging what I saw to be obvious needs. "If I let the door swing, it could knock a patient on crutches on his can," I protested. The physician correctly replied: "Until he gets knocked on his can a time or two, he'll never figure out how not to let it happen." I learned something not only about working with rehabilitation patients, but something about life as well.

When I first entered Ward 5-B, a cheer went up. Some of the beds were occupied by Marines I had helped medevac from the battlefield. One reminded me that when the medevac chopper brought in enemy fire, I was lying on top of him, clothed in my flak jacket, to protect him from incoming artillery fire and shrapnel, while he was shouting at me: "Be careful of my leg!"

Chaplains were promised that if they had volunteered for Viet Nam duty, they would be given their first choice of follow-on duty. I filled out my Preference Card with a red felt pen in a foxhole at Cam Lo. I wrote in bold print: "Too much blood out here. *No Naval Hospital!* West Coast. 12th Naval District (San Francisco Bay Area), please."

Yes, you've got it! I was sent to the National Naval Medical Center, Bethesda, Maryland. But I know it was all the result of God's Detailer overriding my mind and the decisions of the Navy Detailer, because I was where I needed to be. As chaplain to postcombat veterans (among others in the wards I was assigned to care for), I was "coming down" emotionally at the same time they were. Our many conversations served as therapeutic debriefings. We ministered to each other unashamedly.

The hospital corpsmen on those wards at Bethesda had come to that duty primarily from two sources: those who knew they would be going to Viet Nam (some of whom were new graduates from Corps School), and those fortunate enough to be among the twenty-five percent of those who had survived a tour there without having been killed or having suffered disabilities which had consigned them to patient lists themselves. Those facing imminent assignment to combat units while caring for the wounded, disfigured, and those in pain were understandably anxious.

One fine young Hospitalman I knew serving on the ward had never revealed the depth of his anxiety, but, apparently to avoid combat duty, he faked a suicide attempt one sunny Saturday morning in the barracks with an overdose of pills. What may have been a gesture sadly became a permanent solution to his fears, a great loss to his family, and a loss to the Navy. From this I deduced that even when it was not expressed, the high degree of anxiety among those male caregivers must be shared, and needed to be taken into account as part of ministry to staff as well as to patients.

As I approached the ward duty desk on one occasion, a corpsmen cried out to me in a desperate whisper: "When do these guys stop fighting the war?" He was referring to the banter among the patients in the orthopedic ward where he was on duty. I was able to answer his question (if not his desperation) by saying, "See that screen door at the end of the ward (leading out onto the grass)? They stop fighting the war when they pass through it. They don't discuss the war, because they know that the folks outside either don't understand or don't want to hear about it. They share their feelings here inside that screen door because they need to, and because here it is safe to do so."

"Chaplain, we've got a problem." The Nurse Officer told me that one of the ward patients in a spica body cast had a fiancée who had come to visit him. During his Viet Nam tour of duty, even though it was shortened by his being wounded, her pregnancy was becoming increasingly obvious. The couple wanted to marry, but he was months from becoming ambulatory. "What can be done for them?" asked the concerned woman Lieutenant.

Soon thereafter, when his visitor came, we pulled the curtain around the patient's bed so I could begin a brief series of premarital counseling sessions with a degree of privacy. When the day arrived, Judy stood at the left side of George's bed, and they held hands. The tray table became a makeshift Altar. Amidst the other occupants of the beds in the long ward, surrounded by the ward medical staff, with one of his Marine buddies acting for her family to give the bride away, we had a wedding on 5-C! The Nurse Officer who had brought the need of this couple to my attention then wheeled in a cart which held a large wedding cake, and the reception (with refreshments minus alcohol) began. Although the honeymoon would have to be delayed, the birth of their first child came some weeks later in our hospital. As far as I know, the canon law of the Church was not offended, and I believe they all lived happily ever after.

As the Medical Center buildings were designated at the time, the Sick Officers' Quarters, V.I.P. wards (with the exception of the second floor Presidential suite) and the women's wards were in the landmark tower at the center of the sprawling hospital. As inefficient as such a plan was for the delivery of medical care, it had pleased President Franklin D. Roosevelt, and it remained that way pending later significant additions that have now been made to the complex.

Bars had been added to the tower windows after our first Secretary of Defense, James Vincent Forrestal, had leaped from the 14th floor during an episode of severe mental depression in 1949. The NNMC Tower that has always been the distinguishing feature of the Bethesda medical center was an entirely different world inside, compared to the "outrigger" three floors of enlisted wards that surrounded it below.

Betty Moore, one of the civilian nurses who augmented the medical staff of the hospital, was dedicated to her tasks in the tower wards. The then-Vice President Hubert Humphrey came to the hospital one afternoon, and the Navy staff was alerted to observe all possible protocols on his behalf. While military personnel were buzzing about this visit, Betty was preoccupied with her rounds and responsibilities, quite oblivious to the excited banter about this anticipated presence. She was balancing a tray of medications en route from the 8th Floor nursing station to the patient rooms, when she passed directly in front of the elevator bay. One of the doors opened momentarily without discharging a passenger. Her military nurse counterpart at the desk behind her called excitedly as Betty stood directly in front of the open door: "Betty! Look! Look! There's Humphrey! There's Humphrey!" Betty, with tray in hand, whirled around just a few feet from the Vice President and his party in the elevator, and asked with some honest irritation at being interrupted: "Humphrey who?" I was standing where I could see a very chagrined look on the face of our distinguished patient as the doors automatically closed between them. Betty, still unaware of what had just transpired, rushed on to deliver her pills. I guess the V.P. may have had a little starch taken out of his collar. I had a good belly laugh, as I thought all this was just a part of another routine day in the hospital tower.

"Damn it, General! Just sit down and shut up!" I had just stepped off the elevator on the 14th floor. I was startled to see a tall, thin, elderly Alzheimers patient meekly follow these orders. I was amazed even more to see who was giving the orders. It was a non-rated Hospitalman who was evidently temporarily in charge of patient care while the commissioned supervisor was off the ward. But I guess this World War II hero (whose name would be familiar to many readers), confused by his dementia, was becoming a liability on the floor. The Corpsman was just doing what he had been told to do. Yes, it did take me a little while to adjust to the tower.

On the Sick Officers' Quarters (SOQ) floor in a very small single room, a Marine Second Lieutenant (who had been a Platoon Commander in Viet Nam) lay on his back in a body cast in a position of virtual helplessness— which was extremely frustrating to this previously active gent. To complicate matters for him, the ward supervisor was a middle-aged female nurse, Lieutenant Commander in rank and First Sergeant in demeanor. These two personalities clashed. But the Marine Officer found himself in a position of severe disadvantage, which added considerably to his physical discomfort. According to his complaints to me, the nurse saw to it that there was a glass of apple juice on his tray at what seemed to him like every meal, and he quickly developed a hatred for apple juice. The more he appealed for something else, the more the disputed apple juice was forced upon him by this superior officer.

In his small single room, the hospital bed was against an outside wall. The window sill (which was a bit of a ledge that could hold small items) was within his reach. On it stood an empty graduated glass container for the collection of samples of his urine for testing. There being no flower pot handy, he emptied the apple juice from his lunch tray into this flask when he was not under surveillance. It seems that the nurse supervisor entered his room that afternoon and observing the liquid on the window ledge from a distance, commented (with the air of teacher to child) something to the effect that as a sign of his progress it looked a bit clearer. At that, he grabbed the glass and exclaimed: "That's not good enough! Like good navy coffee, let's run it through a second time," promptly gulping it down.

As I came on the floor, she came running down the hall screaming: "He's *crazy!* That Marine is *crazy!*" I ran to his room to find him laughing hysterically inside his immovable body cast. "I got her! At last I got her! It took me six weeks, and I finally got her!" he triumphed.

As I left the room he was singing with great gusto: "From the halls of Montezuma...." Fortunately no disciplinary charges were filed in the aftermath of that event in the hospital tower.

The Women's Wards were several floors below the SOQ. In those days (before Rowe v. Wade), all abortions were illegal. I counseled with young Navy Women (then still known as "Women Accepted for Volunteer Emergency Service" or WAVES) who had come to our Emergency Room after unsuccessful attempts to abort themselves with wire coat hangers or knitting needles.

These frantic and very tearful sessions I shall never, never forget. These girls were so alone in their plight as they faced their consciences and an uncertain, perhaps fearful future. They etched in my memory their tragic desperation, and on my heart a pastoral concern for which I had no clear solution. I knew that something had to be changed in the medical and legal world. The Seventh Commandment was not just "a suggestion," but neither was the Sixth. Definite change was urgently needed to make responsible forgiveness an alternative to suicide or fetal murder, or dangerous attempts to perform either one.

On the foot of each bed in the hospital there was a metal frame in which a card was inserted which identified in large print an abbreviated indication of the religious affiliation which the patient had identified as his or hers upon admission. This expedited the daily calling ministry of the chaplain teams as they made their rounds.

In the surgical area on the Women's Floor, I visited with a lady who seemed to enjoy a rather intellectual line of conversation. Because it seemed to be helpful to her (and pleasant for me), I took a little extra time talking with her at the risk of shortening other patient visits. In one such conversation she asked me why I was so interested in extrasensory perception. I replied that I knew little about it, but because the bed tag that identified her spiritual interests was marked "ESP" I was inquiring to learn more about the subject as well as showing interest in her as a patient. She was surprised, and responded with gusto: "Oh no! ESP? I'm an Episcopalian!"

Amusement covered my embarrassment, but, as the Episcopal Chaplain to the Medical Center, I had missed what probably would have been a more helpful line of dialogue, given the limited time that we had.

An official from the Presidential Suite in the hospital came to the Chaplain's Office asking for Father Fitzpatrick (I have changed the name here). The Chaplains' Secretary said that we had a Chaplain Fitzpatrick, but asked just who it was that was being summoned. It seems that this Protestant Chaplain, much senior to me, had been identifying himself in the V.I.P. suites as an Episcopalian, because many who were treated there were Episcopalians. The motto of the Navy Chaplain Corps is "Cooperation without Compromise." This was the first and, happily, the only time in my 26 years in the Chaplain Corps that this vow was compromised in this manner. I think I was more sad than I was furious at the time.

In this case, I was able to respond to the needs of the Johnson family and expedite seeing that their daughter Lucy, who had just given birth, was able to receive Holy Communion. She insisted on coming to the Chapel in a wheelchair to receive with the congregation on a Sunday morning, rather than receiving privately from the Reserved Sacrament. I appreciated this act of devotion and her understanding of what the Church is all about. Yet in their publicized search for a name for little newborn Lucinda, my suggestion of "Baby Bird" (after grandmother Lady Bird Johnson), was politely ignored.

The lovely, well-appointed hospital chapel then had an outside entrance with a convenient circular drive and parking area. This accommodated the significant number of high-ranking active duty and retired military officers, their families, Members of Congress, and various diplomats who lived on the Maryland suburban side of Washington and who enjoyed worshipping at the chapel. On the "inboard" side, the chapel was accessible to the first floor of the medical center, of which it is structurally a part, through doors from the passageway (Navy talk for "hallway"). The combination lectern and pulpit stood at the Altar Rail and adjacent to one of the doors leading into the hospital corridor.

One Sunday morning as I was preaching, I remember making a gesture to emphasize an important point in my message. As I made my point, I spontaneously brought the palm of my hand down hard on the wooden pulpit stand. "Bang!" Simultaneously the fire alarm in the hall right outside the door went off. In turn this excited the psychiatric patients who, with their escorts, traditionally occupied the last two rows of pews. Some, convinced that I had summoned the end of the age, stood on the pews and began shouting, some wept, and some began beating their chests. This was a sermon I wanted to forget, but it was a worship service that the distinguished visitors who regularly augmented our congregation of staff and patients will probably always remember!

After fourteen months of ministering to "all sorts and conditions" of patients—from leaders who were moving the world to the "snuffies" who had carried the world on their backs in battle—I felt compelled to return where I felt my work was yet unfinished. I had missed the Tet Offensive of 1968.

In January 1969, I left this wonderful house of healing miracles to head westward to language school, then back to help carry the burdens of war.

Saint Mary's Medical Center, McAuley Neuropsychiatric Institute, San Francisco, California, 1972–73

Part of my postgraduate study plan was to earn first the Master of Arts in Pastoral Psychology, and then the Doctorate. The Master's program included practicum in counseling and an internship in psychology at one of the major psychiatric hospitals in the San Francisco Bay Area.

It was my good fortune to be selected for the year at McAuley under the supervision of Miss Pat Jones, L.C.S.W., the intake supervisor for the institute. She was such an able mentor through that clinical year, that at my request, she was appointed Adjunct Professor to serve as my guide through my doctoral dissertation. Thus I had several years of access to the resources of that hospital, and I performed an academic year of counseling with clients in the outpatient clinic. Pat saw to it that my patients were those who manifested a wide variety of symptomatologies and ages so as to broaden my learning and provide opportunities for critiquing treatment strategies. It was an outstanding environment that challenged professional growth in my Vocation.

By "growth in my Vocation," I am referring to the priesthood. Even though, as the result of this internship, and the degrees I earned, I gained qualifications for the California license of Marriage and Family Therapist, I viewed my acquired skills in counseling as adjuncts to ministry. Clergy must be counselors, and I wanted to "hold my feet to the fire" of responsible professionalism in the counseling field. In the counseling situation, the client or parishioner comes because of a vulnerability and a need. It is usually a fragile time of life for the seeker, and I wanted to honor this precious trust with the best insights and the best skills that I could acquire. I was not seeking a substitute occupation. However, when not obligated to a full-time church commitment, I have used my license as a means of continuing a ministry to persons in need.

I was at McAuley in a role that was unique for me. I was familiar with the hospital setting and even that of psychiatric wards. But I had always been the chaplain and the priest in that environment. The time at McAuley was spent, not with collar and pyx, but with smock and tie. It was not unlike my days as a seminarian, when I returned to ship's boiler rooms as just another sailor. In that situation, I was without the protection of being known as "of the cloth," yet committed to living as a follower of Christ in the merchant seamen's environment—to be known only by "my fruits" (cf. St. Matthew 7:20).

Although this was a Roman Catholic hospital, the professional community was secular, in that each professional was "on his own" as far as religious expectations were concerned. It was a challenge that gave me an indelible understanding of the strength of character that was expected of lay people on the job.

When I was in training at Herrick Memorial in Berkeley, I gained insights into the life stresses of those in medical vocations, insights that became an enormous resource for ministry in Viet Nam and thereafter. Now I was in another role which would sharpen my pastoral skills for ministry to both clients and providers. It caused me to experience, from the inside, common experiences and feelings of those in vocations of mental health. (At the time I did not expect that this was simultaneously preparing me to serve in the remote future in that capacity.)

An additional insight with which I was endowed from this experience seemed to have some application in the pastoral ministry. In the Church, it is properly stressed that the Grace of God and His Sacraments are free for the asking. As a corollary to this concept, I was trained as a priest to ignore financial requirements for my time and efforts. But in the clinical setting, where clients paid directly for therapy, I discovered that they tended to work harder to assimilate what I was able to provide for them. Clients who contributed to their own progress generally experienced greater and more rapid improvement in their lives and families.

I began to see that many who sought my counsel in the pastor's office seemed to be less committed to making life changes when compared to those who paid for the same services in my office as a licensed therapist. Further, I learned to "listen with an intense ear" to those who said they were seeking "a *Christian* therapist," to discern whether or not they were seeking an easier path to change by means of what is called "cheap grace."

I gained greater compassion for ministerial colleagues who, for conscientious reasons, were abandoning the parish for the rapidly developing professions in the field of secular counseling. It is certainly not universal, but, in general, what I am describing represents a conflict that is frustrating for trained pastoral counselors. On the other hand, this gives credence to the establishment of parish- and diocesan-sponsored counseling centers which provide clergy and lay counselors who are psychologically trained and professionally licensed for this specialized ministry, and where a scale for compensation can exist.

My experience in the clinical setting gave me a greater appreciation for parish stewardship endeavors (even though they seemed too far removed from individual pastoral counseling cases that needed commitment for their own sake). One of the Deans of our National Cathedral is reputed to have said: "Living waters are free, but the plumbing costs."

An additional illustration of this is that, in my parish experience, I discovered when placing books or pamphlets on the tract rack in the narthex, folks will obligingly pick them up. But when a price, even a small one, is expected by having it marked on each item, the purchaser is much more likely to read and make use of the literature once it has been acquired.

Working in the hospital, even as a volunteer intern, I learned that even as a minister, "the laborer is worthy of his hire" (St. Luke 10:7a and I Timothy 5:18). This amendment to my concept of the role of the minister and priest gave me new potency as God's person, and by setting greater limits on what I would tolerate, I found that my effectiveness was greatly enhanced by being *the person* who wears the collar.

Naval Hospital Oakland, Oakland, California, 1985–87

Following sea duty on what was the world's largest ship and its battle group, I was assigned to the Naval Hospital, Oakland as Director of the Department of Pastoral Care and Chaplain Services. We had a number of clergy on the team, and I was excited to have the first female Rabbi and her Rabbi husband join us.

Our enlisted staff of Religious Program Specialists possessed extremes on both ends of the scales of dependability and reliability. In addition to being an acute care medical facility with outpatient clinics for military active duty and retired personnel and their dependents, our emergency room was designated as the trauma center for all of East Oakland.

An inpatient Alcohol Rehabilitation Center was also located on our campus. This was also a teaching hospital for Medical, Dental, and Medical Service Corps for both commissioned and enlisted personnel. The Chaplain Corps part of this was to provide annually several two-week classes of instruction for Naval Reserve Chaplains. There were 20 or 30 participants in each of these classes. As a result, in addition to patient care, the "Department of Pastoral Care" became a provider for hospital ministerial education for experienced clergy from all over the United States.

Although I required of myself a place on the 24-hour duty roster equal with that of the other chaplains and a presence on the ward assignments, and although I had a chaplain of senior rank as my administrator, the ultimate leadership responsibilities were certainly mine. These included the Fitness Reports for all the staff and for the transient student chaplains. I enjoyed facilitating a weekly therapy group at the Alcohol Rehabilitation Center (ARC). I relished the fact that our struggling efforts to pioneer in this field fifteen years before at Naval Air Station, Alameda, which had met with such resistance from the command, had come to fruition throughout the entire Navy and Marine Corps. The psychiatrist in charge of the ARC knew of my previous efforts and respected me for them.

My passion was patient care. I did not eschew the leadership role nor was I hesitant about being pastor to my shepherds. But I felt a growing frustration when confined to a desk and the constant need to correct support staff incompetence, especially in a hospital with sick and dying fellow humans. I was coming to terms with the conflict between the career advancement I had achieved and my Vocation as a pastor. I knew I would rather be on the wards and in the trauma center than shuffling papers in the office or mediating cat fights behind the counter in the reception area. Hospital duty here was very different for me than when I was in Bethesda, ministering to the wounded in the open wards and with patients in the rarefied atmosphere of "The Tower." The following stories illustrate how I kept involved in pastoral care.

—⟋⟋⟋—

There was a crash of breaking glassware. "Jesus Christ!" someone yelled. My immediate response, even though not in view of the calamity, was to yell in response: "No! Just His humble servant."

I had just emerged from the elevator on one of the upper ward floors when a male nurse in one of the corridors nearby had dropped a tray of beakers; hence the spontaneous oath. What began as crisis promptly turned to humor. Loud laughter resounded from the rooms and echoed down the corridors surrounding the nursing stations on either side of the elevator lobby.

The chaplain's presence had evidently saved somebody's day, and had made the day for others.

It was Saturday night about midnight. I had the 24-hour duty, and I was making my rounds of the quiet floors and the intensive care units. The service elevator opened on the surgery floor and a patient occupied gurney was pushed out en route to the operating suite. I blessed the young sailor, inquired privately of the corpsmen of the case, and let them proceed with dispatch. And now "for the rest of the story."

It seems that there had been an argument in the Enlisted Club at the Naval Air Station, Alameda. In the midst of this confrontation the sailor, our patient, responded to a Marine with an obscene gesture. Whereupon the Marine thrust the sailor's extended middle digit into his mouth and bit it so hard that it was going to require amputation. I never found out if his opponent was ever identified or if any legal action was pending, but I am confident that the sailor will be using his right hand differently the rest of his life.

The old veteran had gone to the bathroom, and when he returned to his bed, the sheets had been changed for his comfort by the ward corpsman with such military precision that the patient's weakness prevented him from pulling the covers apart to return to his resting place. Coming down the hall, I heard a loud string of blue language coming from this single bed room. I rushed to the door, and, as I flung it open, I immediately observed the gentleman's dilemma as he was hanging onto the side of the bed and swearing loudly. "What have you got to be grateful for this day?" I inquired. "Father," he responded, "I thank God I can still cuss!"

Friday and Saturday nights in the Emergency Room, which also served the East Oakland community, provided us all with a journey into the civilian world beyond the protection of the Uniform Code of Military Justice—to which we "insiders" were subject.

Although our Trauma Center responsibilities were not limited to the weekends, these were the times when our case load was heavily augmented by the presence of commercial ambulances with Oakland Police Officers guarding patients they unloaded into our triage. Some of the scenes grimly reminded me of "Charlie Med" in ways I never expected to witness in my homeland and in the city of my birth.

East Oakland was a battleground, principally in a war over drugs. As an example, I remember a young man in his early twenties who was evidently extracted from his very expensive sports car after bullets had paralyzed him permanently from the waist down. The Police Inspector called me into the Trauma Room to be a witness when he emptied his pockets. Rolls of hundred dollar bills bound in rubber bands scattered across the tile floor. "Father, I needed you to see what was about to happen, and to verify my inventory of his 'possessions' as well," the plain clothes officer explained as he thanked me for my presence.

Sadness filled my heart as I compared what I saw in Viet Nam with what I was seeing in Oakland. At least most of the wounded who came to our Medical Battalion in Viet Nam believed they were making sacrifices in the interests of others, while the drug merchants were risking their lives only in the service of themselves while they were destroying those whom they served.

———————

When Naval Hospital Oakland served as a major medical facility during World War II, scores of temporary buildings were erected throughout the canyon that had once been the location of the Oak Knoll Country Club. I dare not venture a count of them, but aerial photographs I have seen display an enormous collection of structures that housed the wards, clinics, schools and administration facilities which were linked by sheltered walkways and by what must have been miles of roadways.

At the Mountain Boulevard main gate was a large, well-appointed Navy Chapel. The velvet padded pews in the main nave would seat in excess of 400, and the chapel was equipped for multifaith use. The building also housed a 40-seat Blessed Sacrament Chapel with a separate entrance. This structure had served well as a worship center for patients and staff members of various Faith Groups when the hospital served the medical needs of that great war and before inpatient services were centralized in a main hospital building. Its size and location fulfilled planning for the command at the time the census was so large, the rehabilition stays were long, and when the facility was so dispersed throughout the large complex.

With the advent of a new well planned high-rise hospital in the middle of the land area still surrounded by some of the old wooden buildings that served as clinics, administration and recreation facilities, the large old dignified chapel at the gate was almost a mile downhill from the main hospital and virtually unavailable to patients and to staff on duty. A smaller but lovely chapel was included in the construction of the high-rise hospital one story above the lobby, away from activity and noise, and easily available to ambulatory patients, wheelchairs, and to staff. The five chaplain offices, sacristy and the reception area for the chaplaincy were adjacent to this chapel in the hospital.

The Roman Catholics were quick to move their Masses and programs from the old chapel to the new one, once the new hospital could be occupied, but the Protestant chapel worship programs remained behind in the comfortable old setting. Thus, attendance at Protestant worship services, similar to the attendance at the Bethesda hospital chapel, was augmented by retired personnel and their families who resided in the area. They added a semblance of continuity and stability to the Protestant Chapel Congregation, and they provided a valued presence.

But, unlike at the Bethesda Medical Center Chapel, it was at a cost of making the Protestant Chapel worship ministry less available to the parent Navy Hospital command and its personnel. Further, six civilian churches in a very inclusive spectrum of Christian denominations (including a Roman Catholic retreat center) were located within a radius of only six blocks from the chapel at the Main Gate. These provided alternatives for those residing outside the hospital compound, should they not wish to drive another mile up the hill and enter the main hospital building to attend church.

Several months after assuming the duty as Senior Chaplain, I asked those who attended from the surrounding community, and whom I recognized had volunteered to perform many valuable tasks to perpetuate a permanent

Protestant chapel program for an otherwise transient congregation, to join me for worship and Eucharist in the chapel in the hospital proper. I suggested to them that by moving our services to the hospital building, we had a great opportunity for service to the patients and to staff members by bringing Sunday and other services within their reach. All were willing, and we mobilized our constituents to bring patients who wanted to worship in their wheelchairs and even on gurneys from the wards to the chapel on Sundays, and, when practical, to the weekday noontime devotions. Initially, this plan was met with both success and wholesale satisfaction.

When news spread that the old chapel was being abandoned, the telephones started to ring. From both near and far, objections were expressed to the Commanding Officer and to me as the Command Chaplain. Most of the objections came from the wives of retired senior officers who did not attend either of the congregations identified with the chapel. The common complaint was that there were hopes that daughters might be married in the old chapel. This did not improve my standing with the command, but I was following my conscience.

Queries came from as far away as offices of influence in Washington, D.C. The administrative side of the command approved the decommissioning of the old chapel, so that the space could be used for other purposes. This involved clearing it of all ecclesiastical and consecrated materials. I saw to it that various sacred objects were returned to proper judicatories, and I distributed unused and unclaimed cassocks and choir robes to some foreign missions in need of them. Most of these articles had not seen the light of day since the late 1940s, and many were mildewed, faded, and obviously unusable.

The stained glass windows in the Sanctuary area of the main chapel were identified by brass donor plates as having been given in 1945 by "The Chinese Benevolent Society of San Francisco," which represented a population that, at the time, may have wanted to be identified as separate from Japanese-Americans. My research yielded no trace of this organization. With the approval of the command, I had the windows removed, crated, and donated to "True Sunshine Episcopal Church" in San Francisco, which gratefully received them, stored them, and designated them for the new church they were building to replace their old convent school building in Chinatown.

I had great hopes of providing several of the struggling churches, especially in essentially minority neighborhoods in East and West Oakland, with the lovely pews and church furnishings, knowing that they would be valued and in the hope of encouraging congregations that were demonstrating honorable leadership in the community. After my tenacious protests and to my great disappointment, the chapel furnishings had to go to a Survey Yard in Alameda for bids that I knew would never be expedited. I lost track of these precious articles with their heavy walnut construction and velvet seat pads after their second winter standing out in the weather and the rain.

The steeple was removed, and the decommissioned chapel became a functioning personnel office and Badge and Pass Office for base security, advantageously located by the compound entrance. It remained so until the Naval Hospital, Oakland was closed because of the need to retrofit the structure against earthquake threats in accordance with new technology (it is on a fault line) and as the result of "downsizing" of the American military. I regret the scattering of the chapel congregations that gave such support to the hospital ministry, but I have no regrets about moving all the hospital chapel activities to the hospital proper where they belonged.

—◦◦◦—

It was a brisk and sunny Sunday afternoon. I returned to the hospital to take the Reserved Sacrament to patients who wanted Holy Communion. As I entered the delivery entrance which afforded easy access to the chapel and to my office, the electric doors opened as expected, and I began my march down the long corridor.

Suddenly I was down and out, returning to consciousness only when medics from the emergency room were crawling to me on sheets spread down the long slippery hallway. The maintenance crew had taken advantage of a Sunday abandonment of that part of the building to spread wax stripper (about the consistency of 10-weight motor oil) on the asphalt tile flooring from wall to wall, but they had failed to set up warning signs at either end of the passage. I had injured my left shoulder, had an irreparable Colles' fracture of my left wrist, and compression fractures of three vertebrae. After initial examination and cursory treatment, I was sent home to rest.

A week later I experienced severe chest pain, and Marjorie delivered me back to the hospital in the middle of the night, where I spent three days in the Coronary Intensive Care Unit to await the end of the Veterans' Day holiday and the return of the examining physicians. I was in too much pain on the right and on the left and full of tubes in mouth and nose to perceive the pathos of my Veterans' Day dilemma. I could not speak, with my airway so intruded upon with intubation hardware.

Tuesday morning following the four-day weekend, the Administration Officer of the hospital command, a pathologist, visited my bedside before Grand Rounds, announcing that he had been sent by the Commanding Officer to inform me (in these exact words): "You can't sue us, because you are on active duty."★ He then left the unit. At the time of his visit, my primary concern was staying alive in the midst of unrelenting pain. I had no thought of anything other than that. I later learned that the maintenance department had claimed that my fall was due to a lack of lighting, and changed the florescent tubes in the back hallway.

When the Cardiac Resident and his covey of interns surrounded me in my helpless state, I heard the Resident introduce "my heart case" and finally call for discussion. An intern from the back, after the others had made observations, offered a timid suggestion of a differential diagnosis. He thought that perhaps an inflamed gall bladder had been overlooked, and that my problem may not have been with the heart.

It was just minutes later that I was on a gurney, with handlers running as they rushed me from the Intensive Cardiac Care Unit to surgery. Six-and-a-half hours later, my anxious wife was waiting for my return on the postsurgical ward, when she overheard a conversation in normal voices at the nursing station. A man in "greens" was talking to the nurses and corpsman, saying:

"Boy, that Chaplain! His gall bladder was so hot I thought twice we were going to lose him on the table." Marjorie was livid, and, when she got her emotions under control, she approached this informal debriefing, excused herself for interrupting them, introduced herself, and demanded an explanation.

This certainly gave me a patient's view of what could happen *in my hospital!* During my confinement in the CICU that long weekend before my surgery I had endured intense pain. I was wondering what was wrong with me. As a Department Head, I was worrying about the state of my responsibilities in the hospital while I was incapacitated. When I heard what the "Admin" Officer had to say to me on behalf of my Commanding Officer, I thought to myself, "I guess my work for Jesus in the Navy has run its course." I began to consider how much I really missed the Episcopal parish ministry and worshipping freely in ways so familiar to me.

My traditions had to be muted in the military ministry (without compromising essentials) for the greater good of leading ecumenical congregations. I missed some of the enrichments which had given me joy: ancient hymns, Eucharistic vestments, chanting, sanctus bells, incense, and the beautiful teachings that had nurtured me and that could nurture others in the Apostolic Faith as I had known it. I missed the mystical and the numinous, so essential to distinctly Anglican devotion. I missed the spontaneous liturgical responses of Episcopal congregations. I missed not having to apologize for my fondness for such things. I had fought and won battles for addiction rehabilitation, for family counseling, for multiracial celebrations of the birth of Martin Luther King, Jr., and for moral entertainment in the clubs of the Navy and the Marine Corps. I had faced enemies, both foreign and domestic.

I was coming to the realization that I was growing tired of all those battles for progress. During my convalescence and after returning to my office, I came to the conclusion that in all of this the Lord was once again trying to get the attention of this hardheaded priest. His message seemed to be: "It's time to move on. I Called you into the Navy as my priest, and now I am Calling you out."

I began the process of searching for a diocese and a parish that would, in a sense, welcome me back home from what had been, I believe, a very productive ministry "in exile." I was proud of what I had done, but I knew the Lord had spoken to me in the CICU through the voice of a "lesser command."

★ Statement of the Naval Hospital Command was justified by the half-century-old Feres Doctrine codified by the U.S. Congress in the Federal Tort Claims Act of 1946. However legal, the timing of the notification was anything but considerate.

Redding Medical Center, Redding, California, 1987-96

When I came to Redding as a parish priest, I visited parishioners in the many convalescent hospitals and care facilities in town. In 1987 there were two general hospitals functioning in the community, plus a county hospital. Now two more specialized hospitals have been added, but the county no longer maintains an inpatient facility for physical medicine.

I was no longer a chaplain with hospital staff privileges as I had been in the Navy. I visited my parishioners who were acute care inpatients, keeping my former disciplines of being with them at least once a day for a chat and/or prayer, and anointing them just before surgeries. But now I was obliged to request permission to enter Intensive Care Units by corridor telephone (with frequent delays), and I lacked access to patient records. I behaved as a guest, and I was humbly grateful when there was a convenient designated parking space marked "Clergy Only."

In this role, it was helpful that I was familiar with hospital routines, because this guided me to time my visits when they would be most beneficial to patients and convenient for the nursing staff. Rather than offering here a repetition of stories somewhat typical of those previously related, I have chosen to single out two incidents at R.M.C.

Mercy Medical Center had its chaplaincy and Sisters of Mercy. But at R.M.C. (before this hospital happily recruited a retired clergyman, followed by a trained professional chaplain), after visiting the patients I knew, I would drop by the Oncology Ward occasionally on my rounds, just to see if there were any special needs, or to offer a greeting to a patient or two.

As I entered a room one afternoon, the gentleman in the bed sat up with a smile on his face, and greeted me with: "It's a *great day today,* Father!" "What's great about it?" I asked, returning his smile. "What's great," he said, "is that I'm looking down at the blossoms instead of up at the roots." This was followed by a very thoughtful conversation which reflected his positive yet realistic attitude reinforced by a hearty faith.

Patients often give to us so much more than we are able to offer them!

It was always my practice when a death occurred on a ward to stop by the Nursing Station and spend a few moments with staff members who I knew had invested so much of themselves in providing care to the expired patient. This I did on the Oncology Ward following the death of a chronically ill parishioner of mine. I thanked the staff for their assistance.

The Charge Nurse shared with me a most valuable insight. She said that this ward is different from all the others, and the nursing staff has different goals. I listened and learned as she continued.

The others, she explained, were dedicated to keeping their patients alive, whereas patients who entered Oncology and those who nursed there, all knew that the patients were terminal. Therefore, their goal was to help their patients die as comfortably, as painlessly, and as easily as possible. "Frankly, we are here to help them die," she shared with me. "When such a patient we have been helping passes away and has found peace at last, the nursing staff usually feels that they have not failed, but rather that they have done their job."

This solemn testimony ministered to me at this time, because I also was grieving the loss of a friend. I found this conversation to have been of lasting help as I continued to offer pastoral care to others.

All Saints' Episcopal Church, Redding, California, 1987-95

When I returned to ministry in a civilian setting, there were several adjustments I needed to reconcile with the changes that had taken place in my denomination in the United States during my "migrations."

I asked Bishop John Thompson, my new diocesan in Northern California, his justification for having infants and small children who had been baptized receive Holy Communion at the Altar Rail long prior to Holy Confirmation. I had not observed this before. He was unwilling to simply state that it was common practice in the Eastern Orthodox Church, and it had become so in the Episcopal Church. Instead, he stated his personal reasons for advocating this. "I want Christian children to be so used to receiving Communion by the time they mature that they will not remember when this began in their lives."

That made sense to me as a pastor in a new age (as long as instruction and Holy Confirmation were not neglected). I made it a practice to meet with the parents of newly baptized youngsters to review the meaning of Holy Communion with them, to discuss means by which they could help their children receive and grow into better understandings of the Blessed Sacrament. I also encouraged them to see that their children would come to Inquirer's Classes and be Confirmed by the bishop when they reached middle school age. I found administering Holy Communion to children under these conditions to be a new joy in my ministry.

I followed this pattern in an additional matter. Even though Holy Unction was a Sacrament to be administered "by the Elders of the Church," thus reserved for the clergy, Saint James also adds: "the prayer of faith will save the sick." From this, I adopted the custom in the parish of asking the permission of individuals who were facing major medical procedures or experiencing significant health crises if they might be willing to be anointed with prayer in the midst of the congregation. (Often I, as pastor, would be the only one to know of this matter, and I was always very careful to honor each person's privacy at such times.) If and when permission was given, I would ask that person to kneel before me in the center aisle at a point in the main Sunday service when we are accustomed to "pass the Peace of Christ." I would then invite members of the congregation to gather around and to lay their hands with mine upon the person (or on the shoulder of one in front of them in the surrounding circle), and, at the time of the anointing, to pray with me for healing by the Savior.

This, too, was a new experience for me in ministry—one that I found to be very powerful for "the healing of the sick" (as well as for the support of the minister). Without diverting from the functions of the ordained clergy, this seemed to have a logical relationship to the service of parish Lay Eucharistic Ministers. Participation in home Communions and in Healings serves to reawaken in the lives of the laity their rightful place in ministry, a place firmly incorporated in the vows each of us takes in Holy Baptism.

—⊷⊶⊷—

What an enormous honor it has been for me to be able to commune, anoint, pray, counsel, comfort and to be present with many whose journey has taken them through pain of body or mind, to witness miracles of Christ, and to be Christ's chosen representative in times of illness and death. This is priesthood! The healing and hospital ministry is a spiritual experience of constantly learning how to love and how to trust. Each setting is different and each patient is unique. However, what constantly remains is the message announced by Saint Gabriel to a scared little girl twenty centuries ago, a chosen mortal who would be God's instrument to bring Christ to us all: "...for you have found favor with God" (St. Luke 1:30).

I have never felt alone in the ministry of healing. Indeed, the Lord has been the Source of Power, but the others on the team have been my colleagues, companions, and source of encouragement and caring for me as well in this miraculous adventure. We have been reminded by Saint Paul that there are diversities of talents and diversities of services (I Corinthians 12:4ff).

"Minister" is a generic term, referring to all who serve the Lord. St. Matthew 25:40 records Jesus' teaching that those who care for and serve others in need are indeed ministering to Him. Thus, those who celebrate the Holy Eucharist and anoint the infirm, those who wash the feet or empty bed pans, physicians who labor to restore our bodies and ease our pain, those who nurse and nurture the sick, those who do research to equip others to do the work of healing, and those who mend broken hearts and families—all are God's ministers. Whether they acknowledge it or not, all these are agents of the One from Whom all knowledge, healing and wholeness comes. "Behold, I make all things new," says the Lord.

A Christian pastor has been chosen by God to deliver His healing love, often in fear-filled situations. Our very *presence* as His ministers at bedsides and at gravesides speaks beyond any words we might utter.

In modern translation, I believe that God speaks through us, saying: "Do not be afraid. You are not alone. You are not forgotten. You are My child. With Me, you are special. You are loved, and always will be! Accept, obey, then trust the Savior for the outcome. You are *safe* with Me."

As God's messengers on Saint Gabriel's Team, ministers are ordained to deliver God's messages of hope, healing, and Eternal Life, ...and *to be* that message as well.

—JOB 42:1-5; ST. LUKE 1:30; 10:17, 23f; JAMES 5:14ff

CHAPTER TEN

Return to Civilian Life and Ministry

The World is My Parish

The "Church" is the Body of Christ. A "church" is a building where a congregation meets. A "parish," according to Anglican Church traditional thinking, is a geographic area within which all persons, irrespective of their religious sentiments, are considered to be the concern of the parish congregation and clergy. This is a definition of unselfish compassion and obligation to serve, not one of proselytizing demands.

I had enjoyed the military ministry because it fit with this concept. Likewise, I was thrilled to be back home in a parish of my own denomination. However, I was to discover that even with my brother and sister Episcopalians, there was a continuing need to unscramble the differences between "church boundaries" and "parish boundaries." Had I not found this my dilemma at the church school in Manila?

This story's title, "The World is My Parish," is a proclamation accredited to Anglican priest, Father John Wesley, whose evangelistic challenge still needs recognition in many of the same and succeeding parishes and episcopal palaces he was addressing in the 18th Century.

I have the vivid memory of my last Parish Senior Warden (who recognized that his congregation was *not* being neglected), telling me that he considered my participation in local benevolent community projects to be my hobby, and that the congregation should consider such activities to be on "my own time"—not related to ministry. I was appalled. Since I worked at least 80-hour weeks, such projects could be considered "on my own time." But to have them thought to be unrelated to the parish ministry was heresy in my book. This opened for me another great challenge for Christian education in my own congregational support family!

All year around the Sacramento Valley, when in public, I always wore a clerical shirt, black slacks, the distinctive white clergy collar, adding a black top coat in winter. "Why, in all this summer heat, would you insist on wearing black?" I was asked—even challenged—frequently. My standard reply: "I am advertising for Jesus."

Availability is the ministry of presence. More than once have I had people in need identify themselves, ask questions, even seek guidance on the street. Many times people, young and old, have stated that they had never spoken with a priest before; even had never met one. Sometimes we are the personification of someone's guilty conscience (which is not my objective!), but we can be reminders that our God is alive and with us in all that we do and say and think. That should be the joy of being visible as God's servant—if we can avoid expectations of perfectionism.

I remember a motion picture entitled, "O God!" George Burns played the part of God, who was present among people in the common events of life. Here was God in the checkout line at the supermarket, on the sidewalk, engaging folks in conversation, and the like. But in this film—which presented an incarnational image of God—He was presented primarily as an observer of the human condition, rather than one who made interventions in the lives and history of those among whom He lived. I think a great opportunity was overlooked by the screenwriters in this production.

To focus on the theology of ministry, I believe the pastor must be present in the community and be willing to take risks when appropriate interventions have a potential for improving things. Sometimes our task is simply to witness to Truth, to plant seeds in the hope that such a witness may be acted upon by others in the future, with the result that things might develop in better directions.

I say "risks," because one who acts as a change agent is not always welcome. Saint Paul was frequently flogged, jailed, and run out of town in response to his ministry. Jesus was crucified for the changes He advocated. To be effective, ministers must sometimes take risks when choosing potentially effective strategies. But we dare not expect rewards greater than those of the Savior, nor even those of our spiritual ancestors.

We are not in our communities to be merely observers, just to see and play the "Oh How Awful!" game. On the other hand, we are the Savior's representatives—not the Savior Himself! He is the One who saves.

—〰—

I have always followed the annual tradition of holding the Blessing of Animals on or near Saint Francis' Day, October 4th. This is not an event with great theological implications, but rather a reminder of injunctions of kindness and a means of joyful gathering. Often the Blessing of Animals is full of surprises and lots of happiness, and folks of all ages always seem to enjoy it.

To expedite this in each church where I have served, I have constructed a small Saint Francis shrine mounted on a redwood 4-by-4 in the adjacent churchyard. After the church building was completed in Redding, the initial services were popular. Even seniors in wheelchairs came from the nearby rest home to have their mascot bird blessed.

But on a Saturday morning in early October, the excitement seemed to be wearing down. The last group that gathered at the Saint Francis bird feeder/shrine was composed of four mature parishioners with four almost identical bull dogs. It was fun, but also time to reevaluate the event.

I engaged the Haven Humane Society's director in conversations. They were holding a fund-raiser pet walk at another time of the year in the park across the boulevard from the new church. I proposed that we join forces— that the pet walk commence with a blessing of the assembled animals for those who wished, and that a certificate marking the blessing be issued for each of the animals who participated with their owners. I asked that the date for the pet walk be switched to early October to remember Saint Francis and his love of God's creatures (as well as to obtain pledges for the support of the Humane Society).

The pact was sealed, and on a Saturday morning the following October, at least one hundred fifty dogs, cats, snakes, and even a llama (who refrained from spitting back) got a quick splash of holy water from an evergreen sprig, a prayer, and a paper for its master to frame.

—◦◦◦—

My nickname in the Redding Rotary was "Padre," which seemed to choke no one's religious sensitivities, and I served consistently on the community projects committee for much of my time in the club. This gave me an opportunity to be an advocate for projects that would benefit the poor and the dispossessed. For the most part, my participation in service clubs (such as the West Berkeley Lions Club for four years in the late 1950s, and in Rotary for eight years in Redding) provided me with a circle of friends, an influential support community, and gratifying opportunities to be of help to those within the membership as well as those in the communities the clubs are pledged to serve.

—◦◦◦—

I was a Volunteer Chaplain to the Redding Police Department for eight years, which will be detailed in a later vignette.

—◦◦◦—

The Salvation Army suddenly had a change of local command in late summer, discontinuing their ten years of service providing for the winter homeless shelter. I went to Fresno to find out how they had mobilized their community to do this work. They had formed a "No Name Coalition" to provide such services, so named to avoid any participating church, service club or business from seeking notoriety by means of their helping. Although the name was not duplicated in Redding, the model was.

I participated in the recruitment and incorporation of the Shasta County

Winter Homeless Shelter Coalition, which had a monumental task to organize and to get equipped in time for the heavy seasonal rains and very cold weather. However, this was all accomplished and the National Guard Armory readied in time to prevent another person from freezing to death on the streets that winter in "our town" (as had happened the previous year in a city nearby). Many resisted this project with the slogan expressed or implied: "Not in my neighborhood!"

Melinda Brown, Director of the helping organization called "People of Progress," was the head of the executive committee and the courageously true leader throughout the five winters that this lifesaving project survived in our local armory. Volunteer Church groups, businesses, and groups of friends rotated nights on a schedule to provide hot meals, unfold cots with cleaned blankets (required bathing to be taken in the armory shower rooms) for a hundred guests from November through March. Social workers and a Public Health Nurse were regular visitors, offering help and assistance to those in need of such. The "Good News Rescue Mission" expanded with new and progressive leadership, an enlarged facility, and now has assumed responsibility for the homeless shelter—the National Guard Armory no longer being available for this use in winter.

—◦◦◦—

Together with a lay member of the Seventh Day Adventist Church who had lost her son, I organized and wrote a liturgy for the first local HIV/AIDS Memorial Service on the national day set aside for this, December 1st. We held the first of these services in the parish church where I was rector, and many pastors participated in the event. It was designed to be perpetuated by rotating to other churches/synagogues, and it has become an annual event in the city. Each year this service provides a time for heartrending and therapeutic testimonials by surviving family members and friends.

—◦◦◦—

As a participant in the organizing committee for the annual celebration of the birthday of the Reverend Dr. Martin Luther King, Jr., I suggested that, as in the past, confining this event to the park and center in the primarily Black neighborhood tended to neutralize it as just a "Black Event." To be true to Dr. King's dream that involved every race in America, this event is worthy of visibility and participation by citizens throughout the entire city. It now comes on a *holiday* when working people and students can come!

Having observed this annual event become increasingly "segregated" as a Black celebration in the Navy, I wanted to reverse a trend which I believed was making this celebration racially isolated. I organized and led the first King Day March from the steps of the Shasta County Courthouse to the Martin Luther King, Jr. Center, where other events then took place. It began with a great prayer circle of the marchers. This annual march now involves people of all ages, ethnicities, and faiths, and it is now a routinely expected event in the city which is well covered in the media. I counted this a victory for King, for his dream for true harmony among us, and for the City of Redding. I believe this was a victory for God!

—◊◊◊—

On the green of the Close of the 13th Century Cathedral of the Blessed Virgin Mary in Salisbury, England, there is a remarkable sculpture by the late Dame Elisabeth Frink entitled "The Walking Madonna." There on the lawn, a youthful Saint Mary appears to be striding briskly toward Saint Ann's Gate and the city and the world beyond. I interpret this artwork to symbolize God's driving force in the life of His Church and all of us, His saints, to reach out and to carry the Good News into the "highways and the byways" where people live and travel and do business. The message of faith, like that ancient, towering, Gothic House of God that stands behind Our Lady depicted on her way with determination to accomplish her errands, is too beautiful to be contained, too urgent to be kept isolated—only for "insiders."

Community outreach and the ministry of presence in "every corner of the realm" is essential to the Great Commission: "Go into all the world…." I have attempted to relate some projects and events which I believe have benefited the community, and also in which the ministry of presence has been expressed.

As stated previously, some of these efforts were controversial in the community and even in my own congregation. Nevertheless, doing God's work requires one to be prophetic (but not reckless). Some battles must be lost so that eventual victory may be achieved. Rarely can we anticipate where and how God will act to bring to us the lonely and the distressed, that they may be ministered to appropriately. On the other hand, many who do not know the Lord but who wish to celebrate a success or a victory, wander, seeking how and to whom thanks can be truly offered. May we be present in such ways that we can be channels through which such unexpressed prayers may be answered.

—St. Matthew 22:9f

Happy Birthday, Happy Memories

*O*ctober 19, 1990 was my 60th birthday. Dan Spiess, Senior Warden of All Saints' Parish, informed us that the Vestry had planned a small informal gathering at a restaurant with this celebration in mind. He and the Junior Warden came by our house at dusk to pick up Marjorie and me for this occasion, which we accepted as a very nice courtesy.

Once on our way, they apologized for a necessary diversion. There had been a report that someone had evidently neglected to lock the door of the new church building, and they had to pass by the property to secure it before dinner. It was getting dark when we stopped at the front entrance of the church. The two wardens stepped out of Dan's car, and invited us to join them to see that the interior of the building was not disturbed.

When I opened the church door, Marjorie and I stepped into a darkened nave lighted only by sixty candles. The pews had been moved to one side, and tables had been set and decorated in several rows the length of the building. The candles were part of the table decorations. "Happy birthday to you," was our boisterous greeting. "Surprise!" cried the Church Wardens. And indeed it was!

These were the days before the construction of our parish hall, thus the multiple use of the church building was a temporary routine. Usually, for fellowship events, a portable screen was placed in the center of the sanctuary between the High Altar and an audience (except for sacred music concerts). More screens were used to subdivide the rear of the nave when Sunday School classes were conducted, and that area, behind the pews, was used for "coffee hour" gathering after worship services.

The wonderful evening of the surprise birthday banquet was but one of numerous positive parish events that strengthened our teamwork. But this one was especially heartwarming for me, because its focal point was an expression of appreciation for my presence and that of Marjorie in the parish, and our efforts to serve the congregation well. It propelled me forward with a fresh wind of the Spirit at my back, because it came from those I wished to continue serving through the years, reassuring me that we were together and on the right track.

A roast beef dinner was catered, and singing cheered the gathering. My birthday gift was presented after dinner—an Academic Doctoral Gown, something that I had always wanted for my ecclesiatical wardrobe but could never afford. But the real birthday gift was the event itself, because it gave credence to the objectives to which I had dedicated my life.

There is a healthy selfishness which Jesus directed in the second part of His Summary of the Law (St. Matthew 22:37-40). Specifically, "You shall love your neighbor *as yourself.*" It is self-respect! One has to *receive* in order to keep giving. That includes receiving from God and from those to whom He Calls us to minister, for they need to minister to their pastors. True love runs in both directions, and I am convinced that it is just as blessed to receive as it is to give.

—PROVERBS 25:11; ST. JOHN 4:7–15; I JOHN 4:16–19

Always a Novice in the Pulpit

*N*othing has been so terrifying for me, and simultaneously so thrilling, as the ministry of preaching. From the very start I have approached this task with a sense of personal inadequacy, but invariably I discover the grace of God through preaching!

I have always admired the long-suffering patience of the congregations to whom I have preached. I have been conscious that they were praying for me at times, and at other times, praying for me to finish. There have been times when my dear wife has said after worship that my homiletical offering was "the best three sermons" she had ever heard in a given Sunday service (implying that it was much too long).

The most honest comment I ever received was from an usher at Saint Peter's Church in Redwood City when I was a very new priest and curate. At the recessional, when the celebrant reached the narthex, it was the usher's duty to lift the chasuble from the priest's shoulders and replace it with a cloak over his cassock in cold weather. This was so that the priest might be more comfortable when greeting the people as they left the church. This dear man, as he assisted me, whispered in my ear ever so gently during the singing of the final hymn: "Honestly, Father, that sermon was awful!" (He did not mean awe-inspiring!) Of all of the responses I have heard at the close of a service in fifty years of preaching, this is the one comment I shall never forget—because it was honest, and we both knew it. Still, Christ's Commission includes the ministry of preaching, so it was destined to be my sacred responsibility for the rest of my life, and I have always worked hard at it.

There is a thrill to preaching, and it comes both in the process of preparation and in the experience of delivery. It has always been my practice to prepare sermons where I could find a place and time devoid of distraction. In parish life, I have made every effort to set aside a day in the middle of the week which I booked as a day with the Lord. My parishioners have needed to respect that day as a day of work, not a "day off." It is a day for meditation, study, and sermon building.

When I was a circuit rider in the Mountain Province of the Philippines and in the Mekong Delta, conducting one or two services a day, I made preparations for the service visitations by coming to a central place where I had a degree of privacy. Even before going to Viet Nam, I spent every spare hour I could collecting ideas and sermon illustrations in advance and writing them in a large bound notebook for use when I would be composing homilies in the year ahead under pressure and without my library at hand.

Every sermon must have a reason for being, whether to teach, to motivate, to inspire, to celebrate, or to mourn. But each sermon needs to come from the Lord and to be directed to a particular congregation, speaking to their current needs. I discovered through the years that, given a time and place for the discernment of His Will in sermon writing, God usually comes through. When ideas come and a sermon develops in one's study, *it is a humbling and exciting experience!*

For me, it usually requires about an hour of time in preparation for each minute in the pulpit. I usually spend between twelve and eighteen hours for each preachment to a congregation. The only exception to this is that shorter sermons usually take more time than longer ones. This can be compared to taking a journey. If you have a shorter time in which to cover a given route, more care must be given in the planning and execution of the trip. If more time is available, one can be a little more careless with one's use of time, and therefore with one's planning.

The excitement in the delivery of a sermon comes when the preacher feels the guidance of God as he proceeds. If the sermon was motivated by selfish reasons, such as to impress the congregation, or when it is a digression from the Will of the Divine Author for any reason, its weakness is apparent in the delivery. When the sermon has the confirmation of the Divine Will, its strength is revealed to both the preacher and the congregation. Not every sermon is going to be popular, because the truth is not always something to be enjoyed. No sermon should be offered with the specific intent of pleasing the hearers, and no sermon should be designed to avoid criticism if telling God's truth might provoke such a response.

There is another manifestation of Divine Guidance in which the action is with the hearers rather than with the speaker. I recall vividly the first time this happened in my ministry. I was a seminarian in my senior year, assigned to Saint Mark's Mission in Tracy, California. Obviously these were the very developmental days of my preaching ministry, and I did my very best to prepare. I wish I could remember the name of the lady who left church one Sunday telling me: "That sermon *really helped me!*" Naturally I thanked her for her words, but I had wisdom enough to inquire: "What was it that you heard that *really* helped you?" What she related in detail and with great seriousness I do not think was included in my oratory. But what she heard really helped her, and for this we were both grateful.

This initial experience of having communicated something that was relevant and helpful to a listener, yet knowing it did not come from me (although it may have come *through* me), was for me a pentecostal experience. That is to say, it gave me a new and, I believe, quite valid interpretation of the second chapter of the Acts of the Apostles. Many find in that text a justification for a glossolalia (speaking in tongues) phenomena—which may communicate a very valid religious experience to another. However, when those ancient pilgrims who understood different languages were given an understanding of the same gospel through the utterances of only Aramaic-speaking Apostles, I think it was much like what happened in my first encounter with such communication when I preached that Sunday to a small congregation in Tracy. It was the transmission of a greater meaning than what I recall either planning or delivering. Surely the Holy Spirit played His omniscient part in this—as He has *many times since!*

Preaching is like "casting bread upon the waters," or similar to the experience of the youngster who offered Jesus five barley loaves and two small fish and saw Him multiply them to feed the multitude. People have received so much more than I have delivered during the fifty years I have been preaching. What used to take me as a complete surprise, I have learned to accept and rejoice in as a miracle of God.

I shall always be grateful for this experience, but I never came to rely upon it as a substitute for offering my own best efforts. When God speaks His greater meaning through my preaching and I know it, it is a most inspiring demonstration of God's overriding Presence. Preaching always requires complete dedication, but once I learned that God was there as "my backup," much of the timidity and fear of the pulpit experience left me.

In the preaching ministry of the Prophet Jeremiah (described in the opening verses of the *Book of Jeremiah*), God promised that He would be there for him as he spoke. God purified the lips of Isaiah (Isaiah 6:5–8), that he might speak for Him. The other Prophets also testify they were given strength and wisdom to speak for God. The ancient Prophets, the Christian Martyrs, and the Holy Apostles were Called to witness. Today's preachers are ordained to witness to God's forgiveness, love, and power. God guides us in our preparations, then He speaks through us in this preaching ministry. Had this been stressed in my seminary training, my initial sermon delivery would have been much more relaxed, and I would have been much less anxious.

However, I still approach the pulpit ministry with "some fear and trembling" that may result from a recognition of the responsibility entailed, and serve as a constant reminder not to be reckless in my reliance upon "God's backup." Although I am reluctant to admit it, it may reflect some lack of faith on my part as well.

There is a legitimate exhaustion that is experienced after preaching. It is as though the preacher is a conduit through which a rushing torrent has passed. As such a conduit sustains some erosion from the contents passing through it, so the preacher undergoes feelings of expended energy as he or she acts as a channel of God's grace.

———

Not every worshipper listens intently to the sermon. I was invited to preach at a service of thanksgiving for the return of our Prisoners of War from North Viet Nam. It was held on Veterans' Day of 1974 in Saint Luke's Episcopal Church in San Diego. The congregation was composed of a sprinkling of parishioners and civilian visitors from the community at large, but the majority of those attending were combat veterans, including some of the former prisoners.

The sermon I gave was "gutsy" and filled with vivid illustrations to which most of those who were assembled there could easily relate. In bold terms my sermon underscored the reasons why we who had returned from hell could be thankful. At the close of the service I stood on the church porch, flanked, as I remember, by the parish rector, the mayor of San Diego, and several of the POW returnees. As the worshippers filed past us with the customary handshake and greeting, one of the nice ladies of the parish smiled cordially and said: "I certainly enjoyed your sermon." My instant response went unheard as she passed on down the stairs: "I didn't see you laughing." Those who surrounded me did laugh heartily. My sermon was *not* one designed to amuse, and it was obvious that it "went right over her head."

———

Although many preachers prefer to open their sermons with a prayer which they share with the congregation, there is a prayer from an anonymous source that I recommend for the preacher to offer privately before ascending the pulpit. "O Lord, fill my mouth with worthwhile stuff, then nudge me when I've said enough."

I bring to a close this section about preaching with the memory of the 3rd Sunday in Advent in 1955 at Saint Peter's Church in Redwood City. I was a deacon then. As I entered the pulpit to preach, the choir and congregation were singing the sermon hymn, which on that particular Sunday complied with the lectionary's subject of Saint John the Baptist. As I ascended the lofty podium, all intoned: "Hark! a thrilling voice is sounding." Knowing that I had picked the hymns for that day, members of the congregation were amused by the thought that there may have existed some confusion regarding the intended subject of those words. It took months to live that down.

Preaching is truly a thrilling experience, but the Source of the thrill needs never to be forgotten by preachers nor by parishioners alike.

—JEREMIAH 1:4–9; ACTS 26:15b-18;

II CORINTHIANS 4:5–7

Photo by Happy Warren

"The Rose Wall" being lifted into place. Author is second from left. (Page 384)

Photo by Air Photo, Inc., Everett, WA

All Saints' Episcopal Church, Redding, California and future office building (temporary parish hall and Sunday School), the first two units of a planned quadrangle, constructed during the Author's tenure as Rector of the parish. - May 1994 (Page 392)

The Rose Wall

The year was 1991. Louis Edmund Rose's diabetes had required progressive amputations of his left leg up to the thigh, and several strokes had left him partially blind. He sat in his wheelchair in the living room, straining to read and watch television. In addition, with telephone in hand, he shared with his wife Susan the duties of a Neighborhood Pastoral Shepherd for the parish, keeping track of church members, comforting the lonely, cheering people who seemed in need of it, and referring matters to me that seemed to require priestly interventions. Sue went about her work as an interior decorator for the local J. C. Penney Store. They belonged to a neighborhood Bible study. They shared a beautiful Christian life.

When Louis died in late October, Sue was devastated. She broke from her customary demeanor when she cried out: "I am so angry! I don't know what to do next." Now Sue was and is a very well-educated lady, and was far beyond needing a lecture on the stages of grief. We wept together. She knew where she was emotionally, but the problem was that of finding her way out of the maze.

Our parishioner volunteer builder Pat Nickerson provided me with a 12-ounce framing hammer. I gave it to Sue, explained to her that the parish hall we were building needed the east wall to be fabricated, and that I believed she needed to do some pounding. Pat showed her the pattern and gave her some lessons in nailing two-by-sixes in place to frame the wall lying on the cement floor. Sue took up the challenge. She took shorter hours on her job and came down to the church to beat nails into studs and headers.

Some few weeks later on a Saturday morning, 35 church members assembled to raise from its horizontal resting place into vertical position the 70-foot-long "Rose Wall" that had been hammered together by Susan C. Rose. Today, as one drives into the plaza of that church in Redding, the wall of the parish hall that faces the drive has been finished with stucco and steel casement windows, and is indeed a thing of beauty. Although few may remember, it is a living memorial to a love that will never die.

"I feel good now. I have never done anything like that before, but I really needed to do that," said Sue with a sense of satisfaction when the heavy frame of the east wall was up and in place, awaiting the completed ends to replace the temporary anchors holding it. In my office, she handed me back the hammer. "I put my anger to work, and now I am ready to live again."

Once back at work, Sue soon earned a raise and a promotion with an assignment to a new store in another city. It was as though the nails, the wood, and the pounding had crucified her loss and had brought her through the tomb to the resurrection.

—St. John 19:30

The Codependency Trap

*S*ailors, from the dreamer Walter Mitty (in a short story by James Thurber*) to the newest Seaman Recruit, may have visions of becoming the commanding officer of a ship of the line, but the secret held by each C.O. is that the Captain always eats alone. Yes, others may be invited to join him for a meal in his private mess, but in a sense the one who has that terrible responsibility for decision-making that could involve life or death, promotion or dishonor, for those he leads, must always be his/her own person. It is unavoidably lonely "at the top."

This is but a parable. However, even though we may not want to accept the idea that a position of ministry is a "place at the top," clergy are in positions of leadership, and leadership requires making decisions that involve or influence others. In short, a minister may be surrounded by people as the captain is surrounded by his/her crew, but leadership regrettably demands subtle boundaries of privacy that have to be guarded to maintain effectiveness.

The most obvious example of that is confidentiality. I was trained not only to forget revelations given in conditions of Sacramental Confession, but also to drop down a well or let float heavenward what I might have heard. As a priest, I must act as a channel of God's Grace, knowing always that confessions are never mine to keep—nor mine to remember or retain in any way.

But there are many other matters that one hears or observes as a clergy person that must be retained under a guarded seal. And even though this privilege is constantly under siege by judicial authorities, they have yet to invade the fortress of honest "loss of memory" on the part of the confessor/minister. For the penitent, Sacramental Confession is Reconciliation with God and with one's human brothers and sisters by *God's* Action, with the ordained confessor acting exclusively as God's ambassador. Confession is not in-depth counseling. A referral for counseling at another time and place, either with the minister or with another trusted professional, can be offered the penitent as an Act of Contrition. But counseling, or the counseling ministry, must establish its own guidelines.

One of the most important functions of the bishop in the Episcopal Church (or of any judicatory overseer in another denomination) is to have the trust of clergy and to be available to them with an open heart, rather than as a judgmental authoritarian.** This is the safety valve that keeps both pastors and their flocks safe!

There are times in the lives of ministers when pastors need a pastor to revive and to reinforce that necessary grace-filled relationship with Our Savior. "Under the stole" of Sacred Ministry, a trusted and available bishop can *be there* to drain the pressure—acting with understanding, compassion and objective wisdom, for the benefit of a minister and the clergy family when they might feel isolated and/or misunderstood. At times like these, without genuine caring amidst the social, financial, and emotional pressures of clergy life, the hazard of a dreadful leak or even an explosion is predictable.

There is a degree of "aloneness" that is integral to the ministerial life. Why such urgency in regard to the matter of isolation? It is because the demands of total control of the balance between the private and public domains of a minister's life require superhuman resources, and isolation can gnaw away the boundaries between them. There are inner dwellings of the heart and mind of a pastor that, when invaded, place a pastor's people as well as his/her Vocation at risk. The minister, in search of consolation, may be tempted to seek counsel in unreliable places with undependable persons who seem to "understand me." The psychological phenomenon of transference easily enters such a scenario.

In my denomination it is common for clergy in Priest's Orders to be addressed by such familiar terms as "Father" or "Mother." Jesus (in St. Matthew 23:9f) objected to the use of the term "Father"—in His time commonly used to show respect for men of past generations. Such identities as "Master" (then the equivalent of "Doctor," "Teacher," "Rabbi," and most certainly "Mister") were not titles to hide behind as substitutes for one being a person of integrity, according to Jesus. If these were prohibitions for the use of titles or rank, I guess we would all be in trouble!

As a young boy, I learned from my rector, Father J. Henry Thomas, a most humble man, that "Father" was to be considered an earned title, earned from those who acknowledged that they were loved and cared for by one who had been to them a true Father in God (rather than Father in heaven). The term demonstrates endearment; therefore, it is not to be expected or required. Other ecclesiastical bodies have similar positions and titles that would be relevant to this discussion, such as Elder, Pastor, Doctor, and that adjective (that is so improperly and dreadfully used as a noun)—"Reverend." Being known in public as "Joe," "Mike" or "Mary" may help the minister feel less lonely and more humble. On the other hand, I believe this is a reflection of a bygone youth-driven generation in which respect became passé, a concept which was heralded by bumper stickers with the logo: "Question Authority!" Such superficial bids for familiarity originate from a demand for personal independence. If it had not been modified, this movement would have resulted in a "Cultural Revolution" that would have threatened our national future.

The routine avoidance of acknowledging courtesies can become barriers that result in distancing people from qualified professional resources for help, healing, and growth. Some years ago, a priest in Australia told me: "Our bishop wants to be just 'one of the chaps', but we would much rather have him as our bishop." Authority should be the recognition of ability, skill, talent, which is not the same thing as the "authoritarianism" that has been so feared since the 1960s.

Transference is a "mistake in identity" that occurs commonly in the unconscious functions of the mind that misidentifies one person in the place of another, especially where the roles may have been thought to be similar.

Countertransference exists when the object of the transference reciprocates in the misidentified relationship by unconsciously responding to the other in the role expected of him or her. The clergy titles that I have defended can serve as invitations for transference to occur, and the minister needs to be aware when this may be happening, so that it may be handled carefully and appropriately.

Countertransference can be a setup for vocational tragedy. If the unprepared pastor finds him/herself acquiescing to the seduction of being accepted as the object of love (or wrath) that originated with another, then responds as appropriate to that imagined relationship (for example, responding as father, mother, or absent or shunned lover of another), damage has usually been done. Some of my married seminary classmates were lost from productive ministries when they fell in love with an "understanding" secretary, Director of Religious Education, or a parishioner. There are always those close to us in the work of the ministry (whether we be clergy or lay persons), whose company we grow to enjoy, especially when involved together in common benevolent endeavors. Such activities bring people together frequently, sometimes beyond the circle of one's own home and family. There are also times in which good people are emotionally vulnerable. Clergy and lay leaders need supportive team workers and good friends of both genders. But keeping a good and constant self-inventory in such relationships will avoid domestic mistakes.

It is difficult to resist such blunders in ways that preserve the dignity of the perpetrator, especially when one detects this kind of attraction happening in one's flock, either involving oneself or when observed to be developing between parishioners. A wrathful member of one's Vestry or congregation needs to be confronted privately with the question: "What do you think is happening to us (or between you two)?"

Some years ago, a recently widowed employee once entered my closed office at noontime and suddenly began to disrobe. Even though I was caught by complete surprise, I told her that I thought she was a pretty lady, that I knew that she missed her late husband, and that this was not appropriate. I continued by saying that I was on my way home to have lunch with my wife. Fortunately, and to her credit, this behavior never recurred, and she continued to serve well with no further mention of the incident.

When such an encounter occurs as an isolated episode, we are not necessarily looking at mental illness or a character disorder. Transference is present in the unconscious mind and in human relationships more than we imagine, especially where misinterpretations of authority might be imagined or perceived.

I once heard a sailor say: "I think every enlisted man should own his own Captain." By that, I understood him to mean that it would be advantageous for a junior to get himself into a position by which he could influence his senior in ways which would be beneficial to himself and his peers. Sometimes *a conscious manipulation* for affection or for control can exist. However, every congregation has its Borderline Personalities, who cling to the pastor. These persons willingly run errands and provide for a pastor's needs in exchange for the personal acceptance and appreciation they so desperately need. A thing to remember: "There ain't no free lunch!" Such persons can monopolize a minister's time and availability, and this can gradually wear away the strong façades that protect the pastor's privacy and dedication—catching by surprise the minister who lacks training in the identification and handling of such persons. A countertransference response of annoyance or wrath, or the opposite, an inappropriate affectionate attraction, could predictably be provoked.

William Shakespeare said it (*Hamlet,* Act I, Scene 3, Line 75):

"This above all: to thine own self be true,
And it must follow, as night the day,
Thou canst not then be false to any man."

Henry Van Dyke wrote it (*The Prison and the Angel*):
"Self is the only prison that can ever bind the soul."

The minister needs to take constant inventory of the chinks in his/her own armor. Goliath neglected to do so, and went down for the count. No demand for perfection is implied here. Rather one needs to know one's weaknesses as well as one's strengths, so that one can guide around the former and offer the latter when it comes to standing shoulder to shoulder and heart to heart with others. I learned (or thought I did) in seminary that when I took the collar "I would be 2,000 years old." Wow, was I ever in for a shock when I hit my first parish!

The solution lies in knowledge that transference issues can arise. I am not suggesting that undue suspicion is appropriate or urging a defensiveness that would destroy empathetic relationships. What I am stating is that each pastor should have the self-knowledge and self-control to avoid codependency traps that will be found in a small percentage of the encounters required in parish building. This can be done by an awareness that such things occur. When the minister is reasonably sure that a "pull" or "push" of positive or negative energies irrelevant to present relationships are being experienced, he/she can stay in control of the situation by means of dignified yet diplomatic confrontations or intelligent social strategies.

It is important to keep in mind that there are saintly and experienced overseers, reliable colleagues, and licensed psychological consultants who understand clergy. Some licensed psychological clinicians have consultation groups for pastors in which counseling issues are discussed, but in which client's/parishioner's names are withheld. I have participated in several of these. They can be objective, confidential, and available resources for ministers who need not stand alone nor believe that they have no right to seek help with their own private matters.

Human life is fragile; the human soul is God-given and divinely precious. The pastor and the individuals of his flock are human; all are vulnerable and all are precious. The minister is indeed one of them—as well as being their spiritual leader. God's love requires that we be "wise as serpents, yet gentle as doves."

—GENESIS 25:33f; 27:35f; I CORINTHIANS 9:24–27

★ James Thurber. "The Secret Life of Walter Mitty," *Short Stories from the New Yorker*, New York: Simon and Schuster, Inc., pp. 16-21.

★★ The governing institutions of the Episcopal Church in the U.S.A. were established as a replication of those of the United States by many of our founding fathers, who designed both almost simultaneously. The Metropolitan or Archbishop was to be called "Presiding Bishop," and the General Convention is still bicameral, with a House of Bishops and a House of Deputies—like our Congress. But those who established this system neglected to create an ecclesiastical parallel to the Supreme Court. Recent adjustments in Canon Law to accommodate this need in an era of litigation have placed heavy burdens of judgment on the bishops of the Church which are detrimental to their pastoral role.

Why the Sanctuary Was Made Accessible

When Episcopalians talk about "the Sanctuary," they are referring to a portion of the interior of the church, unlike most Protestants who use this term to describe the whole of the church building. For the former, this is the New Testament equivalent of the "Holy of holies" in the Jerusalem Temple. For the latter, this reflects the concept of "the priesthood of all believers."

Episcopalians believe in "the ministry of all baptized believers," but, with respect to ancient apostolic roots, they also hold to a three-fold ordained ministry which includes Deacons, Priests and Bishops. Thus, the term "Sanctuary" refers to the area dominated by the High Altar within the Altar Rail, where the clergy function in the leading of worship. It is here that the presiding ministers celebrate the Sacraments and preach. In accordance with this definition, the "Sanctuary" is architecturally elevated somewhat above the Nave, where the congregation worships. In Gothic style, the Sanctuary stands above the "Choir," which in turn stands above the Nave. In reverse order, this makes for easy catechetical illustration of the Church Militant (here on earth), the Church Expectant (with the Dead in Paradise), and the Church Triumphant (where Christ will gather the blessed in Heaven after His Return). This does not imply any hierarchy of authority or importance in the temporal Church!

Now, having explained this, I questioned why the Department of Rehabilitation (Mobility and Communications Barriers Section) of the State of California requires that the Sanctuary of a church building must be wheelchair accessible. We were in the midst of planning a new church building for All Saints' Parish, Redding, California, when a myriad of regulations were hurdles to be leaped, long before construction and a Use Permit would ever be ours. Where would a wheelchair ramp find a graceful place in our Tudor Gothic structure? The architects, however, had the answer. The ambulatory (which is the passageway behind the scenes that leads from one side of the Sanctuary to the other) would be inclined, so as to connect the choir room and, through it, the far side door to the Altar area, at the higher level. So we built an accessible Sanctuary and Choir Room in a way that pleased the building inspectors and the law, but the true reason for this was yet to be revealed.

After the new edifice was completed, and on a bright Easter Sunday, as the congregation was gathering for the High Celebration, a newcomer transited the main aisle to a place beside the front pew. The smile on his face revealed the joy of the Paschal Celebration. It was obvious that he was no stranger to the Church, and his demeanor diverted one's attention from the fact that, missing one leg, he propelled himself in a wheelchair. We would later discover that through a system of pulleys, he was able to board his van and store the chair in it quite without assistance.

The Sunday after Easter this gentleman reappeared, still sporting his Easter smile. As he welcomed this newcomer, Jack, a member of the congregation, asked "Bill" if he was a priest. "How could you tell?" Bill asked. Jack said: "You just look like one." "Well," he replied, "I haven't functioned as a priest for seventeen years. As a matter of fact, I just sent my vestments back to Trinity Cathedral in Newark, New Jersey to see if anyone might be able to use them."

It seems that "Bill" was indeed Father William MacBeth, who had been successively a vicar, curate, school chaplain, and rector, throughout New England. Father MacBeth was Canon assistant to Arthur C. Lichtenberger when he was Dean of Trinity Cathedral, Newark (before Dean Lichtenberger became a bishop, and later the Presiding Bishop of the Episcopal Church).

While serving as Archdeacon of the Diocese of Newark, this gentle priest was mugged and robbed while making his urban pastoral rounds. His vascular system was damaged, eventually causing the loss of his leg. Prostheses seemed not to fit and only caused him pain. For seventeen years, Bill MacBeth had been managing motels. He had come to Redding to retire, and had taken an apartment not far from a young couple who had "adopted" him, and who had moved to the area in response to an employment opportunity.

Initially when I approached Father Bill about assisting me at services or in any way he might desire, he graciously refused with the comment: "I could never serve again, but thank you." However, it seemed as though he had rolled into our congregation to make sense out of the requirement of making the Sanctuary of All Saints' Church accessible to all.

His old friends at the Newark Cathedral returned Father's vestments to him with great joy. Leon and Mary Lewis, my Navy friends from former days, donated a public address system with a portable microphone. Thus, Father MacBeth's voice could be projected while he was seated in his wheelchair. In front of the Altar, a table from the parish hall was set up for him with fair linen, candles, and vested Chalice. Several weeks later this priest was restored to his life's Vocation as he celebrated the Holy Eucharist for the entire congregation. On occasions thereafter, using the special P. A. equipment, he preached inspiring messages. In full vestments, he would roll down the aisle with the entering procession, and during the recessionals (with proper timing), he would leave the Sanctuary by the Choir Room door and shoot down the ambulatory ramp, all in time to join me in the clergy position behind the Acolytes and Choir.

Father Bill even made occasional hospital calls on patients who were members of the parish, and his presence stimulated a return to communicant status of several of our amputees and many fragile persons who responded to his example. One parishioner who owned a motor boat on one of the nearby lakes arranged for Father Bill and me to have a day of fishing with him. During his last fourteen months of life, Father Bill enriched my life beyond belief and the life of the entire parish.

As a memorial to Father William MacBeth and his ministry, the parish established a tradition of welcoming retired priests into its Sanctuary and its Pulpit as stipendiary part-time clergy. Indeed, he was the first in a succession of clergy associates who would follow. The intent was to demonstrate to retired clergy that they were valued and loved by the Body of Christ, and to make them accessible to the people of God. All of us were inspired by our association with these priests who had devoted so much of their lives to Christ and His Church. Yes, making the Sanctuary accessible to these clergy made them accessible to the people of God, too. That inclined ramp runs in both directions.

—PSALM 126; JEREMIAH 29:10–14

Code 11-45

*R*edding Chief of Police Robert Whitmer and his wife Jacqueline were enjoying the evening and dinner in our home on March 12, 1988 shortly before his retirement. In the course of the evening he extended an invitation to me to join the small group of volunteer chaplains to his agency. This opened a door for me to enter a world both new and yet familiar at the same time. As a retired Navy Chaplain, I felt comfortable in the assignment and suspected that I might have some organizational background that would be helpful to his paramilitary agency. However, it was new to me because I had yet to be indoctrinated in the world of law enforcement.

I was introduced to a band of five mature ordained clergy who were serving local congregations while volunteering their time on a schedule to be available to the police department. As I began to serve on this remarkable team I would exercise a ministry of presence, spending some swing and graveyard shifts on ride-alongs after my parish work for the day was complete. On my scheduled days I would attend "Roll Call" and briefings in the squad room at the beginning of a shift, where I would become familiar with events of importance and get to know who was on duty. I could feel the difference in my life as I entered "the Blue Circle." When I was driving in town and would spot a police car, now I looked to see who was driving it rather than automatically focusing on my speedometer to see if I was within the law.

The five members of this chaplaincy team shared an unselfish fellowship of devotion and service. We served citizens on call in times of emergency, and expedited referrals to the local pastors of those who had an affiliation— even just a potential one. We learned what a fellow chaplain could or could not do because of his denomination. Frequently I was called upon by another chaplain to perform an infant baptism (especially in an Emergency Room), and I had occasion to refer for marriage civilian and police-related couples whose nuptials were beyond my canonical restrictions.

Riding hours on patrol with officers made for small talk, often during which the officer was subtly probing the chaplain's reliability. Such ride-alongs were not infrequently followed in subsequent days, weeks, or on future patrols by a disclosure of personal needs or invitations to offer personal advice. Expressing such a need is often difficult for such assertive persons, and it was a privilege to feel gradually accepted by the officers as a trusted resource.

I designed a blue blazer jacket with a Department Chaplain patch on the pocket which chaplains could wear over their normal civilian attire. The presence of an identified chaplain with an officer at a door instantly signaled an unsuspecting host that an urgent message or notification of death was to be delivered. When the chaplain entered a house with officers in the middle of the night, it had a remarkably calming effect on a family fight in progress.

I elected to obtain professional training at my own expense from the national organization that addresses the Posttraumatic Stress Debriefing (PTSD) program, and was instrumental in providing several of the first debriefings for the Fire Department personnel after tragic events or rescues. They were given according to the prescribed syllabus. Initially they were minimally successful because supervisors had yet to learn of their importance and did not require attendance. But this launched a developing program among emergency services first responders in my city for whom it has great potential for resolving professional "burnout." The ongoing effects on both survivors and rescuers at the Pentagon and the World Trade Center subsequent to the attacks on September 11, 2001 have impressed upon local agencies throughout the nation the importance of this program.

When Officer Chris Darker "laterally transferred" from the Riverside (California) Police Department, he brought with him the concept of the *Blue Santa* which had been useful in his previous agency. From their rounds, patrol officers have special knowledge of families and foster children who lack resources for a happy Christmas or Hanukkah. In the Pediatric Units of local hospitals, there are always children needing encouragement at that emotional time of the year. As we adopted the program, I rode with the police escort for *Santa* to homes in a police car with flashing light bar. A van followed with specifically selected and wrapped gifts with a Cadet dressed as *McGruff the Anti-Crime Dog* to help with the distribution. These gifts were previously purchased with donated funds and money from the Peace Officers' Association. In some cases we would deliver Christmas meals, and even a tree. During our initial planning sessions, Officer Darker told us of an incident that happened in his previous department in the form of a warning. It seems that when *Blue Santa* arrived at a residence, a family member escaped through the back window of the dwelling, thinking that the assembled force was really after him instead of their being on a charitable mission. It was a joyful privilege to be a participant in the replication of this annual project.

One of the Police Officers always wore his uniform hat, whereas in our mostly temperate climate none of the others did outside formal ceremonies. On one occasion I commented on this to him, whereupon he removed his head cover to show me that fixed inside his officer's hat was his yarmulke. In a quiet voice but with pride in his eyes, he replied: "I'm Jewish."

As a pastor in the community, I was able to advise the department and especially the Shift Sergeant of special needs of which I was aware in the city, and to suggest extra patrols where I knew them to be appropriate. When a police dog needed some "seek and find" training on graveyard shift, I secretly made the church facilities available to his K-9 Officer for some midnight "hide and seek". This came to light with my Vestry when one night a silent intruder-alarm was triggered at the church. Four police cars, six Officers and brave *Beano* arrived on the premises within four minutes, and the intruder was successfully apprehended.

Every ten days or so on a warship, mass casualty drills are held without warning. When I joined the public arena, I looked for an equivalent in my community, and found none activated. I was informed that there was a plan in a file drawer, but was also told that an interagency drill had not been held for a number of years. I accepted this as a personal challenge in a city served by a railroad mainline, an interstate highway, and a commercial airfield that also served as *Bingo Field* (alternate emergency landing field) for commercial aircraft. We also have two General Aviation airfields—one in the midst of a residential neighborhood. My covert quest was rewarded with the establishment of such drills as annual events in which I was an enthusiastic participant. However, I confronted resistance from fire and emergency medical personnel who had yet to interface with chaplains as military people routinely do.

Chaplains need police and fire training if they are to participate in meaningful ways with public safety agencies and not become liabilities. Some agencies require that their chaplains choose either to minister to offenders and in the jail or to citizens and agency personnel—not both simultaneously. I never encountered this restriction, however. I found the national chaplains' organization that assumed the task of training chaplains to be reliable on the agency side, but unreliable when it came to the pastoral side. I was told on two separate occasions by trainers that baptizing a SIDS-death baby in the morgue would be a comfort to parents of the infant. *I was shocked!* Pastoral Training would be better handled by local resources, I thought.

The benefits of my eight years as a volunteer police chaplain were mutual. I gained valued colleagues, and performed an effective outreach ministry in the name of my congregation. It gave me a wider world of reality beyond the confines of the parish, it broadened my horizons as well as my circle of friends, and it offered satisfactions (and, frankly, a measure of excitement) sometimes absent from the life of a parish leader.

Clergy who are *want-to-be cops*, or who are excitement *seekers*, must be disqualified from this chaplaincy! Some agencies have recruited well-meaning lay people as chaplains, and in known cases have them wearing clergy garb.★ Many agencies take a shortcut by choosing an unordained police officer, firefighter or staff member to be chaplain "because they understand cops or firefighters," even though they lack theological training and pastoral experience. These persons quickly lose their identity as either officer or chaplain, and confidentiality within the agency's chain-of-command and under subpoena becomes suspect.★ This ministry has the precious task of caring for those who "serve and protect" others and who encounter a great deal of stress in the process. Such clergy must be persons whose lives are so well in the Hands of God, that they have room in their hearts for others. This is the challenge that confronted me while I was in this chaplaincy!

Having been a military chaplain for over two decades, I recognized bravery and commended it when I observed it in even the unheralded routine actions of the police officers. I could see the mutual advantage of having a small number of chaplains (with one volunteer chaplain in charge) for our local agency of 100 "sworn officers" and an equal number of support staff.** Our lead chaplain, a Seventh Day Adventist Minister, had died, and his replacement, a splendid Baptist Minister, was promoted to another city and church. The old team had scattered. A larger number of volunteer chaplains, both ordained and lay persons, were being recruited. Our chaplaincy undertook obligations to the other public safety agencies and the Highway Patrol as a means of soliciting financial support for a combined independent chaplaincy organization with an office and stipendary leader. This expansion had the effect of depersonalizing the relationship between the agency members and the chaplains. It served the purpose of using chaplains for outreach to citizens on behalf of the various agencies, but it distanced the chaplains from the emergency workers and staff, and it inhibited a relationship which allowed chaplains to be valued as advisors to their agency and to its Chief. It appeared to me to be "empire building." As these trends developed, a new breed of chaplains became competitive and the thrust shifted from being non-directive and pastoral to evangelical and proselytizing. I felt I had completed what contribution I could make after eight years of volunteer service.

I strongly recommend Police or Fire Chaplaincy as an adjunct to parish ministry. The experience was splendid for me and for my parish—which was never neglected because of it—when the climate was right. The time came when I wanted less conflict of interest than the chaplaincy provided. The external policies of the national association of police chaplains began driving our local team, and junior police officers took over the department liaison position which limited our influence on the agency and communication with its leaders. I explore these issues here for the consideration of the clergyperson before making a commitment (or before a lay person encourages a pastor to volunteer) to participate in the support of a particular agency. For eight years it was a good fit for me. But the time came when I was shown that offering my time, expertise, and efforts in the community would be better directed elsewhere.

—Psalm 89:14; Amos 5:24, 7:7f;
St. Matthew 8:5–10; Acts 10:1–4

★ For example, California Evidence Code, Section 1030-1034, defines "clergyman," and grants the privilege of refusal to disclose penitential communications specifically to the clergy. Lay chaplains are unprotected in this regard, and can become a legal and ethical liability to the agency and to its members.

★★ The benefit of personal bonding with identified chaplains was observed as the entire nation mourned the loss of FDNY Chaplain Father Mychal Judge. He was killed when giving Last Rites at the World Trade Center to Firefighters to whom he was Chaplain.

Stop or I'll Shoot

I want to change my major," said the soft plaintive voice on the telephone. It was Karen, our youngest, from Humboldt State, where she was a Senior in Marine Biology.

Her ambition "to talk to Flipper" came from her inherent love of animals, and from elementary school days on Guam when I was chaplain in the submarine tender and the submarine squadron. Our home was near palisades that towered above the white sand beaches on the northwest part of the island. Our children would frequently descend a jungle canopy-covered pathway halfway from our house to the shoreline, where a natural inverted cone in the coral cliffs collected rain water. This pool was clear to a depth of twelve feet or so. There in that jungle-shrouded playground they would swing from a rope or vines out over the clear warm water pool, to drop into it screaming like Tarzan (or Jane).

Their neighborhood swim team challenged teams from Japan and the Philippines in meets on Saipan. At beaches there, a child can swim a mile to sea in the clear turquoise-colored ocean waters, accompanied by a myriad of harmless exotic tropical fish, and still stand up in the shallows within atoll-protected lagoons. It is no wonder these memories had sustained Karen through most of her undergraduate academic endeavors. Declining grades were indicators that inspiration was failing, however. Seemingly late in the game she came to terms with the fact that her need to communicate with human animals had taken precedence over her career choice, relegating scuba instead to career adjunct or to sport. With God, there are no blind streets!

Upon hearing Karen's request, my mind skidded to a sudden stop. I was a parent, but a busy one—much as my parents had been when I was a young student. I was in the midst of building a congregation, overseeing the construction of buildings, and I was surrounded by a multiplicity of community endeavors.

Yet, I was given to guilt-whipping myself for my years at war and at sea when I missed so many precious developments in the lives of my family members. I was trying to put pages back on the calendar, hearing echoes that I had extended myself to save others at the expense of those closest to me. Was I replicating parenting patterns that, though borne of love, had victimized me in ways I had never dared to guess? Had my family of origin prepared me for ministry in this peculiar unconscious way?

Whirling in my own memory were pressures I had experienced in a tug-of-war between my elders who loved me dearly; father urging me to study mechanical engineering; mother urging me to be a physician—when I wanted to be a priest. College preparatory high school had cost them years of labor and long days at their professions. In response, I had passed my freshman year at Stanford (where I entered at age 16) with grades sufficient to be invited back—but far from an "honors" grade point average. I literally felt compelled to escape to sea as a Merchant Mariner—where I had found peace in an engine room the summer before university matriculation. As a youth, I had felt torn and confused. College Senior or not, I would not allow my daughter to be trapped in a similar dilemma.

When I heard her plea on the telephone, my own life passed before my mind in the split second her reality collided with my own. Only by God's grace was I able to conquer the natural ambition that well-intentioned parents vicariously wish upon their children. I answered: "Okay, Karen. We're with you. What is it that you want to do?" After a protracted silence, she timidly offered: "I want to be a cop."

"Come on home; try out the major at the local junior college and see if you like it." I surprised myself that I had not suggested that she try to graduate before making the proposed change (as I had been taught: "Finish what you start!") "Are you willing?" "Sure, Dad. (long pause)...Thanks."

For Karen, this has been a success story. She made the Dean's List immediately at Shasta Community College, held several security and parking enforcement jobs, then went on to Sacramento State University to achieve her degree in Criminal Justice. She served four years on patrol, then was made Detective in one of California's leading law enforcement agencies.

But the success story most prominent in this pastor's mind was his own. I had ample memories of developmental years *seeking* to find myself as a young person, then those of being an absent and often preoccupied pastor parent. The Lord played them back to me in that instant when I heard my daughter's tears, and He gave me the grace to stop in my tracks, then to respond with hope— the same hope that I so frequently dispensed beyond my family's circle.

Indeed, his/her own family is the minister's most immediate opportunity to extend compassion by acting for the Master.

—St. Matthew 5:48*

---

* Note regarding the Biblical citation: An accurate translation of the Greek word *teleioi/teleios (τέλειοι/τέλειός)* includes "fulfillment," "brought to completion," as well as "perfect." For this vignette, I prefer to also translate this as "mature," which implies reaching one's goal or objective.

Changes

At least once a year when I have been in my homeland, I have made every effort to make a pilgrimage to the place where I first met the Christ—the Chapel of Saint Savior at the Harvard (Episcopal) School in North Hollywood, California. It was in this place that God called me to be His Child, and where I learned to love serving the Altar as an Acolyte. It was in this place that the Holy Savior summoned me to prepare to be His Priest. Here in the pew where I had once knelt as a twelve-year-old military school cadet, I come to quietly pause in prayerful awe and gratitude.

As I was in this posture several years ago, two young men entered from the sacristy area and began a discussion. One may have been a representative of the school, the other perhaps an interior decorator or an architect. They were as seemingly oblivious to my presence in this small shrine as I was trying to be to theirs. I fought to retain my thoughts in meditation. However, their audible conversation captured my attention as they crossed the nave to the baptismal font where I had been baptized.

Its concrete pedestal has a concave dish cast into the upper surface to receive water to be poured and blessed, and the font was topped by a carved wooden decorative cover which was raised when the Sacrament of New Birth was to be administered.

"Let's start by getting rid of this ugly thing," said one self-styled innovator to the other. "Agreed," came the instant reply. They progressed to the Altar Rail where I had been Confirmed and knelt to receive my first Holy Communion, and often thereafter. It was subjected to the same verdict as their planning progressed. Soon the entire chapel, like the Church which it represents, would be made acceptable to a new age.

My meditations had come to an abrupt end. I left with a saddened heart. I had travelled hundreds of miles to revisit the holy place where life really had begun for me. Suddenly I was not only ignored, but I was allowed to overhear that things that were sacred treasures to me were seen as ugly in the eyes of those who would continue where I would one day leave off.

Traditions have their foundations in teaching as well as in beauty. But of greater value than any is the value of the heart. Changes can bring new perspectives and enlighten horizons beyond. But changes that fail to bridge the generations can lose more than they gain. What is more, to observe the enforcement of such changes while being ignored can sadden the heart of those who have possessed endangered treasures, and who have lovingly shared them with others in the past.

—I Samuel 3:1-10; Psalm 137:4ff

The Mutiny—A Parable

*T*he story you are about to read, though fictional, is secretly replicated with varying details in the Christian Church more often than is commonly known. As the last century came to a close, such experiences had become increasingly commonplace. This is so even in "my beloved" Episcopal Church, as its polity shifts from a church of order and collegiality to one of congregational governance and independently acting bishops. This parable is a montage of actual events in nameless congregations. It is included so that clergy may not be devastated by such experiences, and so that congregations may take measures to avoid them. Let both be armed with the knowledge that the Ministry is not ours, but Christ's—His gift for the benefit of *all* of His Children and for the world beyond any boundaries.

Truly, the Church is larger than one congregation, one parish, even one diocese, judicatory or denomination. We need to be fortified with the knowledge that our Holy Mother Church is composed of *both* the perfect Son of God *and* His fallible Baptism-adopted Siblings.

From His Cross, Jesus struggled to redeem us. From His Throne, His saving struggle with us and for us continues hourly. The minister would be well advised to guard against an idealization which elevates to the position of idol (of the Church, or members of the clergy, or even one's own ego) to a height from which the idolized can easily topple and fall. Realism strengthens one to see beyond the limitations of a single situation, as catastrophic as it may seem in a moment of time, to the beatific Vision of one's indelible Call to serve.

The Parable

Once upon a time, a town called Prideville struggled with the growing pains that seem inevitable as rural America "grows up." Prideville's history is one of individualism related to rough-and-ready cultural independence. Where once stood trees and wildlife, speculators are now building as many houses as they can. Where the main highway once brought business into town as Main Street, now a freeway circumvents Prideville, and new motels on its outskirts have usurped the travellers' trade once enjoyed by the stately old downtown hotels. "Mom and pop" shops are slowly surrendering to huge chain discount stores with well-advertised products and cheaper prices, but fewer services. The locally-owned department store that had enjoyed a monopoly, a privilege that it had carefully maneuvered to protect for years, watched helplessly as several new malls were erected in apparent defiance, away from the city's center, each anchored by large well-known department stores—corporate in name and size. The old store shared the fate of many of its downtown neighbors and quietly closed its doors.

The population of Prideville has almost doubled in the last decade. The descendents of a few old families feel the control of the policies and the politics of the town slipping through their fingers as the town grows into a city, but the means of manipulating from behind the scenes still work politically in some organizations and institutions. Old money and a prevailing nepotism still have power. A succession of qualified local governmental and business professionals, recruited from outside, will only serve for what will be a limited period. Then, for "undisclosed personal reasons," they will join the passing parade, to be replaced by others. Power is still retained in the hands of a few.

One lifelong member of "Old Trinity" Church, a gentleman in his late seventies, can remember having worshipped under the leadership of nineteen rectors! Father Joseph has served in that position at Trinity Church for nine years, a tenure that is the longest in the known history of the parish. Each in the series of recent clergy vacated the position after making initial contributions to the church and the town. In turn, each minister was criticized or intimidated out of his pulpit—then discarded. This allowed the old guard to maneuver yet another "steering committee" in the selection of their own next chaplain—one whose eventual popularity would hopefully not compete with their own. More than a few good pastors had left with broken hearts—some with broken careers.

Father "Joe" had accepted the invitation of the bishop before he retired, to come to Prideville "to provide leadership for a church that was 'circling the drain'." It was at a time when such an invitation was not attractive to other clergy who knew the history of how the parish had treated its ministers, and, in a few cases, driven them to misbehave.

During Father "Joe's" tenure, his vigorous program of home and hospital visitations doubled the participating congregation. Soon financial stability was achieved, a significant building construction program succeeded, and "Old Trinity" reestablished itself as a benevolent leader in the civic community. Father "Joe" became a prominent figure in Prideville, serving in the community at large, as well as within the Church, projecting his own role as a visible representative of the People of God. Many in Prideville who wanted acceptance by a church family, and many who needed the shelter from the storms of life, a comfort that a church can provide, swelled the active membership rolls, received instruction in the Faith, and worshipped in the new facility. They brought with them to "Old Trinity" new ideas and new methods of doing things that challenged the Vestry and the congregation in ways that were not always welcomed. Before long, Father "Joe," himself, was confronted with resistance that was not always anonymous.

Trivial discussions occupied more and more time in meetings of the Vestry, which resisted progress. The rector diplomatically invited an outside presenter to hold a "retreat" for the Vestry. Since the parish was growing, part-time help was needed. An ordained deacon moved into the community to take a secular position during weekdays. He was employed part-time to assist the rector. Deacon Absalom was initially a positive asset to both the parish and to Father Joseph, although his ideas were quite liberal in comparison to those of the self-proclaimed "traditional" rector. Father "Joe" found this acceptable, and a healthy expression of the inclusiveness typical of the Anglican ethos. The rector hoped this openness would prevent the parish from becoming a liturgically "specialized" congregation in a single Episcopal Church town.

However, after several years, three or four "old guard" families, feeling it was time for another change of command for "Old Trinity," seduced Deacon Absalom into gathering a group around him. (Clergy have come to know such divisive parishioners as "Curate's Men.") Father Joseph went to the newly installed bishop for several consultations, but found him to be pleasantly passive (cf. Exodus 1:8ff). Father "Joe" perceived this to be the new bishop's subtle support for those who had greater longevity at "Old Trinity" than did the incumbent rector, and he accepted the fact that this bishop was wooing lay persons in the parish likely to support future diocese-wide projects of his own choosing. He suspected that the bishop already had his replacement in mind from his former "team."

During the rector's annual vacation, a secret meeting of the Vestry was called by the Parish Warden, and to it several parish members were summoned to witness against the rector in what was in reality a "kangaroo court." Nothing definitive could be produced (no immorality or heresy), and there was no denying that Father Joseph had saved the parish and that he was a devoted pastor. Perhaps the rector had done his job too well, and he was outshining the sparkle of lay community stars. If the truth be told, a self-chosen few were spreading the word that Father Joseph was now too old to carry on for "the new" Old Trinity.

Without notifying the rector, the Parish Warden invited the new bishop to the next Vestry Meeting. At the "Announcement Time" during Sunday services just after Father Joseph had returned from vacation, the Warden volunteered in public that Father Joseph would retire early and leave "Old Trinity." (Under these circumstances, the parish would not be obliged to provide severance compensation.)

By this time in his participation at Trinity Church, Deacon Absalom had declined to serve at the Altar, and during church services would sit with a small cluster of church members who talked aloud during the sermon and stood as a group when most of the parish knelt. The latter posture is allowed by the Prayer Book, but the changing of this parish tradition was in fact a means of gathering allies for a protest. When the new bishop came to the meeting of the Vestry, the presence of a spontaneously gathered group that "crashed" the meeting in support of their rector made it clear that the parish was polarized over this growing conflict.

Father Joseph, knowing he was too old to find another challenging parish, retired before the required time in order to preserve the unity of the parish he and his family had devoted themselves to rebuilding. By leaving them, he chose to protect from conflict people whose lives he had shared and whom he loved.

The bishop sent expert interim rectors to the congregation to bind up any wounds, and a new and younger rector was selected and moved into place. Father Joseph, an experienced priest, would not interfere with the future of "Old Trinity," because he wanted it to succeed, and he was well aware of appropriate protocols. Yet he received a letter from the bishop (endorsed by the parish Warden and by Deacon Absalom) ordering him, under Holy Obedience, to make no future contact with the parish or any of its members. No pastoral assistance was ever offered to Father Joseph or to his family by the new diocesan.

Father Joseph was financially and spiritually exhausted when he left Trinity Church, but he left to preserve the unity of the congregation. Holy Church had been the center of his entire life, and Father Joseph had served with devotion.

Although at great cost and with sad feelings that he had been betrayed by many whom he loved, he left with dignity to join the procession of clergy that had gone before. He would tell us: "That is sometimes the price of Ministry. The gift one gives of years of life and love can have no strings attached. If it was no less for Jesus the Savior, how can we expect more?"

Summary

An Ordination is a lifetime, even an eternal commitment—the result of a Vocation, a Divine Selection. An Ordination *is* a marriage. In the Anglican tradition, marriage of a clergyperson to a spouse is permitted only if such will be adjudged an asset to one's ministry. (At the time when I hoped to marry Marjorie, that judgment for clergy was reserved for one's bishop.) Further, like the Sacrament of Holy Matrimony, receiving Holy Orders must be only at the bidding of an individual and very personal Call from God to do so. The vows of both Sacraments, I reckon, must prevail "for better, for worse, in sickness and in health."

When and where we believe the Church to be in trouble, the clergy must be Her bold prophets and minister to Her with their lives as well as by their lips. The Church is the bride of Christ. As such She deserves our loyalty. Thus, She also deserves to be told the truth, and to have it modelled by her leaders as well. In this prophetic role, the minister needs to use every skill that can be mustered to communicate truth, but we clergy dare not expect to be understood at every turn. Our souls need to be strong enough to carry secret discernments, even at the cost of internal anguish. The trust of comrades that I experienced in combat and the loyalty which Prisoners of War depended upon from each other to stay alive in North Korea and in Viet Nam is a model from a most unfortunate resource, but is nonetheless a model for the Church of Jesus!

The above tale is told because such conflicts do recur in every denomination, and thus needs to be related in the hope that it may serve as a deterrent to pain and loss. When divisions in a congregation or in an entire denomination occur, once adoring families and friends become divided by the very Body that Christ gave to unify the world and to bring peace, and the shelter for wanderers is brought down. Clergy are also victims of schism.

A national news column* reported a survey that determined that every month in our country, 1,300 pastors are fired or forced to resign, and that 30 percent of all pastors have been terminated at least once. The survey adds that in the last 25 years, the divorce rate among pastors has increased by 65 percent. It is no wonder that many of my old friends have "left the ministry," and I am sure that many more carry burdens which they think will lift when the Church Pension Fund (or its equivalent) provides them with a magic date.

In the fifty years I have devoted to the Sacred Ministry, I have known far too many talented and dedicated brother and sister clergy who have put aside their stoles, feeling defeated and disillusioned. This has been a tragic waste! It all seems so unnecessary, and the result of allowing comparatively trifling matters and egotism to eclipse the Son of God. Real controversies often elude resolution in the Church because they take on falsely justifying disguises of theological, liturgical, or administrative differences.

Ministers are not perfect. We are well aware of this! But should we momentarily forget this, there will be some parishioners who are quite capable of reminding us of our imperfections. There is but one *Good* Shepherd (St. John 10:11). But this Master Calls His ministers to be good sheepdogs, and always as such, to follow the bidding of the Shepherd—the *Good* and *Perfect* One.

Wherever our Savior leads, even through dark, dangerous, and lonely valleys, we are to follow! Spiritual warfare can endanger our souls in more grave ways than can the blue green tracers of an AK–47. I know. I have seen too much of both. Whether we classify our endeavors as sacred or secular, every person will find fulfillment when his/her labors are in response to God's unique Will for the use of that person's life. I believe strongly that each of us has a Call to be discerned and through which to offer one's talents and energies. That is the meaning of "Vocation"—one's Call from God. That will stand before the test of any storm or trial, if we dare to go where He Calls us to go and do what He Calls us to do—without expectation of tangible response or earthly reward.

—II Samuel 15:2-6; St. Matthew 10:13f;
I Corinthians 11:17-22; 13:1-13; Ephesians 2:14-18

⋆ Scripps Howard News Service, 1999.

N.B. In I Corinthians 6:7, Saint Paul urges Christians to accept unfairness rather than taking fellow Christians to civil law courts.

Retirement

*I*f that dog that chases cars in your neighborhood ever caught one, what would he do with it? Some things we work for may never fulfill our expectations once they have been achieved.

When I was struggling to complete my doctoral dissertation after having invested three years in the project, I can remember a colleague telling me that when it was finished, I would miss it. I thought that was a crazy notion until it happened to me. It had so structured my life, that I felt lost without the demands it made upon me. I went through a period of grieving after the degree was awarded. Many who nurse a chronically ill loved one over months and years may be surprised by similar feelings of missing the demands, once the time for parting has past.

The event of retirement is usually marked by celebrations, but after the party is over, what does one do next?

Fathers Westling and MacBeth with the catch of the day. (Page 394)

Father Wes and Marjorie at home in retirement. (Pages 413 & 423)

I stepped off the treadmill on January 1, 1996, when I departed from my last parish and retired from what is called "the active ministry." Feeling lost without the demands of an 80-hour workweek, I returned to work as a psychotherapist with County Mental Health. The schedule was not as strenuous, because off-duty hours and weekends were covered by other qualified staff, but the commute to neighboring Tehama County added two additional hours to each workday.

My body needed some surgical repairs that could not be delayed any longer, so I finally left the workforce on May 1, 2000. But, then I had this book to write, requiring six-hour days over the following eighteen months, and the house beckoned with endless tasks that had been long delayed for other priorities. Active lives are hard to slow down.

All those delayed projects and goals keep us going for a while. I have heard it said often by retirees: "I am so busy now, that I long for the old job." Activity can be a cover for an emptiness in "life after full-time ministry." In all honesty, "we have been to the mountaintop!" One may have the reassuring knowledge that he/she is a "Priest Forever" (Psalm 110:4; Hebrews 5:6b). But duties and obligations once cursed can become reframed and mysteriously missed, and all the things we enjoyed are often predominantly remembered when one is in a position to deny those "former burdens" that have vanished. Retirement brings both immediate and lasting satisfactions, but retirement for the pastor may require the exercise of perception and patience to find these satisfactions with an easy acceptance.

When retirement sets in, one is required to evaluate oneself in this new condition, if spiritual and emotional (even physical) health are to be preserved. Suddenly those pesky telephone calls at all hours of the day and night disappear. Another minister now answers the telephone. There comes the realization that one was living on what might be described as a one-way thoroughfare. Folks were "always there." However, this was primarily because the pastoral caller was usually welcome, but the clergyperson was the one primarily taking the initiative and doing "the leg work." People freely came to the office or to the rectory seeking help or advice, the pastor's wife served on the Altar Guild or taught Sunday School, and the "parson's kids" participated in youth events or Christian Education classes. But routine social life, especially in large parishes, usually centers at the parish hall, the men's barbecue, or within one of the women's guilds. Who casually "comes calling" on the parson?

When retirement status is reached, formerly intense friendships suddenly appear to be fewer and less energetic. Courtesies formerly received must now be extended to the new incumbent, and the retiree begins to recognize that most who had gathered around resulted from his/her being the prime mover, an action that seems no longer appropriate.

I am suggesting that strong forces in the life of the clergy promote symbiotic relationships with one's flock. There, I wrote it! "One's Flock!" "My Flock!" "My parish!" Now just whose flock is it? The cognitive answer is immediately obvious, but the emotional answer is not so easy for us to accept. They are *God's* flocks, *not ours!*

Yet, we have "fed them" as a shepherd feeds his flock, and *they feed us* in more ways than we recognize when we are in the midst of our pastoral duties. Suddenly, there is an emptiness in our lives that even rushing to do errands for our family and volunteering for community projects fail to fill. "Who needs me?" we may ask ourselves—even when surrounded by obvious answers. There are those close to us who do need us and always have, but who may for some time have been neglected in our race to support others. It is important for us to take a fresher look at them when we retire. And perhaps our new availability may require some adjustments from them as well.

Grieving is not only an experience resulting from the death of a loved one, or even the loss of a limb. Grieving can result from any major loss in one's life. That includes the time when the minister who has been "joined at the hip" with a congregation is suddenly replaced by another who has been called to fill the pulpit. Spoken and written comments that the minister has "made a difference" in lives or to the church at times like these are "like apples of gold in a filigree of silver" (Proverbs 25:11). They bring comfort and reassurance to those who have spent decades bringing comfort and reassurance to others. However, the retired pastor needs to be open to hearing and assimilating the sincerity of those who say such things or who write occasional notes or send cards after he/she has been "displaced." Scholars on death and grieving have published wise theories about the steps of adjustment to loss, from denial and anger to eventual acceptance, and these certainly can be valid here. This experience of clergy retirement tests the spiritual resilience of even the most saintly.

Some never manage to say goodbye to their former flock. They hang around in the wings, are available for marriages and burials, and split the allegiance of the people—giving hidden grievances to the new rector (which he/she may never dare to admit aloud).

In the Navy, neither the Captain nor the Chaplain returns to a command without a formal invitation, once there has been a change of command or Military Orders for replacement have been executed. Caution is an appropriate watchword for the retired rector or vicar who remains in his old neighborhood, even when requests for assistance are extended. There will be new "rules" and changes preferred by the incumbent that need to be followed and honored. Some of these changes may have motivated the selection of the new pastor by the Search Committee of the congregation. There are, indeed, departing pastors for whom acceptance of inevitable changes under new leadership is too difficult, or who discern that their continued assistance after retirement may not be welcome. If it is necessary to move out of town to find peace or to avoid conflict, so be it. Retirement for the clergy is not as easy as it is usually anticipated to be.

There are many ways to say goodbye. If they are not recognized in advance, they may "play sport" with us, rather than our controlling them. Some can bid *adieu* with a gracious hug and exchange of love messages. Some make the break by simply walking away, perhaps with a casual wave. Some have to be kicked out, and some conflict has to be provoked to dissolve the pastoral relationship. Those who die in the pulpit, on the contrary, are usually canonized in the eyes of survivors. It is easier for a new pastor to follow one perceived as a liability than to follow a predecessor who appears to have ascended directly from the parish altar to heavenly places. One who retires in apparent disgrace, or is deposed, has done a secret favor for the one who follows. But there *is* a time to say "goodbye," and that is when the Lord who has Called us to a place has revisited us with His Call to go away. There are times when we need to say to ourselves: "I have done what I could to teach them to fly, and if I stay longer I will just be stepping on their wings."

Another gremlin in the mix is the factor of age in the life of older clergy. Oriental cultures honor age and seek wisdom at the feet of experienced elders. Asians learn from infancy that there is merit in caring for aging parents and honoring mentors. In contrast, our Western ways differ, and the American Church is strongly affected by our mores.

Clergy approaching their senior years, who wish to make a change, cannot expect the same opportunities offered younger and more modern minded clergy. (The introduction of female clergy and their proven effectiveness in the last quarter century in many previously less accepting church bodies has not only challenged theological notions, but has impacted employment opportunities as well.) One who leaves a parish in one's late 50's or early 60's, will discover that selection committees of searching churches dare not admit *in writing* that only younger clergy need apply (even if the asterisk in the position advertisement reassures that the Church is "an equal opportunity employer"). One must also keep in mind the age ceiling that is required by church pension plans. This artificially limits the time one can serve, even when one is able to continue an effective pastorate. Selection committees are certainly cognizant of such time constraints, and they commonly harbor doubts about the health as well as the vigor of "senior" applicants. Years in the exercise and sometimes turmoil of ministry claim their price on the minister. As an aging colleague once told me: "My get-up-and-go has got-up-and-went!" Problems accepting one's own age limitations complicate the graceful acceptance of retirement.

Age cuts both ways. It may oblige an older rector (especially one who has a legal contract or where the canons provide legal lifetime tenure) knowingly to overstay his effectiveness because there is no place else to go. The alternative is to retire prematurely from the active ministry to protect self and/or the flock, but with jeopardy to the future security of the family and self. Yes, there are many "part-time positions" that invite the retiree to serve with partial stipends and/or housing suitable to that part-time definition. But any priest or minister worth his/her salt, once in place, would be tempted to give full-time devotion and availability in exchange for the privilege of having a pulpit and an altar "at *your* age." I believe there is a lack of dignity in such disguised offers.

If a congregation were to advertise a part-time stipend with expectations of full-time ministry, the retiree would be well advised at least to investigate the matter, and only accept the position in an atmosphere of mutual honesty, that good feelings might prevail.

Ministry must have its own rewards, and the perception of those rewards is our responsibility as clergy. If, on the other hand, we recognize with God's help that our work is finished or devoid of joy, then it is time to go elsewhere and do something else. When a minister retires, leadership in the Church is left to one's successors as the Lord directs them. What they do or how they follow the Lord's bidding is *their gift* in their turn, and entirely *their* opportunity.

When one retires, one needs to adjust to the role of Follower. When leadership has for years been expected by oneself and by one's "audience" and title, this transition requires courage and faith. It requires the trust that we have made our contribution (for better or for worse) to the objectives of each milestone along our way. Hope comes when that same intensity of trust in the Lord applies to a search for and an openness to the next milestone, and the faith that He has a new goal for each of us. The Lord knows who we are, and where we need to go to follow Him.

This new chapter in life's journey may take a new and unexpected form, requiring new resources of learning or of patience. Further, ministry extends beyond the boundaries of time and space in the Eternal Life we preach and share. How we offer our retirement, with every inner struggle that may be involved, is our witness to our Faith. "The Lord gives, and the Lord takes away"...and the Lord of the Resurrection then gives again. "Blessed be the Name of the Lord!"

—EXODUS 12:31, 41f, 51; PSALM 37:3-7a; PSALM 39:7, 12f
[BOOK OF COMMON PRAYER TRANSLATION, PSALM 39:8, 14f;
MASSORETIC HEBREW TEXT, PSALM 39:8, 13f]; ST. MARK 9:2–9

Those Who Live in Glass Houses

Two years after I had retired and left the parish, I failed a treadmill stress test in a big way, and my physician refused to allow me to return home from the hospital—even for a toothbrush. Fortunately good heart surgeons were on duty, and I had the very best of care and prognosis.

Within hours after finally leaving my hospital bed of pain, I was reclining on the couch in the living room of my home in a state of extreme discomfort. The telephone rang, and my wife left her station beside me to pick it up in the kitchen. From where I was lying, I could almost hear the loud protesting voice on the other end of the line. From Marjorie's responses, I could easily put it all together.

"Why didn't you tell me?" the voice of a former parishioner yelled in a demanding manner. In an attempt to answer with civility, Marjorie stated that I had not wanted visitors, and since I had no current ties to the parish, we had a right to our privacy. She added that I was in pain, and had asked not to be disturbed at the hospital.

The point of this story is to illustrate that ministers forego many of the rights of privacy, even though the modern Church—through its clergy training seminaries—now routinely seeks to introduce business time-management concepts that waive the importance of total availability of pastors. Remembering "the good old days," and by way of comparison with the pastoral ministry, I asked my family physician if he ever made house calls. He replied that if it were within the city limits and in the case of an identified and rare emergency with one of his patients, he would—for a minimum of two hundred fifty dollars—make a brief home visit. Father Thomas, my Rector from boyhood through the seminary years, taught me in regard to pastoral responsibilities: "a doorbell punching parson makes a growing parish." The ministry of presence can yield to no substitutes, but it impacts the minister's private and home life.

Like it or not, it is a fact that the pastoral role extends to the personal life of the clergy. There is an adage that says: "There are no secrets in a small town." The same is true in a warship, and in a civilian parish. The minister's private life can only be protected to a degree (in spite of what we consider appropriate or just). Limited privacy goes with the privilege of public life and public leadership. More than once I was called upon to follow clergy who had misbehaved in positions they had vacated. The common excuse that the offending clergypersons offered themselves was: "What I do on my own time is no one else's business."

What I am claiming loud and clear is that our time is the Lord's time. Even though we must defend our right to direct our own lives, maintain self-respect, and listen to our own consciences, we will always be subjected to unavoidable scrutiny. The common concept is that there are many privileges that automatically come with ordination. The truth of the matter is that nothing comes automatically except the expectation that one is Called to serve, and that there are many sacrifices that must be willingly offered. Invasions of privacy for the minister and the clergy family is not right, and this escalates where the rectory is on church property. A Vestry (or Offical Board) needs to teach their congregation that their spiritual leader is a Servant of God, and they do not own him/her. But clergy need to be constantly mindful that their behavior does reflect on their flock.

The "Special Report" issue of *Time* dated August 31, 1998 had on the front cover a nice color photograph of President Clinton, his wife and daughter.

Emblazenoned across the photograph were words of a recent quote of the President's: "It's nobody's business but ours." Of course it was the country's business! Their "private life" cost us millions of dollars in court fees and investigations, and even if the shame of his private behavior and bold disclaimers under oath did not seem to bother the polls of public opinion in our nation, he embarrassed us in the international arena. Public life is public life!

Part of the unfortunate truth is that this commonly spills over onto the members of the minister's family. Marjorie and her sister of the same age were daughters of an Episcopal Priest, thus, they were raised in a rectory. They recalled how difficult it was during school days to hear that parents of their peers had preached to their offspring: "Follow the example of the Clark Twins; their father is the preacher." I must confess that it was much easier for my children, because only once during their lives did we live in military or church provided housing (with the exception of Karla's first seven years in the Philippine Mission). Our residences, in 19 moves, were usually in large population areas. My children were not ashamed that I was a minister, but when asked by peers what their father did, the common answer was that I was a Naval Officer. We wanted them to avoid the title of "Parson's Kid" (or P.K.). After years in the military chaplaincy, when we returned to a civilian parish, they were already adults. At least they avoided the stigma of unwanted "expected behavior" because of living in their father's shadow. Thus they were able to make maturing choices on their own. I thank God daily that my wife has a Vocation to be not only my wife, but a clergy wife. My children did not have their choice of parents, but fortunately they endured into productive adulthood by God's grace! These issues of privacy are *essential considerations* for clergy aspirants, because some loss of privacy just "goes with the territory."

Make no mistake about it: since retirement from the naval chaplaincy and from the parish ministry, we thoroughly enjoy eating meals without as many as six telephone interruptions. Yes, we failed to set some limits—especially before the advent of telephone answering machines. Some of these calls were just routine matters from day workers who knew when and where to find us.

Some interruptions were unthoughtful. But within the total number of them, many emergencies that required my response thereby came to my attention. They could not have been sorted out by an answering machine! Our mailbox at the house now receives either refreshing personal communications, personal business, or junk mail. We do not miss the commanding tenor of much of the ecclesiastical business or complaints of the dissatisfied, and we only read the articles in the church media that are of real interest to us as Christian people. We are free to go where we please, and all those church meetings and community outreach projects are now entirely voluntary—no longer required by the "Eighth Commandment for Clergy Only." We are discovering that the conduct of our personal lives has enjoyably returned to our total possession under God. When folks intrude on those barriers, we can let them know as diplomatically as we did before, but now with greater boldness. But the truth of the matter is that ministers are unavoidably in public life, and what they do affects their leadership and reflects in the lives of those they are committed to lead to the Master.

In the *Examination* at the Ordination of an (Episcopal) Priest,★ the Candidate is asked by the bishop: "Will you do your best to pattern your life and that of your family in accordance with the teachings of Christ, so that you may be a wholesome example to your people?" An acceptable Candidate will answer: "I will." There can be no demand for absolute perfection in the lives of clergy and their families. That Puritan injunction is obviously unachievable, and living under the threat to conform to it will lead to failure at the least, or to mental illness at the extreme. Saint Paul said, "We have this treasure in earthen vessels, to show that the transcendent power belongs to God and not to us" (II Corinthians 4:7). Christian theology teaches us that the efficacy of the Sacrament is not dependent upon the moral character of the ordained celebrant.★★ However, there are no implied excuses herein. We are not "to sin, that grace may abound!" "By no means!" (according to Romans 6:2).

The even greater sin is in the injury, be it moral, physical, or financial—but always spiritual—to others that result from the breach of trust by a minister. Scandal can devastate individuals, parishes, dioceses, denominations, even international communions of the Church.*** Ethical failures of Christians take unavoidable tolls on the cause of Christ, be they secret or publicized, be the perpetrator prominent or obscure. But the clergy will always bear a special burden in this regard.

—St. Mark 3:31–35; 10:35–38; I Timothy 3:1–13

---

* The *Book of Common Prayer*, 1979, p.532.
** As illustrated in "The Articles of Religion," XXVI, *Book of Common Prayer*, p.873.
*** No Faith group can claim a monopoly on sexually errant clergy. But the enormity of the problem was brought to light when the Pope summoned the American Cardinals to the Vatican for a meeting on April 23, 2002 over the issue of pedophile priests.

Beulah Land, Sweet Beulah Land

*R*etirement provided time to reexamine my ties to Christ my Savior and my ties to home as well. After leaving the parish, I continued to provide services for somewhat remote Saint Philip's Mission congregation in Weaverville, California, which I did for almost seven years.

Holy Eucharist was held in the afternoon on alternate Sundays, so I began taking walks on Sunday mornings. I encountered a surprising amount of spontaneous friendliness on those anonymous neighborhood meanderings without the prompts of ushers or greeters. The "outside world" was a friendly place, and I felt relieved of the responsibility of making it so. I began to discover joy in my lovely home—at times previously considered to be so much extra work. Now I could watch the Rose and Super Bowls and the World Series, if I chose. No longer did I worry about the weekend weather or the effect Daylight Saving Time adjustments might have on Sunday attendance. I began to enjoy my freedom to go and come without feeling I was neglecting parishioners. After all, they were God's parishioners—not mine. I did not miss all of the church and community meetings I had been obliged to attend! I quit them all! (at least temporarily).

But my previous belief that the Church was having a vital influence on the community was shattered as I observed the many activities that seemed to be occupying a majority of the population on the Lord's Day. Had they all attended services, there would never have been enough room for all of them in the worship centers in town, or in the world beyond for that matter! This came as a bit of a shock to me, thrust as I was beyond the ecclesiastical boundaries within which I had previously confined myself for decades.

The night before I wrote this vignette I was sitting in the living room of the house I had built for the comfort of my family but also as a rectory that would accommodate an occasional open house and vestry dinner gatherings. I sat in the big easy chair with my feet on the ottoman. My dear wife was resting on the sofa, and my dog was sleeping nearby. I was engrossed in reading a book of my choice, not cramming for a sermon. Beyond the "picture windows," the setting sun was casting purple hues on the snow on Mount Shasta. As I glanced up from my book to scan the room and gaze out the window, this idea came to me: "I am 72 years of age, yet this is the first time that I can remember sitting in this chair without feeling I should be somewhere else, doing something else!" I thought of the five tall file cases packed with a half century of my sermons and writings in the family room, and I began to think: "If they have a value, how might that be perpetuated?"

I began to consider how I would love to continue to write on several subjects I had always reserved for that future that never seemed to come. Now Marjorie and I could disconnect the telephone at mealtime, because no one was depending on us any more. Planting petunias and washing the dog were becoming more shared pleasures and less of a duty. Marjorie was gradually relinquishing more of her kitchen dominion to accommodate my presence. With fewer complaints, she graciously relocated washed dishes I mistakenly stored on the wrong shelves. Home life was becoming more of a honeymoon as well. I felt a surprising contentment in a new surrender to a slower pace, a change from my previously driven self, and I sensed that my beloved wife was also enjoying this change in the tempo of our lives.

The late psychologist Fritz Perles used to advise: "Don't push the river." Virginia Satir, my mentor in family therapy and my departed friend, taught those around her: "Plant your flowers where the earth is fertile." As these thoughts paraded through my memory, seated as I was in my comfortable parlor, it was revealed to me quite profoundly that at last it was time, ...our time, ...my time, and that God was blessing us, because this is His time for us as well.

—◦◦◦—

Upon Church retirement, I spent two months contacting friends long neglected due to previous ministerial duties. We visited the graves of three generations of Marjorie's missionary family on the Rosebud Reservation on the plains of South Dakota, and I made visits to my parents' and my great aunt's graves in Oakland to honor them.

My boyhood buddies were falling like autumn leaves: Jerry as a passenger in a car wreck; Ewald, Charlie and Bob with cancer. Richard is struggling so courageously with MS and his wheelchair. As a survivor in the midst of these recollections, I began to feel a revival of that compulsion to seek further service for the Lord who had still blessed me with vigor, health and memory. I began to get a mixed message from the Lord, and I began to feel myself in a "double bind": be content to relax and enjoy what has been earned, as opposed to the need to continue to be helpful and productive. I fell victim to what I have observed to be a common adjustment to the vacuum in newly retired lives which drives many to fill the vacant space with volunteer activities or a return to compensated employment.

I began to struggle to find a new Church parish or institution that could use me full-time, and thereby justify deferring my Church Pension Fund benefits. I had years of pastoral experience in a broad range of situations. I could "grow programs" and analyze mission outreach strategies quickly. When still in the Navy, was I not a semifinalist nominee in a search for a diocesan bishop? I believed I had a responsibility to be a good steward of God-given talents and experiences.

I accepted the gracious invitation of the Right Reverend Peter H. Beckwith to be his house guest, and toured with him some of the Diocese of Springfield (Illinois) as a candidate to replace his retiring Archdeacon. I admired this bishop and I would have loved the job, but it would have been at half salary, and, with the resulting loss of my church pension, we could not afford to accept the position.

As the desire for professional activity accelerated, I found myself compulsively searching for a suitable challenge. Marjorie, too, was ready to sell our house and join me anywhere that we might be Called and could be creative. My daily anxious trips to the mailbox in search of replies to my many applications for positions advertised in church publications only brought fading hopes. Letters that were answered were "boiler plate" stereotypical replies wishing me well while offering me nothing. This continued for eighteen months. I had a good resumé, and I never lost confidence in my abilities, but between the lines of those rejection letters, the Lord was making His Will evident. The Church had no more need of me; it was time for a new generation to carry on. While working in my garden I pondered: "One must pick the spent rose flowers that the new buds might blossom."

"Why set yourself up for more rejections?" Marjorie kept asking me. Was it not time now to practice what I was preaching? I had reiterated to others through the years: "God always answers our prayers. Sometimes it is with a 'yes'; sometimes the answer is 'no'; sometimes He just tells us to wait." On the other hand, I was still very much alive, and I knew that God was not finished with me yet.

Why then, I asked myself, was I trying to put pages back on the calendar? Was it not time just to be grateful for the past? Yet I was unable to find satisfaction in giving up on future ministry, future service. What was driving me so? What was feeding this passion? Was it "survivor guilt" over the loss of lifelong friends and battlefield casualties? Was it of the Lord or of self, or a combination of both? I knew in my heart and had often repeated: "With God there can be no blind streets!"

I came to one awkward conclusion that there was a thrill in ministering with the Savior. Could that be too selfish or self-centered a motive for a desire to return to this work? As we serve the Lord, with or without human acknowledgement, *we feel valued*. When expressing God's love as a pastor, preaching His Word and giving Holy Communion as a priest, I have always known an elation—an elevation to the Mount of Transfiguration with my Lord. This exaltation transcends all others, and provides a resource in life and in ministry that shows the way through sadness and tragedy—even in war— with the Light of Christ. I am sure this experience is shared by all whose lives in any way are touched by the Holy One, and through whom that love is conveyed to others. This experience comes to me now when invited to hold "supply" services for vacationing or ill clergy, or to bring the Blessed Sacrament to a home or hospital. However, in retirement, one misses a parish family that values its minister. The joy of being valued is something every human needs. The other name for this is "Love."

I was in search of comfort in my new status as "retired priest without portfolio"—diplomat without an embassy. Where should I turn to answer that restlessness? I asked the Lord: "Am I wandering in a wilderness, or had I reached my Promised Land but was refusing to accept it?" I looked back- ward into my own ministerial history, and I discovered an experience of effectiveness that I had enjoyed. This was what was described in this writing under the title: "Therapy is Ministry, and Ministry is Therapy."

I began a serious review of the *Diagnostic and Statistical Manual of Mental Disorders* (DSM IV), and I casually explored private practice exercising the professional "Marriage and Family Therapist" California State license I had earned while in San Diego. If I were to find a position working for a County Mental Health Agency, it would have to be beyond the borders of the county where I had ministered and the community where I was so well known. This would avoid any continuation of former expectations, avoid "church-state" conflicts in the minds of others, and I would want an anonymity that would be impossible in the midst of a population I had previously served. I accepted what I interpreted to be the voice of the Lord, and instead of pleading for a place in the Church, I applied for positions which would allow me to express ministry by another means and in another role.

The Lord Calls with one voice. He tells us when and where to go, including when and where to start and when and where to stop. Once the angel that wrestled with Jacob had blessed him, Jacob had to let him go (Genesis 32:24-29). But once Jacob was given a new direction, his name was changed to "Israel" as well. It is hard to let go of the angels that have blessed us. But when the blessing has been given, God Calls us to find His next angel, and new blessings to be bestowed as well. Jesus Calls us ever onward, never backward.

A new name is not a new identity, but it can be symbolic of a new direction in our journey. One answers God's new Calls in new ways that, with faith, unfold with time, and then God gives us the growth to meet His new challenges for us. It was so with the Exiles returning from Babylon to Palestine to rebuild old ruins into a new nation. They called their old homeland by a new name: "Beulah Land" (Isaiah 62:4).

—◦◦◦—

The telephone rang. The voice on the other end said: "Lester, this is June from Tehama County Mental Health. We liked your resumé, you have a State License to practice, and we are inviting you for an interview with the possibility of joining our team of professional psychotherapists full-time. We need you." This was in June 1997, eighteen months after leaving the parish because it was God's time to go. I had spent much of that time searching for a new Church home, but this new opportunity only surfaced when I had given up my own efforts and accepted whatever the Lord might have in mind. Is this not the kind of surrender that I had been preaching to others for a half century?

A new angel came to bless me with new work for our loving God who never abandons us. He heard my prayer, but He waited until I stopped telling

Him how I wanted it answered. Truly, I wanted to be useful. I wanted to help people, but in a place where I was needed and could be effective. And, like Jacob, I was given a new name. I had been called Father, Captain, Chaplain, or Doctor, because I spent my entire adult life representing the Church, the Navy, or one of their institutions. I loved representing them, but in return, my life was theirs. What's in a name? Well, I had leased my identity. Few laymen understand that this can be a sacrifice rather than a privilege. I have often said that titles are like curls on the tail of a pig. They add nothing to the stature of the animal, but they make him look nice.

"Lester, this is June from Tehama County Mental Health....We need you." She called me by my baptismal name, and she said I was needed. I guess that is all I heard. Her message echoed in my brain. I was elated. I rejoiced that I was "invited" to be myself and to be on a team with colleagues that needed me to serve others with them. Although not without their own internal politics and institutional problems, for the most part my new colleagues proved to be caring professionals with great wisdom and talents. It was indeed a privilege to work among them. I was older than they and had earned my therapist's credentials the hard way twenty years before, but there had been many changes in the field of psychotherapy during that time. My experience and my doctorate were in the related fields of pastoral ministry and family therapy, rather than in clinical mental health and social work. As a result, I had much to learn from my bright young colleagues. They graciously accepted me and shared with me both on and off the job, and I gladly sat at their feet.

I especially remember Don Smith, a devout Mormon and recent Master of Social Work graduate, who took me "under his wing," so to speak. I frequently had in excess of 50 weekly clients. I served as one of the Clinicians for almost two years in two increments. My work there was interrupted by a sudden need for heart bypass surgery, but I was permitted to return, joyfully with the additional task of mental health consultant to Social Workers at Adult Protective Services. "Yes June, this is Lester. You can count on me. I will come right away. Thank you for calling." Thank you, Jesus, for Calling! I needed to hear from You.

I eventually felt the need for a complete rest from the long days at the office and a long round-trip commute. But the work as a Mental Health Clinician gratified my needs to love and serve others. I had found a "ministry beyond Ministry," and that is what I have chosen to call my "Beulah Land." However, I believe God's current Call for me is to write this book in order to share insights of a half century at the Altar, in the Pulpit, and at the side and in the confidence of thousands.

What will be the next direction for me to take? I know it will be revealed when He wants it to be. Ministry has many avenues, but the right one for each of us and the right time for it are best known in the Mind of God. He reveals His Will to us when we need to know it. I candidly relate my experiences in retirement—as well as those throughout all my years in God's Ministry—in the sincere hope that others will be reassured that God is tracking our abilities, pacing each of our journeys, and at each milestone God will open before one who listens what *He* desires of us. Such revelations come to us only "in His time." For me, now, God's message is:

"Stay, stay at home, my heart, and rest;
Homekeeping hearts are happiest...."★

—Genesis 32:24–30; Psalm 139:7-12;
St. Matthew 25:29

★ Henry Wadsworth Longfellow, "Song." *The Complete Works of Henry Wadsworth Longfellow.* Cutchogue, New York: Buccaneer Books, 1993, pp. 340f.

CHAPTER 11

Coda

All that Glitters

Some things that glitter are pure gold. Some are "fool's gold." Some things do not glitter at all because they are hidden.

For centuries the Golden Buddha of Bangkok was hidden from invading vandals beneath beautifully painted plaster. When the huge image was being moved, it was damaged. A crack in the plaster revealed that beneath it there was a priceless treasure which was covered by a disguise intended for the world to see. When the solid gold inside was discovered, the painted plaster—as beautiful as it was—was stripped away, and the real Golden Buddha was revealed!

Christ gave us a Church of priceless beauty, a source of peace, and He doesn't do His work twice! Our Blessed Savior sees the best in people—even those who betrayed and nailed Him. He sees beneath the image we display to the world, because He knows there is within us precious gold that is greater than we can imagine. It is the image of God in which we were created. His mission is to restore us to His Image. Likewise, the mission of the Church is to redeem the world. As Christ's disciples, we are guardians of His Church. It is our constant, vigilant, yet often thankless mission to strip the painted plaster off the surface, so that the solid integrity of the Church may be continually revealed and restored to power.

The priest cannot function unless he is first a prophet—that is, one who is unafraid to tell the truth for God. Every Christian is Called to such action by the commission of Holy Baptism, as agreed to in the Covenant of our response. We are not only to keep the Faith, but to defend it as well!

I learned in the seminary that Satan's strongest ally is the rumor that he does not exist. In ascetic theology class (well over five decades ago) we were taught to spell Satan's name with a capital letter, so as to keep that in mind. I believe Satan has no power of his own. Thus, for Satan to work his mischievous and iniquitous will, he must seduce good people to redirect the power and the talents God gave them. The Church is such a potent instrument for good that it does scare Satan into fighting hard against it. The fact that the Church includes our fallible humanity as well as the perfect Lord should motivate us to serve within the Church in allegiance with Christ when problems are encountered, rather than to cause us to retreat from the Church in disillusionment.

When God sent the rainbow to Noah, He vowed never to visit humankind with evil, even for the purpose of teaching or punishing. But He did not promise to keep us from harming or destroying ourselves. I believe we can identify three reasons that bad things happen. The most obvious is the result of one's own erroneous behavior. Secondly, and sometimes more obscurely, evil can be the consequence of the behavior of others. A third possible reason is that which confronted poor Job. He did not get an answer to the question, "Why me?"—and many times we do not either. Job refused to blame God for his misfortune, and in that trust he was upheld. Our faith tells us (using the words of the *Book of Common Prayer*★) that God "dost not willingly afflict or grieve the children of men." Sometimes the reason bad things happen is not revealed to us, but we know that God cannot do that which is contrary to His Good Nature.

By revealing in this writing some of the experiences I have had or which I have witnessed in ministry, experiences that have required tenacious ethical struggles, it is my purpose to explain that, even though all that glitters is not gold, pure gold is there to be found by all Christians in service for Our Redeemer. This gold is worth discovering, and it is worth the struggle for its triumphant revelation.

In my years as a priest, I have communed hundreds of thousands, baptized on every continent but Antarctica and South America, been party to God's miracles of healing, married the devout, buried the faithful, reconciled countless souls, mended broken hearts, and I have offered the shelter of the Church to the homeless and hope to the seemingly hopeless. I have planted congregations, built churches, schools, and clinics, blessed, preached and taught in the Name of Our Blessed Lord. As His servant, I have loved and been loved by many. I am warmed by memories too countless to be documented in my "Priest's Personal Record" book. It is in ministering, in serving, that I have found the sacred treasure—the pure, refined, and solid gold.

In St. Matthew 25:35–40, my favorite text, Jesus said to his followers: "Inasmuch as you have done (service) to one of the least of these my brothers (and my sisters), you have done it unto Me."

At times I have failed in my perceptions and in my efforts, and at times I have succeeded in my objectives and in the causes I have espoused. Many times when I knew in my heart that I had succeeded for the Lord, it looked to others as though I had failed. Did Calvary seem to be a victory to the observers? (Dare we ask more than Jesus was given?) Irrespective of applause, I believe the Master Calls us to action, and that motivates us to look for cracks in pretty plaster façades—even in the Holy Church, where politics, ambition, secularism or indifference can, on the surface, hide God's Holy Spirit. When we find such a crack in an unworthy or unloving veneer, even in ourselves, we need to see through it to view the treasure beneath. Then we are duty bound to sound the alarm and summon the others to share the vision and uncover what is eternally precious for the world to see and know. I believe we are Called by God to tear false icons away, to unmask all that is less than worthy, to *let His Gold shine through.*

The Church is the gift of Christ to us—the Family of God for us. In it, God struggles with us humans in community to perfect The Body of His Christ and to preserve His continuing mission. Truly, we know that Jesus is risen and among us in the struggle we experience as He works with us daily, urging each of us to become more like His own precious Self. This has been my experience in the ministry of His Church. This has been my experience in my own life: God struggles with me to guide me and to make me better.

Gold must be refined to siphon off its impurities. When the fire gets hot, it hurts us when and where it touches us. But the price Jesus paid for our redemption is beyond human comparisons! God has taken me "over the rainbow," the rainbow God showed to Noah, and He has taken me far beyond it. He has chosen to share with me treasures that never could be measured in earthly gold, and my years in His Service have far surpassed any imagined expectations of my own. It has been a wonderful life, and, with every word that I write, I thank Him for it!

In Holy Baptism we are Called by God the Father to put our earthly lives on the line to serve others. Sometimes, for us as humans, it is easier to die for a cause than it is to live for and serve it. Nothing is more glorious than to discover in our Gethsemanes that we have found the Father's Will. Nothing is so satisfying as to follow it.

—GENESIS 9:14–16; MALACHI 3:2–4; I CORINTHIANS 4:1f;
II TIMOTHY 4:7f; I PETER 1:3–9

★ *Book of Common Prayer,* Prayer 55: "For a Person in Trouble or Bereavement," p.831.

The Appendices

Appendix A: Index of Biblical Texts for Reflection

Note: "f" indicates verse following, likewise "ff" indicates two following verses; "a" indicates first part of a verse; "b" indicates the last part of a verse.

From the Apocrypha

From the New Testament

Appendix B: Index of Maps

Appendix C: The Author's Chronology

Birth: October 19, 1930, Oakland, California.

Baptism: October 1, 1944, St. Savior's Chapel, Harvard (Episcopal) School, North Hollywood, California by The Rev. Fredrick M. Crane

Confirmation: March 22, 1945, St. Savior's Chapel, Harvard (Episcopal) School, North Hollywood, California by The Rt. Rev. W. Bertram Stevens

Postulant: May 15, 1951, Missionary District of San Joaquin (Sponsor: The Rev. Morgan S. Sheldon)

Candidate: January 12, 1954, Missionary District of San Joaquin (Sponsor: The Rev. J. Henry Thomas)

Deacon: June 13, 1955, St. Paul's Parish, Bakersfield, California by The Rt. Rev. Sumner Frank Dudley Walters

Priest: January 7, 1956, St. Peter's Parish, Redwood City, California by The Rt. Rev. Karl Morgan Block

Marriage: November 1, 1958, Good Shepherd Mission, Berkeley, California to Marjorie Clark

Children: August 3, 1959—Karla Nancy; August 20, 1966—Lester Leon III; August 13, 1968—Karen June

Ministry:

  Sept.1950–June 1951: Lay Vicar, Emmanuel Mission, Terminous, California

  Sept.1952–June 1953: Seminarian Intern, St. Clement's Parish, Berkeley, California

  Sept.1953–June 1954: Seminarian Intern, St. Peter's Parish, Redwood City, California

  Sept. 1954–May 1955: Lay Vicar, St. Mark's Mission, Tracy, California

  Aug.1955–Sept. 1956: Curate, St. Peter's Parish, Redwood City, California

  Sept. 1956–Jan.1960: Vicar, Good Shepherd Mission, (West) Berkeley, California

  Jan.1960–Nov.1960: Director, Easter School, Baguio City, Philippines Director, St. Elizabeth's School, Acupan, B.C.I. Mines, Benguet

Subprovince, Philippines; Assistant Priest (Circuit Rider) Epiphany Mission Outstations, Benguet Subprovince, Mountain Province, Philippines

Nov.1960–May 1966: Assistant Priest, St. Stephen's (Chinese) Parish, Manila, Philippines

Nov.1960–Dec.1961: Assistant Chaplain, St. Stephen's High School, Manila, Philippines

Jan.1961–May 1966: Chaplain & Dir. Dept. of Christian Education, St. Stephen's High School, Manila, Philippines

Sept.1961–May 1966: Founding Vicar, Emmanuel Mission, Tondo, Manila, Philippines

Dec.1963–May 1966: U.S. Naval Reserve Chaplain LT(jg) assisting at U.S. Naval Air Station, Sangley Point, Cavite, Philippines (one day/week, except 2 weeks annual Training Duty in the fleet during school vacation)

June 1966–Aug.1966: Student Chaplain, Naval Chaplain School, Newport, Rhode Island, U.S.A.

Oct. 1966–Apr.1967: Chaplain, 3d Medical Battalion, "Charlie" Company (Da Nang); "Alpha" Company (Phu Bai)—3d Marine Division; & 1st Medical Battalion (Da Nang)—1st Marine Division, FMF (Reinforced), Viet Nam

May 1967–Sept.1967: Chaplain, 3d Battalion, 9th Marine Regiment, 3d Marine Division, FMF (Reinforced), Quang Tri Province/DMZ, Viet Nam

Nov. 1967–Jan.1969: Chaplain, National Naval Medical Center, Bethesda, Maryland

Feb. 1969–May 1969: Student, Defense Language Institute (West Coast), Viet Nam (South) Class, Monterey, California, U.S.A.

May 1969–May 1970: Chaplain, Naval Support Activity, Saigon (Mekong-Bassac Delta Riverine Circuit Rider), Viet Nam

June 1970–Aug.1972: Chaplain, Naval Air Station, Alameda, California

Aug. 1972–Sept.1973: Student, Naval Postgraduate School attached to San Francisco Theological Seminary, San Anselmo, California

Feb. 1973–Aug.1973: Interim Rector, St. Andrew's Parish, Oakland, California

Oct. 1973–June 1976: Chaplain, Naval Training Center, San Diego, California (included founding family counseling unit, also research at the Joint Center for Prisoner of War Studies, Point Loma)

Aug. 1976–Sept. 1978: Command Chaplain, USS *Proteus* (AS 19) and Staff Chaplain, Commander Submarine Squadron FIFTEEN, Guam, Marianas Islands, U.S.A.

Oct. 1978–May 1980: Command Chaplain, Naval Weapons Station, Concord, California (including Marine Barracks, Concord)

July 1980–Jan.1983: Staff Chaplain, Commander Service Squadron THREE (Circuit Rider on 8 ammunition [AE] ships), Home Port at Mare Island, Vallejo, California

Feb. 1983–Aug.1985: Command Chaplain, USS *Carl Vinson* (CVN 70) and Staff Chaplain, Commander Battle Group "C," Home Port transferred from Norfolk, Virginia to Alameda, California on 1983 around the world maiden voyage.

Aug. 1985–May 1987: Command Chaplain & Director of Pastoral Care, Naval Hospital, Oakland, California

May 1987–Dec.1995: Rector, All Saints' Parish, Redding, California

Nov. 1992–July 1999: Priest in Charge, St. Philip's Mission, Weaverville, California

Post Retirement from Episcopal Church
Jan. 1, 1996–July 7, 1997: Temporary sabbatical

Licensed Marriage and Family Therapist:
Aug. 25, 1975: License issued by Board of Behavioral Sciences

Feb. 3, 1981: Clinical Member, California Association of Marriage & Family Therapists

July 1997–Sept. 1998: Psychotherapist, Tehama County (Calif.) Health Agency, Mental Health Division, Red Bluff, California.

Sept. 1998–Aug. 1999: Recuperation from heart surgery

Sept. 1999–Apr. 2000: Return to Psychotherapist position at Tehama County Health Agency, Red Bluff, Calif.

Retirement:
May 1, 2000–Present: At my desk to write.

Appendix D: Author's Awards, Decorations, and Degrees

Military Personal Decorations (in order of precedence):

Bronze Star Medal (with Combat "V")

Purple Heart Medal

Navy Commendation Medal (with Combat "V")

Navy Achievement Medal

Combat Action Ribbon

Sea Service (major deployment) Ribbon (3 awards)

Combat Air Crew Wings (3 stars)

Submarine Deterrent Patrol Pin

Military Unit Awards

Presidential Unit Citation (2 awards)

Navy Unit Commendation (3 awards)

Meritorious Unit Commendation

Battleship Efficiency Ribbon

Vietnamese Presidential Unit Citation

Vietnamese Meritorious (Civic Action) Unit Citation

Military Campaign Medals

National Defense Service Medal

Viet Nam Service Medal (with 6 campaign stars)

Viet Nam Campaign Medal

Ecclesiastical Recognition

1985 Episcopal Church Presiding Bishop's Jubilee Award for Humanitarian Service (for USS *Carl Vinson* civic action projects in Africa and Asia during 1983 and 1985 deployments)

Civic Awards

"Paul Harris Fellow" awarded by the Rotary Foundation of Rotary International in 1996

Senior Police Chaplain, awarded in July 1991 for achievement by the International Conference of Police Chaplains

Silver Star Alumnus of the Alpha Tau Omega Fraternity

Academic Degrees

Bachelor of Arts, University of the Pacific, Stockton, California. 1952.

Master of Divinity, Church Divinity School of the Pacific, Berkeley, California. 1955.

Master of Arts (Pastoral Psychology), San Francisco Theological Seminary, San Anselmo, California. 1973.

Doctor of Ministry, San Francisco Theological Seminary, San Anselmo, California. 1974.